The Global Football Industry

T0358853

In recent years, football's status as "the world's sport" has shown little sign of waning. From increasing participation at grassroots levels and to the highly lucrative media rights deals secured by the top elite clubs, the game appears to be thriving as it continues to excite and enthral billions of people around the globe. Nevertheless, there are a number of challenges and opportunities facing the football industry today that warrant further examination.

This book brings together leading international researchers to survey the current state of the global football industry, exploring contemporary themes and issues in the marketing of football around the world. With contributions from Europe, Asia, and the Americas, it discusses key topics such as football club management, the economics of the football industry, match-fixing, social media, fan experiences, the globalized marketplace, and the growing popularity of the women's game.

Offering insights for researchers, managers, and marketers who are looking to stay ahead of the game, *The Global Football Industry: Marketing Perspectives* is essential reading for anyone with an interest in international sport business.

James J. Zhang is a Professor and Director of the International Center for Sport Management (ICSM) at the University of Georgia in Athens, Georgia, USA.

Brenda G. Pitts is a Professor of Sport Management and Director of the Sport Business Research Laboratory at Georgia State University in Atlanta, Georgia, USA.

World Association for Sport Management Series

Series Editors:
Brenda G. Pitts
Georgia State University, USA
James J. Zhang
University of Georgia, USA

The World Association for Sport Management (WASM) was founded to facilitate sport management research, teaching and learning excellence, and professional practice, across every continent. The WASM book series is designed to support those aims by presenting current research and scholarship, from well-established and emerging scholars and practitioners, on sport management theory, policy, and practice. Books in the series will explore contemporary issues and key challenges in sport management and identify important new directions for research and professional practice. Above all, the series aims to encourage and highlight the development of international perspectives, international partnerships, and international best practice in sport management, recognizing the globalized nature of the contemporary sport industry.

Available in this series:

1 **Global Sport Management**
   Contemporary Issues and Inquiries
   Edited by Brenda G. Pitts and James J. Zhang

2 **Contemporary Sport Marketing**
   Global Perspectives
   Edited by James J. Zhang and Brenda G. Pitts

3 **The Global Football Industry**
   Marketing Perspectives
   Edited by James J. Zhang and Brenda G. Pitts

The Global Football Industry

Marketing Perspectives

Edited by James J. Zhang
and Brenda G. Pitts

Routledge
Taylor & Francis Group

LONDON AND NEW YORK

First published 2018 by Routledge

2 Park Square, Milton Park, Abingdon, Oxfordshire OX14 4RN
52 Vanderbilt Avenue, New York, NY 10017

Routledge is an imprint of the Taylor & Francis Group, an informa business

First issued in paperback 2019

British Library Cataloguing-in-Publication Data
A catalogue record for this book is available from the British Library

Library of Congress Cataloging-in-Publication Data
A catalog record for this book has been requested

ISBN: 978-0-8153-6056-8 (hbk)
ISBN: 978-0-367-89412-2 (pbk)

Typeset in Sabon
by Apex CoVantage, LLC

Contents

SECTION II
Marketing perspectives

Contributors

Christian Alfs, Johannes Gutenberg University Mainz, Germany

Christoph Breuer, German Sport University Cologne, Germany

Kevin K. Byon, Indiana University, USA

Dan Drane, Winthrop University, USA

Dana Ellis, Laurentian University, Canada

Iris an der Heiden, Johannes Gutenberg University Mainz, Germany

Chris Henderson, Miami University, USA

Chris Horbel, University of Southern Denmark, Denmark and Norwegian
   School of Sport Sciences, Norway

Noah Y. Hsu, Aletheia University, Taiwan

Craig Hyatt, Brock University, Canada

Adriano M. Lamberti, Brock University, Canada

Becca Leopkey, University of Georgia, USA

Su Liu, China Pharmaceutical University, China

Tobias Nowy, German Sport University Cologne, Germany

Boris Osorio, Brock University, Canada

N. David Pifer, Texas Tech University, USA

Brenda G. Pitts, Georgia State University, USA

Bastian Popp, Saarland University, Germany

Holger Preuss, Johannes Gutenberg University, Germany

Glaucio Scremin, University of West Georgia, USA

Natalie L. Smith, East Tennessee State University, USA

Scott Tainsky, Wayne State University, USA

Yan Wang, Shanghai University of Sport, China

Liang Wei, Jinan University, China

Herbert Woratschek, University of Bayreuth, Germany

Jie Xu, University of Illinois, USA

James J. Zhang, University of Georgia, USA

Mandy Y. Zhang, Shanghai University, China

Global football industry

Chapter 1

Contemporary global football industry

An introduction

N. David Pifer, Yan Wang, Glaucio Scremin,
Brenda G. Pitts, and James J. Zhang

Introduction

In recent years, the sport of football, also known as soccer in North America, has managed to further entrench itself as "the world's game." Buoyed by an increasingly diverse array of participation at the grassroots level, and spurred forward at its highest professional ranks by bankrolling owners and lucrative media rights deals, this relatively simple, yet beautiful game has continued to excite and enthrall billions of people around the globe. Its premier tournament, the FIFA World Cup, has grown into the largest, single-event sporting competition in the world, with an estimated 3.2 billion people tuning in to watch the 64 matches that were played in Brazil during the summer of 2014 (FIFA, 2014a). The English Premier League (EPL), considered by many to be the most popular professional sports league in the world, recently agreed on a television deal that will distribute over $7.3 billion in revenues to its member clubs over the 2016–2017 to 2018–2019 seasons (Premier League, 2015b). The grassroots level, too, is experiencing growth, with nations that have been reluctant to football's influence in the past now boasting some of the sport's highest participation numbers (Johnson, 2015; King, 2014).

Nonetheless, even in the midst of football's financial and fundamental successes, there remains a need for continued research and recommendation in all areas of the sport. FIFA, after all, finds itself embroiled in scandal and corruption, and mega events such as the World Cup continue to raise questions about the benefits and financial burdens that are left to the host communities. At the top levels of the club game, the influx of new money means that team administrators must find the most efficient and effective ways to transform these funds into on-field success. It also means that the leagues must deal with assertions that the competition is becoming more unbalanced as the revenue gaps between the big and small clubs widen. Therefore, clubs of all sizes can benefit from explorations into potential sources of new revenue and whether or not their current arrangements are providing an adequate amount of capital. Similarly, the businesses and corporations relinquishing these funds through television and sponsorship deals should be concerned with whether or not these ventures are providing the best value for the money. With some of the payments made by these organizations reaching record-breaking levels, analyses into whether or not they are receiving adequate returns on their investments become warranted.

In regions of the world where football's influence is not as pronounced, fledgling leagues are looking for ways to grow and market their product so that they, too, can claim a share of football's lucrative revenues. Some of the teams in these leagues have resorted to paying high wages and transfer fees for current and former star players (Atkins, 2016), believing that these signings will raise both the competitive quality and consumer awareness of their clubs. Others have employed unique marketing promotions in order to attract an increasingly perceptive group of consumers (Jowdy & McDonald, 2002). Nations in these parts are also hoping to increase the success of their national teams while developing and tapping into the rising levels of grassroots participation. Numerous opportunities and challenges currently exist in emerging football economies and across the industry as a whole. The purpose of this chapter is twofold. First, it seeks to provide an overview of football's growth in order to frame the current situation and build a context for the overall examination. Second, it highlights and discusses the opportunities and challenges that currently exist within football's international and club environments, paying special attention to developing football nations. As such, the authors were able to offer suggestions to researchers, managers, and marketers who are looking to explore the opportunities and address the challenges that currently exist within the global football industry. Collectively, this all-encompassing review provides an overview of the world's game and a platform from which future football-related studies can proceed.

Growth of football

Origins and evolution

With an ancient origin dating back to the second and third centuries B.C., football has managed to withstand the tests of time and propagate its legacy amidst the rise and fall of empires, the outbreak of deadly diseases, and the conflicts brought forth in back-to-back, world wars (FIFA, 2016b). That it has survived in some form or fashion over these 2,000-plus years lends credence to both its inherent durability and its longstanding ability to capture the attention of the masses. Although England is typically credited with establishing and popularizing the modern form of the game, historical records indicate that ancient China actually created the earliest version of the sport around 200 B.C. Known as *Tsu' Chu*, this sport required players to fend off opponents while maneuvering a leather ball filled with feathers and hair through a small opening on their opponents' end of the playing field. Use of the hands was not permitted, leaving the feet as the most efficient means of guiding the ball to its intended destination (FIFA, 2016b).

Other primitive versions of the sport were subsequently recorded in Japan and Greece, but FIFA (2016b) credits England for giving structure to the game during the 1800s. Initially, the sport consisted of a mob of participants moving the ball from one end of a field to another, and it was usually played by students at schools and universities. However, the game was rough and informal, and it seemed as though each group of participants had a different interpretation of the rules. Some, such as the school at Rugby, allowed the ball to be carried by hand and tolerated the more aggressive features of the sport such as tackling and tripping. Others, like the school at Cambridge, disallowed the use of the hands and placed more emphasis on the technical ability of the participants. Following years of disorganized and even dangerous matches between rival teams, a subset of organizers finally sought to establish a universal set of rules in order to create consistency and a faction that was separate from the Rugby-style version of the game. These representatives conducted a series of meetings throughout London in 1863, standardizing a series of laws to regulate play and forming the Football Association (FA) that governs the English game to this day. From here, association football distinguished itself from "rugby" and spread quickly throughout Britain and the rest of Europe. By 1872, over 50 English clubs were participating in the sport and the first FA Cup was played out between them. That same year, England played Scotland in the first-ever international match, leading the latter to establish its own governing body for the sport in 1873. Wales (1875) and Ireland (1880) were the next to form their respective governing bodies, and when the Netherlands and Denmark did so in 1889, the game officially left British borders. Prominent football nations such as Argentina (1893), Italy (1898), Uruguay (1900), and Germany (1900) announced the formation of their associations shortly thereafter, and in 1904, the Fédération Internationale de Football Association (FIFA) was created in Paris, France (FIFA, 2016b).

FIFA and the World Cup

FIFA was created with the goal of unifying the various national associations that had formed across Europe and the rest of the world at the turn of the nineteenth century. Branding itself as football's international governing body, the association set out to lend further clarity to the laws of the game while providing a more official means through which international matches and competitions could be staged. As part of its early mission, FIFA sought to establish an international football competition that could determine a world champion and bolster the growing popularity of the sport. Initially, FIFA held its world championship in conjunction with the Olympic Games, where it proved to be an immense success from 1908 to 1928. However, the amateur nature of the Olympics cast doubt on its long-term viability as a platform for the highest level of football competition, and prompted FIFA officials to devise an alternative. Jules Rimet, FIFA's president at the time, accordingly took it upon himself to spearhead a movement that would provide football with a championship event of its own. Per his efforts, the FIFA World Cup was born, and the inaugural tournament took place in Uruguay during the summer of 1930. That July, the hosts went on to win the first edition of the tournament with a 4–2 victory over Argentina in the final match (FIFA, 2016a).

Since its inception, the World Cup has lived up to Rimet's billing and grown into the largest, single-event sporting competition in the world. The number of teams participating in the final stages of the tournament has increased considerably from 13 at Uruguay in 1930 to 32 from 1994 onward. The viewership numbers have also attested to its rising popularity. During the 2014 World Cup in Brazil, an estimated 3.2 billion people tuned in to watch the 64 matches that were played throughout the tournament, with one billion of those viewers tuning in to watch the final alone (FIFA, 2014a). To put these numbers in perspective, the 2014 edition of the National Football League's (NFL) Super Bowl was watched by 160 million viewers worldwide (Both, 2015), and the opening ceremony of the 2012 London Olympics garnered a global audience of 900 million (Ormsby, 2012).

As an event that is played just once every four years across cities in a designated host country, there is an element of scarcity that surrounds each tournament. The infrequent nature of the World Cup, combined with its position as a showcase for the world's most popular sport, make it an exclusive event for both the rising number of viewers and the corporations that hope to profit from them. Indeed, commercial sponsors and advertisers pay large sums of money for the opportunity to associate their brands with the World Cup, and television networks engage in extensive bidding wars for the rights to broadcast the event's matches. In 2014, commercial sponsors partnering with the World Cup contributed $1.6 billion in revenues to FIFA, while broadcasting rights to the tournament fetched upwards of $2.4 billion. Adding in its other sources of income, FIFA raked in close to $5.7 billion in total revenues during the 2011–2014 budgeting cycle. This total set a new record of earnings and represented an increase of over 26% from the $4.2 billion that was accrued over the 2007–2010 period (FIFA, 2010, 2014b). "The [2014] FIFA World Cup was a veritable success," said former FIFA president Sepp Blatter, "concluding the 2011–14 financial period on a great high" (FIFA, 2014b). With profits of $338 million and financial reserves in excess of $1.5 billion, FIFA appears to be operating on a healthy margin.

Youth and societal development

Today, ensuring the continued success of inspirational tournaments like the World Cup remains at the forefront of FIFA's overall mission. Nonetheless, the ever-growing popularity of the sport has also led the association to identify a new primary objective of improving the game and promoting it globally, particularly through the advancement of youth development programs (FIFA, 2016c). For this reason, FIFA now donates proceeds from World Cup revenues to developmental projects in each of its 209 member associations. Many of these programs exist in third world countries, and therefore depend on these funds for day-to-day operations. The latest financial reports from FIFA (2014b) show that 72% ($3.8 billion) of the association's $5.3 billion in expenses over the 2011–2014 budgeting cycle were directed toward FIFA events and grassroots development projects. FIFA also claims to care about society and the environment, citing the need for its programs and events to not only enhance the lives of football-playing youth, but to leave behind a positive legacy in its World Cup host communities (FIFA, 2016c). Accordingly, FIFA has created a Legacy Fund that provides the hosting association with $100 million to help cover developmental and infrastructural costs that last beyond the duration of the tournament.

FIFA also positions itself as a key player in the quest to provide everyone with the equal right to play. Having seen the ways in which the sport can overcome social, political, and economic barriers, FIFA founded the Women's World Cup in 1991 and embarked on a recent "Say No to Racism" campaign in an effort to eliminate inequality and prejudice from the game. Ironically, the women's game has taken off in past decades, particularly in nations such as China and the United States where the men's game has been slower to catch on. As a result, the sport is now providing a platform for female athletes to showcase their skills and cultivate followings similar to those enjoyed by their male counterparts (Kim, 2015). For its part, FIFA earmarked around $200 million in its latest budgeting cycle for improvements in women's football and other solidarity projects (FIFA, 2014b).

The club game

Although the World Cup stands out as football's premier event and dominates the sporting headlines once every four years, the various club systems that exist across the globe are what truly cultivate and carry the sport on an annual basis. According to global management consulting firm, A.T. Kearney, the worldwide revenues derived from the ticketing, media, and marketing efforts of professional football events amounted to a staggering $28 billion in 2011 (Zygband, Collignon, Sultan, Santander, & Valensi, 2011). To put this figure in perspective, the 2011 combined revenues of the four major North American sports of football, baseball, basketball, and hockey, along with the more global games of tennis, golf, and Formula 1 racing, totaled $32 billion (Zygband et al., 2011). The fact that football alone was able to generate just $4 billion less in annual income than a combination of the world's remaining, popular sports speaks volumes to the level of affluence on which it operates. It also highlights the importance of the club game in supplying the demand that is regularly craved by consumers and corporations around the world.

Indeed, the cyclical nature of the World Cup and other international competitions means that these mega events account for just a fraction of the revenues that are persistently generated by the sport. In reality, the European club scene lends fundamental and financial relevance to football on a more consistent basis. Nearly 79% ($22 billion) of football's total revenues in 2011 were attributable to European club football, with Europe's top five club leagues – the EPL (England), Bundesliga (Germany), La Liga (Spain), Ligue 1 (France), and Serie A (Italy) – accounting for nearly half of this sum. These 2011 estimates also preceded many of the lucrative revenues that have since flowed into the sport through the updated media rights deals and sponsorship arrangements. In the United Kingdom, for example, the domestic rights for live television broadcasts of the EPL's 2016–2017 to 2018–2019 seasons were recently sold for over $7.3 billion ($2.4 billion per season) to the highest bidders (Premier League, 2015b). Even in countries that are not traditionally associated with the sport, such as the United States and China, foreign EPL broadcasting rights were able to fetch revenues of $1 billion and $92 million, respectively (Harris, 2016; Sandomir, 2015).

In addition to the rising tide of broadcasting revenues, many of the world's top leagues and teams are also benefiting from the commercial partnerships that have become more common in recent years. Total commercial revenues across the EPL and Ligue 1 rose by $990 million and $250 million, respectively, between the 2012–2013 and 2013–2014 seasons (Deloitte, 2015) as corporations looked to profit from the rising popularity of these leagues' teams. Nowhere was this trend more visible than in the record-breaking kit deals that Manchester United was able to obtain prior to the starts of the 2014 and 2015 seasons. The first of these was a $560 million kit-sponsorship agreement with American car manufacturer, Chevrolet, which saw the company's chevron logo earn a prominent place across the front of Manchester United's game-worn and replica jerseys (Baxter, 2014). "Chevrolet as a global brand is really trying to strengthen our position in a lot of emerging markets," said Megan Stooke, Chevy's director of global marketing. "When you look at the fan base of Manchester United, one of the world's most popular sports brands, we saw a great alignment in those markets" (Baxter, 2014). The deal, which runs through the end of the 2020–2021 season, is not even the most rewarding portion of Manchester United's kit. That honor belongs to apparel magnate Adidas and the ten-year, nearly

$1.3 billion deal it agreed with United to be the official manufacturer of its kits through the 2024–2025 season (Bandenhausen, 2015). With these, United will rake in close to $200 million a year for allowing the Chevrolet logo to be emblazoned across its Adidas-supplied jerseys for the next several seasons. As seen in Table 1.1, many of Europe's other top clubs also take advantage of exorbitant kit deals in order to bolster their finances.

Pursuit of success

Even as revenues continue to pour into the club scene, the reality is that very few of these teams are out to pocket their financial profits. Rather, they intend to use the money to fund wins (Szymanski, 2015). As such, clubs in leagues across the world are splashing the cash on the transfer fees and wages that are necessary to attract and retain the top players in the world. The annual reports published by Deloitte on the financial status of clubs in the top five European leagues have shown that the average wage-to-revenue ratios of these teams is nearly 60%, indicating that over half of their revenues are being reinvested in the on-field product (Deloitte, 2015). These wage figures do not even account for the transfer fees – the sums of money paid to purchase an under-contract player from another team – that often accompany player acquisitions and now reach into the hundreds of millions of dollars (Cunningham, 2013; Frick, 2007). But are these expenditures necessary? A study by Hall, Szymanski, and Zimbalist (2002) tested

Table 1.1 Ranking of European football's most valuable kit deals by annual revenues (2015–2016)

Team	Manufacturer	Sponsor	Total
Manchester United	Adidas ($117m)	Chevrolet ($79.9m)	$195m/year
Chelsea	Adidas ($47m)	Yokohama ($62.3m)	$109.3m/year
Arsenal	Puma ($47m)	Fly Emirates ($47m)	$94m/year
Liverpool	New Balance ($43.6m)	Standard Chartered ($39m)	$82.6m/year
Manchester City	Nike ($18.7m)	Etihad Airways ($62.3m)	$81m/year
Real Madrid	Nike ($46.7m)	Fly Emirates ($32.8m)	$79.5m/year
Barcelona	Nike ($36.1m)	Qatar Foundation ($32.8m)	$68.9m/year
Bayern Munich	Adidas ($27.3m)	Deutsche Telekom ($32.8)	$60.1m/year

Note: Adapted from "Premier League, 2015–16 Most Valuable Kits," and "Europe's Most Valuable Kits, 2015–16," by J. Tyler and M. Yesilevskiy, 2015, *ESPNFC.com*, Retrieved May 2016 from http://espn.go.com/espn/feature/story/_/id/13357293/english-premier-league-most-valuable-kits-2015-16 and http://espn.go.com/espn/feature/story/_/id/13455547/european-football-most-valuable-kits-2015-16.

the link between team payroll and performance within the EPL from 1974 to 1999 and found strong correlations between a team's winning percentage and how much it spent on wages compared to the league average over time. These results are visualized in Figure 1.1. Tomkins, Riley, and Fulcher (2010) showed a similar relationship between team success and transfer fee expenditures. In both situations, those who spent heavily appeared to reap the associated rewards.

This buyer's mentality has long been modeled by clubs like Real Madrid in Spain, where each season seems to mark the arrival of a new *Galactico*. As the richest club in the world, Madrid is seldom afraid to flaunt its wealth in the face of its La Liga and European rivals by purchasing some of the biggest names on the market. Unsurprisingly, Madrid has set and broken the world transfer record five times since 2000 by bringing in star players like Luis Figo, Zinedine Zidane, and Cristiano Ronaldo (Cunningham, 2013). Most recently, the club spent a record amount on Gareth Bale despite having a number of attacking options already present in its squad (Marcotti, 2013). "I must repeat that my policy is to try to sign the best players in the world," says Real Madrid president Florentino Perez, "in every position where we do not already have that" (Simons, 2004).

Perez's actions at Madrid highlight a trend that has also taken place within the EPL over the last couple of decades as wealthy, often foreign owners arrive on the scene and inject large amounts of cash into their clubs' payrolls. Bankrolling owners such as Roman Abramovich at Chelsea and Sheikh

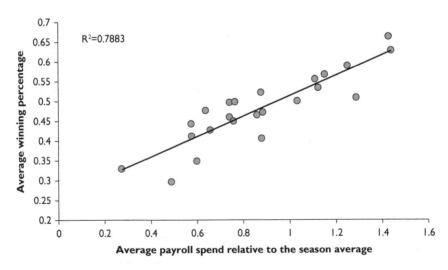

Figure 1.1 A scatterplot depicting the relationship between the average payrolls spend of EPL teams (1974–1999) relative to the season average and the average winning percentage of these teams

Adapted from "Team Average Spending in the English Top Division: 1974–1999," by S. Hall, S. Szymanski, and A. Zimbalist, 2002, *Journal of Sports Economics*, 3, p. 155.

Mansour at Manchester City serve as prime examples of this phenomenon, as both took relatively mediocre clubs to new heights by serving as their benefactors in the transfer market (Szymanski, 2015). The cash they pumped into these clubs was an asset unrealized by teams of less affluent ownership, and it helped them outbid their rivals for the world's top talents. In the process, a unique facet of the European league structure was also revealed; that is, it is free from the labor market restrictions that impede the fluid movement of players in other professional sport leagues (Frick, 2007). In North America, for instance, the NFL and National Hockey League (NHL) require all of their member teams to keep payrolls beneath a designated salary cap. Similarly, the National Basketball Association (NBA) and Major League Baseball (MLB) tax teams who spend above a mandated salary threshold and redistribute these taxes to teams who do not (Howard & Crompton, 2014). As noted by Hall et al. (2002), "The absence of these restrictions in English football make it more likely that teams can buy success" (p. 166).

The formula for success seems rather straightforward, namely the possession of a bankrolling owner who will buy the top players at will or use the growing revenue streams to make smart decisions in the transfer market. Fledgling teams in less-developed leagues such as the Chinese Super League (CSL) seem to have bought into the former strategy. As shown in Figure 1.2, the 2015–2016 winter transfer window saw CSL teams spend nearly $296 million on player acquisitions (FIFA Transfer Matching System, 2016). To put this total in perspective, teams from the EPL, the wealthiest league in the world, spent a comparatively less $181 million on player transfers, and the sum total of all transfer expenditures in the top five European leagues during this period was just $58 million higher (ESPNFC.com, 2016). Jiangsu Suning FC, a mid-level CSL team for the better part of the last decade, ignited the spending spree with the $32 million acquisition of Brazilian midfielder Ramires from Chelsea. They were outdone shortly thereafter by Guangzhou Evergrande's $48 million purchase of Jackson Martinez from Atletico Madrid (Spain), but returned to the top of the CSL spending charts with a $57 million move for Shakhtar Donetsk's (Ukraine) Alex Teixeira (Atkins, 2016). Teixeira was a reported target for EPL giant Liverpool at the time, but apparently opted for a move to China after hearing that Suning would pay him nearly $11.5 million a year over the duration of his four-year contract (Atkins, 2016). Overall, money certainly seems to have a heavy influence in the proceedings of modern football clubs.

Opportunities and challenges

Winning without money

Spending exorbitant amounts of money on elite-level athletes seemed to be the easiest and most assured method of finding success in European club football over the past several seasons. In England, for example, the strong

CSL Transfer Spending, 2014–2016

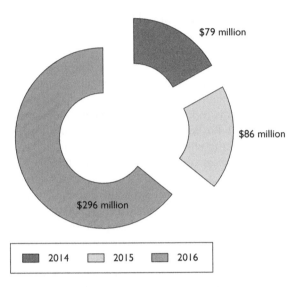

Figure 1.2 A chart illustrating the comparative differences in CSL transfer spending over the 2014 ($79 million), 2015 ($86 million), and 2016 ($296 million) seasons

Data was retrieved from FIFA Transfer Matching System (2016).

correlations between money and performance saw the same teams competing at the top end of the table on a regular basis. In fact, no team ranked outside of the top-four in terms of wage expenditures for a given season had ever won a championship in England's top flight (Szymanski, 2016). At the end of the 2015–2016 season, however, something happened that shattered these commonly held assumptions and offered hope for the financially less-endowed. Leicester City, competing with a squad whose total, monetary value prior to the start of the season was less than the transfer fees paid for individual players on some of the EPL's wealthier clubs, won the EPL title. Having begun the season as 5000–1 outsiders, Leicester cruised to victory on the wings of undervalued players and a coach that was considered past his prime (Figueira, 2016). Table 1.2 shows just how far back the team was ranked in terms of payroll relative to its EPL competitors.

How was a team with so little financial backing able to upset the odds and run the table on England's elite? Although it is perhaps too soon to tell, some are crediting the club's rise to the efficient and effective use of data analytics (Bahia, 2015). The field of analytics, in many ways, represents one of the biggest opportunities for advancement in professional football

Table 1.2 2015–2016 estimates of club wages (in millions of U.S. dollars) relative to Premier League finish

Club Name	Wages ($)	Wage Rank	EPL Finish	Club Name	Wages ($)	Wage Rank	EPL Finish
Chelsea	245.8	1	10	West Ham	79.23	11	7
Man. United	231.4	2	5	West Brom	78.09	12	14
Man. City	220.9	3	4	Aston Villa	74.214	13	20
Arsenal	218.9	4	2	Southampton	67.83	14	6
Liverpool	173.3	5	8	Crystal Palace	61.902	15	15
Tottenham	125.9	6	3	Swansea	58.14	16	12
Newcastle	86.4	7	18	Leicester City	54.948	17	1
Everton	85.2	8	11	Norwich	42.18	18	19
Stoke City	82.4	9	9	Watford	33.06	19	13
Sunderland	80.9	10	17	Bournemouth	28.5	20	16

Note: Estimated wage data pulled from "Premier League Club Wage Bills for 2015–2016 Season," by TotalSportek2, 2016, *TotalSportek.com*, Retrieved May 8, 2016 from www.total sportek.com/money/english-premier-league-wage-bills-club-by-club/.

management and research. By using a host of statistical methods to model the performances and interactions of players and teams, analysts are able to supplement a manager's observed knowledge with statistical facts and figures that can help guide decision-making. The game of football, though, is inherently difficult to model. It contains a relatively high number of players (22) compared to other sports and is more free-flowing in nature. Gerrard (2007) highlighted the difficulties that can occur while attempting to quantify the contributions of individual players in complex, invasion team sports like football where the discrete actions of the athletes are not as pronounced. Some have also viewed the use of analytics as a means of outsmarting the transfer market. If a team can properly price a player who is over or undervalued by the competition, then it possesses a unique advantage that should aid in its bidding strategies (Carmichael & Thomas, 1993; Dobson & Gerrard, 1999). Again, difficulties arise while attempting to assess athletes in a sport where the traditional statistics are rather limited. The most widely examined metric of football success – goals scored – occurs rather infrequently and as the result of a combination of numerous, seemingly independent events (Sally & Anderson, 2013; Szymanski, 2015). Statistically-minded researchers therefore have an opportunity to search for the "killer stat" that will help improve the ways in which the players and game are evaluated.

As a relatively poor club whose squad was composed mainly of castoffs, unknowns, and cheap transfers, Leicester's story certainly fits the mold of a team that unearthed some secret store of analytics knowledge. It should come as little surprise, then, that the club was reported to have leaned heavily on analytics throughout its journey to the EPL's summit. However, it was not simply a matter of recording and analyzing data that set the club apart. Rather, it was the manner in which all areas of the organization seemed to embrace the movement and work collaboratively to put the findings to good use. "Our daily meetings bring all of our departments together, and although a small thing, it definitely makes a difference," says Peter Clark, Leicester City's first team performance analyst. "We all help the manager make an informed decision" (Bahia, 2015). Even the Leicester players were introduced to the analytics wave. "It's part of the culture within the club," said Clark, "and by exposing the players to data, they are becoming more familiar with it and the insights it can bring" (Bahia, 2015).

It therefore appears that the analysts at Leicester were able to overcome some of the challenges that have hindered the influence of past analytical movements. Namely, Clark and company were able to bridge the gap between theory and practice while ensuring that the reports they furnished were understandable to coaches and players with limited statistical knowledge. They were also fortunate enough to be immersed in an organizational culture that accepted advanced statistics and the potential value they had to offer. Often times, coaches and owners are reluctant to encourage a new way of thinking, particularly when the data speaks against their commonly held assumptions. As noted by Mark Brunkhar, president of Match Analysis, "I would say that the barriers – the scouts and managers – don't want to cede any of their authority. If you survey football coaches, you'll get the nod, 'Yes, we believe in analytics work, we believe in the study of sport' . . . Just because you have stats available doesn't mean anyone actually uses them to do anything" (Sally & Anderson, 2013, p. 315). Management within Leicester, however, appeared to acknowledge and embrace the insights that solid, practical data analysis could offer.

Time will tell if the insights offered by Leicester's analytics department were pivotal to the team's success, or if they were simple sideshows to factors that played a more vital role in the team's EPL achievements. Luck, after all, has a definite hand in any sport (Sally & Anderson, 2013; Szymanski, 2015), and Leicester seemed to benefit from both a rare lack of injuries and a comparative letdown by many of the EPL's financially and traditionally strong sides. The club also seemed hit on all of its signings, a feat that is seldom accomplished in the whirlwind dealings of the transfer market (Kuper & Szymanski, 2012; Tomkins, 2013). Even if Leicester's analytics department was unique to the sport, many might argue that the club itself was simply primed for such a revolution to take hold. For this reason, some have already equated Leicester's rapid rise to that of Billy Beane's Oakland Athletics in the MLB. As documented in the bestselling book *Moneyball* by Michael Lewis (2004), Beane took an historically bad team with one of the lowest payrolls in the MLB on a remarkable regular season run that included a record winning streak and stellar performances by players whom the scouts had undervalued. Although using previously unheralded statistics, Beane was able to reinvent the game of baseball by fielding a team of affordable misfits that could perform in key statistical areas. However, it was only the Athletics' historical ineptness that provided him with the freedom and environment in which to impart such dramatic changes. As Beane himself said, "We had nothing to lose. We were in a position where we could try anything, and no matter what happened we were probably not going to end up any worse" (Sally & Anderson, 2013, p. 299). The same could be said of Leicester, a financial minnow that had barely managed to survive relegation from the EPL a year before; a club that had just hired an historically mediocre coach who had been fired from his previous job and was relying on the exploits of a former fifth-division striker (Jamie Vardy) and $600,000 midfielder (Riyad Mahrez) to carry his team to glory (Figueira, 2016). It is therefore easy to minimize the influence analytics may have had on Leicester's unprecedented success, or to position the club's achievement as a product of the circumstances. History, after all, has shown that money is imperative for sustained success in England's top flight.

Realizing new revenues and tapping new markets

The very idea that a club of Leicester's status could win the EPL has left many an analyst searching for answers. However remarkable, the club's rise to prominence cannot be attributed to analytics alone. Rather, the story may be better explained in light of the revenues that have continued to pour into the English club scene. As mentioned, the EPL is the recent beneficiary of some massive television deals which have endowed its member clubs with millions of dollars (Harris, 2016; Premier League, 2015b; Sandomir, 2015). It has also installed one of Europe's most equitable revenue sharing procedures, as its member clubs equally split the international broadcast and central sponsorship revenues (Premier League, 2015a). At the conclusion of the 2014–2015 season, these revenues, alone, amounted to almost $40 million per team. As Figure 1.3 shows, the EPL has grown to become the most financially dominant football league in the world. Across Europe, the cumulative revenues of the top five leagues rose by 15% to $12.9 billion between the 2013 and 2014 seasons. The EPL led the way with revenues of $4.45 billion, and its television deals were the largest source of this income (Deloitte, 2015). The gap between the EPL and its next closest competitor, the Bundesliga, is nearly $2 billion, and it currently generates more total revenues than La Liga and Serie A combined (Deloitte, 2015). But what does this mean for its clubs? And what does this have to do with Leicester City's surprise victory?

For starters, it means that all 20 EPL clubs are now ranked in the top 40, globally, in terms of the revenues they bring in (Deloitte, 2015). Even the smallest clubs, like Leicester City, earn enough money through television revenue sharing to rank in the top six, financially, of every other European

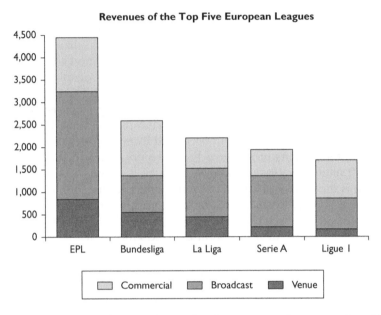

Revenues of the Top Five European Leagues

Figure 1.3 A histogram showing the total and proportional revenues (in millions of U.S. dollars) for each of the top five European football leagues

Data was retrieved from Deloitte (2015).

league. It also means that EPL teams are fully equipped to offer plush contracts to the world's best players. With the talent pool for player prospects widening amidst globalization, law changes, and advancements in technology, English teams stand poised to take full advantage of the numerous recruitment opportunities that now exist. No longer are they limited to domestic or even European players; rather, they can compete to sign high-level talents from across the globe. Football economist Szymanski (2015) noted that the expansion of the global market for playing talent will likely accompany a phenomenon known as talent compression. Citing a prior study by Gould (1983) in which it was shown that there were fewer MLB players with extreme statistical averages following the widening of baseball's talent pool, Szymanski argued that the same is happening in English and European football. Salary dispersion seems to be getting larger over time, implying that teams are becoming more equitable in terms of playing talent (Szymanski, 2015). Leicester City's dream season could therefore serve as evidence of these revenues and this phenomenon simply taking hold.

In essence, the early signs seem to be indicating that the EPL is becoming more competitively balanced. A quick analysis of the league's recent history seems to support this notion. The EPL has had four different champions over the past five seasons compared to three in La Liga, two in Ligue 1, two in the Bundesliga, and just one in Serie A. Other analyses have shown that the unpredictability of EPL matches increased in 2015–2016, reaching the highest levels of uncertainty in over a decade. Indeed, the EPL was also the most unpredictable, top-tier league in Europe based on how teams performed compared to bookmakers' odds (McHale, 2016). Perhaps the television revenues are increasing parity within the league and leading to greater uncertainty in each match. While one season cannot be used to justify the EPL as competitively balanced, the fact that the teams are trending towards equality on the balance sheet and on the pitch makes it a distinct possibility.

As it stands, the growth in the EPL's broadcasting revenues is showing little sign of slowing down. After all, the star-studded and often global composition of EPL rosters means that these clubs are also entitled to the lucrative revenues that exist in foreign markets. Therefore, English clubs and many of Europe's top teams are focusing their current marketing efforts on gathering interest from abroad. For this reason they embark on preseason tours of football's developing fan bases in Asia, Oceania, and North America, selling merchandise and selling out stadiums as they showcase their elite athletes to throngs of adoring fans (Maclurg, 2013). As the interest and viewership numbers continue to rise, so, too, will the payments made through foreign broadcasting deals. This will only pump more money into the pockets of team owners, who will likely then reinvest these revenues in their teams.

Nonetheless, the healthy financial margins and high levels of supporter enthusiasm enjoyed by Europe's top teams have not yet extended to the domestic clubs that operate in developing football nations such as India, China, and the United States. While the financial backing and established pedigree of Europe's top clubs leaves them with a massive competitive advantage, questions remain as to how up-and-coming leagues in other parts of the world can also claim a share of football's wealth. After all, one of the leagues aspiring to reach new heights is the aforementioned CSL. Like the EPL, it seems to be operating beneath the premise that success can be bought, and that in order to market a team, ownership needs to spend millions of dollars to sign top-level talents from across the world. Historically, the evidence does not bode well for China's most recent strategy turning into a success. After all, the league embarked on a similar spending spree several seasons ago, snapping up such prominent names as Didier Drogba and Nicolas Anelka to serve as the catalysts for its reformation. The strategy did not go according to plan, however, as the Drogba experiment lasted just half a season before he returned to Europe. Many within China regarded the failure to retain his services as a national embarrassment (Ramzy, 2013). Even so, simply signing big names in the hope that they will draw attention to a fledgling league or team may not be enough. As one study pointed out, Chinese fans that were aware of and involved with the CSL and its clubs actually possessed negative satisfaction levels toward the league's operative and marketing procedures (Gong et al., 2015).

Ultimately, opportunities abound within professional club football to take advantage of growing football markets that have not yet reached their full potential. As noted by Szymanski (2015), "The four biggest countries on earth, India, China, the United States, and Indonesia – with about 45 percent of the world's population between them – are just starting to switch on to football" (p. xii). Popular European clubs appear to have taken an early step in fulfilling the needs of these markets by embarking on preseason tours and distributing their media rights throughout each of these countries. Although these nations' own domestic leagues appear to be slightly behind the curve in terms of the star power and revenues they exude, many of them are starting to spend the money that is necessary to acquire high-level talent (Atkins, 2016; ESPNFC.com, 2016). However, whether or not the widespread popularity of the top five European leagues is hampering the advancement of these developing domestic leagues is a question worth asking (Fredrick-Brown, 2005). While many of Europe's best practices could be and are being emulated, one has to wonder whether the continent's stronghold on a majority of the game's revenues and best players will weaken any time soon. If not, the gap between Europe's elite and the rest of the world may continue to grow.

Professional football in the U.S.

There have been several failed attempts to popularize professional football in North America. The first known professional football league, the American League of Professional Football, dates to 1894 (Hollander, 1980). The league was a semi-professional league played in the northeast and mid-west regions of the U.S. (Hollander, 1980). The North American Soccer League (NASL), which was the first professional football league with a national reach in the U.S., was launched in the late 1960's and peaked in the late 1970s when football superstars such as Pelé, Beckenbauer, and Cruyff joined the league. The NASL had the major challenge of introducing and winning over the minds and hearts of American sport fans. Although the NASL suspended its outdoor operations in the mid-1980s, it introduced football to millions of Americans and contributed to football becoming one of the most popular youth sports in the U.S.; additionally, it served as blueprints for Major League Soccer (MLS; Tomasch, 2009), the current brand of professional football being played in the States.

Other serious attempts at top-level professional football leagues occurred in 1967 with the launch of two competing leagues, the United Soccer Association (USA) league and the National Professional Soccer League (NPSL). The debut of both leagues in the same year was no coincidence. The USA and NPSL leagues started one year after England's World Cup victory in 1966. The 1966 FIFA World Cup was one of the first major international sporting events to be broadcasted live on television (Chisari, 2006). The event drew a sizable television audience in America. Over one million viewers in the U.S. tuned in to watch England defeat West Germany in the 1966 FIFA World Cup Final (Wilson, 2017). The USA league was sanctioned by FIFA and had the support of the United States Soccer Federation (USSF) as the Division I professional football league in the U.S. The NPSL, on the other hand, was unsanctioned and labelled as an outlaw league by FIFA, which threatened to punish any player who joined an NPSL team. While the NPSL did not have FIFA's and the USSF's support, it did have a ten-year television contract worth $1.0 million per year with the CBS network (Lewis, 2017). After only one season, however, CBS terminated its contract with the NPSL claiming that NPSL games lacked TV appeal due to empty stadiums and foreign players unfamiliar to American spectators (Ludtke, 1976). Without a TV contract and reported losses of $5.0 million at the end of its inaugural season, NPSL executives negotiated a merger with the USA league to form the North American Soccer League (NASL) in 1968 (Lewis, 2017).

NASL executives reasoned that for professional football to succeed in America, football had to look more like other traditional American sports. To create a more exciting, familiar, and ultimately appealing form of football to the average American sport fan, the NASL modified a few century-old FIFA sanctioned rules of the game. The NASL changed the offside mark from midfield to the thirty-five-yard line to cut down on the number of offside infractions and traps. A count-down clock, typical of other American sports, was implemented rather than the traditional upwards to 90-minute clock that was used with stoppage time in Europe. To eliminate a drawing result, the NASL introduced a shootout system. To promote goal scoring, an elaborate point system for wins and losses was implemented, including six points for a win, three for a draw, plus up to three bonus points for each goal scored ("NASL, 1968–1984 – A review of the Golden Era", 2017). These were purposed to cut down on the number of shootouts, ties, and low scoring games, which were considered not appealing to American sport fans (Lisi, Boehm, & Davis, 2017).

The NASL brought football to the forefront of American sports in the late 1970s. The NASL strategy of signing international football stars captured the attention of the American sports media and the public. Péle's debut match for the New York Cosmos was televised nationally on CBS and brought a television audience of 10 million viewers (Ludtke, 1976). The New York Cosmos average home game attendance tripled for the 1975 season – the season Péle joined the Cosmos – and peaked in 1978 with an average of 47,856 fans per game (Jose, 1989). Filled with football icons, which included not only Pelé but Franz Beckenbauer, Carlos Alberto Torres, and Giorgio Chinaglia, the Cosmos frequently played for home and away crowds of more than 40,000 fans (Jose, 1989). The Cosmos playoff match against the Fort Lauderdale Strikers brought a crowd of 77,691 fans to

Giants Stadium (Yannis, 1977). That was not only the attendance record at a football match in the U.S. but also the highest attendance at Giants Stadium (Jose, 2003). By comparison, the Giants Stadium inaugural game on October 10, 1976 between the New York Giants and the Dallas Cowboys of the National Football League (NFL) brought in 76,042 fans. At its peak in the late 1970s, the NASL expanded to 24 teams with an average attendance of over 13,000 fans per game from 1977 to 1983 (NASL, 2017). Five teams averaged over 20,000 fans per game for at least three seasons and the Cosmos average attendance exceeded 42,000 spectators for three consecutive seasons (NASL, 2017). NASL's national TV contract with CBS (1974 to 1976), TVS Television Network (1977–1978), and ABC from 1979 to 1981 introduced football to millions of American viewers (Dewberry, 2010; Tomasch, 2009). In 1977, at the pinnacle of the Cosmos' success and the year Pelé retired, football was the fastest growing sport in the U.S. (José, 2003). Football became one of the most popular youth sports. The number of U.S. Youth Soccer membership grew from 103,432 in 1974 to 1,210,408 in 1985 (U.S. Youth Soccer, 2014). The short-term success on- and off- the field of the NY Cosmos and to a lesser extent the other handful of NASL teams was insufficient to sustain an entire league in the long run. Six years after Pelé's retirement from the Cosmos, the NASL had contracted from 24 to nine teams. By the end of the 1980 season, all NASL teams reported a running deficit and the league lost its national TV deal with ABC (Baker, 1981; Reed, 1980). With no national TV contract, declining gate receipts, and large debts, the NASL folded in 1984.

Four major factors contributed to the rapid decline and eventually demise of the NASL, including rapid and out-of-control league expansion, overreliance and overspending on international players, lack of ownership control, and lack of a league wide profitability model (Francis & Zheng, 2010). From the 1977 to the 1978 season, the NASL expanded from 18 to 24 teams. The NASL front office, keen to capitalize on the rising popularity of football in the mid-1970s brought by the success of Péle and other international football stars, allowed any bidder who could afford the $1 million expansion fee to join the league (Litterer, 2008). The NASL had little governance and oversight over its teams. The league was a collection of team owners motivated by the potential for fast and large profits. To achieve financial success, NASL team owners engaged in an arms' race to sign the next Pelé. Each team was left to fend for itself with little regard for the stability or longevity of the league. The frenzy to match the Cosmos' signing of international football stars triggered an irresponsible spending spree by NASL team owners (Francis & Zheng, 2010). To put in perspective, in 1980 NFL team owners spent about 40% of a team's budget on player salaries, whereas NASL team owners spent over 70% of their budget on player salaries. The money and effort spent recruiting international players and the lack of a strong "home-player" league rule left most teams fielding almost exclusively foreign players (Reed, 1980).

Since the demise of the NASL, a new league known as Major League Soccer (MLS) has attempted to learn from the mistakes of its predecessor and stake its claim on American soil. The MLS capitalized on the success of the 1994 World Cup in the U.S. much like those NPSL and USA investors before who saw the increased visibility and interest on football brought by the 1966 England World Cup as a timely and unique opportunity to market professional football to the American public (Francis & Zheng, 2010; Jose, 2003). By the time MLS debuted in 1996, Americans were already somewhat familiar with the sport of football. Nevertheless, the MLS has faced considerable challenges. First, it has faced the herculean task of starting a professional sport league in a saturated American professional sport marketplace where it had to compete with several major and minor established leagues for the attention and discretionary income of American sport fans. Second, the league has had the improbable mission of creating enough interest in a domestic professional football league to achieve financial prosperity and longevity (Strutner, Parrish, & Nauright, 2014). As part of the bidding process to host the 1994 FIFA World Cup, the U.S. Soccer Federation pledged to establish a top-level men's professional football league in the U.S. In 1993, the U.S. Soccer Federation selected the MLS to be the top level of professional football in the U.S. MLS was officially formed in 1995 as a limited liability organization and made its debut with ten teams in 1996, 12 years after the collapse of the NASL (Fraser v. MLS, 2000). Now, in its 21st season, the MLS is the second iteration of a top-level domestic professional domestic football in America.

One of the biggest challenges MLS has faced from its inception was not to repeat the mistakes that led to the demise of the NASL. That preoccupation has led MLS leaders to structure the league with an "anti-NASL" philosophy (Trekker, 2006). To avoid the dencentralization that allowed the NASL to expand uncontrollably and team owners to outspend one another in a destructive manner, MLS leaders set up the league as a single-entity. In a single-entity structure, the MLS retains centralized control over both the league and its teams. The league owns the intellectual property, tickets, and broadcast rights of all its teams. Moreover, revenues are shared and player contracts are negotiated by the league and not individual teams (Fraser v. MLS, 2000). These measures are set to limit spiraling costs, reduce expenditure competitions, prevent disputes over shared revenues, and avoid exploiting salary cap loopholes (Lubove, 1995). In addition to the single-entity legal structure, MLS leaders adopted a strategy of slow and controlled growth with respect to league expansion. The league started with ten teams in 1996 and expanded to 12 in 1998, with two teams being folded in 2002. It was not until 2004, eight years after its inaugural season, that the MLS began a slow and controlled expansion process. Since 2004, the MLS has more than doubled in size, expanding from ten to 22 teams by 2017. Careful consideration was given to award MLS franchises in large and small markets (Francis & Zheng, 2010; Owen, 2005). To control the over-reliance and over-spending on international players, the MLS limits the number of foreign players to four per team and instituted a hard salary cap for every team. MLS leaders reasoned that the strategy of relying on international talent was short-sighted and a major reason for the collapse of the NASL (Francis & Zheng, 2010). The strategy was to recruit domestic players with the conviction that fans would respond more positively to American players (Gilbert, 1995). Those policies remained in place until 2007 when the league modified its international player rule and made salary-cap exceptions to draw high-profile and talented international players (Thomaselli, 2009).

MLS team valuation and revenues have increased considerably in recent times. In 2016, the average MLS franchise was worth $185 million, an 80% increase when compared to 2013 and a 400% increase when compared with 2008, when the average MLS franchise was worth $37 million. The Los Angeles Galaxy is MLS's most valuable franchise, worth $315 million (Smith, 2017). Yet, although MLS has grown tremendously in these past 20 years, it continues to be stigmatized as a "second-tier" sport in America. MLS's TV ratings, media coverage, popularity, and profitability have all grown steadily over the past ten years, but professional football is still far from being considered a "major" sport in the U.S. MLS's financials pale in comparison to the other Big Four professional sport leagues in the U.S. For example, the LA Galaxy franchise would be ranked in the bottom quarter of the 122 teams in the Big Four professional sport leagues (Sports Money: 2016 Valuations [Smith, 2017]). The total revenue of the MLS is almost seven times lower than that of the National Hockey League (NHL), the lowest revenue generating league among the Big Four leagues, and 20 times lower than that of the NFL (see Table 1.3). The average revenue per franchise of MLS in 2015 was $30 million while the NHL average revenue per franchise was $136.70 million – 4.5 times higher than that of the MLS. The NFL average revenue per franchise in was $380 million, 12.6 times higher than that of the MLS (see Table 1.3).

Although the financial shortcomings of the NASL provided valuable lessons to MLS leaders, the path to financial stability has been long and treacherous. MLS commissioner Don Garber attributed this challenge to the fact that "the league has an inverted economic model. In most other leagues in the U.S. and probably in England as well, the dominant revenue comes from television. Today the majority of our income comes from the gate. After that comes sponsorship and television and then merchandising" (Francis & Zheng, 2010, p. 562; Owen, 2005). Recently, MLS has tried to diversify its revenue streams to get in a path of financial stability. The construction of football-specific stadiums, which reduce stadium leasing fees and allow for a better fan experience, help increase gate-receipt revenue and sponsorship deals (Wahl, 2007). Nonetheless, MLS's actions to increase profitability

Table 1.3 Revenue comparison: MLS and Big Four leagues

Professional Sport League	Season	Number of Teams	Total Revenue ($B)	Average Revenue per Franchise ($M)	Average Franchise Valuation ($B)
National Football League	2015	32	$12.20	$380.00	$2,338.40
Major League Baseball	2016	30	$9.00	$301.00	$1,536.83
National Basketball Association	2015–16	30	$5.87	$195.53	$1,355.33
National Hockey League	2015–16	30	$4.10	$136.70	$0.517
Major League Soccer	2015	20	$0.61	$30.60	$0.185

have yet to reach a point where the league is self-sustaining and profitable. Despite charging expansion clubs upwards of $150 million in league expansion fees, the league has reported annual operating losses for most of its existence.

Growth at the grassroots

If developing football nations like the United States and China intend to grow their domestic products from within, then perhaps they should start with an examination of their youth development systems. As mentioned before, both of these nations were latecomers to a modern form of the game that was developed primarily in England, and football's subsequent spread to the rest of Europe and South America was much more rapid and pronounced than it was in either of these nations. Therefore, European and South American nations have long benefited from a steady supply of youth football talent. Children have grown up wanting to emulate the success of famous stars like Pele (Brazil), Diego Maradona (Argentina), Franz Beckenbauer (Germany), and Sir Bobby Charlton (England). Likewise, established systems have been put in place to help discover, develop, and determine which players are good enough to represent their teams at the club and international levels.

Nonetheless, the full effects of globalization and emigration have shown that football's reach has no limits. As seen in Table 1.4, China and the United States currently rank number one and two, respectively, in terms of player participation at all levels of the game (FIFA, 2006). Recent viewership figures and the aforementioned media rights deals also attest to the game's rising popularity within these countries (Johnson, 2015; Premier League, 2012; Sandomir, 2015). However, research has shown that youth participation numbers have tended to fall as children move from childhood to adolescence. In the United States, for example, nearly 21% of all six-year-olds

Table 1.4 Top 20 FIFA associations ranked by total player participation

Association	All Players	Registered Players	Unregistered Players	Clubs	Officials
China PR	26,166,335	711,235	25,455,100	2,221	129,057
USA	24,472,778	4,186,778	20,286,000	9,000	796,300
India	20,587,900	384,900	20,203,000	6,540	38,640
Germany	16,308,946	6,308,946	10,000,000	26,837	159,172
Brazil	13,197,733	2,141,733	11,056,000	29,208	61,000
Mexico	8,479,595	324,595	8,155,000	311	85,789
Indonesia	7,094,260	66,960	7,027,300	83	1,069
Nigeria	6,653,710	58,710	6,595,000	52	33,122
Bangladesh	6,280,300	271,300	6,009,000	4,100	75,604
Russia	5,802,536	846,736	4,955,800	14,329	259,830
Italy	4,980,296	1,513,596	3,466,700	16,697	78,481
Japan	4,805,150	1,045,150	3,760,000	2,000	249,603
South Africa	4,540,410	1,469,410	3,071,000	900	20,557
France	4,190,040	1,794,940	2,395,100	20,062	285,723
England	4,164,110	1,485,910	2,678,200	42,490	168,186
Ethiopia	3,474,245	56,245	3,418,000	1,004	310,600
Egypt	3,138,110	52,110	3,086,000	608	18,270
Colombia	3,043,229	291,229	2,752,000	2,773	15,800
Pakistan	2,975,400	64,400	2,911,000	720	9,900
Spain	2,834,190	653,190	2,181,000	18,190	62,573

Note: Data was retrieved from the FIFA Big Count (2006).

play football in some form, but by the time they turn 12, this number has shrunk to 14%. At age 17, it is only 9% (King, 2014). Therefore, one of the pressing needs within these countries involves finding a way to translate the high participation numbers into sustained interest at the more advanced grassroots levels. Cultivating the skill of the athletes who do progress to the highest levels is equally important. To this end, more efficient developmental systems and administrations that better educate young players on the technical and tactical elements of the game could prove beneficial in the long run. In addition, the integration of these platforms with the players' everyday lives – as seen in Europe's youth academies – would allow the players to get the practice repetitions that are necessary for increased skill (Helsen, Hodges, Winckel, & Starkes, 2000).

World Cup legacy

Many world leaders, national and local governments, and public figures have considered the World Cup to be a means for economic, social, infrastructural, and political advancement. With this viewpoint, though, comes a need to justify to one's constituents just how beneficial the hosting of a World Cup will actually be. This is particularly important since taxpayer dollars and government resources are often used to erect the stadiums and develop the infrastructure that is necessary to host a tournament of this magnitude (Howard & Crompton, 2014). As seen with the two most recent World Cups in Brazil and South Africa, many of these resources can end up being wasted on stadiums that will see little or no use after the final whistle blows (Douglas, 2015). Such wastefulness can be particularly troubling within emerging economies, like Brazil and China, which could have used the money elsewhere. Therefore, proper planning is necessary to ensure that these tournaments will leave behind a positive legacy. To this end, a variety of studies have been conducted to show the true benefits that actually accrue to a host community (Cornelissen, Bob, & Swart, 2011; Lee & Taylor, 2005; Pillay, Tomlinson, & Bass, 2009), with some going so far as to suggest that the positive economic impacts of mega events and facility construction projects are often overstated (Howard & Crompton, 2014; Hudson, 2001).

Ultimately, it seems that for all of the attention and money that flows through the FIFA World Cup every four years, significantly less consideration is given to the long-term effects that these events will have on their host communities. FIFA attempts to downplay these issues by highlighting the existence of its Legacy Fund or by positioning the World Cup as a key instrument in societal development (FIFA, 2014b, 2016c), but the reality is that many are starting to question the merits of hosting a World Cup in countries that cannot afford it. Many are also starting to question the reputation of FIFA itself after the association became immersed in a series of recent scandals. The first and most pronounced of these indignities saw 30 prominent FIFA officials indicted on the grounds of "rampant, systemic, and deep-rooted corruption" (BBC.com, 2015). The corruption in focus revolved around a series of criminal schemes that saw FIFA officials exchange over $200 million in bribes and kickbacks. Many of these illegal payouts were disguised as developmental costs that were supposed to be applied toward infrastructural improvements in poorer football communities (BBC.com, 2015).

The currently held assumption is that many of these payments were made as bribes to buy the votes of FIFA officials during the bidding processes for the 2018 and 2022 World Cups. Initial concerns, after all, were ignited when the tiny but wealthy nation of Qatar was awarded the rights to host the 2022 World Cup. Qatar contains a population of just 1.5 million and reaches an average temperature of 110 degrees in the summer months when World Cups are normally held (Carlson, 2010). It has almost no club system or suitable facilities to speak of, and its national team has never qualified for a FIFA World Cup. In addition, reports have surfaced of the horrible conditions that are being faced by its migrant construction workers (Gibson & Pattisson, 2014). All of these issues have factored into the negative light that is now being cast on FIFA. Although time is needed for the full line of facts to emerge in each of these situations, the transparency and honesty of FIFA's bidding process and financial management are both under question. Those in charge of football's global governing body are now faced with the challenge of replacing the top executives and repairing the damages that have been done.

The women's game

Despite the issues that have plagued FIFA in recent years, the World Cup as an event still holds a power that extends far beyond the field of play. In 2005, for instance, the Ivory Coast's qualification for the 2006 World Cup in Germany initiated peace talks between the two parties that had been waging a civil war in the country for years (Rainbow, 2013). Similarly, the 2014 World Cup final inspired the Vatican to call for a global ceasefire on social media amidst rising tensions in Ukraine and the Middle East (Blumberg, 2014). These examples are just two in a long line of scenarios that have seen the World Cup bring joy, hope, and unity to countries around the world. "Sport can reach parts politicians can't reach," said former U.K. Prime Minister Tony Blair. "It can help in bringing divided conflicts together in a way nothing else can" (Rainbow, 2013).

Many assert that football, the world's most popular sport, can bring about positive changes to a nation. Although it may not arrive in the form of lavish World Cup stadiums or a club league that is on par with Europe's elite, the sport as a whole presents plenty of opportunities for societal enrichment. In the past this was seen through football's positive impact on gender equality, as the spread of the game presented new opportunities for females to enjoy the benefits of team sports. Ironically, nowhere was this more evident than in nations such as China and the United States; nations where the men's game had not taken complete hold. However, some recent setbacks have been suffered by the women's game within both of these countries. The Chinese women's national team, one of the strongest sides in women's football throughout the 1980s and 90s, fell out of form at the turn of the century as members of its golden generation retired. A thinned-out pool of talent proved inadequate at replacing the resigning veterans and highlighted the lack of foresight that existed within the national team system (Halsley, 2015; Su, 2015). As such, they have already begun enacting a series of measures that should see the women's team return to prominence. Amongst these are an overhaul of the youth system, improvements in elite training, and logistic support. A recent appearance in the quarterfinals of the 2015 Women's World Cup has offered a glimmer of hope that brighter days may lie ahead (Su, 2015). Speaking after the team won in the round of 16, CCTV commentator Shen Fangjiang said, "No matter how far they go, these women deserve applause for their dedication, persistence, and hard work during a tough time for the game in China" (Su, 2015). To reward their efforts, the CFA created the largest-ever pool of prize money in the history of the women's game.

However, the improvements being made in China stand in stark contrast to the current status of the women's game in other parts of the world. Members of the United States women's national team, for instance, recently filed a discrimination complaint against the United States Football Federation (USSF) on the basis of unequal pay for equal work. The complaint alleges, amongst other things, that the women receive considerably less in performance-related bonuses than their male counterparts and are forced to play and travel under worse conditions (Spies-Gans, 2016). It also argued that the team, which won the 2015 Women's World Cup, was not being duly compensated for its achievements. "In this day and age, it's about equality," said goalkeeper Hope Solo. "It's about equal rights. It's about equal pay. We're pushing for that. We believe now the time is right because we believe it's our responsibility for women's sports, and specifically for women's football, to do whatever it takes to push for equal pay and equal rights. And to be treated with respect" (Spies-Gans, 2016).

Again, it appears as though football is giving a voice to those who seek positive change; however, the issues presented here do not start with the USSF. Rather, they stem from FIFA and the secondary nature with which it has treated women's football over the years. This is seen simply by comparing the prize monies that are distributed to male and female teams in their respective World Cups. The U.S. women's national team, for example, took home $2 million for winning the 2015 Women's World Cup while the 16 men's teams that were eliminated in the group stages of the 2014 FIFA World Cup were awarded $8 million (Isidore, 2015). Sexist remarks were also a hallmark of former FIFA president Sepp Blatter's controversial tenure. He was once quoted as saying that in order for the women's game to attract more viewers, the players needed to "have tighter shorts" (Isidore, 2015). The fact that the women were forced to play on turf fields – a traditionally rougher surface – at the most recent World Cup was the source of further controversy; the men, after all, played all of their World Cup games on natural grass.

While such remarks and playing conditions are inexcusable, the financial disparities can be more easily justified. This is due to the fact that the revenues brought in by the men's and women's games vary immensely. Even within the United States, where the women's team has enjoyed more on-field success than the men's team, the female version of the sport on average attracts fewer fans and lower television audiences. Despite the recent claims of the U.S. women's national team, a simple review of facts, figures, and the USSF's latest financial reports will show that the men sell more tickets, accrue higher television ratings, and ultimately earn more revenues during the standard four-year budgeting cycle (Dure, 2016; Kennedy, 2016; United States Football Federation, 2016). Marketers and managers are therefore presented with both a challenge and an opportunity to improve the appeal of women's football to fans, media members, and corporate sponsors. Up to now, most strategies have sought to build on the popularity of the women's game at the grassroots level by turning these young players into fans. One way in which this has been done is by hosting fan festivals that allow young girls and their families to interact with the players before or after games. These events bring the sport's heroes down to a more personal level and allow meaningful connections to be made (Jowdy & McDonald, 2002). Others have also highlighted the need for marketers to portray female athletes as role models while offering a wholesome experience to those who attend (Funk, Ridinger, & Moorman, 2003). However, it is becoming clear that more effective measures need to be taken. The global and financial advancement of football at the women's level depends on it.

Closing remarks

Overall, football appears to be operating healthily at its highest levels. Europe's top five leagues, and in particular the EPL, are as popular as ever and awash with lucrative television, commercial, and merchandising revenues (Deloitte, 2015). These revenues, coupled with the presence of bank-rolling owners, have allowed the top teams in these leagues to spend lavishly on star recruits in their pursuit of success. Prior to the 2015–2016 season, it seemed as though the wealthiest teams were locked into a cycle of dominance (Szymanski, 2015); however, the emergence of Leicester City offers an opportunity for researchers to explore for factors that may have contributed to the club's unlikely EPL triumph. Opportunity also abounds beyond European borders in the domestic leagues of nations that are just beginning to tap into football's popularity and wealth. The Chinese Super League is one such league, and if freed from the corruption and bureaucratic measures that have hindered its development and operation over the past few years, it could begin marketing itself in a new light (Gong et al., 2015). If it could find a way to increase American interest and overall profitability, the MLS might also find its way into club football's upper echelons.

On the international scene, FIFA is certainly facing its fair share of administrative challenges, but the World Cup continues to entertain billions of people around the globe. More research is needed, though, in the areas of legacy and development. After all, the costs that are incurred by a host community make it important for FIFA to ensure that it is acting responsibly toward the cities and nations that publicly fund these tournaments. In addition, football's far-reaching influence means that it is capable of positively impacting numerous areas of society. The women's and grassroots levels of the sport are therefore ripe with opportunity from a development standpoint. Figuring out how to effectively manage and market these segments is imperative to an emerging football nation like China as it attempts to turn itself into a global powerhouse at every level of the game (Gibson, 2015).

As evidenced by the rising number of participants at the youth and recreational levels, and the record-breaking television deals that are funding
and promoting the top international leagues and competitions, the sport
is continuing to make strides at a variety of levels. In fact, football, which
has always been popular in Europe and South America, is now garnering
increased attention in Africa, Asia, and North America, where professional
football has historically been less structured and popular. The overall attention devoted to the sport is also bridging numerous socio-economic, racial,
and gender-related gaps, powering forward a global phenomenon that has
been able to stand the tests of time and culture. In lieu of football's continued
dominance in global sport, appeal to a wide variety of audiences, and persis-
tent expansion into the market frontiers of Africa, Asia, and North America,
it has become highly pertinent for scholars and practitioners to look into the
managerial forces that drive its growth and sustainability across all levels.
Beginning with the grassroots systems that are in place for youth development, and culminating in the billions of dollars in revenues that drive the
highly competitive professional leagues in Europe and abroad, the spectrum
in which management and marketing theories can be applied and analyzed
is ripe with new prospects. In fact, football's continued growth has brought
forth new opportunities and challenges as teams and programs operate in
an increasingly competitive environment and promote their products and
services in a complex, globalized marketplace.

In an effort to critically examine contemporary issues, formulate theories,
identify best practices and guidelines, and contribute to football's continued
growth, the co-editors of this book have selected research papers that focus
on a variety of marketing perspectives as they pertain to the football industry at all levels. Formatted into book chapters, they are empirical, theoretical, critical, and/or case studies covering a wide spectrum of research
questions in local, national, regional, and global settings. There are a total
of 12 chapters in this book that are divided into two sections: (a) global
football industry and (b) marketing perspectives. It is necessary to highlight
that a total of 29 authors from seven countries or territories contributed to
this book, representing a diverse background of scholars.

References

Atkins, C. (2016). *Jiangsu Suning shock world football with Alex Teixeira and Ramires
deals*. Retrieved February 6, 2016, from www.espnfc.us/blog/espn-fc-united-blog/68/
post/2802268/jiangsu-suning-shock-football-with-alex-teixeira-and-ramires
Bahia, R. (2015). *Inside Leicester city*. Retrieved October 15, 2015, from www.
optasportspro.com/about/optapro-blog/posts/2015/blog-inside-leicester-city/
Baker, C. (1981). Soccer: Is it still the sport of the 80s. *The Telegraph*, p. 30. Retrieved
August 21, 2017, from https://news.google.com/newspapers?nid=2209&dat=1981
1112&id=qaErAAAAIBAJ&sjid=hfwFAAAAIBAJ&pg=6924,2551485
Bandenhausen, K. (2015). Manchester United kit launch generates millions in social
media value for Adidas. *Forbes*. Retrieved August 21, 2017, from www.forbes.

com/sites/kurtbadenhausen/2015/08/05/manchester-united-kit-launch-generates-millions-in-social-media-value-for-adidas/#14361eef5ad4

Baxter, K. (2014). *Manchester United uniform is pricey real estate, as Chevrolet knows*. Retrieved July 21, 2014, from www.latimes.com/sports/football/la-sp-manchester-united-20140722-story.html

BBC.com. (2015). *Fifa corruption crisis: Key questions answered*. Retrieved December 21, 2015, from www.bbc.com/news/world-europe-32897066

Blumberg, A. (2014). *Vatican calls for global ceasefire during world cup final with #pauseforpeace hashtag*. Retrieved July 11, 2014, from www.huffingtonpost.com/2014/07/11/vatican-ceasefire-world-cup_n_5578546.html

Both, A. (2015). *Super bowl has ways to go in captivating global audience*. Retrieved January 24, 2015, from www.reuters.com/article/us-nfl-international-idUSKBN0KX0KK20150124

Carlson, N. (2010). The 7 reasons a World Cup in Qatar is so outrageously stupid. *Business Insider*. Retrieved August 21, 2017, from www.businessinsider.com/the-7-reasons-a-world-cup-in-qatar-is-so-outrageously-stupid-2010–12

Carmichael, F., & Thomas, D. (1993). Bargaining in the transfer market: Theory and evidence. *Applied Economics*, 25(12), 1467–1476.

Chisari, F. (2006). When football went global: Televising the 1966 World Cup. *Historical Social Research*, 31(1), 42–54.

Cornelissen, S., Bob, U., & Swart, K. (2011). Towards redefining the concept of legacy in relation to sport mega-events: Insights from the 2010 FIFA World Cup. *Development Southern Africa*, 28(3), 307–318.

Cunningham, S. (2013). *From a £100 scot to Ronaldo for £80m, and now Bale – look at the history of the world's record transfer*. Retrieved August 21, 2017, from www.dailymail.co.uk/sport/football/article-2399897/Gareth-Bale-signs-Real-Madrid – world-transfer-record-broken-42nd-time.html

Deloitte. (2015). *Annual review of football finance*. Retrieved August 21, 2017, from www2.deloitte.com/content/dam/Deloitte/global/Documents/About-Deloitte/gx-deloitte-uk-arff-2015-highlights.pdf

Dewberry, E. (2010). *Framing Soccer for the network era: ABC and the challenge to nationally broadcast the North American Soccer league, 1979–1981*. Retrieved May 27, 2017, from http://mediacommons.futureofthebook.org/imr/2010/11/12/framing-soccer-network-era-abc-and-challenge-nationally-broadcast-north-american-soccer-l

Dobson, S., & Gerrard, B. (1999). The determination of player transfer fees in English professional football. *Journal of Sport Management*, 13(4), 259–279.

Douglas, B. (2015). *World cup leaves Brazil with bus depots and empty stadiums*. Retrieved March 29, 2015, from www.bbc.com/sport/football/32073525

Dure, B. (2016). The US women's football pay dispute: A tangled web with no easy answers. *The Guardian*. Retrieved August 21, 2017, from www.theguardian.com/football/2016/apr/11/uswnt-womens-football-pay-gamble-gender-equality

ESPNFC.com. (2016). *Premier league January spending trumped by Chinese super league*. Retrieved March 8, 2016, from www.espnfc.us/chinese-super-league/story/2824777/premier-league-spending-topped-by-chinese-super-league

FIFA. (2006). *Big count*. Retrieved August 21, 2017, from www.fifa.com/worldfootball/bigcount/allplayers.html

FIFA. (2010). *Financial report 2010*. Retrieved August 21, 2017, from www.fifa.com/mm/document/affederation/administration/01/39/20/45/web_fifa_fr2010_eng[1].pdf

FIFA. (2014a). *2014 FIFA World Cup reached 3.2 billion viewers, one billion watched final*. Retrieved August 21, 2017, from www.fifa.com/worldcup/news/y=2015/m=12/news=2014-fifa-world-cuptm-reached-3-2-billion-viewers-one-billion-watched-2745519.html

FIFA. (2014b). *Financial report 2014*. Retrieved August 21, 2017, from www.fifa.com/mm/document/affederation/administration/02/56/80/39/fr2014weben_neutral.pdf

FIFA. (2016a). *History of FIFA – the first FIFA world cup*. Retrieved August 21, 2017, from www.fifa.com/about-fifa/who-we-are/history/first-fifa-world-cup.html

FIFA. (2016b). *History of football – the origins*. Retrieved August 21, 2017, from www.fifa.com/about-fifa/who-we-are/the-game/index.html

FIFA. (2016c). *What we stand for: About FIFA*. Retrieved August 21, 2017, from www.fifa.com/about-fifa/who-we-are/explore-fifa.html

FIFA Transfer Matching System. (2016). *Monthly insights: China PR*. Retrieved August 21, 2017, from https://reports.fifatms.com/wp-content/uploads/2016/03/Monthly-insights_China-PR_JanFebTransfer-window-2016.pdf

Figueira, J. (2016). *Leicester city win the premier league: Their remarkable title by the numbers*. Retrieved May 3, 2016, from www.espnfc.com/blog/five-aside/77/post/2863760/the-numbers-behind-leicester-city-premier-league-title

Francis, J., & Zheng, C. (2010). Learning vicariously from failure: The case of major league Soccer and the collapse of the North American Soccer league. *Group & Organization Management, 35*(5), 542–571.

Fraser v. Major League Soccer, 284 47 (US 1st Cir March 20, 2002).

Fredrick-Brown, S. (2005). Can European football spur interest in American football? A look at the champions world™ series and major league football. *Football & Society, 6*(1), 49–61.

Frick, B. (2007). The football players' labor market: Empirical evidence from the major European leagues. *Scottish Journal of Political Economy, 54*(3), 422–446.

Funk, D. C., Ridinger, L. L., & Moorman, A. M. (2003). Understanding consumer support: Extending the Sport Interest Inventory (SII) to examine individual differences among women's professional sport consumers. *Sport Management Review, 6*(1), 1–31.

Gerrard, B. (2007). Is the Moneyball approach transferable to complex invasion team sports? *International Journal of Sport Finance, 2*(4), 214.

Gibson, O. (2015). *China's focus on football could tilt the global game on its axis*. Retrieved September 8, 2015, from www.theguardian.com/football/2015/sep/08/china-focus-football-global-game

Gibson, O., & Pattison, P. (2014). Death toll among Qatar's 2022 World Cup workers revealed. *The Guardian*. Retrieved August 21, 2017, from www.theguardian.com/world/2014/dec/23/qatar-nepal-workers-world-cup-2022-death-toll-doha

Gilbert, N. (1995). Kickoff time for Soccer. *Financial World, 164*(4), 78–86.

Gong, B., Pifer, N. D., Wang, J. J., Kim, M., Kim, M., Qian, T. Y., & Zhang, J. J. (2015). Fans' attention to, involvement in, and satisfaction with professional football in China. *Social Behavior and Personality, 43*(10), 1667–1682.

Gould, S. J. (1983). Losing the edge: The extinction of the 400 hitter. *Vanity Fair, 120*, 264–278.

Hall, S., Szymanski, S., & Zimbalist, A. S. (2002). Testing causality between team performance and payroll: The cases of major league baseball and English football. *Journal of Sports Economics, 3*(2), 149–168.

Halsley, B. (2015). *The once great, now unknown China women's national team.* Retrieved June 3, 2015, from http://screamer.deadspin.com/the-once-great-now-unknown-china-womens-national-team-1708675354

Harris, N. (2016). *New year, new TV billions: Premier league rules the world, with foreign sales of games set to hit £1billion a year in 2016 deals.* Retrieved August 21, 2017, from www.dailymail.co.uk/sport/football/article-3382281/New-year-new-TV-billions-Premier-League-rules-world-foreign-sales-games-set-hit-1billion-year-2016-deals.html

Helsen, W. F., Hodges, N. J., Winckel, J. V., & Starkes, J. L. (2000). The roles of talent, physical precocity and practice in the development of football expertise. *Journal of Sports Sciences, 18*(9), 727–736.

Hollander, Z. (1980). *The American encyclopedia of Soccer.* New York: Everest House.

Howard, D. R., & Crompton, J. L. (2014). *Financing sport* (3rd ed.). Morgantown, WV: FIT.

Hudson, I. (2001). The use and misuse of economic impact analysis the case of professional sports. *Journal of Sport & Social Issues, 25*(1), 20–39.

Isidore, C. (2015). *Women world cup champs win waaaaay less money than men.* Retrieved August 21, 2017, from http://money.cnn.com/2015/07/07/news/companies/womens-world-cup-prize-money/

Johnson, A. (2015). *Football by the numbers: A look at the game in the U.S.* Retrieved August 21, 2017, from www.nbcnews.com/storyline/fifa-corruption-scandal/football-numbers-look-game-u-s-n365601

Jose, C. (1989). *NASL, a complete record of the North American Soccer league.* Derby, England: Breedon.

Jose, C. (2003). *North American Soccer league encyclopedia.* Haworth, NJ: St Johann.

Jowdy, E., & McDonald, M. (2002). Relationship marketing and interactive fan festivals: The Women's United Football Association's' football sensation. *International Journal of Sports Marketing & Sponsorship, 4*(4), 295–311.

Kennedy, P. (2016). TV viewers: U.S. men vs. U.S. women. *Football America Daily.* Retrieved August 21, 2017, from www.footballamerica.com/article/68281/tv-viewers-us-men-vs-us-women.html

Kim, S. (2015). *The future of American football after women's world cup victory.* Retrieved July 6, 2015, from http://abcnews.go.com/Business/future-american-football-womens-world-cup-victory/story?id=32256814

King, B. (2014). *Football's growing reach.* Retrieved June 2, 2014, from www.sportsbusinessdaily.com/Journal/Issues/2014/06/02/In-Depth/Participation.aspx#

Kuper, S., & Szymanski, S. (2012). *Footballnomics: Why England loses, why Spain, Germany and Brazil win, and why the US, Japan, Australia, Turkey – and even Iraq – are destined to become the kings of the world's most popular sport.* New York: Nation.

Lee, C. K., & Taylor, T. (2005). Critical reflections on the economic impact assessment of a mega-event: the case of 2002 FIFA World Cup. *Tourism Management, 26*(4), 595–603.

Lewis, M. (2004). *Moneyball: The art of winning an unfair game.* New York: Norton.

Lewis, M. (2017). *U.S. pro Soccer's 50th anniversary: 'They called us communists and midgets'.* Retrieved May 25, 2017, from www.theguardian.com/football/2017/apr/17/america-soccer-league-npsl

Lisi, C., Boehm, C., & Davis, J. (2017). *NASL: Arrogant Americans take on FIFA. U.S. Soccer players*. Retrieved 1 June 2017, from https://ussoccerplayers.com/history/the-nasl/nasl-arrogant-Americans

Litterer, D. (2008). *North American Soccer league I (1967–1984). The American Soccer history archive*. Retrieved 1 June 2017, from http://homepages.sover.net/~spectrum/nasl/naslhist.html

Lubove, S. (1995). Soccer socialism. *Forbes, 156*, 259–262.

Ludtke, M. (1976). Soccer is getting a toehold. *Sports Illustrated*. Retrieved August 21, 2017, from www.si.com/vault/1976/08/30/615444/soccer-is-getting-a-toehold#

Maclurg, I. (2013). *FC Barcelona to hold pre-season tour in China, Thailand and Malaysia in August*. Retrieved March 4, 2013, from www.fcbarcelona.com/football/first-team/detail/article/fc-barcelona-to-hold-pre-season-tour-in-china-thailand-and-malaysia-in-august

Marcotti, G. (2013). *How do you put a value on a guy like Gareth Bale?* Retrieved August 21, 2017, from http://espnfc.com/blog/_/name/espnfcunited/id/8858?cc=5901

McHale, I. (2016). *Just how unpredictable is the premier league? Scientists have done the maths*. Retrieved August 17, 2016, from http://theconversation.com/just-how-unpredictable-is-the-premier-league-scientists-have-done-the-maths-59839

NASL. (2017). *Kenn.com. Attendance project*. Retrieved June 21, 2017, from www.kenn.com/the_blog/?page_id=496

NASL. (2017). *1968–1984 – a review of the golden era*. Retrieved April 4, 2017, from www.nasl.com/a-review-of-the-golden-era

Ormsby, A. (2012). *London 2012 opening ceremony draws 900 million viewers*. Retrieved August 7, 2012, from http://uk.reuters.com/article/uk-oly-ratings-day-idUKBRE8760V820120807

Owen, D. (2005, March 28). The beautiful game aims to score in America. *Financial Times*, p. 8.

Pillay, U., Tomlinson, R., & Bass, O. (2009). *Development and dreams: The urban legacy of the 2010 Football world cup*. Pretoria, South Africa: HSRC.

Premier League. (2012). *Super sports media group acquires premier league rights in China*. Retrieved October 30, 2012, from www.premierleague.com/en-gb/news/news/2012-13/oct/super-sports-media-group-acquires-premier-league-rights-in-china-and-macau.html

Premier League. (2015a). *Premier league announces payments to clubs in season 2014/15*. Retrieved August 21, 2017, from www.premierleague.com/en-gb/news/news/2015-16/jun/020615-premier-league-payments-to-clubs-in-season-2014-15.html

Premier League. (2015b). *Premier league awards UK live broadcast rights for 2016/17 to 2018/19*. Retrieved Augsut 21, 2017, from www.premierleague.com/en-gb/news/news/2014-15/feb/100215-premier-league-uk-live-broadcasting-rights-announced.html

Rainbow, J. (2013). *Football as peacemaker? In ivory coast it might just work*. Retrieved March 31, 2013, from www.worldfootball.com/blogs/football-as-peacemaker-in-ivory-coast-it-might-just-work-339960

Ramzy, A. (2013). *Didier Drogba leaves China: Inside a failed football experiment*. Retrieved January 30, 2013, from http://keepingscore.blogs.time.com/2013/01/30/didier-drogba-leaves-china-inside-a-failed-football-experiment/

Reed, J. (1980). It's time for trimming sails in the NASL. *Sports Illustrated*, pp. 22–23. Retrieved August 21, 2017, from www.si.com/vault/issue/70916/24/2#

Sally, D., & Anderson, C. (2013). *The numbers game: Why everything you know about football is wrong*: London: Penguin Group.

Sandomir, R. (2015). *NBC retains rights to premier league in six-year deal*. Retrieved August 10, 2015, from www.nytimes.com/2015/08/11/sports/football/nbc-retains-rights-to-premier-league-in-six-year-deal.html?_r=0

Simons, R. (2004). Real back in for Viera. *The Evening Standard*. Retrieved August 21, 2017, from www.standard.co.uk/sport/real-back-in-for-vieira-6980648.html

Smith, C. (2017). *Forbes welcome: Major league Soccer's most valuable teams 2016: New York and Orlando thrive in first seasons*. Retrieved June 15, 2017, from www.forbes.com/sites/chrissmith/2016/09/07/major-league-soccers-most-valuable-teams-2016-new-york-orlando-thrive-in-first-seasons/#46ec7911270d

Spies-Gans, J. (2016). *USWNT files lawsuit against U.S. football in fight for equal pay*. Retrieved August 21, 2017, from www.huffingtonpost.com/entry/uswnt-wage-discriminatory-suit-us-football_us_56fd33c3e4b0a06d5804ecac

Sporting Intelligence. (2011). *The global game: An A-Z of how the world watches the premier league – China*. Retrieved November 15, 2011, from http://blogs.independent.co.uk/2011/11/09/the-global-game-an-a-z-of-how-the-world-watches-the-premier-league-%E2%80%93-china/

Strutner, M., Parrish, C., & Nauright, J. (2014). Making Soccer "major league" in the USA and beyond: Major league Soccer's first decade. *Sport History Review*, 45(1), 23–36.

Su, X. C. (2015). *Football buzz rises with women players' victory*. Retrieved June 22, 2015, from www.womenofchina.cn/womenofchina/html1/news/sports/1506/1978-1.htm

Szymanski, S. (2015). *Money and football: A footballnomics guide*. New York: Nation.

Szymanski, S. (2016). *Leicester city and Donald trump: A new era for the premier league?* Retrieved March 24, 2016, from www.footballnomics-agency.com/?p=890

Thomaselli, R. (2009). Soccer in the U.S. reaches its goals a step at a time. *Advertising Age*, 80(13), 14.

Tomasch, K. (2009). *NASL TV: A short history*. Retrieved June 16, 2017, from www.kenn.com/the_blog/?page_id=553

Tomkins, P. (2013). *These turbulent times: Liverpool FC's search for success*. London: GPRF.

Tomkins, P., Riley, G., & Fulcher, G. (2010). *Pay as you play: The true price of success in the Premier league era*. London: GPRF.

Trekker, J. (2006). *Chelsea, MLS, and the NASL*. Retrieved May 20, 2008, from http://community.foxsports.com/blogs/JamieTrecker/2006/08/04/Chelsea_MLS_and_the_NASL

U.S. Youth Soccer. (2014). *Annual registration of players*. Retrieved June 2, 2017, from www.usyouthsoccer.org/media_kit/keystatistics/

United States Football Federation. (2016). *U.S. Football 2016 annual general meeting*. Retrieved August 21, 2017, from http://media.philly.com/documents/2016+U.S.+Football+Annual+General+Meeting+Minutes.pdf

Wahl, G. (2007). *Anatomy of a blockbuster: The story behind the Beckham deal and the economics*. Retrieved May 20, 2017, from http://sportsillustrated.cnn.com/2007/writers/grant_wahl/01/17/beckham.qa/index.html

Wilson, B. (2017). USA 1967: When American Soccer's summer of love ended in tears. *BBC News*. Retrieved June 5, 2017, from www.bbc.com/news/business-38904513

Yannis, A. (1977). *Cosmos triumph at giants stadium before record Soccer: Crowd of 77,691*. Retrieved August 21, 2017, from www.nytimes.com/1977/08/15/ archives/cosmos-triumph-at-giants-stadium-before-record-soccer-crowd-of. html?nytmobile=0

Zygband, P., Collignon, H., Sultan, N., Santander, C., & Valensi, U. (2011). *The sports markets: Major trends and challenges in an industry full of passion*. Chicago, IL: A. T. Kearney.

Chapter 2

European grassroots football

Structural and managerial peculiarities

Christoph Breuer and Tobias Nowy

Introduction

The governance system of European football can be considered hierarchical and is often described as a pyramid in which international governing bodies such as the Union des Associations Européennes de Football (UEFA) sit at the top, national member associations beneath them, and then, below that, the grassroots represented by voluntary amateur football clubs (Breuer, Feiler, & Wicker, 2015; Gratton & Taylor, 2000; Peeters & Szymanski, 2014). Within that pyramid there is an internal (vertical) solidarity to protect the sustainability of the game (Brown, 2000). Grassroots football clubs, as the foundation of football (Vos et al., 2012), support professional football by developing and providing playing talent, coaches, and officials while the professional sector as the "*tip of the iceberg*" (UEFA, 2015) serves as the promotor of the entire sport. Arguably, the more solid the foundation of the pyramid is – i.e., the better the grassroots football clubs are in shape – the better are the chances for a sustainable development of the sport (Breuer & Nowy, 2015).

Football's importance as a social and economic phenomena within Europe is underlined by some 20 million men and women registered as players in more than 50 national football federations (Crolley & Hand, 2013) and the impact of grassroots football clubs goes beyond the sheer provision of the game (Hoye, Smith, Nicholson, & Stewart, 2015). The clubs' role as the "*key architectural structure*" (Adams, 2011, p. 85) for the creation of social capital to accrue and as the "*democratic infrastructure*" (Enjolras & Waldahl, 2010, p. 215) of democracy has been increasingly cited in public policies (Doherty & Misener, 2008; Nicholson, Hoye, & Houlihan, 2011; Tacon, 2014).

In order to deliver such benefits to society, European grassroots football clubs rely on their organizational capacity. Organizational capacity can be understood as a multi-dimensional concept which represents an organization's ability to draw upon different types of organizational capital, i.e., human, financial and structural resources (Hall et al., 2003). In a climate of austerity across European countries (Collins & Haudenhuyse, 2015), a football club's capacity to solve organizational problems is more than ever critical, as the participation in and consumption of football is affected in new and often unclear ways (Breuer, Feiler et al., 2015; Breuer & Nowy, 2015; Brown, 2000). It is likely that external factors – such as the demographic development in a country – vary across Europe and that football clubs in different countries experience different organizational problems to a different extent.

Previous research on organizational problems has shown that European grassroots sports clubs particularly have problems with the recruitment and retention of members, volunteers, and coaches and their overall financial situation, moreover, they are increasingly challenged in their attempt to justify substantial public subsidies (Breuer, Feiler et al., 2015; Breuer & Nowy, 2015; Hoye et al., 2015; Wicker, Vos, Scheerder, & Breuer, 2013). Many originally volunteer-based grassroots clubs face increasing pressure for more professional management (Adriaanse & Schofield, 2014; Ferkins & Shilbury, 2015), which is leading towards business-like management, which is, in turn, characterized by the strengthening of institutional management (Nagel, Schlesinger, Bayle, & Giauque, 2015).

Managers and boards of grassroots football clubs need argumentative and action knowledge (Breuer, 2013) about the relationship between organizational capacity and problems. While Balduck, Lucidarme, Marlier, and Willem (2015) concluded that the relevance of the concept of organizational capacity in the grassroots clubs context has been proven, Doherty, Misener, and Cuskelly (2014) suggested that the relative strength and weakness of single capacities alone and in concert still needs more empirical validation with larger samples and in different contexts. The lack of comparative data on the organizational capacity levels at the bottom of the European football pyramid leads to the following two-folded research aim of this study: in a first step, differences in organizational capacity and problem levels of football clubs across Europe are assessed. Second, the influence of all dimensions of organizational capacity on various organizational problems is empirically tested. The statistical analysis is based on data from an online survey of $N = 5,100$ grassroots football clubs in Germany, Poland, Italy, Norway, and France.

Organizational capacity

The concept of organizational capacity was originally conceptualized by Hall et al. (2003) for the Canadian non-profit sector following extensive focus groups. The three-dimensional framework – consisting of human resources, financial and structural capacity – has received increased attention in the non-profit sport context as a theoretical framework that allows a holistic analysis of the factors involved in an club's ability to achieve goals and meet stakeholders' expectations (e.g., Doherty et al., 2014; Millar &

Doherty, 2016; Misener & Doherty, 2009, 2013; Sharpe, 2006; Svensson & Hambrick, 2016; Wicker & Breuer, 2011, 2014). In the following paragraphs, the key components of the model are introduced (Figure 2.1).

External factors affect the organizational capacity and performance of a grassroots football club and include environmental constraints and facilitators, such as public policy frameworks, demographic development, and levels of competition among non- and for-profit organizations (Hall et al., 2003). *Human resource capacity* can be considered the key element that affects all other capacity dimensions and refers to "*the ability to deploy human capital (i.e., paid staff and volunteers) within the organization, and the competencies, knowledge, attitudes, motivation, and behaviors of these people*" (Hall et al., 2003, p. 37). This capacity dimension has been a primary research focus with the sports club context (Millar & Doherty, 2016), and different types of human resources have been found to be important determinants of various organizational problems (e.g., Koski, 1995; Nowy, Wicker, Feiler, & Breuer, 2015; Wicker & Breuer, 2013; Wicker, Breuer, & Hanau, 2012; Wicker et al., 2013).

The primary focus of grassroots football clubs might not be on making profit; however, they still need to break even as a first requirement for their

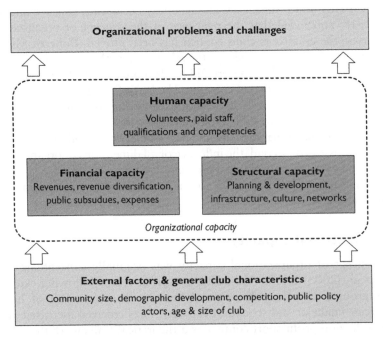

Figure 2.1 Conceptual model of organizational capacity – modified after Hall et al. (2003) and Land (2001)

financial sustainability (Nowy et al., 2015; Winand, Zintz, & Scheerder, 2012). The second crucial dimension of organizational capacity is, therefore, *financial capacity*, which can be understood as the ability to develop and deploy financial capital (Hall et al., 2003). Previous research suggests that grassroots clubs across countries are likely to report notoriously low financial resources and financial problems (Breuer, Hoekman, Nagel, & van der Werff, 2015; Gumulka, Barr, Lasby, & Brownlee, 2005; Wicker & Breuer, 2014). Revenue diversification and resource acquisition were suggested to be critical, as they give grassroots clubs more flexibility to achieve their organizational goals (Doherty et al., 2014; Millar & Doherty, 2016; Wicker & Breuer, 2013)

Structural capacity includes three sub-dimensions and is referred to "*the ability to deploy non-financial capital that remains when the people from an organization have gone home*" (Hall et al., 2003, p. 5). The first sub-dimension, infrastructure and process capacity includes policies and organizational culture. Wicker and Breuer (2013) report that the use of own and/or shared facilities determines organizational problems in mixed ways. Organizational culture is manifested in cultural systems and socio-structural systems (Allaire & Firsirotu, 1984). Generally, sports clubs emphasize values such as fair play, tradition, and companionship (Breuer, Feiler et al., 2015). Maitland, Hills, and Rhind (2015) provide an extensive overview on organizational culture in the sports clubs context. A strong emphasis on tradition and companionship and conviviality was found to be beneficial for higher social cohesion within the clubs which in turn has the potential for lower organizational problem levels (Wicker & Breuer, 2013). The ability to develop and carry out strategic plans is part of the second sub-dimension, i.e., an organization's planning and development capacity. Planning was found to be a critical issue for grassroots clubs (Misener & Doherty, 2009), however, Wicker and Breuer (2013)reported that only a few clubs have strategic plans in place. Moreover, Doherty et al. (2014) showed that the implementation of such plans represents another challenge for the clubs. The third sub-dimension, *network and relationship capacity*, refers to an organization's ability to build and maintain relationships with external stakeholders and includes the engagement with partners (e.g., federations) and balanced relationships (Doherty et al., 2014; Hall et al., 2003; Svensson & Hambrick, 2016).

A grassroots football club's *outputs* and its intended *outcomes* depend upon its capacities and external environment (Hall et al., 2003). Typically, outputs can be defined as measures of the quantity of services delivered and outcome measures include client characteristics – or, in the case of grassroots football clubs, member characteristics such as age, income level, race, and gender (Land, 2001). Organizational problem levels are used as a proxy for organizational performance levels. In this context, it is assumed that organizations with less severe problems demonstrate higher performance levels (Breuer & Nowy, 2015).

Method

Data collection, sample size, and response rates

The empirical analysis of this study is based on a cross-sectional study that drew primary data from football clubs in Germany, Poland, Norway, Italy, and France through an online survey in 2014. The selection of participating associations was made in accordance with the project partner (UEFA) and was based on geographical and feasibility considerations. To ensure a qualified assessment of the current condition of the grassroots, the corresponding national federations were asked to provide contact information, i.e., e-mail addresses, of board members. E-mail addresses from more than 12,500 clubs were provided to the research team. For the survey of German clubs, Germany's federation invited board members via its internal mail-system. The sampled French clubs are part of the FondaCtion du Footbal, a project organization comprising of 282 clubs that are considered to be representative by and for the Fédération Française de Football (FFF). Potential respondents were assured the anonymity and confidentiality of the gathered data in an invitation e-mail in the respective language. This e-mail also included a personalized link to the questionnaire. To increase the completion rate of the survey, it was possible to suspend and complete it at a later point in time. Moreover, the link could be forwarded to other board members, for example, to the treasurer to fill out the financial questions. Incorrect e-mail addresses and strict spam-filter reduced the sample. As a result, 34,806 invitations to the survey were eventually delivered, and 5,100 clubs began the survey, with a total response rate of 15 % (Table 2.1).

Table 2.1 Sample sizes, actual participants, and response rates

Variable	Germany	Poland	Italy	Norway	France	Total
Population	26,836	5,891	16,397	3,218	20,062	72,404
Sub-population	23,632	4,333	6,080	1,808	282	36,135
Dropouts	271	140	815	93	10	1,329
Sample size	23,361	4,193	5,265	1715	272	34,806
Participants	3,382	697	703	230	88	5,100
Response rate	14 %	17 %	13 %	13 %	32 %	15 %
Share of respondents in statistical analysis	67.9 %	13.1 %	13.3 %	4.1 %	1.7 %	100 %

Notes:
Population: # of clubs registered in respective national association (Source: www.fifa.com/worldfootball/bigcount/clubs.html)
Sub-population: # of e-mail addresses provided to research team (Germany: # of individual links provided to national football federation)
Dropouts: # of clubs that could not be reached under the provided e-mail address
Sample Size: # of invitations successfully delivered
Participants: # of participation in responding to the online questionnaires

As the focus of this study lies on the grassroots of European football, clubs that compete in the four highest divisions were dropped from analysis. Comparing key characteristics of the resulting sample with the grassroots football club population in the respective countries is challenging, as appropriate data are scarce. It is not possible to claim that the drawn sample is completely representative even though there are some positive indications for representativeness.[1] Following the procedure suggested by Bartlett, Kotrlik, and Higgins (2001), the sample size can be considered big enough to infer the research findings back to the population.

Operationalization of variables

External factors

In order to control for country specific effects, dummy variables for the respective countries were formed. The size of the municipality / city the club is based in is assessed by the ordinal variable *communitysize* (1 < 20,000; 2 = 20,001–100,000; 3 = 100,001–500,000; 4 = more than 500,000 inhabitants) and respective dummy variables. The extent to which a club is challenged by the current demographic development is captured by the variable *demographic* (5-point Likert scale ranging from 1 = no problem at all to 5 = a very big problem). To assess the power of public policy actors, clubs indicated on a 5-point Likert scale, whether the public subsidies they receive are subject to specific conditions (*conditional_subsidies*). Also, they reported their subjective perception of the power of local sports authorities to manifest their sports policy through strict regulations for the provided subsidies (*PLSA*). The perceived level of competition is assessed through an additive index ranging from 0 (no problem at all) to 100 (very high problem) which is based on the components competition with other football clubs, for-profit, and public sport institutions (*competition_index;* Cronbach's α: 0.7).

General club characteristics

Following the procedure of Vos, Wicker, Breuer, and Scheerder (2013), a set of background variables, i.e., general club characteristics, was included. Since previous research in the grassroots sports context has suggested that age of the club might be associated with the ability to generate income (Wicker et al., 2013), the variable *age_orga* was included. Wicker, Breuer, Lamprecht, and Fischer (2014) found evidence that organizational size is critical with respect to various organizational problems, therefore, board members were asked to report membership numbers in four age /gender categories leading to the variables *member, member²* (included to detect non-linear effects), and shares of female (*f_members*) and youth members (*y_members*). *Competitive* is the variable that captures a club's emphasis on competitive football and not just on recreational aspects (5-point Likert scale ranging from 1 = do not agree at all to 5 = totally agree). The number of active teams in the club is assessed with the variable *numberteams*. When a club has at least one team for kids and teenagers under the age of 18, *youthteam_dummy* takes on the value of 1, otherwise 0. A dummy variable for clubs with a senior team (i.e., only players above 30 years) was formed (*seniorteam_dummy*).

Organizational capacities

To assess the human resource capacity, clubs provided information on the number of core volunteers (any volunteer in a formal position, such as president, treasurer, coach, physio, etc.) and whether those positions were financially rewarded or not. A club's core voluntary engagement (*cv*) was then obtained by dividing the number of core volunteers by the total membership number of the club. Since research of Adriaanse and Schofield (2014) and Nagel, Schlesinger, Bayle, and Giaque (2015) suggests that clubs more and more implement paid staff, *cv_paid* is included in the analysis. The competencies and knowledge of the deployed human capital is operationalized by the two variables *qual_staff* (the share of training staff with a formal qualification) and *com_skills*. The latter variable was assessed by the level of agreement of board members on the statement "*Our club has sufficient computer skills*" (5-point Likert scale ranging from 1 = do not agree at all to 5 = totally agree). The final variable within this capacity dimension is *sv*, which represents the share of volunteers in the club which has no formal position, yet, occasionally volunteers for the club.

For the financial capacity dimension, clubs were asked to provide information on their total revenues and expenses in 2013 and the respective proportions of several revenues categories to total revenues. The revenue categories included revenue streams from membership fees (*rev_mem_share*), public subsidies (*rev_pub_share*), other forms of subsidies (*rev_ofs_share*), subsidies from federations (*rev_fed_share*), revenues from commercial activities (*rev_com_share*), donations (*rev_don_share*), restaurant operations (*rev_res_share*), social and sporting events (*rev_soc_share* and *rev_sev_share*), credit and loans (*rev_cal_share*), and other forms of revenues (*rev_ofr_share*). Revenue diversification (*rev_diversity*) is calculated by adding up the squared shares of a club's revenue categories and subtracted from 1 (Carroll & Stater, 2009; Wicker & Breuer, 2014). Respectively, clubs indicated their expenses in the categories players (*exp_ply_share*), coaches and training staff (*exp_cts_share*), facilities (*exp_fac_share*), administrative staff (*exp_adm_share*), equipment (*exp_equ_share*), insurances (*exp_ins_share*), taxes and fees (*exp_taf_share*), membership in federations (*exp_mif_share*), and other expenses (*exp_ofe_share*). Other financial indicators include per capita revenues (*rev_pc*), and the dummy variable *BE*, which takes on the value of 1 when revenues were greater or equal to expenses in 2013.

Within the structural capacity, infrastructure is operationalized through four variables: *f_own*, *f_shared*, *f_both*, and *it_infra*. While the first three variables are objectively measured by a board member's indication whether the club uses own and/or shared facilities, the latter was assessed on a 5-point Likert scale on the statement "*Our club's IT-infrastructure is sufficient*" (1 = do not agree at all – 5 totally agree). Two variables capture cultural systems of a grassroots football club: *v_tradition* and *v_companionship*. A club's emphasis on those two values was again measured on a 5-point Likert scale. The sub-dimension planning and development is operationalized through *strategy* and *develop*. Board members reported their level of agreement on the statement "*Our club has a strategic policy*" (5-point Likert scale ranging from 1 = do not agree at all to 5 = totally agree) and whether the club specifically had a person in charge for the development of training staff and volunteers. Clubs indicated whether they cooperated with another institution in 2013 (*coop*), and – if they did – also the type of institution they cooperated with. This led to the variables *coop_fpo* (cooperation with a for-profit institution), *coop_preschool* (cooperation with a kindergarten), *coop_school* (cooperation with a school), *coop_club* (cooperation with another sports club), *coop_public* (cooperation with a public institution), and *coop_other* (other institution). Additionally, clubs that cooperated with another institution also stated the nature of cooperation, i.e., common offers (*coop_offer*), shared use of facilities and/or equipment (*coop_usage*), shared employment/development of training staff (*coop_tstaff*), sharing experiences and knowledge (*coop_experience*), or other forms of cooperation (*coop_oform*). To assess whether the relationship with one key stakeholder is balanced, clubs were asked to indicate their level of agreement on the statement: "*Our club works hand in hand with football federations*" (5-point Likert scale; *federation*).

Organizational problems

All considered organizational problems are assessed on 5-point Likert scales (ranging from 1 = no problem at all – 5 = a very big problem). They include attracting /retaining members (*p_member*), training staff (*p_trainingstaff*), young competitive athletes (*p_youngtalent*), volunteers (*p_volunteer*), referees (*p_referees*), the costs of running the sport (*p_opcostgame*), the condition and timely availability of facilities (*p_f_condition* and *p_f_time*), uncertainty of future public subsidies (*p_uncertain_subs*), and the general financial and overall situation of the club (*p_finance* and *p_outlook*). *Shadow of the game* problems cover discrimination (*p_discrimination*), racism (*p_racism*), and violence (*p_violence*) incidents on match day. When clubs indicated that a particular problem was very big, they were asked in a second step whether that problem poses a threat to the sustainability of the club. The variable *1tts_dummy* takes on the value of 1 when a club reports at least one such threat to its sustainability.

Data analyses

Statistical analysis was performed with STATA 11. After checking data for plausibility, content validity, and extreme outliners, implausible values were set to missing values. Factor analysis was used to identify patterns in the considered organizational problems and to reduce them into a structured handful of dimensions (Hair, Anderson, Tatham, & Black, 2009). This led to three problem dimensions (labeled *strategic, operative, shadow of game*), for which additive indexes ranging from 0–100 were constructed. Their internal consistency is acceptable with Cronbach's α levels above the suggested threshold of 0.7 (Andrews, 2010). Descriptive statistics include one-way ANOVAs for the external factors and general club characteristics, organizational capacities and problems and challenges to portray country-specific differences. To analyze the impact of organizational capacities in concert with each other while controlling for external factors and general club characteristics, 15 OLS-multivariate regression models within three problem dimensions were constructed. Within each problem dimension one model is carried out for the combined sample of German, Polish, Italian, Norwegian, and French clubs (Models 1, 2, and 3), where the German clubs serve as the reference group. Additionally, country-level regression models were constructed, e.g., for the *strategic* problem dimension Models 1 a-d. No country-specific regression models for France are reported as the number of observations was too small for the complex regression models. An α-level of 0.1 is used for the multivariate regression models. Multicollinearity was not a problem, as tolerance values for each independent variable in the five regression models were above 0.1, and the variance inflation factor for each independent variable was below 10 (Belsley, Kuh, & Welsch, 1980).

Results

Descriptive statistics

External factors

Roughly 72% of the sampled German and Polish grassroots football clubs are based in small municipalities/cities that have less than 20,000 inhabitants, while this number amounts to 60% of Italian and 58% of Norwegian clubs. The public subsidies that football clubs receive from local authorities are subject to relatively high conditions across all countries. Restrictions are highest for German ($M_G = 3.78$) and lowest for French clubs ($M_F = 3.18$).

The actual power of local authorities to implement their intended sports policy through their subsidies is lowest in Germany ($M_G = 2.52$) and highest in Poland ($M_P = 3.19$). For Polish clubs, the competitive environment is most pronounced ($M_P = 42.52$); Norwegian ($M_N = 29.88$) and German clubs ($M_G = 31.95$) consider competition to be less of an issue (Table 2.2).

General club characteristics

Italian clubs are particularly young compared to their European counterparts. French clubs are biggest in size (on average 387 members) – almost five times bigger than Polish clubs (79 members). The share of female members is astonishingly low for Italian ($M_I = 3.4$ %) and Polish ($M_P = 5.7$ %) clubs and extraordinary high for Norwegian clubs ($M_N = 29.8$ %). The sampled Italian clubs appear to focus on young players as more than four out of five members are under the age of 18. German clubs demonstrate the lowest emphasis on the competitive aspect of football ($M_G = 2.26$), while for Norwegian ($M_N = 3.16$) and French clubs ($M_F = 3.54$), this aspect is more important. The relative small size of football clubs in Poland is also reflected in the total number of active teams ($M_P = 5.36$), which is only a fourth of the number of teams in Norwegian clubs ($M_N = 14.57$). Nine out of ten sampled clubs have at least one youth team, and seven out of ten have a team particularly designed for players over the age of 30 years. As the

Table 2.2 ANOVA – external factors and general club characteristics

Variable	Germany	Poland	Italy	Norway	France	Combined	F	Sig.
			External Factors					
sizeofcommunity1	73.37	71.54	59.87	57.26	64.71	69.90	7.67	***
demographic	3.32	3.45	2.74	2.34	2.43	3.21	45.90	
subs_conditional	3.78	3.65	3.38	3.46	3.18	3.69	10.42	***
PLSA	2.52	3.19	2.68	3.18	2.67	2.67	31.94	***
competition_index	31.95	42.52	38.10	29.88	33.18	34.09	23.35	***
			General Club Characteristics					
age_orga	76.48	38.22	31.91	74.44	48.48	65.17	249.55	***
totalmembers	272.33	78.99	164.28	276.51	386.50	230.74	123.71	***
share_f_members	12.24	5.71	3.44	29.84	8.06	10.82	90.23	***
share_y_members	41.59	48.03	81.82	69.83	59.89	49.56	213.70	***
competitive	2.26	2.84	2.88	3.16	3.54	2.48	68.24	***
numberteams	10.74	5.36	14.57	20.15	19.29	11.03	73.29	***
youthteam_dummy	89.25	83.76	99.39	91.13	98.04	89.94	13.62	***
seniorteam_dummy	78.22	75.00	41.59	46.77	62.75	71.55	61.27	***

*** $p < 0.001$, ** $p < 0.01$, * $p < 0.05$.

ANOVAs indicate all external factors and club characteristics differ significantly across countries.

Organizational capacities

Turning the focus on the organizational capacities of the sampled grassroots football clubs, Norwegian, German, and French clubs show similar figures regarding core volunteers (around 13%); this figure is almost twice as high for Polish ($M_p = 20.2\%$) and Italian ($M_I = 21.3\%$) clubs (Table 2.3). The

Table 2.3 ANOVA – human resource and structural capacity dimension

Variable	Germany	Poland	Italy	Norway	France	Combined	F	Sig.
			Human Resource Capacity					
cv	12.91	20.15	21.27	13.18	12.43	14.87	52.35	***
cv_paid	15.09	10.30	30.48	5.70	18.32	15.73	42.39	***
qual_staff	35.72	79.50	53.54	45.87	60.63	45.14	164.91	***
com_skills	3.66	3.30	3.66	3.24	3.32	3.59	18.20	***
sv	27.77	43.02	42.79	43.14	38.31	32.71	42.80	***
			Planning & Development					
strategy	3.44	3.22	3.82	3.72	3.40	3.47	21.11	***
develop	32.27	17.26	23.53	23.58	46.81	28.94	11.91	***
			Infrastructure & Culture					
f_own	63.05	41.48	20.57	82.89	50.00	55.78	90.03	***
f_shared	74.51	86.07	85.96	76.92	95.16	78.02	15.47	***
f_both	39.26	32.75	12.50	61.18	45.16	36.36	38.61	***
it_infra	3.03	2.41	3.29	2.87	3.06	2.97	38.58	***
v_tradition	3.49	3.63	3.82	3.32	3.44	3.54	13.61	***
v_companionship	4.17	4.01	4.51	4.42	4.28	4.20	24.85	***
			Relationship & Networking					
coop	53.62	85.11	66.45	64.00	72.55	60.56	36.42	***
Club cooperates with . . .								
coop_fpo	4.71	27.39	26.45	27.20	31.37	12.17	76.84	***
coop_preschool	20.67	21.28	13.23	12.80	11.76	19.32	3.92	**
coop_school	36.39	70.48	42.58	30.40	62.75	42.28	43.45	***
coop_club	38.86	69.15	49.03	56.80	33.33	45.20	33.27	***
coop_public	14.98	50.80	39.35	35.20	43.14	24.58	78.15	***
coop_other	7.35	19.41	15.16	7.20	25.49	10.37	18.42	***
Club cooperates by . . .								
coop_offer	37.66	66.22	44.19	12.80	39.22	41.40	39.38	***
coop_usage	40.41	75.00	53.55	54.40	52.94	47.89	41.51	***
coop_tstaff	25.20	40.96	29.68	31.20	43.14	28.65	11.11	***
coop_experience	27.32	63.56	51.61	42.40	41.18	36.44	58.52	***
coop_oform	26.87	30.32	20.97	32.80	25.49	26.92	2.52	*
federations	3.64	3.95	4.14	3.83	4.30	3.76	28.30	***

*** $p < 0.001$, ** $p < 0.01$, * $p < 0.05$.

share of paid core volunteers ranges from 6% in Norwegian to 30% in Italian football clubs. Formally qualified training staff is by far most likely to be found in Polish clubs (M_p = 79.5%), followed by their counterparts in France, Italy, and Norway – German clubs display the lowest respective share (M_G = 35.7%). German and Italian clubs are most likely to be convinced that their clubs can count on sufficient computer skills (M_G = M_I = 3.66); Norwegian clubs perceive such skills to be below average (M_N = 3.24). The share of secondary volunteers is lowest in German clubs (M_G = 27.8%) and around 43% in Italian, Norwegian, and Polish grassroots football clubs.

Italian (M_I = 3.82) and Norwegian (M_N = 3.72) clubs are most likely to follow a strategic concept, French (M_F = 46.8 %) and German (M_G = 32.3 %) clubs are most likely to have a person in charge for the development of their training staff and volunteers. Substantial differences in the infrastructural resources from which the clubs can draw upon exist: while only one out of five Italian clubs uses its own facilities, four out of five Norwegian clubs practice football within own facilities. Furthermore, 78% of all investigated clubs – and almost all French clubs – use shared facilities. About 36% of the sampled clubs use their own facilities and shared facilities. The IT-infrastructure of European grassroots football clubs still has room for improvement, particularly in Polish clubs. Of all sampled federations, Italian clubs value tradition and companionship/conviviality the most – Norwegian clubs value tradition least, Polish clubs companionship/conviviality, respectively. About one-half of the German clubs cooperates with another institution; in other countries, the share is significantly higher: for example, 85% of the Polish clubs report at least one institution they work together with. While only less than 5% of all sampled German clubs cooperate with a for-profit institution, this share is at least four times higher in the other sampled countries. On average, four out of nine clubs cooperate with another sports club, four out of ten with schools, a fourth cooperates with public institutions, a fifth with kindergartens, and roughly a tenth with other institutions. More than half of the sampled clubs share their knowledge and experiences with another institution; for Polish clubs, this amounts to almost two-thirds. Additionally, many sampled clubs (48%) cooperate in the form of sharing equipment. French (M_F = 4.30) and Italian (M_I = 3.95) clubs perceive their relationship with their governing federations to be more balanced than German clubs (M_G = 3.64).

Turning the focus on the financial capacity and, in particular, the revenue structure of the grassroots football clubs, substantial differences can be observed (Table 2.4). With the exception of Polish clubs, revenues from membership fees are the most important revenue stream for the sampled clubs. Polish clubs heavily depended on public subsidies (almost 64% of total revenues) and also demonstrate the highest share of revenues from other forms of subsidies. Italian clubs report the highest share of revenues from commercial activities (M_I = 25.0%) and credit and loans (M_I = 1.2%). Norwegian clubs lead in revenues from sporting events (M_N = 4.2%) and

Table 2.4 ANOVAs – financial capacity dimension

Variable	Germany	Poland	Italy	Norway	France	Combined	F	Sig.
Share of revenue category to total revenues (in %) ...								
rev_mem_share	39.30	11.90	45.26	31.21	28.05	35.14	98.64	***
rev_pub_share	6.98	63.61	8.20	10.45	27.74	16.49	958.4	***
rev_ofs_share	1.38	2.61	0.21	0.62	2.07	1.41	7.17	***
rev_fed_share	3.49	0.54	0.71	2.17	2.63	2.63	13.74	***
rev_com_share	14.73	7.56	24.98	19.85	12.51	15.02	48.27	***
rev_don_share	8.50	7.99	4.78	3.47	4.91	7.67	11.89	***
rev_res_share	8.05	0.36	2.93	6.06	0.23	6.01	42.01	***
rev_soc_share	7.59	1.22	4.32	6.04	15.14	6.29	39.33	***
rev_sev_share	7.04	1.45	4.20	9.12	3.42	5.87	39.50	***
rev_cal_share	0.65	0.29	1.22	0.22	0.28	0.63	3.42	**
rev_ofr_share	2.18	2.48	2.61	10.78	3.02	2.70	22.85	***
Share of expense category to total expenses ...								
exp_ply_share	4.84	2.70	6.19	0.32	3.33	4.42	8.50	***
exp_fac_share	16.54	13.27	20.16	18.84	2.12	16.27	16.14	***
exp_adm_share	1.13	2.30	2.04	4.00	12.05	1.77	35.63	***
exp_equ_share	15.76	20.57	18.70	19.07	21.26	17.13	12.53	***
exp_ins_share	6.61	5.19	7.09	6.14	4.47	6.38	5.54	***
exp_taf_share	7.08	8.14	6.74	3.13	1.67	6.92	14.95	***
exp_mif_share	9.83	11.34	3.90	2.48	14.33	9.12	34.76	***
exp_ofe_share	10.07	12.90	4.89	23.78	17.37	10.70	30.47	***
Financial performance indicators								
rev2013 pc	116.01	181.02	550.13	538.82	294.39	200.46	12.02	***
rev_diversity	0.65	0.36	0.51	0.67	0.70	0.58	139.94	***
breakingeven	76.36	60.12	72.05	81.55	74.42	73.51	10.59	***
exp_cts_share	22.68	21.55	23.52	14.99	22.56	22.23	4.14	**

*** $p < 0.001$, ** $p < 0.01$, * $p < 0.05$.

other forms of revenues ($M_N = 10.8\%$), German clubs in the revenues categories federations ($M_G = 3.5\%$), donations ($M_G = 8.5\%$), and restaurant activities ($M_G = 8.1\%$). French clubs have the highest shares of revenues from social events ($M_F = 15.1\%$) across the sampled countries. The financial capacity of a football club also includes the ability to deploy financial capital. Comparing the different expense categories reveals that Italian clubs have the highest share of expenses for players ($M_I = 6.2\%$), training staff ($M_I = 23.5\%$), facilities ($M_I = 20.2\%$), and insurances ($M_I = 7.1\%$). French clubs, on the other side, have the highest shares in the categories administrative staff ($M_F = 12.1\%$), equipment ($M_F = 21.3\%$), membership in federations ($M_F = 14.33\%$), and other expenses ($M_F = 17.4\%$). The expenses for training staff are the biggest expense category for all sampled clubs – except for Norwegian clubs. Per-member revenues are highest for Italian clubs ($M_N = €\ 550.13$) and lowest for German clubs ($M_G = €\ 116.01$). Revenue diversity is lowest in Polish clubs ($M_P = 0.36$) – as their high dependence on public subsidies already suggests – and highest for French ($M_N = 0.70$) and Norwegian clubs ($M_F = 0.67$). Norwegian clubs demonstrate the best financial management since almost 82% of the sampled clubs were able to break even – compared to 60% of the sampled Polish clubs.

Organizational problems

Within the first problem dimension (*strategic*), Polish clubs report the highest ($M_P = 68.51$) and Norwegian clubs the lowest ($M_N = 38.89$) index scores. Uncertain future subsides are perceived to be more problematic than any other problem in this dimension in all sampled countries (Table 2.5). Attracting/retaining volunteers is the most problematic challenge ($M = 3.98$) that the sampled clubs are facing within the *operative* problem dimension. German clubs show particularly high problem levels for all three problems and the respective index ($M_G = 75.07$), while Polish clubs perceive this dimension less problematic ($M_P = 51.16$). The sampled clubs do not perceive the

Table 2.5 ANOVAs – problems and challenges

Variable	Germany	Poland	Italy	Norway	France	Combined	F	Sig.
Problem Dimension 1 ($\alpha = 0.8$) – Strategic								
p_finance	3.05	4.01	3.49	2.34	3.11	3.21	79.30	***
p_outlook	2.69	3.54	2.86	2.14	2.05	2.80	62.23	***
p_uncertain_ subs	3.31	4.03	3.93	2.92	3.98	3.48	53.74	***
p_member	3.25	3.41	3.18	2.82	3.18	3.24	7.34	***
Index PD1	51.91	68.51	59.11	38.89	52.01	54.48	69.51	***
Problem Dimension 2 ($\alpha = 0.7$) – Operative								
p_trainingstaff	3.75	3.06	2.85	3.03	3.32	3.50	76.43	***
p_volunteer	4.20	3.38	3.57	3.56	4.02	3.98	74.81	***
p_referees	4.06	2.71	2.45	3.39	3.16	3.63	218.99	***
Index PD2	75.07	51.16	48.98	58.15	62.50	67.62	202.55	***
Problem Dimension 3 ($\alpha = 0.8$) – Shadow of the Game								
p_discrimination	1.50	1.61	1.90	1.45	1.93	1.57	20.54	***
p_violence	1.35	1.52	1.91	1.22	2.07	1.45	54.53	***
p_racism	1.23	1.13	1.71	1.25	1.73	1.28	52.66	***
Index PD3	9.05	10.56	21.06	7.67	22.73	10.87	49.90	***
Other Problems and Challenges								
p_opcostgame	3.45	3.86	3.65	2.84	3.82	3.51	27.55	***
p_f_condition	2.59	3.39	3.59	2.50	3.05	2.82	63.18	***
p_f_time	2.18	2.69	3.25	2.83	2.75	2.42	56.24	***
p_youngtalent	3.26	3.53	3.07	2.22	2.89	3.22	34.25	***
Share of clubs with at least one threat to its sustainability (in %)								
Itts_dummy	57.13	67.93	62.18	26.43	64.29	57.95	20.10	***

*** $p < 0.001$, ** $p < 0.01$, * $p < 0.05$.

shadow of the game to be problematic; French (M_F = 22.73) and Italian (M_I = 21.06) clubs demonstrate index scores that are at least twice as high as the scores of German (M_G = 9.05), Polish (M_P = 10.56), and Norwegian (M_N = 7.67) clubs. The costs of running the game (M = 3.51), the condition of the used facilities (M = 2.82) and the attraction/retention of young talented (M = 3.22) are least problematic for Norwegian clubs. Italian clubs suffer the most from the condition (M_I = 3.59) and timely availability of facilities (M_I = 3.25), and Polish clubs from the operative costs (M_P = 3.86).

Analytical results

Strategic problem dimension

As can be seen in Table 2.6, Norwegian and younger clubs per se, clubs in smaller municipalities /cities, clubs that are less affected by the demographic development and the competitive situation as well as clubs facing powerful local sports authorities demonstrate lower problem index scores in the strategic problem dimension (Model 1). Moreover, more (male) members and a weaker focus on the competitive aspect of football can be associated with lower problem levels (Table 2.6).

Several of the 18 considered organizational capacities have the potential to contribute to lower problem index scores, including higher shares of secondary volunteers, breaking even, higher shares of expenses on training staff, following a strategic concept, a stronger emphasis on companionship and conviviality (and less on traditional values), a sufficient IT infrastructure, cooperating with other institutions, and a balanced relationship with federations. The normalized beta coefficients indicate that the most influential capacity is following a strategic concept.

Controlling for external factors and general club characteristics, a country-level analysis of the strategic problem dimension reveals for German clubs (Model 1a) that the two most beneficial organizational capacities are breaking even and following a strategic concept. For the Polish clubs (Model 1b), the respective capacities are cooperating with another institution and breaking even. Sufficient computer skills and IT infrastructure appear to be the most beneficial determinant for Italian clubs (Model 1c) with respect to this problem dimension. Norwegian clubs (Model 1d) report lower problem index scores when they have higher shares of core volunteers and more balanced relationships with federations.

Operative problem dimension

The analysis of the second problem dimension shows that all country-dummies have negative coefficients – this means that problem levels in the reference country Germany are significantly higher than in any other considered

Table 2.6 Regression models: strategic problem dimension

	(1)	(1a)	(1b)	(1c)	(1d)
	Combined Sample	Germany	Poland	Italy	Norway
			External factors		
dummy_poland	**14.576*** (0.225)**				
dummy_italy	**14.741*** (0.196)**				
dummy_norway	**-4.858* (-0.049)**				
dummy_france	**7.404*** (0.050)**				
sizeofcommunity2	**3.597** (0.060)**	**3.875** (0.063)**	-0.237 (-0.004)	2.310 (0.048)	0.535 (0.013)
sizeofcommunity3	**5.647*** (0.065)**	**7.350*** (0.088)**	-1.903 (-0.021)	-1.250 (-0.016)	-5.062 (-0.089)
sizeofcommunity4	3.633 (0.033)	3.356 (0.034)	10.374 (0.085)	-1.335 (-0.005)	-3.125 (-0.040)
demographic	**4.271*** (0.234)**	**5.159*** (0.282)**	2.306 (0.118)	0.870 (0.051)	1.192 (0.077)
conditional_subsidies	0.657 (0.036)	0.651 (0.036)	0.555 (0.037)	2.156 (0.120)	-1.326 (-0.074)
PLSA	**-1.929*** (-0.102)**	**-3.579*** (-0.182)**	**2.428** (0.155)**	-1.846 (-0.106)	-0.681 (-0.047)
competition_index	**0.274*** (0.268)**	**0.271*** (0.260)**	**0.247*** (0.252)**	**0.337*** (0.431)**	**0.375*** (0.378)**
		General club characteristics			
age_orga	**0.060*** (0.096)**	**0.061*** (0.092)**	0.027 (0.037)	0.088 (0.131)	0.066 (0.113)
totalmembers	**-0.019*** (-0.160)**	**-0.035*** (-0.298)**	-0.011 (-0.034)	0.028 (0.235)	-0.023 (-0.298)
member^2	**0.000* (0.085)**	**0.000*** (0.243)**	0.000(0.065)	0.000 (-0.403)	0.000 (0.264)
share_f_members	**0.065* (0.042)**	0.007 (0.004)	0.136 (0.078)	0.189 (0.139)	**0.247** (0.247)**
share_y_members	-0.019 (-0.023)	-0.039 (-0.040)	-0.081 (-0.108)	-0.030 (-0.024)	-0.002 (-0.003)
competitive	**0.953* (0.047)**	**1.160* (0.056)**	-0.210 (-0.011)	0.898 (0.042)	1.272 (0.061)
		Organizational capacities			
cv_engagement	-0.076 (-0.037)	-0.032 (-0.013)	-0.131 (-0.089)	-0.217 (-0.125)	**-0.590** (-0.329)**
paid_share	-0.044 (-0.039)	-0.015 (-0.013)	-0.108 (-0.077)	**-0.186** (-0.211)**	**0.658** (0.263)**
qual_staff	-0.015 (-0.022)	-0.005 (-0.007)	-0.001 (-0.002)	-0.054 (-0.077)	-0.137 (-0.244)
com_skills	0.126 (0.006)	-0.098 (-0.004)	1.589 (0.105)	**-5.777** (-0.250)**	0.416 (0.024)

(Continued)

Table 2.6 (Continued)

	(1) Combined Sample	(1a) Germany	(1b) Poland	(1c) Italy	(1d) Norway
sv	-0.042** (-0.051)	-0.042 (-0.044)	-0.030 (-0.048)	-0.002 (-0.004)	-0.105 (-0.188)
rev13_pc	0.000 (-0.020)	0.004 (0.032)	-0.003 (-0.036)	0.000 (-0.030)	0.005*** (0.403)
revdiv	1.305 (0.012)	-1.203 (-0.010)	7.834 (0.080)	6.131 (0.067)	5.747 (0.039)
BE	-5.750*** (-0.116)	-5.519*** (-0.115)	-10.062*** (-0.218)	-4.317 (-0.091)	1.750 (0.040)
exp_cts_share	-0.051* (-0.043)	-0.045 (-0.040)	-0.023 (-0.019)	-0.053 (-0.045)	-0.184 (-0.162)
strategy	-2.674*** (-0.120)	-2.609*** (-0.119)	-1.709 (-0.094)	-3.108 (-0.120)	-4.305 (-0.200)
develop	0.056 (0.001)	0.354 (0.007)	2.655 (0.045)	4.389 (0.081)	10.559** (0.267)
v_tradition	1.475** (0.062)	1.850** (0.080)	1.158 (0.058)	-3.586 (-0.120)	5.737** (0.273)
v_companionship	-1.820** (-0.064)	-3.149*** (-0.112)	0.575 (0.025)	2.857 (0.071)	1.876 (0.060)
f_own	-1.114 (-0.024)	0.044 (0.001)	-5.934* (-0.135)	-3.241 (-0.052)	-12.837 (-0.247)
f_other	1.33 (0.023)	2.303 (0.043)	-7.603 (-0.099)	-5.038 (-0.056)	-2.941 (-0.076)
it_infra	-1.169** (-0.061)	-0.572 (-0.030)	-1.617 (-0.097)	4.641* (0.217)	-2.524 (-0.149)
coop	-2.368** (-0.051)	-2.238* (-0.050)	-15.512** (-0.258)	-7.708** (-0.173)	3.899 (0.101)
federations	-1.371*** (-0.064)	-0.988* (-0.048)	-2.119* (-0.112)	-2.747 (-0.101)	-6.497** (-0.367)
R-squared	0.40	0.40	0.41	0.45	0.69

Normalized beta coefficients in parentheses; *** p < 0.01, ** p < 0.05, * p < 0.1.

country (Model 2). The demographic development and competitive environment are again significantly affecting problem index scores, while powerful local public authorities appear to be beneficial. Older clubs are specifically challenged by this problem dimension (Table 2.7).

Statistically significant and beneficial organizational capacities in this model include higher shares of core volunteers and qualified training staff, better computer skills and higher shares of secondary volunteers. Following a strategic concept and having a person in charge of the development of training staff and volunteers and a stronger emphasis on traditional values is beneficial, too. The two capacities with the strongest influence are shares of secondary volunteers and qualified training staff.

On a country-specific level, higher shares of core volunteers and having a person in charge for the development of training staff and volunteers is particularly beneficial for German clubs (Model 2a). The problem index score for Polish (Model 2b) clubs is significantly lower when the share of core volunteers is higher and when clubs can use their own facilities. Only one significant (and beneficial) capacity for Italian clubs was found, i.e., the share of qualified staff (Model 2c). For Norwegian clubs, balanced relationships with federations seem to be the key contributor to lower problem index scores (Model 2d).

Shadow of the game problem dimension

The statistical analysis of the problem dimension *shadow of the game* shows that external factors are significantly determining problem levels (Model 3). The problem dimension's index scores are significantly higher in Italian and French clubs and more than 6% higher in clubs that are based in big cities compared to those clubs that are based in municipalities/cities that have less than 20,000 inhabitants. Again, the demographic development in the corresponding region and the level of competition contribute to higher problem index scores. General club characteristics do not significantly determine the index score of this problem dimension (Table 2.8). Two beneficial organizational capacities were found, i.e., higher shares of secondary volunteers and better computer skills. However, it has to be acknowledged that the explanatory power of this model is relatively low.

German clubs with higher shares of qualified training staff and secondary volunteers, as well as clubs with better computer skills and clubs that use their own facilities and emphasize traditional values perceive this problem dimension less challenging (Model 3a). Following a strategic concept is particularly beneficial for Polish (Model 3b) and Italian (Model 3c) clubs. Moreover, revenue diversification appears to be the capacity that managers of Italian football clubs should turn their attention to with respect to lowering problem levels in this dimension. Norwegian clubs may want to consider increasing the shares of paid staff and emphasizing companionship/conviviality as those capacities (next to using own facilities) are beneficial for lower problem index scores.

Table 2.7 Regression models: operative problem dimension

	(2) Combined Sample	(2a) Germany	(2b) Poland	(2c) Italy	(2d) Norway
			External factors		
dummy_poland	-20.375*** (-0.305)				
dummy_italy	-18.880*** (-0.242)				
dummy_norway	-8.626*** (-0.084)				
dummy_france	-4.202 (-0.027)				
sizeofcommunity2	-2.216 (-0.036)	-1.150 (-0.021)	-2.858 (-0.045)	-1.841 (-0.036)	4.091 (0.086)
sizeofcommunity3	-2.367 (-0.026)	0.539 (0.007)	-8.124 (-0.082)	-7.318 (-0.087)	-10.127 (-0.151)
sizeofcommunity4	0.569 (0.005)	4.844 (0.053)	-1.695 (-0.013)	-31.666 (-0.119)	-11.486 (-0.125)
p_demographic	3.693*** (0.196)	3.936*** (0.236)	5.215*** (0.247)	3.811** (0.206)	1.714 (0.094)
conditional_ subsidies	0.229 (0.012)	0.305 (0.018)	-0.688 (-0.043)	4.739*** (0.243)	-5.913** (-0.280)
PLSA	-0.954** (-0.049)	-1.074* (-0.060)	-0.651 (-0.038)	-3.451** (-0.183)	-2.609 (-0.153)
competition_ index	0.195*** (0.184)	0.186*** (0.196)	0.207*** (0.195)	0.285*** (0.336)	0.159 (0.136)
			General club characteristics		
age_orga	0.039** (0.061)	0.038* (0.062)	-0.020 (-0.025)	0.090 (0.124)	0.102 (0.149)
totalmembers	-0.002 (-0.019)	-0.014 (-0.129)	-0.087 (-0.255)	0.080** (0.625)	-0.084** (-0.937)
member^2	0.000 (0.012)	0.000 (0.138)	0.000 (0.212)	-0.000*** (-0.724)	0.000** (0.821)
share_f_members	-0.008 (-0.005)	0.024 (0.016)	-0.222 (-0.117)	0.124 (0.084)	0.067 (0.058)
share_y_members	0.016 (0.018)	0.056* (0.063)	-0.098 (-0.121)	-0.041 (-0.030)	0.311** (0.402)
competitive	-0.568 (-0.027)	-1.338** (-0.071)	0.972 (0.047)	-1.292 (-0.055)	-1.879 (-0.076)
			Organizational capacities		
cv_engagement	-0.160*** (-0.075)	-0.216** (-0.098)	-0.306** (-0.193)	-0.217 (-0.115)	-0.332 (-0.158)
paid_share	0.012 (0.010)	0.027 (0.025)	-0.042 (-0.027)	-0.085 (-0.089)	0.663 (0.226)
qual_staff	-0.059*** (-0.086)	-0.052** (-0.075)	-0.009 (-0.013)	-0.125* (-0.165)	-0.109 (-0.165)

	(1)	(2)	(3)	(4)	(5)
com_skills	-1.133* (-0.052)	-1.536** (-0.075)	-0.385 (-0.024)	0.216 (0.009)	1.252 (0.061)
sv	-0.087*** (-0.102)	-0.116*** (-0.132)	-0.063 (-0.093)	-0.006 (-0.008)	-0.135 (-0.206)
rev13_pc	-0.000 (-0.024)	0.003 (0.028)	-0.006 (-0.068)	-0.000 (-0.020)	0.004* (0.285)
revdiv	-2.008 (-0.018)	-3.604 (-0.031)	15.182* (0.142)	0.065 (0.001)	5.087 (0.030)
BE	-1.448 (-0.028)	-2.182 (-0.050)	1.566 (0.031)	-6.453 (-0.125)	4.626 (0.089)
exp_cts_share	0.004 (0.004)	0.002 (0.002)	-0.008 (-0.006)	0.110 (0.088)	0.267 (0.200)
strategy	-1.331** (-0.058)	-0.453 (-0.023)	-1.714 (-0.088)	-2.266 (-0.080)	1.539 (0.061)
develop	-2.390* (-0.046)	-4.175*** (-0.095)	6.459 (0.100)	7.666 (0.132)	1.742 (0.038)
v_tradition	-1.812*** (-0.074)	-1.540** (-0.073)	-2.011 (-0.093)	-4.358 (-0.135)	1.417 (0.057)
v_companionship	-0.803 (-0.027)	-0.842 (-0.033)	-0.780 (-0.032)	-1.762 (-0.040)	3.267 (0.089)
f_own	-0.533 (-0.011)	1.303 (0.031)	-7.857** (-0.165)	3.262 (0.050)	-4.474 (-0.073)
f_other	-0.451 (-0.008)	-0.080 (-0.002)	-8.044 (-0.097)	7.941 (0.087)	0.040 (0.001)
it_infra	-0.430 (-0.022)	0.208 (0.012)	-0.272 (-0.015)	-3.034 (-0.132)	2.056 (0.104)
coop	-0.475 (-0.010)	-0.186 (-0.005)	-9.293* (-0.142)	-1.267 (-0.026)	6.142 (0.136)
federations	-0.207 (-0.009)	0.043 (0.002)	-1.191 (-0.058)	-0.577 (-0.020)	-8.831** (-0.424)
R-squared	0.38	0.24	0.37	0.44	0.59

Normalized beta coefficients in parentheses; *** $p < 0.01$, ** $p < 0.05$, * $p < 0.1$.

Table 2.8 Regression models: shadow of the game dimension

	(3)	(3a)	(3b)	(3c)	(3d)
	Combined Sample	Germany	Poland	Italy	Norway
	External factors				
dummy_poland	-1.066 (-0.024)				
dummy_italy	**9.535*** (0.182)**				
dummy_norway	0.467 (0.007)				
dummy_france	**16.935*** (0.163)**				
sizeofcommunity2	**3.555*** (0.086)**	**4.552*** (0.121)**	-0.680 (-0.019)	7.794 (0.136)	-5.542 (-0.194)
sizeofcommunity3	2.182 (0.036)	**3.677** (0.072)**	3.426 (0.060)	-0.765 (-0.008)	-8.458 (-0.211)
sizeofcommunity4	**6.382*** (0.083)**	**7.762*** (0.127)**	5.874 (0.077)	-22.655 (-0.076)	-6.322 (-0.115)
demographic	**0.895** (0.070)**	0.432 (0.039)	1.346 (0.111)	2.451 (0.119)	-1.452 (-0.134)
conditional_ subsidies	-0.298 (-0.024)	-0.543 (-0.049)	0.374 (0.041)	0.972 (0.045)	-0.511 (-0.041)
PLSA	0.374 (0.029)	0.293 (0.024)	0.659 (0.068)	1.412 (0.067)	1.271 (0.125)
competition_ index	**0.110*** (0.154)**	**0.103*** (0.162)**	-0.043 (-0.071)	**0.189** (0.201)**	**0.461*** (0.663)**
	General club characteristics				
age_orga	-0.009 (-0.020)	0.001 (0.001)	-0.007 (-0.017)	-0.016 (-0.020)	**0.150* (0.365)**
totalmembers	-0.001 (-0.014)	-0.007 (-0.093)	0.081 (0.411)	-0.003 (-0.018)	0.017 (0.319)
member^2	0.000 (0.021)	0.000 (0.014)	-0.000 (-0.354)	-0.000 (-0.043)	0.000 (0.125)
share_f_members	-0.042 (-0.039)	0.001 (0.001)	-0.129 (-0.119)	-0.236 (-0.143)	0.020 (0.028)
share_y_members	-0.018 (-0.030)	-0.007 (-0.011)	-0.005 (-0.012)	**-0.366** (-0.240)**	-0.012 (-0.027)
competitive	0.128 (0.009)	0.124 (0.010)	-0.279 (-0.024)	3.321 (0.127)	2.963 (0.201)
	Organizational capacities				
cv_engagement	0.035 (0.024)	-0.057 (-0.038)	0.137 (0.151)	0.341 (0.163)	0.217 (0.172)
paid_share	**0.052** (0.066)**	**0.062** (0.089)**	-0.036 (-0.041)	0.077 (0.072)	**-0.622** (-0.355)**
qual_staff	-0.014 (-0.030)	**-0.044*** (-0.095)**	-0.002 (-0.004)	0.081 (0.096)	-0.002 (-0.006)

	(1)	(2)	(3)	(4)	(5)
com_skills	**-0.935** (-0.063)**	**-1.206*** (-0.088)**	0.202 (0.022)	-5.458 (-0.196)	1.595 (0.130)
sv	**-0.034** (-0.060)**	**-0.042** (-0.071)**	-0.047 (-0.121)	-0.010 (-0.012)	0.051 (0.130)
rev13_pc	-0.000 (-0.024)	-0.004 (-0.047)	**0.007* (0.152)**	-0.000 (-0.026)	-0.000 (-0.010)
revdiv	-0.998 (-0.014)	**6.297** (0.082)**	-3.041 (-0.050)	**-21.759* (-0.196)**	9.260 (0.091)
BE	-0.229 (-0.007)	-0.745 (-0.025)	0.430 (0.015)	0.059 (0.001)	-0.748 (-0.024)
exp_cts_share	-0.030 (-0.037)	-0.029 (-0.043)	0.007 (0.009)	-0.103 (-0.073)	0.045 (0.057)
strategy	-0.239 (-0.016)	**0.855* (0.064)**	**-2.505** (-0.225)**	**-5.143* (-0.164)**	0.980 (0.065)
develop	1.190 (0.034)	**2.363*** (0.081)**	-3.791 (-0.102)	-4.305 (-0.067)	-2.735 (-0.099)
v_tradition	-0.794 (-0.048)	**-1.020* (-0.072)**	0.116 (0.009)	-4.681 (-0.130)	2.477 (0.168)
v_companionship	-0.580 (-0.029)	0.264 (0.015)	0.405 (0.029)	-6.649 (-0.137)	**-5.719* (-0.260)**
f_own	0.251 (0.008)	**-1.778* (-0.063)**	0.446 (0.016)	**16.621* (0.227)**	**-14.751* (-0.405)**
f_other	0.147 (0.004)	0.043 (0.001)	-4.184 (-0.087)	4.272 (0.042)	-0.954 (-0.035)
it_infra	0.389 (0.029)	0.327 (0.028)	-0.129 (-0.013)	**5.681* (0.222)**	-2.246 (-0.190)
coop	1.336 (0.041)	0.745 (0.027)	1.776 (0.047)	3.533 (0.066)	2.649 (0.098)
federations	0.285 (0.019)	-0.131 (-0.010)	0.872 (0.074)	3.167 (0.096)	-1.486 (-0.120)
R-squared	0.13	0.12	0.16	0.34	0.56

Normalized beta coefficients in parentheses; *** $p < 0.01$, ** $p < 0.05$, * $p < 0.1$.

Conclusion

The first aim of this study was to assess differences in organizational capacity and problem levels of football clubs across Europe. The descriptive results showed that clubs differ substantially across all considered organizational capacities. The second aim was to analyze the influence of all dimensions of organizational capacity on various organizational problems while controlling for external factors. The standardized beta coefficients in the regression models revealed that some capacities have a stronger influence than others and are, therefore, more important in predicting organizational problem levels. For example, while emphasizing companionship/conviviality is beneficial for reducing index scores in the strategic problem dimension, it appears to be less influential than other capacities such as breaking even or following a strategic concept. It can be argued that the effect of human and financial resources on organizational problems is relatively straight forward, i.e., *beneficial* – with the exception of more paid staff. The effect of structural capacities, however, provides mixed results, i.e., some capacities have a positive effect on one problem dimension and a negative effect on another. Capacities that never showed a harmful effect on problem levels are more core and secondary volunteers, better qualified training staff and better computer skills, breaking even, and higher shares of expenses on training staff, emphasizing the values companionship and conviviality, as well as the use of shared facilities and balanced relationships with federations.

This study has some limitations. Specifically, the relatively low response rate and a lack of appropriate comparative data make the claim of representativeness for the obtained results difficult. Surveys were generally completed by one board member of the football club, and her/his assessment on the current condition of the club might not reflect the opinion of other board members. Additionally, this study is based on cross-sectional data which does not allow analyzing dynamic cause-and-effect relationships.

Note

The authors would like to thank the UEFA for supporting this research within the UEFA Research Grant Programme 2014/15. The content of this chapter is the work of the authors alone and does not necessarily represent the views of UEFA opinion.

1 For example, revenues from membership fees and expenses for training staff of the sampled German clubs are similar to what is reported in Breuer and Feiler (2013). Norwegian clubs report similar shares of female members as official statistics from the Norwegian Football Federation for 2011 (Haavik, 2012).

References

Adams, A. (2011). Social capital in England. In M. M. Groeneveld, B. Houlihan, & F. Ohl (Eds.), *Routledge research in sport, culture and society: Social capital and sport governance in Europe* (pp. 85–107). New York: Routledge.

Adriaanse, J., & Schofield, T. (2014). The Impact of gender quotas on gender equality in sport governance. *Journal of Sport Management*, 28(5), 485–497. doi:10.1123/jsm.2013-0108

Allaire, Y., & Firsirotu, M. E. (1984). Theories of organizational culture. *Organization Studies*, 5(3), 193–226. doi:10.1177/017084068400500301

Andrews, R. (2010). Organizational social capital, structure and performance. *Human Relations*, 63(5), 583–608. doi:10.1177/0018726709342931

Balduck, A. L., Lucidarme, S., Marlier, M., & Willem, A. (2015). Organizational capacity and organizational ambition in nonprofit and voluntary sports clubs. *VOLUNTAS: International Journal of Voluntary and Nonprofit Organizations*, 26(5), 2023–2043. doi:10.1007/s11266-014-9502-x

Bartlett, J., Kotrlik, J., & Higgins, C. (2001). Organizational research: determining appropriate sample size in survey research. *Information Technology, Learning, and Performance Journal*, 19(1).

Belsley, D. A., Kuh, E., & Welsch, R. E. (1980). *Regression diagnostics: Identifying influential data and sources of collinearity. Wiley series in probability and mathematical statistics*. New York: Wiley-Blackwell.

Breuer, C. (2013). Theoretischer Hintergrund: Produktion von Handlungs- und Argumentationswissen. In C. Breuer (Ed.), *Sportentwicklungsbericht 2011/2012* (pp. 842–848). Cologne, Germany: Sportverlag Strauß.

Breuer, C. & Feiler, S. (2013) Situation und Entwicklung der Fußballvereine [Situation and development of football clubs]. In C. Breuer (Ed.), *Sportentwicklungsbericht 2011/2012 – Band II [Sport Development Report 2011/2012 - Vol. II]*. (pp.7–68). Köln: Sportverlag Strauß.

Breuer, C., Feiler, S., & Wicker, P. (2015). Germany. In C. Breuer, R. Hoekman, S. Nagel, & H. van der Werff (Eds.), *Sport clubs in Europe* (pp. 243–272). New York: Springer.

Breuer, C., Hoekman, R., Nagel, S., & van der Werff, H. (Eds.) (2015). *Sport clubs in Europe*. New York: Springer.

Breuer, C., & Nowy, T. (2015). *A comparative perspective on European football: Organizational capacity of European football clubs*. Köln: Deutsche Sporthochschule Köln, Institut für Sportökonomie und Sportmanagement.

Brown, A. (2000). European football and the European union: Governance, participation and social cohesion – towards a policy research agenda. *Soccer & Society*, 1(2), 129–150. doi:10.1080/14660970008721268

Carroll, D. A., & Stater, K. J. (2009). Revenue diversification in nonprofit organizations: Does it lead to financial stability? *Journal of Public Administration Research and Theory*, 19(4), 947–966.

Collins, M., & Haudenhuyse, R. (2015). Social exclusion and austerity policies in England: The role of sports in a new area of social polarization and inequality? *Social Inclusion*, 3(3), 5. doi:10.17645/si.v3i3.54

Crolley, L., & Hand, D. (2013). *Football, Europe and the press: Sport in the global society*. Oxon, England: Routledge.

Doherty, A., & Misener, K. (2008). Community sport networks. In M. Nicholson & R. Hoye (Eds.), *Sport and social capital: An introduction* (pp. 113–142). Heidelberg, Germany: Butterworth-Heinemann.

Doherty, A., Misener, K., & Cuskelly, G. (2014). Toward a Multidimensional framework of capacity in community sport clubs. *Nonprofit and Voluntary Sector Quarterly*, 43(S2), 124S–142. doi:10.1177/0899764013509892

Enjolras, B., & Waldahl, R. H. (2010). Democratic governance and Oligarchy in voluntary sport organizations: The case of the Norwegian Olympic Committee and Confederation of Sports. *European Sport Management Quarterly*, *10*(2), 215–239. doi:10.1080/16184740903559909

Ferkins, L., & Shilbury, D. (2015). Board strategic balance: An emerging sport governance theory. *Sport Management Review*, *18*(4), 489–500. doi:10.1016/j.smr.2014.12.002

Gratton, C., & Taylor, P. (2000). *Economics of sport and recreation*. New York: Spon.

Gumulka, G., Barr, C., Lasby, D., & Brownlee, B. (2005). *Understanding the capacity of sports and recreation organizations*. Toronto, Canada: Imagine.

Haavik, Y. (2012). *Facts and history about Norwegian Football*. Retrieved August 6 2015, from http://gamle.fotball.no/toppmeny/english/Facts-and-history-about-Norwegian-Football/

Hair, J. F., Anderson, R. E., Tatham, R. L., & Black, W. C. (2009). *Multivariate data analysis* (7th ed.). Englewood Cliffs, NJ: Prentice Hall.

Hall, M. H., Andrukow, A., Barr, C., Brock, K., Wit, M. de, Embuldeniya, D., & Vaillancourt, Y. (2003). *The capacity to serve: A qualitative study of the challenges facing Canada's nonprofit and voluntary organizations*. Toronto, Canada: Canadian Centre for Philanthropy.

Hoye, R., Smith, A., Nicholson, M., & Stewart, B. (2015). *Sport management* (4th ed.). London, England: Routledge.

Koski, P. (1995). Organizational effectiveness of finnish sports clubs. *Journal of Sport Management*, *9*(1), 85–95.

Land, K. C. (2001). Social indicators for assessing the impact of the independent, not-for-profit sector of society. In P. Flynn & V. A. Hodgkinson (Eds.), *Nonprofit and civil society studies. The private nonprofit sector. Measuring its impact on society* (pp. 59–76). New York: Kluwer Academic/Plenum.

Maitland, A., Hills, L. A., & Rhind, D. J. (2015). Organisational culture in sport – A systematic review. *Sport Management Review 18*(4), 501–516. doi:10.1016/j.smr.2014.11.004

Millar, P., & Doherty, A. (2016). Capacity building in nonprofit sport organizations: Development of a process model. *Sport Management Review 19*(4), 365–377. doi:10.1016/j.smr.2016.01.002

Misener, K., & Doherty, A. (2009). A case study of organizational capacity in non-profit community sport. *Journal of Sport Management*, *23*, 457–482.

Misener, K., & Doherty, A. (2013). Understanding capacity through the processes and outcomes of interorganizational relationships in nonprofit community sport organizations. *Sport Management Review*, *16*(2), 135–147.

Nagel, S., Schlesinger, T., Bayle, E., & Giauque, D. (2015). Professionalisation of sport federations – a multi-level framework for analysing forms, causes and consequences. *European Sport Management Quarterly*, *15*(4), 407–433. doi:10.1080/16184742.2015.1062990

Nicholson, M., Hoye, R., & Houlihan, B. (2011). *Participation in sport: International policy perspectives*. London, England: Routledge.

Nowy, T., Wicker, P., Feiler, S., & Breuer, C. (2015). Organizational performance of nonprofit and for-profit sport organizations. *European Sport Management Quarterly*, *15*(2), 155–175. doi:10.1080/16184742.2014.995691

Peeters, T., & Szymanski, S. (2014). Financial fair play in European football. *Economic Policy*, *29*(78), 343–390.

Sharpe, E. K. (2006). Resources at the grassroots of recreation: Organizational capacity and quality of experience in a community sport organization. *Leisure Sciences, 28*, 385–401. doi:10.1080/01490400600745894

Svensson, P. G., & Hambrick, M. E. (2016). "Pick and choose our battles" – understanding organizational capacity in a sport for development and peace organization. *Sport Management Review, 19*(2), 120–132. doi:10.1016/j.smr.2015.02.003

Tacon, R. (2014). Social capital and sports clubs. In A. Christoforou & J. B. Davis (Eds.), *Routledge advances in social economics: Social capital and economics. Social values, power, and social identity* (pp. 236–261). New York: Routledge.

UEFA. (2015). *Football development*. Retrieved November 25, 2015, from www.uefa.org/football-development/index.html

Vos, S., Breesch, D., Késenne, S., Lagae, W., van Hoecke, J., Vanreusel, B., & Schreeder, J. (2012). The value of human resources in non-public sports providers. *International Journal of Sport Management and Marketing, 11*(1/2), 3–25.

Vos, S., Wicker, P., Breuer, C., & Scheerder, J. (2013). Sports policy systems in regulated Rhineland welfare states: similarities and differences in financial structures of sports clubs. *International Journal of Sport Policy and Politics, 5*(1), 55–71. doi :10.1080/19406940.2012.657665

Wicker, P., & Breuer, C. (2011). Scarcity of resources in German non-profit sport clubs. *Sport Management Review, 14*(2), 188–201.

Wicker, P., & Breuer, C. (2013). Understanding the importance of organizational resources to explain organizational problems: Evidence from nonprofit sport clubs in Germany. *Voluntas, 24*(2), 461–484.

Wicker, P., & Breuer, C. (2014). Exploring the organizational capacity and organizational problems of disability sport clubs in Germany using matched pairs analysis. *Sport Management Review, 17*(1), 23–34.

Wicker, P., Breuer, C., & Hanau, T. von. (2012). Gender effects on organizational problems – evidence from non-profit sports clubs in Germany. *Sex Roles, 66*(1–2), 105–116. doi:10.1007/s11199-011-0064-8

Wicker, P., Breuer, C., Lamprecht, M., & Fischer, A. (2014). Does club size matter: An Examination of economies of scale economies of scope and organizational problems. *Journal of Sport Mangement, 28*(3), 266–280.

Wicker, P., Vos, S., Scheerder, J., & Breuer, C. (2013). The link between resource problems and interorganisational relationships: A quantitative study of Western European sport clubs. *Managing Leisure, 18*(1), 31–45.

Winand, M., Zintz, T., & Scheerder, J. (2012). A financial management tool for sport federations. *Sport, Business and Management: An International Journal, 2*(3), 225–240. doi:10.1108/20426781211261539

Chapter 3

Economic importance of football in Germany

Holger Preuss, Iris an der Heiden, and Christian Alfs

Introduction

Sport and physical activity (referred to as "sport" in the following pages) are one of the central leisure activities in Western societies, and many people spent time and money to participate in sport activities or passively consume sport as fans (Preuss, Alfs, & Ahlert, 2012). For Germany, Preuss et al. (2012) and later an der Heiden et al. (2015) have determined that football as one out of many sport-related activities has induced private household expenditures of about €11.1 billion in 2010. Sport overall contributed €77.4 billion to the gross value added of the German economy representing 3.5% of GDP in 2010 (Ahlert & an der Heiden, 2015). This overall economic dimension is essentially shaped by the sport-related consumption of German private households being determined by the money being spent by the households on sports, more specifically, on the different types of sport.

Preuss et al. (2012) have shown that the consumption patterns of the participants and fans of different types of sport vary remarkably and that football is the type of sport that creates the highest overall private household expenditures of all types of sport in Germany. Later, an der Heiden et al. (2015) have manifested these findings. The importance of football is caused mainly by the dominance of football in regard to the interest in sport, with 19.8% of the German population spending money on their interest and passion for football without necessarily participating actively in it. This private household consumption is expanded by other significant economic activities induced by football. The football Bundesliga (highest football league in Germany) alone had a turnover of €2.62 billion in 2014/2015 (DFL, 2016). Football is by far the most relevant type of sport as far as sponsorship deals und media rights are concerned (an der Heiden et al., 2012a; Angenendt et al., 2009). Additionally, we have to consider the public investments in football such as the construction of football pitches and stadia.

Until 2012 (Preuss et al.), no representative and detailed information on the structure and volume of the overall football consumption in Germany was available (see also Alfs, 2014; an der Heiden et al., 2015). For example, the consumption of those doing grassroots/sport-for-all football or even those who passively consume football by purchasing pay TV, football magazines, go to the stadia or bet money on football has not been focused upon in detail. As far as the participation in football is concerned, more or less reliable data on club-organized football is available from the German Olympic Sport Confederation (Deutscher Olympischer Sportbund – DOSB). At this point, it has to be mentioned that clubs are the main and most common form of organized sports in Germany, with much higher participation numbers compared to school or university sports, for example. Preuss et al. (2012, p. 105) have also shown that only 55.2% of football players say that they play football in organized sports clubs. The remaining share is played in other organizational forms (self-organized or in commercial settings).

Accordingly, little was known about the volume and structure of football participation and the related consumption outside of sport clubs in Germany. In other words, the statistics on club football or the Bundesliga turnover nor data from professional football sponsorship can provide a complete picture about the money spent on football. Even when we add up all figures, we have no idea who is earning the money, what is counted double, or which of the goods and services are imported and therefore not produced in Germany. Thus, a reliable determination of economic importance of football for a national economy is rare.

Method

The data for this investigation is based upon was collected to determine the economic dimensions of sport consumption of the German private households completed in 2012 (Preuss et al., 2012). Furthermore, data was used from two additional studies regarding the sponsorship and media rights markets in Germany (an der Heiden et al., 2012a) and the sport-related infrastructure in Germany (an der Heiden et al., 2012b). The data of all three studies were taken together to produce the satellite account sport (Ahlert, 2013; Ahlert & an der Heiden, 2015).

All studies are grounded on representative data. For example, the sport-related consumption of the German population is based on a total sample of $N = 19,396$. On top of being able to analyse the total sport-related expenditures, the data also enabled precise analyses of aspects of participation and fandom related to individual types of sport. Besides precisely investigating the number of people actively playing football and/or who are interested in football and spend money on their interest on a sample of $n = 7,031$, which is representative of Germany in the dimensions age, gender, and state of residence, a total of $n = 824$ data sets of football consumers were analyzed. Regarding consumption in sport we follow consumption categories that go in line with the "broader Vilnius definition of sport." That defines the economically relevant categories connected to sports (SpEA, 2007). This definition describes sport as corresponding with the current NACE (statistical classification of economic activities in the European Union) category 92.6 ("sporting activities"), plus all products and services which are necessary as inputs to produce sport as an output plus all products and services which have a (direct or indirect) relation to any sport activity but without being necessary to do sport. Accordingly, these data provide a very useful basis for evaluating the football demand and consumption of the German population.

The study on sponsorship and media rights was conducted in 2011 by realizing 1,500 CATI (computer-assisted telephone interview) interviews in all industry branches, 508 CATIs with sport organizations, and 133 CATIs with agencies and experts. The last study was about the maintenance and construction of sport facilities. It was conducted in 2012 using 455 CATIs with public authorities and 204 expert interviews.

Several studies have been conducted in Germany in order to determine the economic dimensions of sport, which includes the sport-related consumption of the private households. The first major studies were done by Weber, Schnieder, Korlücke, and Horak (1995) and Meyer and Ahlert (2000). These studies were followed by the research of Preuss et al. (2012) and an der Heiden (2012a, 2012b), who provided data on the overall sport-related consumption, sponsorship, media rights, and sport facility investments in Germany. All those data were used to construct a satellite account sport (Ahlert, 2013). The satellite account sport (Ahlert & an der Heiden, 2015) is part of the national accounting system. Its calculations have been recorded on the basis of a sport specific extra analysis of the Input-Output Tables by the Federal Statistical Office for reporting year 2010. It enables us to precisely determine the gross value added of football for a national economy.

Results

Participation and interest in football

In regard to participation in football in Germany, the official numbers of the German Football Association (Deutscher Fußballbund) have mostly been cited. These numbers are also used in the statistics of the DOSB and show that 6.9 million people (5.8 million males and 1.1 million female) have been members of football clubs in the year 2015. Concerning the age structure of the football players in Germany, the DOSB numbers say that 52% of the members of football clubs are younger than 27 and 64% are younger than 41 (see Table 3.1). These numbers do not include the participants that are not members of football/sports clubs. As Preuss et al. (2012) have shown recently, 66% of the total sport participation in Germany takes place outside of clubs. So the assumption can be made that a high number of people are playing football not coordinated by clubs. So, in addition to the numbers by

Table 3.1 DOSB data on the number of members of football clubs in Germany in 2015 (DOSB, 2016)

Age Group	Male	Female	Total
< 6	229.711	58.229	287.940
7–14	1,139.250	203.985	1,343.235
15–18	515.364	108.980	624.344
19–26	1,111.512	183.805	1,295.317
27–40	699.360	138.123	837.483
41–60	995.088	197.199	1,192.287
> 60	1,103.925	204.584	1,308.509
Total	5,794.210	1,094.905	6,889.115

the DOSB, which could also be criticized for not being precise in regard to active sport participation because they include passive membership (an der Heiden et al., 2015), double memberships, and are sometimes only rough estimations the club administration does, the total number or participants in football is of high interest.

Other studies have focused more on the total number of football participants, regardless of the organizational form. The results give values between 7% (IPSOS, 2008) and 21% (Köcher, 2009) of the German population. In absolute numbers based on the data of the German Federal Office for Statistics (Statistisches Bundesamt), these values relate to between five million (IPSOS, 2008) and 14.7 million people (Köcher, 2009). These differences in results can be explained by methodological and definitional differences it these studies. This can be seen as another reason why it is necessary to provide reliable data on football participation and consumption in Germany based on representative data and evaluated following a sound methodology and definition of sport and football, respectively.

Only very few studies have focused on the German population's interest in football. The first study that has to be mentioned here was conducted by IPSOS (2008). On a 7-point Likert scale, 33% of the sample of n = 3,000 of the German population 14 years and older have said that they are interested in football with scale values of 5, 6, and 7, and 21% have said to be strongly interested with scale values 6 and 7. Preuss et al. (2012) have shown that 20.4% of the total population are interested in football and spend money on it. This is equivalent to a total number of 16.7 million people.

The total number of people actively participating in football in Germany in the years 2009/2010 is 9.9 million, which equals 12.8% of the German population (Preuss et al., 2012). This number includes all frequencies, which means that people playing football on a weekly basis count just as much as people who claim to only participate once in a while, even including less than yearly participation. However, 11.3% of adults older than 15 years (7.93 million) and 21.8% of the children and juveniles between four and 15 years (1.98 million) said that they play football at least once in a while (see Table 3.2). This places football on rank eight of the most popular types of sport in reference to the total percentage of the population that participates in the types of sports regardless of the frequency. Table 3.3 shows the latest calculation considering all frequencies of sport, showing that the share is a little lower but without a change in ranking. Taking a closer look at the frequency of football participation of the population 16 years and older, it shows that 47.5% of the football participants engage in football at least once a week, which equals an absolute number of 3.77 million people. This is lower than the average weekly participation of 51% over all 71 types of sports (population 16 years and older). Another 26.3% (2.1 million) participate at least once a month and the remaining 26.2% (2.1 million) play football less than once a month.

As far as the gender of the active football players 16 and older is concerned, the results show that 89.6% are male and the remaining 10.4% female. In absolute numbers this equates to 7.11 million men and 0.82 million

Table 3.2 Relative and absolute numbers of football participation of the German population (Preuss et al., 2012)

General Participation (Number)					
≥ 16		< 16		**Total Population**	
Relative	Absolute	Relative	Absolute	Relative	Absolute
11.3%	7.93 million	21.8%	1.98 million	12.8%	9.91 million
Weekly Participation					
≥ 16		< 16		**Total Population**	
Relative	Absolute	Relative	Absolute	Relative	Absolute
5.4%	3.77 million	21.5%	1.95 million	7.3%	5.7 million

Table 3.3 Top 10 sports of the German population (an der Heiden et al., 2015)

Type of Sport	Percent of Population
Cycling	28.7
Swimming	26.0
Hiking/Walking	21.8
Jogging/Running/Nordic Walking	20.6
Fitness	14.5
Bowling	13.6
Gymnastic/Calisthenics/Aerobics	13.0
Football	**12.3**
Skiing	12.0
Health-Fitness Sports	11.8

women actively participating in football. Focusing on the weekly participants, the ratio between the genders is almost the same with 90.1% male
and 9.9% female football players. No information about the gender of the
under 16-year-olds is available. The children and juveniles under 16 play
and practice football with a higher average frequency. Overall 98.4% of
the 1.98 million football participants of that age group have said that they
play football at least once a week, which is equivalent to an absolute number of 1.95 million children and juveniles under 16. This is higher than the
average percentage of weekly participation over all types of sports (69.1%
of children and juveniles under 16). It has to be noted here that the data of
this age group was surveyed through their parents, so the actual number of
children who play football only once in a while is probably higher, since the
parents might have recalled the regularly practiced types of sport more than
the once in a while, leisure time sport activities of their offspring.

Looking at the organizational form of football participation at all age
groups (sport clubs, self-organized or other/commercial settings), it shows
that 55.2% (equals 5.5 million people) of the football participation takes
place in sport clubs, followed by 45.5% (4.5 million) self-organized and
6.4% in other organizational forms (Preuss et al., 2012, p. 105). The sum
of these numbers is more than 100%, since people can play football in more
than one organizational form. About half of the football activities of players 16 and older (50.6%) take place in sport clubs. Just as much is done in
a self-organized way, only 6.6% of the football players said that they also
play football in other organizational forms. The majority of 79.7% of the
football activities of football players under 16 years of age takes place in
sport clubs, which equals an absolute number of 1.58 million people. This is
followed by 22.9% self-organized and 5.2% in other organizational forms.

Taking a closer look at the reasons and motivations people have to play
football, it shows that for both genders the reason "to have fun" is the most
dominant reason (88% of the men and 83% of the women), which is dis-
tinctively above average motivation "to have fun" (68% of the men, 44%
of the women) (Preuss et al., 2012, p. 95). This is followed by the motivation to stay healthy and improve the overall fitness, named as reason to play
football by 43% of both sexes. Significant differences can only be observed
concerning the reason "to be outside in nature". Only 8% of the men but
24% of the women have mentioned this motivation for playing football.
Figure 3.1 shows the results of all reasons/motivations analysed. Figure 3.2
compares the reasons to participate in football with those of all other 71
investigated sports. It is obvious that football is played much more for fun
and to show performance, while fitness and being in the nature is not that
important than in other sports. However, 43% mention that the play football for health and fitness.

Looking at the individual expenditures and consumption patterns of
active sportsmen and sports fans in relation to football, several studies have
to be mentioned. Wicker, Breuer and Pawlowski (2010) have analyzed the

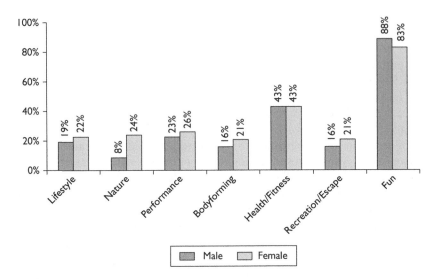

Figure 3.1 Reasons and motivations for participation of active football players in Germany In 2009

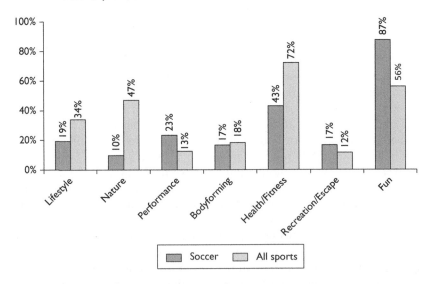

Figure 3.2 Reasons and motivations for participation of active football players in Germany in 2009 compared to the average of 71 other sports

individual expenditures of German sport club members and found that members of football clubs spend on average €692 per year, which is below the average individual yearly expenditures of all sport club members of €1,610. Preuss et al. (2012) and later an der Heiden et al. (2015) have calculated individual expenditures of football players (see Table 3.4).

Table 3.4 Consumption pattern of active football participation (an der Heiden et al., 2015)

Consumption	Active above 16 years		Active below 16 years	
	Share of players who have expenditures in this category	Average expenditures	Share of players who have expenditures in this category	Average expenditures
Shoes	55%	47 €	90%	74 €
Clothing/apparel	45%	35 €	81%	63 €
Equipment	21%	11 €	44%	25 €
Equipment (maintenance and repair)	23%	8 €	17%	14 €
Books and magazines	26%	6 €	–	–
Electronics and software	19%	9 €	–	–
Food and supplements	12%	15 €	–	–
Body care products	42%	49 €	–	–
Medical services and products	11%	3 €	–	–
Internet for active sport participation	63%	33 €	–	–
Membership fees	35%	29 €	–	–
Sport vacations & training camps	24%	26 €	–	–
Sport vacations	–	–	14%	26 €
Training camps and youth trips	–	–	24%	31 €
Transportation to training site	54%	209 €	77%	161 €
Transportation to competitions in Germany	48%	42 €	74%	233 €
Transportation to competitions outside Germany	19%	8 €	–	–
Insurance	5%	6 €	–	–
Average	–	536 €	–	626 €

In 2010, the average football-related expenditures of children and juveniles was €626 and €536 for people 16 years and older. Calculating that up for the total population and considering the frequency of playing football, the overall expenditure for football is €5.5 billion. Table 3.5 shows the same data differentiated by the intensity people play football. It is no surprise

Table 3.5 Consumption pattern active football participation by intensity of participation

Consumption	At least once a week	At least once a month	At least once a year	Less than once a year
Shoes	76 €	40 €	17 €	13 €
Clothing/apparel	54 €	32 €	22 €	19 €
Transportation to training site	395 €	73 €	30 €	– €
Total average	951 €	264 €	165 €	49 €

that the expenditure is high the more often people play. The results show a positive correlation between sport participation and sport expenditures; the higher the intensity of participation the higher the expenditure. These results go in line with those from Taks, Renson, and Vanreusel (1999), Wicker, Breuer, and Pawlowski (2010), and Scheerder, Vos, and Taks (2011).

Football fans in Germany

Besides active participation and the related expenditures, the interest in football is another important economic dimension of football consumption. In this study, the interviewees were asked whether they are interested in football and spend money on it. In total, 19.8% of the German population said they are football fans and spend money on their interest in the sport (an der Heiden et al., 2015, p. 8). This percentage is almost the same for the two age groups of under 16 years old and older than 16 years old. The consumption of fans consists of a variety of consumption categories (Table 3.6). The consumption pattern displayed in Table 3.6 is an average and therefore does not represent a specific expenditure of a fan. However, it provides an overview of the most important categories and it can also be used to calculate the overall Germany-wide consumption.

The average football fan in Germany spends €387 per year for their passion in football. The total amount added up to €5.5 billion in 2010. The figures regarding betting may be underestimated due to a bias caused by direct interception. Some standard deviation of variables in the consumption pattern is high, especially in "betting" or in the consumption of "books and magazines." It is important to remind that the figures presented are only average figures that cannot be used to get any detailed information on the particular individual household consumption.

Football sponsorship in Germany

In professional football, sponsoring is an important factor for the economy. Figure 3.3 illustrates that over 50% of all sponsoring engagements are related to football. Football dominates the sponsorship landscape as it

Table 3.6 Individual and total expenditures of football fans in Germany in 2010 (above 16 years old) (an der Heiden et al., 2015)

Consumption	Share of fans who have expenditures in this category	Average expenditures
Use of internet (computer & mobile) for football	91%	31 €
Merchandise & memorabilia	75%	52 €
Entrance fees/tickets for leagues	40%	37 €
Books and magazines, journals	37%	16 €
Catering, accommodation, & bar visits	32%	28 €
Transportation by car (as driver) to league matches	27%	10 €
Catering, accommodation due to league match visits	27%	8 €
Fees for pay TV	27%	55 €
Passive memberships	21%	12 €
Betting	20%	34 €
Transportation by car (as driver) for football events	18%	6 €
Entrance fees/tickets for football events (EURO, Cup, etc.)	16%	7 €
Transportation public to league matches	15%	11 €
Catering, accommodation for football events	13%	60 €
Computer and games software	12%	8 €
Transportation public for football events	9%	10 €
Donations	5%	2 €
Total expenditures of fans 16 and older	–	**387 €**

is by far the most viewed sport in Germany. However, it is interesting to see that in football more sponsoring is payed for grassroots sport than for the professional part of the sport. In 2010, €1.1 billion was paid for grassroots, while only €700 million went in professional sports (an der Heiden et al., 2015, p. 9). However, the potential is not used entirely. The Bundesliga was able to increase its revenues from sponsorship from 2010 to 2014 by 23% (€523 million), and also the 2. Bundesliga could increase it by 9%, which equals €121 million (DFL, 2016).

Regarding media rights, football is even more dominant as 85% of the overall market is related to football (an der Heiden et al., 2015, p. 9). Overall sport related national Media rights revenue could also be significantly increased in the past years: from €1.1 billion in 2010, a total amount of €1.4 billion was generated in 2014. Most of the money is still from football. The increase in

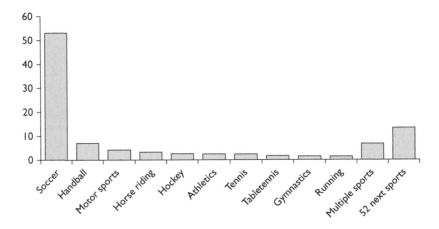

Figure 3.3 Sponsoring of sport organizations in Germany 2010 (an der Heiden et al., 2015)

media rights indirectly shows the interest of football fans in watching the matches. This explains how the Bundesliga was able to double its revenues from national and international media rights in only ten years (from €424 million in in 2006/07 to €835 million in 2016/17) (DFL, 2015, p. 19).

Football-related sport facilities

Even though there is a lot of football in Germany, other sports also need sport facilities. The government invests in a variety of existing sports. Most venues constructed are the ones most needed for schools and the respective physical education classes. It is difficult to explicitly identify which sport venue is dedicated to football or not as many of them are being used for multiple sports. However, in Germany the main purpose of most stadia and outdoor sports fields is football. Table 3.7 shows that top 10 cost-intensive sport facilities constructed and maintained in Germany in 2010. In case we allocate all sports fields and all stadia to football but we do not include any sport halls or other facilities, the share for football facilities would be 19%, representing €4.3 billion. Thus, the consumption/construction of football facilities (19%) is relatively higher compared to consumption of private households (12%).

Pattern of football consumption

Only by comparing the consumption patterns displayed above with different other types of sport, it is possible to visualize the differences. Therefore,

Table 3.7 Sport facilities with the highest costs of infrastructure in construction, maintenance, and personal in 2010 (an der Heiden et al., 2015)

	Facility	In million Euros per year
1	Sports hall (1–3 fields)	5,176 €
2	Swimming pools (open-air/indoor)	4,417 €
3	Sports fields	3,566 €
4	Fitness-centers	2,420 €
5	Cycling roads	922 €
6	Stadia	736 €
7	Horse riding facilities	652 €
8	Shooting ranges	648 €
9	Tennis courts	586 €
10	Swimming pools (hotels)	428 €
	Sport infrastructure total	22,595 €
	Sports fields and stadia	4,302 €
	Estimated share football	19%

we compare the consumption pattern of football with that of other sports. Regarding the consumption of fans compared to the consumption of active football players, Figure 3.4 shows how much football stimulates to spend money for just following the matches.

It is only tennis that has a similar percentage of money being spent for consuming sport as a spectator. But football has almost 50% out of €11.1 billion, the highest out of all types of sport analyzed. The total household consumption amounts for skiing, fitness, and running in combination in each case with related types of sport, however, are comparable with the consumption related to football (Figure 3.5).

In the future, it can be expected that the share of fan and visitor spending will further increase in football. The demographic change in Germany means that there are less people under the age of 16 and many older people. Since football is more often played among the children and juveniles, this will result in less people participating actively and therefore consuming football (an der Heiden et al., 2015). On the other hand, sponsorship and media rights for professional football were constantly growing over the past decade and seem to continue to do so. Another comparison showing the unique characteristics of football is when we compare it with the average consumption of all sports or with the consumption pattern of skiing.

Figure 3.6 shows that the transport to and from active sport participation is almost as high for football as for skiing. Sports vacation related to football is rather rare. It is also no surprise that the sport equipment for football is lower than that for skiing and the average of all other sports. "Others" is much higher than for the average other sports. This can be explained by expenditures for personal hygiene articles (football 9% vs other sports 4%)

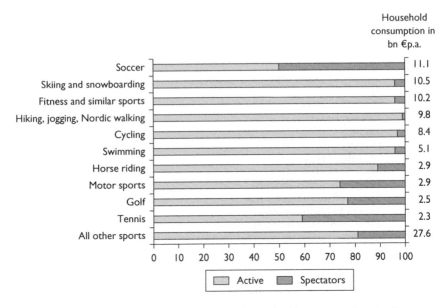

Figure 3.4 Top 10 sports with the highest household consumption in Germany 2010 by share between active sport and spectators/fans (an der Heiden et al., 2015)

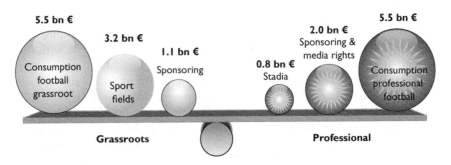

Figure 3.5 Comparison grassroots football consumption with professional football in Germany in 2010

or media and technology costs to support the participation in football (football 8% versus other sports 3%).

Discussion

The results show that professional football consumption by German private households, sponsoring, and media rights, as well as investments in

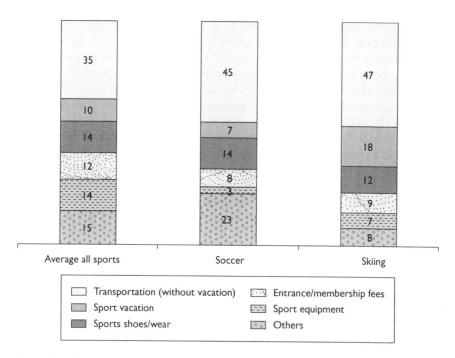

Figure 3.6 Comparison of consumption patterns of all sport with football and skiing over 16 years old in Germany in 2010 (an der Heiden et. al., 2015; Preuss et al. 2012)

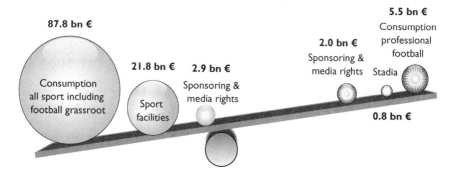

Figure 3.7 Comparison of all sports and grassroots football consumption with professional football in Germany in 2010

sport facilities, dominates other types of sports. However, taking all sports together the consumption of professional football is only a small portion. Figure 3.7 illustrates the economic importance of sport. The private household consumption of sport has a significantly higher impact on the German economy than that of watching and spending for professional football.

Due to the demographic change currently happening in Germany, it is expected that the growth of participation in football will lose in power. Due to the fact that most players are under 16 years, we will see a decrease in active membership. However, because of the close emotional connection to football, many club memberships are probably continued. Already today it can be seen that this happens. For example in the German state of Baden-Wuerttemberg, which has 540,000 members in football clubs, already today, almost 41% of them are passive members (WFV, 2010).

Even though football is the most visible sport in Germany and almost 50% of all money being spent for watching sport or being a fan is related to football, the active, i.e., participation-based consumption is different. Here football as one out of many sports does only constitute 12.3% of the total sport participation. However, of the overall €93 billion spent by private households for sport, the share of football represents, with €11.1 billion, the highest percentage of a single type of sport. By clustering all team sports together €16.8 billion is spent for them, while all winter sports together sum up to €13.5 billion (Ahlert & an der Heiden, 2015; an der Heiden et al., 2013) and €11.4 billion for all water sports.

References

Ahlert, G. (2013). *Die wirtschaftliche Bedeutung des Sports in Deutschland. Abschlussbericht zum Forschungsprojekt Satellitenkonto Sport 2008" für das Bundesinstitut für Sportwissenschaft (BISp).* GWS Research Report 2013/2, Osnabrück.

Ahlert, G., & an der Heiden, I. (2015). *Die ökonomische Bedeutung des Sports in Deutschland: Ergebnisse des Sportsatellitenkontos 2010 und erste Schätzungen für 2012.* GWS Themenreport 2015/01. GWS [Hrsg.], Osnabrück.

Alfs, C. (2014). *Sportkonsum in Deutschland [Sport consumption in Germany].* Wiesbaden: Gabler.

Angenendt, C., Bolten, B., & Krüger, J. (2009). *Sponsor Visions 2009.* Hamburg: Munich Business School.

an der Heiden, I. (2016). *Wirtschaftsfaktor Fußball.* Berlin: Präsentation zur Sonderveröffentlichung des BISp und des BMWi anlässlich des Gesprächskreises Sportwirtschaft.

an der Heiden, I., Meyrahn, F., & Ahlert, G. (2012a). *Bedeutung des Spitzen- und Breitensports im Bereich Werbung, Sponsoring und Medienrechte.* Mainz: www.2hm.com.

an der Heiden, I., Meyrahn, F., Huber, S., Ahlert, G., & Preuß, H. (2012b). *Die wirtschaftliche Bedeutung des Sportstättenbaus und ihr Anteil an einem zukünftigen Sportsatellitenkonto.* Mainz: www.2hm.com.

an der Heiden, I., Meyrahn, F., Preuß, H., & Ahlert, G. (2013). *Wirtschaftsfaktor Wintersport.* Aktuelle Daten zur Sportwirtschaft. Aktuelle Daten zur Sportwirtschaft: Herausgegeben durch das Bundesministeriums für Wirtschaft und Energie (BMWi).

an der Heiden, I., Meyrahn, Repenning, S., Ahlert, G., & Preuss, H. (2015). *Wirtschaftsfaktor Fußball*. Aktuelle Daten zur Sportwirtschaft. Berlin: Herausgegeben durch das Bundesministeriums für Wirtschaft und Energie (BMWi).

DFL. (2015). *Bundesliga report 2015*. Die wirtschaftliche Situation im Lizenzfußball. Retrieved March 21, 2016, from http://s.bundesliga.de/assets/doc/510000/501988_original.pdf

DFL. (2016). *Bundesliga report 2016*. Retrieved March 19, 2016, from http://s.bundesliga.de/assets/doc/1070000/1066689_original.pdf

DOSB. (2016). *Bestandserhebung 2015*. Frankfurt Main: DOSB.

IPSOS. (2008). Backing the right horse. *Sponsoring Perspectives 2009*. www.ipsos.com/sites/default/files/publication/1970-01/ASI_SponsorshipPerspectives_backing_the_right_horse_Dec09.pdf

Köcher, R. (2009). *Allenbacher Jahrbuch der Demoskopie*. München, Allensbach: Saur.

Meyer, B., & Ahlert, G. (2000). *Die ökonomischen Perspektiven des Sports: Eine empirische Analyse für die Bundesrepublik Deutschland*. Schorndorf: Hofmann.

Preuss, H., Alfs, C., & Ahlert, G. (2012). *Sport als Wirtschaftsbranche – Der Sportkonsum privater Haushalte in Deutschland*. Wiesbaden: Gabler.

Scheerder, J., Vos, S., & Taks, M. (2011). Expenditure on sport apparel: Creating consumer profiles through interval regression modeling. *European Sport Management Quarterly*, *11*(3), 251–274.

SpEA. (2007). *The Vilnius definition of sport*. Retrieved from www.esce.at/spea/vilnus/0710%20ESSA%20Vilnius%20Definition%20Sport.xls

Taks, M., Renson, R., & Vanreusel, B. (1999). Consumer expenses in sport: A marketing tool for sport and sport facility providers? *European Journal for Sport Management*, *6*(1), 4–18.

Weber, W., Schneider, C., Kortlücke, N., & Horak, B. (1995). *Die wirtschaftliche Bedeutung des Sports*. Schorndorf: Hofmann.

WFV. (2010). *DFB-Statistik Württembergischer Fußballverband. Stand: 15.* January 2010. Retrieved from July 20, 2015, from www.wuerttfv.de/aurita/Wi-ki::Media_Asset/proxy/media_asset_id=8542

Wicker, P., Breuer, C., & Pawlowski, T. (2010). Are sports club members big spenders?: Findings from sport specific analyses in Germany. *Sport Management Review*, *13*(3), 214–224.

Chapter 4

Nonlocal Portuguese football fans and their love for the "Big Three"

Boris Osorio and Craig Hyatt

Introduction

Sport is a unique phenomenon, as it is simultaneously produced and consumed by society and has the ability to transcend social and political issues, create communities and shared spaces for marginalized people, and unify rival groups (Valeriano, 2014; Bernache-Assollant, Bouchet, Auvergne, & Lacassange, 2011; Stone, 2007). Sport and sport teams have a strong influence on society, and are reflections of fans' perceptions of self and society (Funk, & James, 2006; Lock, Taylor, Funk, & Darcy, 2012). Identifying with a team allows fans to become members of like-minded groups that share strong fan behaviors and attitudes toward their specific team (Funk & James, 2001; Gladden & Funk, 2001). These associations with a team and extensions of self-identity serve as tools to navigate multiple socially constructed categories such as race, gender, and class (Porat, 2010). Further, the influence of these social categories on migration for fans that self-identify with a team may impact their fandom in different social spaces (Knijnik, 2014). This is especially the case for migrants from countries whose national culture and identity is historically integrated with football.

In Portugal, football is a significant part of Portuguese culture and identity. Football influences Portuguese football fans' affiliations, decisions, and activities both in their public and private spaces (Coelho & Tiesler, 2007). Portuguese football dominates the narratives of media production within the nation and reproduces the notion of Portugal as a football nation (Coelho & Tiesler, 2007). Traditionally in the Portuguese football landscape, football fans support one of the "Big Three" teams: Futebol Clube do Porto, Sport Benfica e Lisboa, and Sporting Clube de Portugal. These three teams are based out of the two largest cities in Portugal: Porto in the north, and Lisbon in the center, and have collectively won the Portuguese football league a total of 80 times out of 82 seasons. Although many Portuguese football fans pledge lifelong allegiances to one of the "Big Three" teams and demonstrate behavioral and attitudinal loyalties toward their team, many of these football fans do not attend live matches for various reasons

(Tiesler & Coelho, 2007). Proximity to the stadium plays a role in attending live matches as many fans in Portuguese football are considered nonlocal fans because they reside outside of geographic neighborhoods that the "Big Three" teams are a part of. These nonlocal fans make up the majority of Portuguese league support and have, for the most part, forgone civic allegiance to their local team and instead identified symbolically to a nonlocal team by associating with fan nations, a collective of fans that share attitudes and behaviors of what it means to be a fan (Foster & Hyatt, 2008; Coelho & Tiesler, 2007). As Portuguese football fans continue to support nonlocal teams they directly impact the ability of local teams to compete with the "Big Three" and effect the overall health of the Portuguese Football League (Liga NOS). Furthermore, allegiances to nonlocal teams for Portuguese fans are perpetuated generationally by migrants who take with them their fandom to another country.

In Canada, Portuguese football fans grapple with their sport fandom in relation to retention strategies and fan expression. Although there are many ways in which Portuguese football fans can preserve their identity within cultural space and contribute to the current migration spaces' existing sport landscape, many Portuguese football fans are faced with internal and external tension in regards to their identity and fandom. Through the narratives of migrant Portuguese football fans now living in Toronto, Canada, this research project aims to understand how migration affects nonlocal Portuguese football fans' fandom. The primary research question guiding this research is how do Portuguese migrants in Toronto who regularly visit Portugal retain and express their fandom in comparison to nonlocal Portuguese football fans living in Portugal?

Review of literature

Within sport academia much has been studied on sport fandom. Theoretical frameworks such as the Psychological Continuum Model (Funk & James, 2001) have been used to better understand fan behavior and the processes in which a fan develops over time. The four stages in the PCM are the awareness stage, attraction stage, attachment stage, and allegiance stage. Through this theoretical framework, research has developed to understand push and pull factors that affect team identification (Heere & James, 2007; Wann & Branscombe, 1993), behavioral and attitudinal fan loyalty (Funk & James, 2001; Gladden & Funk, 2001), and civic and symbolic allegiance (Foster & Hyatt, 2008; Lewis, 2001).

Portuguese in Canada

The majority of Canada's Portuguese population arrived during the 1970s and 1980s (Murdie & Teixeira, 2011); however, this immigrant population is increasingly translocal and travel between Canada and Portugal is common, especially amongst first generation Portuguese-Canadians. Ethnic communities within cities influence the spaces that become cultural hubs for ethnic immigrant groups. Most metropolitan cities in Canada have Portuguese ethnic neighborhoods dedicated to Portuguese restaurants, shops, goods, services, and other cultural necessities that meet the needs of the immigrant Portuguese community (Leal 2009; Teixeira, 2001). "Little Portugal" in Toronto is the largest Portuguese community in Canada (Murdie & Teixeira, 2011). Toronto's "Little Portugal" remains a vibrant community representative of Portuguese culture through the use of Portuguese signs and symbols.

Various factors influence immigrant Portuguese identity. When living in a new host country, assimilation and acculturation processes are usually a result of the generational shifts away from traditional and cultural tendencies due to subsequent generations living in multicultural spaces (Sardinha, 2012). As Sardinha (2012) explains the assimilation and acculturation processes may cause strain and tensions on the Portuguese identity as traditions, beliefs, and strong attachments to Portuguese culture by the older generation may not be as important in the second or future generations. One manner in which researchers have been able to understand the effects of acculturation on Portuguese migrants is through sport, specifically Portuguese football (Moniz, 2007; Pereira, 2012; Sardinha, 2012; Tiesler, 2012). Current research includes the use of football as a coping strategy for Portuguese migrants in football-dominant countries (Pereira, 2012), the influence a national sport has on second-generation Portuguese descendants living in Canada (Sardinha, 2012). Further, research on Portuguese football fans in North American cities shows the ways in which football influences ethnic identity and maintenance. For example, Portuguese migrants in New England and Toronto, like Portuguese migrants elsewhere, decide whether consciously or subconsciously to retain, abandon, or negotiate their ethnic identity (Moniz, 2007; Sardinha, 2012). Although the aforementioned studies are pivotal frameworks from which to understand what is known of Portuguese football fandom within a migrant and specifically Canadian discourse, none of the studies focus on the specific fandom of nonlocal Portuguese football fans that are now living in the Greater Toronto area and regularly return to Portugal. Therefore, this study builds on these important studies, but is unique in its methodology.

Nonlocal fandom and Portuguese football

The research on fan behavior for nonlocal and distant fans has been studied from the perspectives of franchise relocation in which fans cheer for their team in the team's new host city (Foster & Hyatt, 2007; Hyatt, 2007), fans living in another country and community (Farred, 2002; Kerr & Gladden, 2008; Sveinson & Hoeber, 2016), and becoming a fan to a distant team when a local alternative exists (Hyatt & Andrijiw, 2008). Much of the literature on how these distant and nonlocal fans support their team focuses on the creation of imagined communities (Anderson, 2006; Stone, 2007; Tiesler, 2012). In football, it is not uncommon for fans to support a distant team or support a nonlocal team. Historically, a person's geographical location to a team formed their allegiance to the team (Brown, Crabbe, & Mellor, 2008). However, football teams that were established early on have benefited from the opportunity to create significant ties to communities outside of their geographical proximity, through the use of names, colors, and class (Heere & James, 2007). This strategy allows teams to appeal to a larger portion of the population, who are more likely to attach themselves to the team that is most representative of the self (Heere & James, 2007). Specifically in Portuguese football, there exists hegemony where the "Big Three" garner most of the support of nonlocal and distant fans that support Portuguese football (Coelho & Tiesler, 2007). Within this specific group of fans, the "symbolic community" and the creation of fan nations (Foster & Hyatt, 2008) have played a major role in forming fan allegiances to one of the "Big Three" teams.

Research on Portuguese fandom has focused on transnational football fans in regards to: their allegiances to their football team within a new host nation (Tiesler, 2012), their contribution to the football landscape within the host nation (Moniz, 2007; Pereira, 2012), the creation of ethnic spaces and markets where the commodification of the "Big Three" merchandise is represented (Leal, 2009), and second generation Portuguese-Canadians grappling with assimilation through the national sport in Canada (ice hockey) and retention of cultural sport (football) (Sardinha, 2012). Through established ethnic communities and markets, Portuguese football fans are able to retain and express their fandom through their behaviors and attitudes by gathering in ethnic spaces to watch football matches, and purchase Portuguese football goods and services that are offered by specialty shops in the "Little Portugal" neighborhood in Toronto.

Portuguese-Canadian football fans have a strong attachment to perceptions of "Portuguese fandom," even though some do not speak or use the Portuguese language often, and even though some are acculturated in Canadian culture (Sardinha, 2012). This is a result of the fact that there is a cultural ambivalence in Canada that provides the space by which individuals can mitigate, negotiate, and form their own identities in relation to their social and cultural needs (Vieira, 2013). Sport-focused cultural centers, such as Casa do Benfica, Casa do Sporting, and Casa do Porto, provide the space that allows for Portuguese football fans to connect to a sense of identity that is tied to their fandom.

Gaps in the literature

The academic literature on the Portuguese in Canada has focused on themes such as gender and work (Giles, 2002; Noivo, 1993), language and identity (da Silva, 2011; Sardinha, 2011), and assimilation and migration (Murdie & Teixeira, 2011; da Silva, 2011; Teixeira & Da Rosa, 2009; Teixeira, 2001). Research on Portuguese football has expanded over the years. Since the 2000s, research has expanded to include knowledge on Portuguese football fans and the effects of migration for both the fan and their new home (Tielser, 2012). Also, researchers such as Tiesler (2012) have conducted thorough literature reviews on what is known of Portuguese football fans on a global scale. Contributions to the study of Portuguese fandom have added to existing literature in regards to the commodification of "home" in Portuguese communities and its influence on fandom retention. Studies on the ways in which first generation Portuguese football fans retain their allegiance to Portuguese football teams including one of the "Big Three" Portuguese football teams once they have emigrated from continental Portugal is limited. Missing in the literature on Portuguese football fandom are the narratives of nonlocal Portuguese football fans living in continental Portugal, the narratives of nonlocal Portuguese football fans who have migrated to Canada, as well as understanding how migration and distance influence fan behaviors and team allegiances.

Method

This exploratory research project is qualitative in nature and involves an interpretive methodology. The aim of this project is to capture the lived experiences of nonlocal Portuguese football fans that have migrated from continental Portugal to Toronto, Canada. In addition to the main research question the following questions were utilized: what strategies are similar and which are different? Is fandom expressed differently depending on where nonlocal fans reside? If so, how? What are the motives for retaining football fandom as nonlocal fans? Are the motives similar/different within these groups?

Between August 2014 and March 2015, the lead researcher conducted four individual semi-structured interviews with Portuguese football fans living in Toronto (Morin, Rui Costa, Gaiteiro, and Ricardo) to understand how each fan became a supporter of a "Big Three" football team, if and why these fans rejected their local alternative team, and how migration effected their fandom. In addition, three semi-structured interviews were conducted with nonlocal fans still living in continental Portugal (Super Dragon, Figo, and Eusébio). Through this, drawing on similarities and differences within both groups of fans provided an in-depth interpretation of Portuguese football fandom. The strategy employed in the interpretive qualitative interviews was borrowed from Hyatt (2007) in which open-ended questions were used to allow the participants to tell their stories in a manner they felt most comfortable with (see Appendices A and B for research questions).

Informed consent was obtained verbally, a strategy similar to a research project involving Portuguese participants in Toronto (Vieira, 2013). The reason for obtaining verbal consent was because in the interviewer's experience with the Portuguese community and culture both in Toronto and in continental Portugal, requesting a signature when there is no transaction can create feelings of obligation and the formalization of a dialogue. In order to create a more natural dialogue between the participant and the interviewer, consent was obtained verbally. Each participant was given a consent form that detailed the expectations of the interview and the level of their involvement in the project. After the participants agreed with the expectation for their involvement, they verbally consented to participate in the research project. After verbally consenting, each fan was interviewed from between 24 and 83 minutes in a mutually agreed upon location.

All interviews were audio taped and transcribed verbatim. The participants included three nonlocal fans currently living in continental Portugal and four nonlocal fans living in Toronto, Canada. The participant ages ranged from 26 to 47. The use of pseudonyms was very important for two reasons. The first reason was to provide a level of anonymity for the participants. The second reason was to further create a more personal and open dialogue between the participant and interviewer. During the interview, participants were encouraged to choose a pseudonym of their liking. Of the seven participants, five participants chose a pseudonym that directly linked them to their football team, while the other two participants used existing nicknames given to them in Portugal (Morin and Gaiteiro). From the five participants that chose a pseudonym that linked them to their favorite football team, four chose the names of former prominent players that had once played on the team (Eusebio, Rui Costa, Figo, and Ricardo), while the other participant chose to be referred to by the name of a member of FC Porto's official supporters section (Super Dragon).

Through the use of personal networks in Toronto and in Portugal one participant from each location was identified that fit the criteria of the study and from there a snowball technique was used to find the rest of the participants (Tracy, 2013). The criteria used for including participants in the study were: all participants had to be considered a nonlocal fan of one of the "Big Three" teams and have access to a local team alternative, be male, be between 25 and 50 years of age, and have never resided in Lisbon or Porto. In addition, the participants in Toronto also required that they be a Portuguese migrant from continental Portugal and frequently return to Portugal to visit. As the sample size is relatively small, it was important to use the selection criteria in order to have a sample of individuals who are more likely to share similar characteristics; excluding female participants was due to the proposed sample size; selecting participants between the ages of 25 and 50 was done to increase the likely hood that these participants have more disposable income to engage in sport related activities; and having the participants who live in Toronto frequently visit Portugal was important to the selection criteria because this allows them the opportunity to consume their local team and favorite team when in continental Portugal.

Throughout the research project, a self-reflexive approach was utilized to allow for a better understanding of the lead researcher's position in relation to the research process. Also, a self-reflexive approach allowed the researcher to better understand how personal biases affect the research. As a second generation Canadian of Colombian and Ecuadorian descent, my status as an insider with the Portuguese participants comes from my upbringing and assimilation into a large Portuguese community in Toronto. Through my experiences within the Portuguese community I have become very familiar with their culture, language, and love for football, specifically, how football is tied to an individual's identity to one of the "Big Three" teams. As an active supporter of one the "Big Three" and an occasional visitor to Portugal, I have gained an insider status with other Portuguese football fans in Toronto and in Portugal, which has allowed me to navigate through the Portuguese football landscape in both spaces and relate to the participants of this research project. However, I am aware that I cannot fully be an insider because I am not of Portuguese descent, I have not experienced migration to another country, and I have only vacationed in Portugal and never taken up residence. For a chart outlining the participants in detail see Appendix C. For a map outlining the location of the participants' hometowns and locations of the Portuguese football teams see Appendix D.

Findings and discussion

From an analysis of all the Portuguese football fans' interview narratives an immediate consensus emerged: geographical locational and proximity to a football team's region had very little effect on Portuguese football fan attraction. Identity formation and demonstrating behavioral and attitudinal loyalty (Funk & James, 2001; Gladden & Funk, 2001) to one of the "Big Three" Portuguese league teams is common place for all supporters of Portuguese league football (Coelho & Tiesler, 2007). This section is divided into four themes that reflect the narratives of the Portuguese fans interviewed.

How many teams do you support?

For each fan in the research project there exists a local team that has played or plays in the first division of the Portuguese league. During each interview the participants acknowledged that there exists a tendency as a Portuguese football fan to have dual fandom in which they support two teams within the same league. Ordinarily, their dual fandom consists of a primary and secondary team, whereby their primary team is one of the "Big Three" and their secondary team is the local team. Although each participant acknowledges the existence of a local alternative to supporting a "Big Three" team, none of the participants support their secondary team as strongly as their primary team. Of the seven fans, only the Super Dragon rejects having any form of secondary team, although an alternative team is present. Twenty-five-year-old Super Dragon's view on Portuguese football fans is shared with the other interviewees whereby many of the interviewees express similar sentiments. The Super Dragon explains:

> In Portugal [it] works like this, you have two teams first is Porto, Benfica, or Sporting. Next is your team from your area. Most people do that they support two teams. Me, no I only support one team because that's how it should be. Supporting your team above everything else is how you show support, you can't decide to support one team today and then when your two teams play each other you split your support, it doesn't work like that.

All of the participants in Toronto (Morin, Rui Costa, Gaiteiro, and Ricardo) express similar understandings of primary and secondary team bonds as a Portuguese football fan norm. The participants in Toronto express feelings of decreased support for their secondary team once they migrated from Portugal and no longer had a direct connection with the secondary team, with the exception of one fan whom trained with his local club's academy as a child. With migration to Toronto the integration into the existing Portuguese football community within "Little Portugal" is similar to Portugal, as the accessibility to secondary teams is difficult because of the hegemony Sporting, Benfica, and Porto have over the majority of Portuguese football activities in Toronto. Gaiteiro, a forty-five-year-old living in Toronto, says:

> It's almost the same. When I came here [Toronto] it was like being in Portugal a bit. Everyone talks about football, Sporting, Benfica, Porto that's it, like in Portugal. The only difference is in our country when you're back in your city you follow the [local] team a bit more. It's in the news, so you kind of give attention, you hope they don't lose too much and stay in the first division you know because that's where you're from. Since I've been here [Toronto] I don't follow my city's team much, it's not the same. I think that's because everyone here [Toronto] just follows one of the [big] three main teams, it's easier.

Further, Rui Costa (28 years old) states:

> I love my city [Coimbra] and I support Academica a lot. I actually played for their academy growing up. So I have a lot of memories with Academica, but sincerely speaking my team is Benfica until the end.

I want them to do well [Academica] but every year I want Benfica to win the title. It would be good if Benfica was in first and Academica get second place but as long as Benfica is first that's all that really matters to me, but I still follow Academica, I have some love for them, but Benfica is in my heart.

Six of the seven participants exhibited some degree of attitudinal and behavioral loyalty toward their secondary team while in Portugal. However, as proximity from the secondary team changed for three of the participants living in Toronto, so did the behavioral and attitudinal loyalties demonstrated toward their secondary team. Although loyalties decreased for the secondary team, loyalties toward the primary team increased.

It's not the same here

In the Portuguese community having one's identity reflect the allegiance to a football club is considered common. For those fans that migrated from Portugal to Toronto, having an allegiance to one of the "Big Three" not only serves as a memento of "home," but also serves as a tool to navigate a new city. With the Portuguese community living in "Little Portugal" in Toronto, the participants in Toronto express how being a fan of a "Big Three" club has provided them with opportunities of employment and camaraderie with fans of the same team. The four participants in Toronto stated they are active consumers of their primary team and seek out various ways to consume their team. Some go as far as to plan their schedules around game times and purposely wear team merchandise on game days. Although all seven participants expressed that their fandom is a symbol of their identity, the participants in Toronto stated a decrease in the level of behavioral and attitudinal loyalty to their "Big Three" team when they returned to Portugal, as the following excerpts from Gaiteiro and Morin illustrate:

Honestly I didn't think about it until now but the only time I've watched Sporting live since I came to Canada was when they came here [Toronto] and played against Juventus. When I go back home I never go watch Sporting play. I've watched Portugal [national team] play a couple of times but when I am there [Portugal] I don't really go out of my way to watch Sporting.

(Gaiteiro, 44)

It's different you know. When I'm here [Toronto] I plan my days around games. I can't tell you how many times I've showed up late to parties, lunches, dinners because my team [SL Benfica] is playing and if they lose forget it I won't even go because I know I'm going to hear it from someone about how my team lost.

(Morin, 45)

Further, Morin states:

> I go back to Portugal at least once a year maybe twice depending on how things are going for me. I never go and watch Benfica play I don't even plan my days around their games like I do here. It's different there [Portugal] you don't have to try hard to look for the game or find out the score, it's everywhere on TV, newspapers, magazines, whoever you see on the street knows the results too.

The participants in Toronto demonstrate a decrease in consuming their primary team when returning to Portugal. As the participants in Toronto return to Portugal the need to actively express their fandom is not as important because being a fan in Portugal does not require as much effort as it does when living in Toronto. Furthermore, the participants in Toronto express that being a fan in Toronto carries more value to them than being a fan in Portugal as it is a point of difference in Toronto. As 26-year-old Ricardo says:

> Everyone is a fan in Portugal and even if you're not really a fan you still cheer for your family's team. In Toronto it makes you different, here, there's not a lot of people that watch football outside of our area, mostly immigrants so it gives you something to share with people that don't know about it. Like an expert because not everyone is a fan of a Portuguese football team in the Toronto.

Do you support your local team?

Each of the seven participants has had the opportunity to follow their local team instead of one of the "Big Three" teams. Of the seven participants, Figo and Eusebio who currently live in Portugal, and Rui Costa, who is living in Toronto, have attempted to actively support their local team. Although the support for their local team is not comparable to the same level of support for their "Big Three" team, these three participants were the only participants to not attribute the lack of quality as the reason why they do not support their secondary team, but instead attributed their lack of support to the local team as a result of being raised as a "Big Three" fan. This can be seen in interview excerpts from both Rui Costa (a 28-year-old SL Benfica fan living in Toronto, Canada) and Eusebio (a 33-year-old SL Benfica fan currently living in Braga, Portugal):

INTERVIEWER: Why don't you follow Academica like you follow Benfica?

RUI COSTA: My dad. He is the reason I support Benfica. Like I was saying I grew up in Coimbra and Academica has a pretty good following, not as big as Benfica, Porto, or Sporting but they have support. I just chose to follow Benfica more than Academica because of my dad. I do have support for them [Academica] but Benfica is my team. It's a family thing; my kids will have to do the same that's how it is.

INTERVIEWER: Why don't you follow Braga like you follow Benfica?

EUSEBIO: I've always been a Benfica fan. The team has my heart. You know. I care about Braga, they should be my team and I do have a connection to them because this is my city but I have a deeper connection to Benfica. It's something that just happens growing up in Portugal. Your dad is the reason you follow your team. Maybe if my dad followed Braga like he follows Benfica things would be different for me but he didn't so Benfica is my first.

Both Rui Costa and Eusebio state that the relationship with their father is the reason they support a nonlocal team instead of the local team alternative. Although Rui Costa and Eusebio acknowledge a level of support for their local team as a result of their residence in Portugal, both fans opted to follow familial ties and support a "Big Three" team. Further, Eusebio feels that if his father supported the local team (Braga) as strongly as his nonlocal team (Benfica) that he, too, would do the same.

In contrast Morin, Gaiteiro, and Ricardo all state that the primary reason for being a fan of a "Big Three" team is winning. The local team is not an appealing option, as they are not as successful and cannot compete for trophies every season on the same level as a "Big Three" team. What is interesting to note is that only two years separate Morin and Gaiteiro in age, and as siblings with similar upbringings in the same household, they do not support the same "Big Three" team. However, both share the same reason for not supporting their local team:

INTERVIEWER: Why don't you follow Uniao like you follow Benfica?

MORIN: When I was a kid there wasn't much excitement about being a Uniao supporter. I remember almost everyone supporting Benfica because they would win all the time. When they [Benfica] would win people in my area would celebrate and have a good time. I liked that, you didn't get that same feeling supporting Uniao, they would be in the first division then second then first. By the time they were in the first division steady I already committed to Benfica.

Gaiteiro began his football fandom with supporting his local team. However, during the interview he recalls why he shifted his primary and secondary team allegiances to support his nonlocal team first (Sporting CP) instead of his local team:

I started to support Sporting because of my brother. He doesn't support Sporting, he supports Benfica. I supported Uniao growing up. I felt like it made the most sense, I'm from there; I can follow them more easily. That didn't last long because I would always have to hear my brother talk about how Benfica is the best and how there was no point in supporting Uniao because they won't win a title. So I chose to support Sporting because they won the league when Uniao got relegated. I thought Sporting would win for a couple of years and that would keep my brother quiet. Since then Uniao never won much and I am still supporting Sporting.

(Gaiteiro, 45)

While the participants retained their loyalty to their "Big Three" team when they migrated to Toronto, it is worth noting that all four participants living in Toronto follow at least one Toronto based sports team. Morin and Gaiteiro recall the playoff rivalry between the Toronto Maple Leafs and the Ottawa Senators as the reason they support the Maple Leafs of the National Hockey League. Similarly, Rui Costa and Ricardo support the Toronto Raptors of the National Basketball Association for the buzz around the team's first Atlantic division title. Although each participant in Toronto supports a Toronto sport team none of the participants support the new local alternative to the "Big Three" (Toronto Football Club); albeit the same sport but in a different league (MLS) entirely. None of the participants claim strong allegiance to Toronto FC. When asked if they support the local football team in Toronto, Rui Costa, Morin, Gaiteiro, and Ricardo responded:

RUI COSTA, 28: No, I came here [Toronto] around the time they started I remember that. But it's hard to go from European football to North American soccer. The quality is not the same.

MORIN, 47: (laughs) For what? The second team of Benfica could beat them [Toronto FC]. My son tries to get me to watch and sometimes I do because I like to make jokes at him. Maybe if they win I would go with him to watch them. I know what's going on with them [Toronto FC] because I enjoy football and I talk to my [son] about them, so I do keep up to date but it's just not the same as Benfica.

GAITEIRO, 45: Not really. You know, I like to watch football. I watch games all the time but it's hard for me to watch North American soccer. It's gotten better. I know teams are spending more money to bring in older players but there's a gap in quality between leagues here and in Europe.

RICARDO, 26: Not really, some of my friends do. I would but it's not the same. It's not like cheering for Porto. When they play [Porto] you expect a win, when you watch Toronto you're hoping they don't lose. I would rather win.

The fans living in Toronto support a Toronto sports team in the sports that they did not follow when living in Portugal such as hockey and basketball. Following a Toronto sport team allows the fans living in Toronto to relate to other fans in Toronto that are outside of their Portuguese community. Although Morin and Gaiteiro express a weak following of the local football team Toronto FC because of the apparent lack of quality, both stated in their respective interviews that their children who are second-generation Canadian in their 20's support Toronto FC. Moreover, because their children consume the local team, Morin and Gaiteiro acknowledge that as a result, they too consume the local team Toronto FC and cheer for them on occasion as a way to bond with their children (Hyatt & Foster, 2015).

Civic and symbolic allegiance

The use of civic and symbolic allegiance in sport literature is used to describe how fans identify with supporting their team either by the city in which their team plays or by the brand of their team (Lewis, 2001). Given that all participants are not from the city that their team resides in, each participant expresses symbolic allegiance to their "Big Three" team. Although four participants state they had civic allegiance, only the Super Dragon expresses civic and symbolic allegiance to the city of Porto. Moreover, Figo, Eusebio, and Rui Costa who support their secondary team more actively than the other participants, show civic allegiance to their secondary local team and symbolic allegiance to their nonlocal primary "Big Three" team. The three fans that have civic allegiance to their secondary team feel a sense of responsibility to support their local team because of the historical ties they feel their local team has with their city, whereas those who did not feel a connection between team and city did not show civic allegiance to their secondary team and only show symbolic allegiance to their primary team. The following excerpts demonstrate how civic and symbolic allegiances play a major role in Portuguese football fandom for these nonlocal fans:

INTERVIEWER: Do you support Academica?

FIGO, 41: I do. I grew up here [Coimbra] but I also support Sporting.

INTERVIEWER: What happens when they play each other? What do you do?

FIGO, 41: It's like this in Portugal everyone has two teams. Mine is Sporting and Academica, but in the end my heart belongs to Sporting. When they play each other I go for Sporting I only really go for Academica when it doesn't affect Sporting. You know, this is my city but Sporting is my team.

In contrast, the Super Dragon who expresses nothing less than complete devotion to his "Big Three" team was asked the question: do you feel any support for the city of Porto? He explained:

SUPER DRAGON, 25: I don't have any ties with Porto except that I support the team, but because I support the team I also support the city. There's a nice place in Lisbon where a lot of people go. My girlfriend wants to go so bad but I won't go. I tell her to take her sister because I refuse to go. It's in Lisbon and I support Porto. I am a Super Dragon, the only time I will go to Lisbon is to walk through the streets to the stadium of Benfica or Sporting when we play them.

The Super Dragon's complete allegiance does not allow him to enter into the rival teams' city of Lisbon as he has civic allegiance to his team and feels that enjoying Lisbon would go against his allegiance to Porto. It is worth noting that S.C. Braga has remained in the first division of the Portuguese league since the 1970s and Academica is the fourth-most supported club in Portugal after the "Big Three" teams. Also, Academica's ties to the University of Coimbra have made the club a staple in the city's identity. This may be a factor as to why Figo, Eusebio, and Rui Costa show civic allegiance to their secondary team. In contrast, the participants from Leiria (Morin and Gaiteiro) and Aveiro (Ricardo) show little civic allegiance to their local team and do not support them to the same degree as the other participants.

Implications

The purpose of this project was to understand the narratives of nonlocal Portuguese football fans in Toronto and continental Portugal. Through the narratives of these seven Portuguese football league fans a number of conclusions were drawn that can provide a better understanding of sport consumer behaviors. First, football in Portugal is embedded in the culture of all residents. With historical ties to regions of the nation, Portuguese football teams have been able to affect the daily lives of football fans and have become an extension of identity and ties to the nation. The "Big Three" teams have capitalized on the creation of fan nations (Foster & Hyatt, 2008) and as a result have remained the primary supported teams for most Portuguese football fans. All of the Portuguese football fans interviewed mentioned that geographic proximity to a "Big Three" team is not a factor in creating allegiances to their team as some fans were closer in proximity to the rival teams. Although these Portuguese football fans acknowledge a dual fandom practice, most did not express equal behaviors for both their primary and secondary teams. This is important for professional teams as the world becomes more closely intertwined due to the advancements in technology, traditions and fan nations become the driving force of fan loyalty in place of civic ties.

Second, when Portuguese football fans migrate they take with them their customs and culture. As football is a large part of Portuguese culture, retaining their allegiance to their Portuguese football team is as important as retaining other aspects of their identity. All of the participants in Toronto feel that the large Portuguese community in Toronto allows them to feel a sense of home away from home, where the only barriers to expressing their fandom are toward their secondary team allegiances, as the ethnic Portuguese spaces in Toronto are dominated by the "Big Three" teams. Although some of the participants in Toronto and Portugal did show some degree of behavioral and attitudinal loyalty to their secondary team, most fans in Toronto did not as accessibility to their secondary team is limited. For migrant fans prioritizing football fan allegiances is important, as loyalty to a "Big Three" team in an ethnic community allows for inclusion in the existing landscape. For teams in the Portuguese league, excluding the "Big Three," it would prove to be a difficult task to gain a strong foothold into Portuguese ethnic communities as hegemony exists. Teams within newer professional leagues such as the MLS should be extremely cognizant of how culture and accessibility to the team play a crucial role in fan attachment. Teams with large ethnic communities must be aware of how leveraging ethnicity can help with attracting those communities that are more likely to consume the team (Moniz, 2007).

Finally, as most first-generation Portuguese sport fans attempt to retain their fandom, they are faced with the reality of acculturating and assimilating into their new home's sports landscape. Typically for the second-generation Portuguese born in Canada, the socialization factors are different in which the old (football) traditions passed on from a previous generation are competing with new (hockey) sports customs introduced by the Canadian sports landscape (Sardinha, 2012). Teams that operate in markets with large immigrant populations should recognize the opportunity that the second generation population provides in which they can influence team socialization within a family's structure by which a new history and tradition can be created and enforced onto first-generation migrants as well as proceeding generations of sport fans.

Conclusion

Limitations

Several limitations must be acknowledged in this research project. Although seven participants provided rich narratives on their experiences of being a Portuguese football fan, it is important to note that only four of the seven participants experienced retaining their fandom in a new country. With only four narratives of migrant Portuguese fans, this project is not reflective of all the Portuguese migrant fans living in Toronto. Another limitation is the way in which the Portuguese participants recognize where they are from within continental Portugal. Of the seven participants only Figo, Rui Costa, Eusébio, and Ricardo are directly from the city centre of their local team while Morin, Gaiteiro, and Super Dragon are from a "Freguesia," a civil parish that acts as a subdivision within the municipality. This distinction can affect the relationship a participant has with their city, as such civil allegiances may be influenced. Of the four participants that are directly from their respective city centers, only Ricardo was uninfluenced by ties to his city which reflected in his limited allegiance to his local team. In contrast Figo, Rui Costa, and Eusébio all expressed strong feelings of pride with their city, which is reflective of their civic allegiance to their local team. Moreover, Morin, Gaiteiro, and Super Dragon who are from a Freguesia in Leiria show little to no civic allegiance to their local team. Although, this study has a small sample of participants there exists a relationship between participants' attitudes towards local teams of those living in a city center versus those living in a Freguesia.

Directions for future research

This research study highlights factors that impact nonlocal fans including those who have migrated to a country where the dominant sport is not football. As the environment changes when fans leave the site where their fandom began, so too do the push and pull factors that impact their consumption particularly when assimilating into the new environment. Although it is common for family to introduce a child to the "family" team, attempts to pass on any secondary team allegiances to the local team in Portugal may be more difficult for second-generation children. This is a result of not being able to replicate the same environment that provided first generation fans the socialization opportunities to their local team in Portugal. North American sports and the "Big Three" teams in ethnic markets are barriers to this because they are the dominate influences on sport socialization for subsequent generations. Future research on Portuguese football fandom may expand the scope of this project by focusing on how fans balance allegiances to two teams in the same league, include the narratives of female Portuguese football fans to understand the ways in which gender influence Portuguese fandom and include the narratives of nonlocal Portuguese football fans from various parts of Portugal not included in this project such as the Azorean Islands and Madeira, where there is a large number of "Big Three" team supporters. Lastly, future research could focus on those Portuguese football fans whose primary team is a team outside of one of the "Big Three" teams. As the competitive balance in the Portuguese football league is skewed towards one of the "Big Three" teams winning, it would be interesting to research what drives those fans that reject having any "Big Three" team allegiance.

References

Anderson, B. (2006). *Imagined communities reflections on the origin and spread of nationalism*. London, England: Verso.

Bernache-Assollant, I., Bouchet, P., Auvergne, S., & Lacassagne, M. (2011). Identity crossbreeding in Soccer fan groups: A social approach. The case of Marseille (France). *Journal of Sport & Social Issues, 35*(1), 72–100.

Brown, A., Crabbe, T., & Mellor, G. (2008). Introduction: Football and community – practical and theoretical considerations. *Soccer & Society, 9*(3), 303–312.

Coelho, J. N., & Tiesler, N. C. (2007). The paradox of the Portuguese game: The omnipresence of football and the absence of spectators at matches. *Soccer & Society, 8*(4), 578–600.

da Silva, E. (2011). *Sociolinguistic (re)constructions of Diaspora Portugueseness: Portuguese-Canadian youth in Toronto* (Unpublished doctoral dissertation, University of Toronto) Retrieved from https://tspace.library.utoronto.ca/handle/1807/30088

Farred, G. (2002). Long distance love: Growing up a Liverpool Football Club fan. *Journal of Sport & Social Issues, 26*(1), 6–24.

Foster, W. M., & Hyatt, C. (2007). I despise them! I detest them! Franchise relocation and the expanded model of organizational identification. *Journal of Sport Management, 21*(2), 194–212.

Foster, W. M., & Hyatt, C. (2008). Inventing team tradition: A conceptual model for the strategic development of fan nations. *European Sport Management Quarterly, 8*(3), 265–287.

Funk, D., & James, J. D. (2001). The psychological continuum model: A conceptual framework for understanding an individual's psychological connection to sport. *Sport Management Review, 4*(2),119–150.

Funk, D. C., & James, J. D. (2006). Consumer loyalty: The meaning of attachment in the development of sport team allegiance. *Journal of Sport Management, 20,* 189–217.

Giles, W. (2002). *Portuguese women in Toronto: Gender, immigration and nationalism.* Toronto: University of Toronto Press.

Gladden, J. M., & Funk, D. C. (2001). Understanding brand loyalty in professional sport: Examining the link between brand association and brand loyalty. *International Journal of Sport Management. 16,* 54–81.

Heere, B., & James, J, (2007). Sports teams and their communities: Examining the influence of external group identities on team identity. *Journal of Sport Management, 21,* 319–337.

Hyatt, C. G. (2007). Who do I root for now? The impact of franchise relocation on the loyal fans left behind: A case study of Hartford Whalers fans. *Journal of Sport Behavior, 30*(1), 36–56.

Hyatt, C. G, & Andrijiw, A. (2008). How people raised and living in Ontario became fans of nonlocal National Hockey league teams. *IJSMM International Journal of Sport Management and Marketing, 4*(4), 338–355.

Hyatt, C. G., & Foster, W. M. (2015). Using identity work theory to understand the de-escalation of fandom: A study of former fans of National Hockey league teams. *Journal of Sport Management, 29*(4), 443–460.

Kerr, A. K., & Gladden, J. M. (2008). Extending the understanding of professional team brand equity to the global marketplace. *International Journal of Sport Management and Marketing, 3*(1/2), 58–77.

Knijnik, J. (2014). Feeling at home: An autoethnographic account of an immigrant football fan in Western Sydney. *Leisure Studies*, *34*(1), 34–41.

Leal, J. (2009). Associativismo e transnacionalismo: Organizações açoriano-americanas na Nova Inglaterra. In D. Melo & E. Caetano da Silva (Eds.), *Construção da Nação e Associativismo na Emigração Portuguesa* (pp. 79–96). Lisboa: Imprensa de Ciências Sociais.

Lewis, M. (2001). Franchise relocation and fan allegiance. *Journal of Sport & Social Issues*, *25*(1), 6–19.

Lock, D., Taylor, T., Funk, D., & Darcy, S. (2012). Exploring the development of team identification. *Journal of Sport Management*, *26*, 283–294.

Moniz, M. (2007). Adaptive transnational identity and the selling of Soccer: The New England Revolution and lusophone migrant populations. *Soccer & Society*, *8*(4), 459–477.

Murdie, R., & Teixeira, C. (2011). The impact of gentrification on ethnic neighborhoods in Toronto: A case study of little Portugal. *Urban Studies*, *1*(48), 61–83.

Noivo, E. (1993). Ethnic families and the social injuries of class, migration, gender, generation and minority group status. *Canadian Ethnic Studies/Etudes Ethniques Au Canada*, *25*(3), 66–75. Retrieved from http://search.proquest.com.ezproxy.library.ubc.ca/docview/61356608?accountid=14656

Pereira, V. (2012). Os futebolistas invisíveis: Os portugueses em França e o futebol. *Etnográfica*, *16*(1), 97–115.

Porat, A. (2010). Football fandom: A bounded identification. *Soccer & Society*, *11*(3), 277–290.

Sardinha, J. (2011). Portuguese-Canadian emigrant descendents in multicultural Canada: Ambiguous identity in a sure-footed nation or cultural awareness in an uncertain country? *Journal of International Migration and Integration*, *12*(4), 371–389. doi:10.1007/s12134-011-0173-9

Sardinha, J. (2012). Negociações identitárias dos luso-descendentes no canadá através do futebol português e do hóquei no gelo canadiano. Etnográfica, *16*(1), 143–162.

Stone, C. (2007). The role of football in everyday life. *Soccer & Society*, *8*(2/3), 169–184.

Sveinson, K., & Hoeber, L. (2016). Female sports fans' experiences of marginalization and empowerment. *Journal of Sport Management*, *30*(1), 8–21.

Teixeira, C. (2001). Community resources and opportunities in ethnic economies: A case study of Portuguese and black entrepreneurs in Toronto. *Urban Studies*, *38*(11), 2055–2078.Teixeira, C., & Da Rosa, M. P. (2009). A historical and geographical perspective. In C. Teixeira & M. Da Rosa (Eds.), *The portuguese in Canada: Diasporic challenges and adjustment* (pp. 3–17). Toronto: University of Toronto Press.Tiesler, N. (2012). Diasbola: Futebol e emigração Portuguesa. *Etnográfica*, *1*, 77–96.

Tiesler, N., & Coelho, J. (2007). Globalized football at a lusocentric glance: Struggles with markets and migration, traditions and modernities, the loss and the beauty. *Soccer & Society*, *8*(4), 419–439.

Tracy, S. J. (2013). *Qualitative research methods: Collecting evidence, crafting analysis, communicating impact.* Hoboken, NJ: Wiley-Blackwell.

Valeriano, B. (2014). Latino assimilation, divided loyalties and the World Cup. *Soccer & Society, 15*(3), 291–313.

Vieira, S. (2013). *"You know what I mean?" Language and cultural retention in Luso-Canadian mothers in the greater Toronto area* (Unpublished master's thesis). Brock University, St. Catharines, Ontario, Canada.

Wann, D. L, & Branscombe, N. R. (1993). Sports fans: Measuring degree of identification with the team. *International Journal of Sport Psychology, 24*, 1–17.

Interview questions for participants in the Greater Toronto area

Background information

1) Age?
2) Where are you from in Portugal?
3) At what age did you leave Portugal?
4) Are you a fan of Sporting, Benfica, or Porto?

Being a fan

1) How long have you been a fan of (team)?
2) How did you become a fan of (team)?
3) Can you tell me what it was like to be a fan of (team) in Portugal?
4) Does being a (team) fan affect the way you interact with your family?
5) Do you support any other teams that are a part of your (team's organization) (i.e., futsal team, handball team etc.)? Why or why not?
6) What are your feelings toward (the other two team names)?
7) How do you compare fans of (team) to the fans of (the other two team names)?
8) Do you cheer for your local Portuguese league football team?
9) Have you been back to Portugal?
10) Have you watched (team) play live?

Being a fan in Canada

1) Do you feel coming to Canada affected the way you are a fan of (team)?
2) How would you describe being a fan of (team) in Canada?
3) Are you a club member of (team)?
4) Do you think there is a difference of being a (team) fan in Portugal?
5) How do you follow (team) in Canada?
6) Can you remember a time when being a (team) fan helped you in Canada?
7) Was there ever a time being a (team) fan worked against you?
8) Do you regularly watch (team) games?
9) Where do you watch the games?
10) How important is watching (team) play?

Interview questions for participants in continental Portugal

Background information

1) Age?
2) Where are you from in Portugal?
3) Are you a fan of Sporting, Benfica, or Porto?

Being a fan

1) How long have you been a fan of (team)?
2) How did you become a fan of (team)?
3) Does being a (team) fan affect the way you interact with your family?
4) Do you support any other teams that are a part of your (team's organization) (i.e., futsal team, handball team etc.)? Why or why not?
5) What are your feelings toward (the other two teams' names)?
6) How do you compare fans of (team) to the fans of (the other two team's name)?
7) Have you watched (team) play live?
8) Do you cheer for your local Portuguese league football team?

Being a fan in Portugal

1) Can you describe what it is like to be a (team) fan in Portugal?
2) How do you follow (team)?
3) Can you remember a time when being a (team) fan helped you?
4) Was there ever a time being a (team) fan worked against you?
5) Do you regularly watch (team) games?
6) Where do you watch the games?
7) How important is watching (team) play?

Participant profiles

Participants Living in Portugal				
Pseudonym	*Age*	*Hometown in Portugal*	*Local Team*	*"Big Three" Team*
Super Dragão	25	Leiria	União Desportiva de Leiria	Futebol Clube do Porto
Figo	41	Coimbra	Associação Académica de Coimbra	Sporting Clube de Portugal
Eusébio	33	Braga	Sporting Clube de Braga	Sport Lisboa e Benfica
Participants Living in the Greater Toronto Area				
Pseudonym	*Age*	*Hometown in Portugal*	*Local Team*	*"Big Three" Team*
Morin	47	Leiria	União Desportiva de Leiria	Sport Lisboa e Benfica
Rui Costa	28	Coimbra	Associação Académica de Coimbra	Sport Lisboa e Benfica
Gaiteiro	45	Leiria	União Desportiva de Leiria	Sporting Clube de Portugal
Ricardo	26	Aveiro	Sport Clube Beira-Mar	Futebol Clube do Porto

Appendix D

Map of Portugal

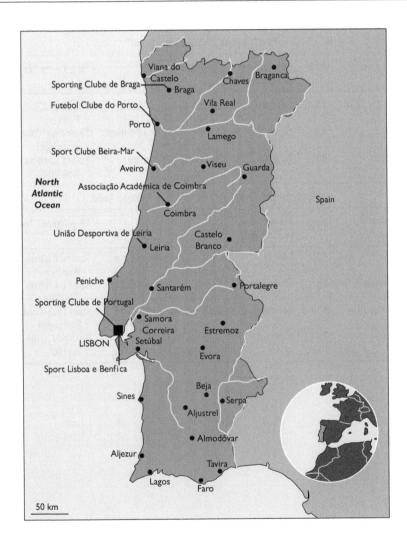

Chapter 5

The driving forces of competitive balance in European football

A review of Europe's top leagues

N. David Pifer

Introduction

Managers of professional sports teams and leagues often concern themselves with the notion of *competitive balance*. Though numerous measures and interpretations are frequently grouped beneath this term, competitive balance, in its most general form, is simply a measure of parity between the competing firms in an industry. Applied to professional sport, it is often defined as the degree of parity between the teams in a league (Leeds & Von Allmen, 2013). Economist Simon Rottenberg is often credited for being the first researcher to integrate this concept with sport in his manuscript, *The Baseball Players' Labor Market*. In this seminal work, Rottenberg (1956) highlighted a unique feature of professional sports leagues that has become one of the focal points of competitive balance research over the years. That is,

> Professional team competitions are different from other kinds of business ventures. If a seller of shoes is able to capture the market and to cause other sellers of shoes to suffer losses and withdraw, the surviving competitor is a clear gainer. But in baseball, no team can be successful unless its competitors also survive and prosper sufficiently so that the differences in the quality of play among teams are not "too great."
>
> (p. 254)

The success that Rottenberg was speaking of was financial success through ticket sales, which were the primary source of income in the decades that preceded sponsorship and media rights deals. History showed that if club owners wanted to optimize their main revenue stream, they needed to cooperate and maintain a credible level of competitive balance across the league (Leeds & Von Allmen, 2013; Quirk & Fort, 1992; Rottenberg, 1956). If a certain game or series was perceived as being too one-sided, then the teams risked drawing lower crowds and losing out on potential revenues.

Measures of competitive balance have therefore become important to leagues due in large part to the belief that the consumers of live sporting events desire a level of uncertainty in regards to which team will win. If games become too predictable or if the same team or group of teams continues to win the championship, then it is argued that the profits associated with ticket sales and television viewership will almost certainly fall. As noted by another economist, Walter C. Neale (1964), "The sporting firms produce an indivisible product from the separate processes of two or more firms. But the product itself is a peculiar mixture" (p. 3). This "peculiar mixture" speaks to the notion that many professional sports leagues operate as monopolized cartels whereby the member teams must engage in a paradoxical form of competitive cooperation in order to produce the enticing matchups that will sustain fan interest and attract more viewers. No team looking to sell a competitive sport product can function in total isolation; rather, it needs the rivalry and drama supplied by its competitors to drive the narrative forward and maximize revenues (Neale, 1964). Because one of the primary purposes of a league is to perform functions that individual teams either cannot do or lack the incentive to do (Leeds & Von Allmen, 2013), it has become common for these cartels to implement policies (e.g., revenue sharing, luxury taxes, player drafts, and salary caps) that will maintain the attractiveness of their competitions.

The issue, though, is that the competitive balance mechanisms imposed by certain professional sports leagues do not fully translate to others. In particular, there is a vast difference between the rules and labor market regulations of the professional sports leagues in North America and those of the largest European football leagues (e.g., the "Big Five" in England, Germany, Spain, Italy, and France). While there are several explanations for this, the main reason is that European football leagues operate as *open leagues* with promotion and relegation systems that shift clubs through a hierarchy of divisions depending on their performance. Conversely, the "Big Four" North American leagues – the NFL, MLB, the NBA, and the NHL – operate as cartels within *closed league* structures that limit franchise entry and distribute revenues and playing talent more equitably to their stable crops of member teams. Whereas North American franchises can strive to coexist in a setting where the threat of entries is limited and one bad season does not signal the end of a team's participation in a league, European football clubs must win in order to simply remain in the top division and sustain relevance with the local fan base. It is therefore hard to imagine the owners of a European football club agreeing to adopt policies that will increase their club's likelihood of being relegated to a less profitable division (Sloane, 1976). As recent court battles have shown, even the implementation of seemingly straightforward policies like collective revenue sharing and spending caps will be met with stern resistance from the traditionally powerful European clubs (Thomas, Duckworth, & Gonzalez, 2015; UEFA, 2015b). In a setting where survival is of the utmost importance, owners can ill afford to substitute their clubs' interests for the greater interests of a league.

It becomes clear, then, that many of the major differences between the open and closed league structures will likely cause the actions and objectives of European football owners to vary from the North American owners that were referenced in some of the earliest economic analyses. Rottenberg's (1956) admonition that the gaps in playing talent should not grow too large and Neale's (1964) assertion that team owners should pray to "make us good, but not that good" (p. 2) will rightly fall on deaf ears in European football leagues that are characterized by cutthroat mentalities in the front offices and on the playing fields. The threat of relegation and the massive losses of income that coincide with the drop should instead motivate clubs to establish a dominant position in their leagues and give little attention to the welfare of opponents that may or may not even feature in the next season's fixtures.

In this regard, studies have shown that the strategic actions of clubs are more closely aligned to win-maximization than profit-maximization (Garcia-del-Barrio & Szymanski, 2009; Késenne, 1996, 2000; Sloane, 1976). Garcia-del-Barrio and Szymanski (2009), for instance, looked at a decade of English and Spanish club data and showed that the choices made by clubs in response to the actions taken by other clubs more closely resembled those of win-maximizing firms. The duo found that clubs tended to occupy positions in the league table that were closer to win-maximizing positions than profit-maximizing positions, as judged by wage expenditures relative to the league average. This led them to conclude that club behavior was better understood through a strategic lens focused on win-maximization rather than pure profit-maximization. This was particularly true in the short term and among clubs that were threatened by relegation. While there were some tendencies over the long run for historically successful clubs to pursue profits, this was largely a product of them having already pursued and achieved win-maximizing strategies.

Further supporting the motivation to win is evidence that European football supporters do not place as much of an emphasis on outcome uncertainty as North American fans (Buraimo & Simmons, 2008, 2009b), and that professional football matches are inherently harder to predict than the games in most other leagues (Anderson & Sally, 2013; Ben-Naim, Vazquez, & Redner, 2006). Indeed, if the profits obtained from consumers are not largely dependent on outcome uncertainty, then there is little need to collude in order to maintain a certain level of on-field parity. Studies have shown that football fans are more drawn to "interesting" matches than "uncertain" ones as high-scoring matches and players, and games in which the home team is a heavy underdog, draw some of the largest crowds (Buraimo & Simmons, 2008, 2009b). The inherent short-run unpredictability of the sport also indicates that the underdog is more likely to win in football than in many other professional sports (Ben-Naim et al., 2006). Therefore, based on these findings and the reality that winning is necessary for revenues, it becomes clear that most European football clubs should, and do, operate as win-maximizing firms.

Nonetheless, even with all of the clubs being ideally suited to act as win-maximizers, dominance by the select few has become an observable feature of modern day European football (Curran, Jennings, & Sedgwick, 2009; Michie & Oughton, 2004; Penn & Berridge, 2016; Szymanski, 2015). Owing much to the gaps that exist between clubs' abilities to attract and pay the top playing talent (Hall, Szymanski, & Zimbalist, 2002; Kuper & Szymanski, 2012; Szymanski, 2015), European football exists as "a competitive enterprise characterized by both dominance and distress" (Szymanski, 2015, p. 28). On one hand there are dominant clubs that have capitalized on their historical success or inherited wealth to become the established leaders in a naturally competitive industry. These clubs are consistently competing at the top end of the table for the domestic league titles and UEFA Champions League positions that will further solidify their reputations and revenues. Whereas, on the outside looking in are the smaller clubs that make up the "competitive fringe" (Szymanski, 2015, p. 21). These clubs seldom break into the dominant group unless they happen upon fortuitous circumstances or the generous investments of a wealthy owner. Though more numerous than the select few that have established themselves at the pinnacle of the Big Five hierarchies, these fringe clubs seem to exist for the sole purposes of providing competition to the elite and entertainment to their local fan bases. Every now and then one of these smaller clubs assumes a place in the highest ranks, but as prior studies have shown (Buzzacchi, Szymanski, & Valletti, 2003), this happens far less often than it should.

In light of the various realities that were just outlined, the current study conducted a thorough review of the extant competitive balance literature and developed a theoretical and data-driven rationale for the current state of competition in European football. Because managers and their teams must operate within the contexts of leagues that are subject to a variety of influencers, it is important for them to know which internal and external factors are working for or against them. Similarly, it is important for them to be aware of their surroundings as they make critical decisions in environments where winning is required for revenues and losing can result in relegation to a lower league. As such, the studies reviewed in this work were derived largely from the analysis of competitive balance (ACB) track. With examinations of outcome uncertainty being less important in the open league structures of European football, where winning and dominance take priority over creating an uncertain outcome, the author chose to focus mainly on analyses that were characteristic of competitiveness on the field of play.

Review of literature

Competitive balance

In its most basic form, competitive balance is a measure of parity that can be assessed within different competitive units (e.g., games, seasons, and multiple seasons) according to various methods that focus on some relevant metric of performance (e.g., pre-match betting odds, point differentials, winning percentages, and championship victories). Over the years, researchers have taken full advantage of the various paths of exploration that are available in this area, creating a vast number of methods for quantifying and conveying the concept with greater specificity. In the beginning, more simplistic approaches to the issue were taken. The seminal study by Rottenberg (1956), for instance, equated competitive balance to the varying number of pennants that MLB teams had won over a 30-year period. Shortly thereafter, Neale (1964) introduced the notion of the "league standing effect" whereby the close proximity of teams in the rankings was more synonymous to a balanced league. El-Hodiri and Quirk (1971) then narrowed the focus even further in developing a model based on the assumption that gate receipts were dependent on the outcome uncertainty of individual league games. Analyses contained in the works of Demmert (1973) and Noll (1974) were then some of the first to test whether or not the point margins from games and the differences in league standings, respectively, were related to actual attendance figures.

Having seen a variety of interpretations come to the forefront in a relatively short amount of time, Sloane (1976) made the preliminary assertion that, in general, a single measure of this construct was inadequate due to the dynamic and time-dependent nature of the variable. Cairns (1987), in his investigation of the Scottish professional football league, echoed these thoughts by showing that competitive balance could be manifested in three distinct forms: uncertainty with respect to individual matches, uncertainty in regards to the outcome of the championship, and the absence of long-run domination by a particular club. Stemming from these distinctions, a plethora of more complex methods began investigating the notion of competitiveness with greater specificity. Some of the measures that rose to prominence included the *ratio of the standard deviation (RSD)* approach developed by Noll (1988) and Scully (1989) to compare the actual standard deviation of winning percentages in a league to an ideal standard deviation in which the percentages are more or less normalized around .500, the *Hirschman-Herfindahl Index (HHI)* employed by Depken (1999) to assess the concentration of wins among the teams in a given league, the use of the *Gini coefficient* as an alternative measure to quantify how equally distributed championships, wins, or points were within a league (Buzzacchi et al., 2003; Quirk & Fort, 1992; Schmidt & Berri, 2001), and the transformation of *pre-match betting odds* into probabilities for the sake of predicting the uncertainty of a specific match (Peel & Thomas, 1988; Peel & Thomas, 1992). These methods and many others have since been summarized in a variety of academic book chapters (Dobson & Goddard, 2001; Leeds & Von Allmen, 2013; Michie & Oughton, 2004; Quirk & Fort, 1992) and peer reviewed journal articles (Bowman, Lambrinos, & Ashman, 2013; Fort & Maxcy, 2003; Fort & Quirk, 1995; Zimbalist, 2002) over the years.

In light of the numerous methods that exist, it can be easy to lose sight of why competitive balance examinations are actually necessary to begin with. "If there is nothing to justify our empirical measure of balance, it is not even clear that the questions are interesting in the first place . . . Whatever the optimal measure, we need to know what we are seeking before we begin to quantify" (Zimbalist, 2003; p. 163). Zimbalist (2002) viewed the most relevant measures of competitive balance as those "to which the consumers show greatest sensitivity" (p. 112). This line of thought echoed the sentiments shared by many of the early researchers who were similarly concerned with competitive balance to the extent that it produced suspenseful, uncertain outcomes in a league's games and championships (El-Hodiri & Quirk, 1971; Neale, 1964; Rottenberg, 1956). In analyses such as these, where the term "competitive balance" is essentially exchanged for "outcome uncertainty," the primary focus is placed on the elasticity between consumer demand and the parity supplied by a given unit of competition. Collectively, these studies are frequently categorized as UOH studies because they are said to be testing the *Uncertainty of Outcome Hypothesis* whereby fans are attracted to a competition in which there is no predetermined winner (Fort & Maxcy, 2003).

For those studies that are not concerned with analyzing competitive balance from the consumer perspective, there exists another label. Known as ACB (*Analysis of Competitive Balance*), this categorization was contrived by Fort and Maxcy (2003) in response to Zimbalist's (2002) assertion that competitive balance is best measured as it relates to consumer sensitivity. In a well-articulated response and review, the duo argued that there are numerous analyses that have been conducted in order to measure the parity in a league for purposes other than consumer demand. While the concerns of the fans and the revenues they provide may be at the root of the concept, there are studies that predominately focus on measuring competitive balance to the extent that it has been affected by league policies, external environmental factors, and business practices over time. So, while the UOH and ACB tracks are inherently related, they should not always be viewed interchangeably. As noted by Forrest and Simmons (2002):

> By competitive balance is meant a league structure which has a relatively equal playing strength between league members. By uncertainty of outcome is meant a situation where a given contest within a league structure has a degree of unpredictability about the result and, by extension, that the competition as a whole does not have a predetermined winner at the outset of the competition.
>
> (p. 229)

Echoing these sentiments, Fort and Maxcy (2003) stated rather plainly that "UOH is aimed at measuring fan welfare and ACB aims at tracking balance itself" (p. 157).

Seeing as European football is not overly concerned with outcome uncertainty, this study chose to look more exclusively at the ACB track and its relevant findings. In doing so, more precision could be directed toward the factors that were driving success and failure in these settings. Because managers are forced to operate in the midst of these constraints and opportunities, knowledge of their existence and impact on performance can prove critical. Rather than reacting to changes in league policy or simply expecting results upon promotion to a higher league, managerial decisions can be made proactively by examining those phenomena which have influenced competitiveness in the past.

Competitive trends in European football

Over the years, there has been no shortage of analyses conducted to assess the levels of parity between the clubs competing in a variety of European football competitions. Ranging from lesser-known leagues in Turkey and Portugal (Inan & Kaya, 2011; Mourão & Cima, 2015), to the more popular members of the Big Five (Michie & Oughton, 2004), competitive balance has become a thoroughly investigated topic in the growing field of football economics. And while the abundance of literature in this area could make for an overcrowded review of the subject, a selection of unique and historical analyses have thoroughly summarized the past and present states of the industry.

In the initial studies, there was a tendency to assess competitive balance in European football leagues through the seasonal measures that had become popularized in North American sports (Quirk & Fort, 1992). The standard deviation of winning percentages, for example, was adapted to the point structure of European football and used to assess how performance had varied within seasons over time. Using this method, Szymanski (2001) showed that the standard deviation of winning percentages in the EPL remained relatively steady from 1977–1998, but that there was evidence of imbalance beginning to creep into the league toward the end of the examined timeframe. In another study, Buzzacchi et al. (2003) used the RSD method to show that the EPL and Serie A had not witnessed any major changes in the spread of their clubs' winning percentages during the decades that lasted from the 1960s to the 1990s. Furthermore, the RSD values during these decades were similar to, and at times lower than, those of three major North American leagues. Feddersen and Maennig (2005) arrived at a similar conclusion in their examination of the EPL, La Liga, Bundesliga, Serie A, and the Big Four, showing that it was difficult to discern any significant differences or trends in competitive balance through various measures that incorporated seasonal winning percentages.

However, Buzzacchi et al. (2003) took their analysis a step further and introduced a "dynamic" measure of competitive balance to show that the actual number of clubs that had won the championship or entered the top five places in the EPL and Serie A was far lower than it would have been in a theoretical scenario where the clubs' probabilities of succeeding had been equal. The measure also accounted for the arrival of new clubs to the top divisions via promotion. After taking these dynamics into account, it became evident that the EPL and Serie A were significantly less balanced than the NFL, NHL, and MLB. In particular, entry to the top five positions appeared to be controlled by a select number of clubs. Within Serie A, for example, the seasons between 1961 and 1999 would have ideally seen 94 different clubs finish in the top five positions; however, only 18 different clubs were able to accomplish such a feat. In the EPL, 78 clubs should have finished in the top five, but only 27 were able to do so. The differences between the actual and theoretical number of league champions painted a similar picture of historical imbalance in both leagues as well. In Italy, 12 out of an expected 33 clubs won the title from 1961 to 1999, while in England, 13 out of an expected 32 teams claimed top honors.

Ultimately, the results of the analyses conducted by Buzzacchi et al. (2003) helped reveal a unique paradox whereby the traditional, more static measures of seasonal competitive balance did not reveal the true disparities of European football. While the contests within each season appeared close in terms of the spread of winning percentages, measures that accounted for the identities of the specific clubs finishing in first place or the top five over time told a different story. As such, more studies began incorporating analyses that measured the dominance of individual clubs and the inequalities that existed between the top teams and their competitors. Michie and Oughton (2004), for instance, measured competitive balance in each of the Big Five leagues from 1947–2004 using variations of the five-club concentration ratio (C5) and the HHI. The duo found that competitive balance had remained roughly constant from 1947 to 1987, but that parity began to experience a significant decline in the EPL during the late 1980s as the top clubs started to dominate more consistently. Similar trends were seen in Germany and Italy, while concentrated dominance had already begun to take shape in Spain about a decade prior. In France, parity remained relatively steady until signs of imbalance began appearing in the early 1990s. Using similar methods, Curran et al. (2009) found that competitive balance in the top flight of English football had gradually decreased in the decades between 1948–49 and 1997–98, but that the decade marked 1998–99 to 2007–2008 had been clearly dominated by four clubs in Manchester United, Arsenal, Chelsea, and Liverpool. Over these ten seasons, 85% of the top four positions had been monopolized by these same four English clubs. The analyses conducted by Brandes and Franck (2007) on competitive balance in the Bundesliga, Serie A, Ligue 1, and EPL revealed a similar pattern of imbalance emerging around the turn of the century.

In what was perhaps the most longitudinal analysis of competitive balance in all of the studies, Penn and Berridge (2016) looked exclusively at

England's top division from 1888–89 to 2009–2010 and used three measures of concentration to assess how representation in the top four (C4) and the spread of points from the league average had changed over time. They found that the early years (1888–1900) of the league were characterized by patterns of dominance as clubs from the larger markets took advantage of their smaller rivals. However, the implementation of a maximum wage and the transfer system in 1901 created a period of relative stability until the wage cap was abolished in 1961. From there, English football trended toward imbalance, ultimately becoming a league that was controlled by a "quadropoly" of clubs in the top four positions. In addition, the seasons lasting from 2007 to 2010 showed the reemergence of a high disparity in points that had not been seen since the earliest years of the examined timeframe.

Taken collectively, it appears as though most of these studies were in agreement that the modern era of European football has been characterized by various sets of monopolies, duopolies, and quadropolies. While the abstract measures of competitive balance within each season and within each game may not reveal clear gaps in performance, it appears as though the same clubs almost always end up winning the title or reaping the rewards of Champions League qualification. Table 5.1 lends further support to this assumption, showing that Big Five championships in the modern era have

Table 5.1 Number of different champions in the Big Five (1992–1993 to 2016–2017)

EPL	La Liga	Bundesliga	Serie A	Ligue 1
6	5	6	5	10
Man. United (13)	Barcelona (12)	Werder Bremen (2)	A.C. Milan (6)	PSG (5)
Blackburn Rovers (1)	Real Madrid (8)	Bayern Munich (15)	Juventus (11)	Nantes (2)
Arsenal (3)	Atletico Madrid (2)	Borussia Dortmund (5)	Lazio (1)	Auxerre (1)
Chelsea (5)	Dep. La Coruna (1)	FC Kaiserslautern (1)	Roma (1)	AS Monaco (3)
Manchester City (2)	Valencia (2)	Stuttgart (1)	Inter Milan (5)	Lens (1)
Leicester City (1)		Wolfsburg (1)		Bordeaux (2)
				Lyon (7)
				Marseille (1)
				Lille (1)
				Montpellier (1)

Notes. Clubs are sorted by the order in which they won their first championship during the observed timeframe. Serie A and Ligue 1 only count 23 championships due to the match-fixing scandals that occurred in the 2004–2005 and 1992–1993 seasons, respectively.

been controlled by a rather small number of clubs. In Germany, Bayern Munich won the Bundesliga in 15 of the 25 observed seasons, while Manchester United (13) and Barcelona (12) similarly hoarded the top honors in the EPL and La Liga. Even in Ligue 1, where there is some semblance of parity, the time period still witnessed Lyon win six consecutive French titles from 2001–2002 to 2007–2008, and Paris Saint-Germain (PSG) win four straight from 2012–2013 to 2015–2016. However, the practical utility that can be derived from this information is limited until the sources of these disparities can be explained in more detail. After all, clubs on both ends of the dominance and distress spectrum are "faced with different but equally exacting sets of challenges" (21st Club, 2016, p. 11). If dynasties are common across European football leagues, a deeper understanding of the factors that both support and disrupt them becomes vital to the formulation of more actionable strategies.

Factors influencing competitive balance

Prior research has indicated that there are two fundamental statistical relationships in football (Michie & Oughton, 2004; Szymanski, 2015). The first is that the more a club spends on players, the more successful it will be on the pitch. The second is that successful clubs generate more revenues, on average, than their less-successful competitors. According to Michie and Oughton (2004),

> The existence of these relationships results in peculiarities in the performance of the industry characterized by the creation of virtuous and vicious circles of sporting and economic performance. On the one hand, good performance on the pitch may enhance the economic performance of clubs. Sporting success – measured by performance indicators, such as league position, share of points or cups and championships won – attracts supporters, sponsors and spectators (both at the ground and on television), all of which boost revenue. Thus, clubs at the top of the league find that sporting success improves economic performance, which in turn provides the club with the resources to invest in players and promote further sporting success in the future. Conversely, clubs at the bottom of the league find themselves trapped in a vicious circle of poor performance on the pitch, leading to a loss of support and revenue streams from match day income, broadcasting rights, sponsorship and cup runs, which, in turn, reduces the resources available for investment in players and may thus lead to a further deterioration in sporting results.
>
> (pp. 22–23)

The causal relationship between players and performance was supported in a study by Hall et al. (2002) where it was seen that English clubs' payrolls, relative to their rivals, explained upwards of 94% of the variation in where they finished in the standings of the top four divisions from 1974–1999. An alternative measure using the clubs' winning percentages as the outcome variable showed that the expected difference in winning percentages between a club spending 50% of the league average on player wages and a club spending 50% above the league average was .191, or about 22 points by today's standards. In regards to the second relationship between wins and revenues, Szymanski (2015) used data from the financial accounts of 100 English clubs over the span of 56 seasons (1958–2013) to show that a club's average position across the four highest divisions, relative to the other 99 competitors, explained close to 83% of the revenues it generated compared to its rivals. Like Michie and Oughton (2004), Szymanski (2015) also highlighted the potentially circular nature of these relationships:

> Successful teams will attract bigger crowds that pay higher ticket prices. More successful clubs sell more merchandise. More successful clubs attract better sponsors who are willing to pay more money to be associated with the club. And better clubs appear more often on TV and therefore receive larger payments from broadcast companies. It is therefore not surprising that greater sporting success generates larger financial rewards. This explanation suggests a clear line of causality from success to revenues. At the same time higher revenues can be used to buy better players and so generate even more success.
>
> (pp. 92–93)

Having made a connection between player wages, wins, and revenues, it becomes clear that money, or rather differences in clubs' abilities to make and spend money, lie at the root of the performance differences that exist. Even when the emphasis shifts from player wages to the transfer fees that are used to purchase players, the results tell a similar story. Analyzing transfer data from the 1992–93 to 2009–2010 EPL seasons, Tomkins et al. (2010) found that the team with the highest "XI" (i.e., the most expensive starting eleven as quantified by the sum of each player's transfer fee) won ten of the 18 titles during that time. When the most expensive team did not win, the second most expensive team would almost always take its place. Outside of Arsenal's 2003–2004 victory with the fourth most expensive XI, the seven remaining EPL winners were all ranked second in terms of the transfer values of their starting 11. On average, over the 18 seasons that were examined, the championship sides were worth at least 89% of the costliest starting 11. Moreover, for English clubs that won a title for the first time in the modern era, an expenditure of at least 94% of the most valuable XI was necessary. "It seems that to overcome this hurdle [of winning the EPL for the first time] an even more expensive team is required; more or less the most expensive in the land" (Tomkins et al., 2010, p. 47).

Therefore, analyses of competitive balance in this area would be wise to incorporate club finances in their assessments. But how are some clubs able to realize substantially more revenues and spending power than others? What obvious and underlying factors have contributed to the income and performance disparities that seem to exist? While no singular answer exists, it can be helpful to look at the historical and structural elements of the EPL and the other European leagues in order to gain a better understanding of the events that have shaped the balance of competition in these environments.

Commercialization

For many, the modern era of European football and the inequalities that have come to characterize it commenced with the start of the 1992–93 season when the English Football League and the European Cup were rebranded into the English Premier League and UEFA Champions League, respectively. The key features underlying both of these rebrands were the broadcast deals that coincided with them, as unprecedented levels of new money became available to the clubs that were able to compete and succeed in these competitions. In the years that have followed, these revenues have only risen as renegotiations have led to even more favorable deals for the involved leagues and clubs. The EPL, for example, is in the midst of a record-breaking broadcast deal that is worth $7.39 billion from 2016–2017 to 2018–2019 (Premier League, 2015). In the Champions League, revenues have soared to a point where the clubs that simply advance to the group stage still earn a minimum of $14 million (UEFA, 2016). However, it is not the rapid growth in revenues that has caused the problem; rather, it is the unequal distribution of these funds and the exorbitant amounts of money that must be spent on player acquisitions that have led to many of these disparities. It is perhaps no surprise, then, that many of the aforementioned competitive balance analyses showed parity declining even further as these merit-based funds became an established feature of the Big Five in the late 1990s.

Table 5.2 uses data from the 2015–2016 EPL season as an example to show how lucrative the broadcast revenues have become at the domestic level. Arsenal, the top earning club, pocketed over $147 million in income from the deal while last place Aston Villa earned upwards of $97 million from a contract that provided each team with a minimum share of nearly $82 million. For the three teams (Hull City, Burnley, and Queens Park Rangers) that had been relegated to the second division at the end of the previous season, the loss of these revenues was significant, even when the parachute payments that helped ease the financial burden of the drop were taken into consideration. According to Deloitte (2016), the parachute payment of $36 million received by these clubs ahead of the 2015–2016 season

Table 5.2 Media rights revenues in the English Premier League (2015–2016)

Club	Market Size	Finish	TV	Appearance	Merit	Shared	Total
Arsenal	8,538,689	2	27	31.449	34.536	81.708	147.693
Manchester City	2,732,854	4	25	29.261	30.900	81.708	141.870
Manchester United	2,732,854	5	26	30.356	29.082	81.708	141.146
Tottenham	8,538,689	3	21	24.884	32.717	81.708	139.310
Leicester City	1,005,558	1	15	18.318	36.353	81.708	136.379
Liverpool	1,391,113	8	23	27.073	23.629	81.708	132.410
Chelsea	8,538,689	10	22	25.978	19.993	81.708	127.680
West Ham	8,538,689	7	15	18.320	25.446	81.708	125.474
Southampton	1,800,511	6	12	15.037	27.264	81.708	124.010
Everton	1,391,113	11	18	21.601	18.176	81.708	121.486
Stoke City	1,111,192	9	9	12.848	21.810	81.708	116.367
Swansea	365,500	12	10	12.848	16.359	81.708	110.916
Watford	1,154,766	13	8	12.848	14.541	81.708	109.097
West Brom	2,808,356	14	10	12.848	12.722	81.708	107.279
Newcastle	1,118,713	18	16	19.413	5.453	81.708	106.574
Crystal Palace	8,538,689	15	10	12.848	10.905	81.708	105.462
Sunderland	1,118,713	17	13	16.130	7.270	81.708	105.108
Bournemouth	759,768	16	8	12.848	9.088	81.708	103.645
Norwich	877,710	19	9	12.848	3.634	81.708	98.191
Aston Villa	2,808,356	20	11	13.942	1.817	81.708	97.468
League Total				381.698	381.695	1634.18	2397.564

Notes: Table adapted from Harris (2016). All money amounts are represented in millions of U.S. dollars ($). *Market size* is based upon the population of the ceremonial county that the club is located in. The *shared* column sums up the equally distributed revenue shares from the sale of domestic media rights (39%), foreign media rights (53%), and central league sponsorships (8%). Due to rounding, the *appearance*, *merit*, and *shared* columns may not sum exactly to the *league total*.

was greater than the average total revenues of the other second division clubs; furthermore, due to the time they had spent in the EPL, the average total revenues of these clubs was over five times that of the clubs they were joining in the division below. The sizeable gap that exists between these revenues in the first and second divisions therefore illustrates why achieving promotion and avoiding relegation at the highest ranks is essential to long-term viability. It also shows why clubs bordering on the relegation zone need to plan and invest accordingly.

Nonetheless, while differences between divisions may explain some of the disparities, it is the growing financial inequalities within the top divisions that paint a clearer picture. From a domestic media rights perspective, these gaps are mostly due to two factors: the merit system whereby clubs earn higher amounts for finishing further up in the league standings, and the additional appearance money that is given to the clubs that play in a greater number of nationally televised games. As Table 5.2 showed, there was a gap of approximately $35 million in merit-based payments between 2015–2016 EPL champion Leicester City and the Aston Villa side that finished at the bottom of the table. In regards to the appearance revenues, it is perhaps unsurprising to see that many of the televised games were awarded to clubs that either played in a larger market or possessed an element of historical success. Therefore, despite the fact that the 2015–2016 contract evenly distributed 61% of its total value to the 20 member clubs, these two features ensured that the ratio between the top (Arsenal) and bottom (Aston Villa) earning teams was still a relatively sizeable 1.5 to 1 ($50 million). Compared to the other members of the Big Five, the EPL actually employed a more equitable revenue sharing system. In the Bundesliga, Ligue 1, Serie A, and La Liga, it was reported that the 2015–2016 ratios between the top and bottom earning teams in these leagues were 2 to 1, 3.5 to 1, 5 to 1, and 8 to 1, respectively (Harris, 2016). In Spain, the traditionally powerful clubs of Real Madrid and FC Barcelona hold a much higher percentage of the cash because La Liga teams have typically sold their media rights on an individual basis. The league recently announced, however, that its 2016–2017 broadcasting agreement would be made collectively in an effort to distribute the money more equally between its member clubs (Thomas et al., 2015).

Separate from the broadcast revenues distributed internally by each domestic league, but still relevant as a merit-based source of income that is dependent on a club's final position in the league standings, are the annual financial rewards for participating in the UEFA Champions League and its secondary competition, the UEFA Europa League. In order to qualify for the Champions League in 2016–2017, a Big Five club had to have finished either in the top three (Serie A and Ligue 1) or four (La Liga, EPL, and Bundesliga) positions of its respective league during the 2015–2016 season. The clubs able to achieve this distinction were subsequently entitled to share in the $1.47 billion in broadcast revenues that had been obtained by UEFA through its various media affiliates (UEFA, 2016). Of this sum, about $14 million was allocated as a fixed share to each of the 32 clubs that simply appeared in the group stages of the tournament. An additional $1.7 million was awarded for each group stage win, while advancing to the round of 16, quarterfinals, and semifinals allowed clubs to obtain sequential payouts of $6.78 million, $7.35 million, and $8.48 million, respectively. The losing finalist was entitled to an additional $12.43 million in revenues, and the winner ended up earning a further $17.5 million. A Champions League winning club, then, could earn upwards of $50 million that would go unshared with its domestic competitors. Even teams that did not win a single group stage match would exit the competition with a minimum $14 million surplus. Realized repeatedly over time, these revenues can lead to an even larger gap between the clubs competing in a domestic league. As noted by Curran et al. (2009),

Reduced competitive balance, or domination by the few, appears to have coincided with the introduction of the Premiership [EPL] and the UEFA Champions League. Both of these competitions generate financial benefits to the successful teams. To qualify for the Champions League it is necessary to finish in the top four of the Premiership. Before the Premiership and the Champions League there was little financial benefit from placing in the top four positions.

(pp. 1677–1678)

Indeed, it was not until the 1992 rebrand that the Champions League allowed multiple clubs to compete in the competition. Prior to that, just the winning team from each league was allowed to participate in an abbreviated version of the tournament. But as the revenues rose and became rewardable to more than one club, the most successful clubs began monopolizing these places in their leagues. It is logical to assume that, over time, the top players then became drawn to the clubs that had established themselves as regular Champions League contenders. After all, the opportunity to play on club football's biggest stage is frequently cited as a factor in players' decisions to join one club over another (Brus, 2016; ESPNFC.com, 2015; Jackson, 2016), and the extra income garnered by these clubs could be invested in higher, more attractive wages.

Furthermore, while the broadcast revenues in the modern era represent the largest source of income to a league and many of its member clubs, some of the widest income disparities have arisen from differences in commercial revenues. In this sector, the money that a club receives from its various sponsorship deals does not have to be shared with any of the other clubs in the league. On a year-to-year basis, commercial deals have represented one of the fastest growing sources of income for European clubs and in particular those with established pedigrees (Deloitte, 2016). One of the more lucrative and recognizable commercial revenue sources is the kit sponsorship deal in which a company pays the club to have its logo emblazoned across a portion of the team's jersey. The manufacturer of the kit will also pay a large sum of money in order to be the official outfitter and equipment supplier to the club. Table 5.3 shows how much these kit deals were worth for each of the teams that participated in the 2015–2016 EPL season. At the top, Manchester United was receiving $195 million from its kit deals with Adidas and Chevrolet while a smaller club like Crystal Palace was earning a comparatively meager $3.6 million from its agreements (Tyler, 2015). In terms of percentages, this gap represents a sizeable 98% difference in revenues.

Across the other members of the Big Five, the inequalities in commercial revenues have told a similar story. In France, PSG's 2014–2015 commercial income amounted to almost half of the Ligue 1 total. In Spain, FC Barcelona, Real Madrid, and Atlético Madrid's combined commercial revenues represented 86% of the total commercial revenues in La Liga (Deloitte,

Table 5.3 Ranking of English Premier League kit deals by annual revenue (2015–2016)

Club	Manufacturer	Sponsor	Total
Manchester United	Adidas ($117m)	Chevrolet ($79.9m)	$195m/year
Chelsea	Adidas ($47m)	Yokohama Tires ($62.3m)	$109.3m/year
Arsenal	Puma ($47m)	Fly Emirates ($47m)	$94m/year
Liverpool	New Balance ($43.6)	Standard Chartered ($39m)	$82.6m/year
Manchester City	Nike ($18.7m)	Etihad ($62.3m)	$81m/year
Tottenham	Under Armour ($16m)	AIA ($25m)	$41m/year
Everton	Umbro ($9.3m)	Chang Beer ($8.3m)	$17.6m/year
West Ham United	Umbro ($6m)	Betway ($8.9m)	$14.9m/year
Aston Villa	Macron ($5.8m)	Intuit QuickBooks ($7.8m)	$13.6m/year
Newcastle United	Puma (Undisclosed)	Wonga ($9.3m)	–
Sunderland	Adidas (Undisclosed)	Dafabet ($7.8m)	–
Swansea City	Adidas (Undisclosed)	Goldenway ($6.2m)	–
Stoke City	New Balance (Undisclosed)	Bet365 ($4.7m)	–
West Brom	Adidas ($2.4m)	TLCBET ($1.9m)	$4.3m/year
Crystal Palace	Macron ($2.5m)	($1.1m)	$3.6m/year
Watford	Puma (Undisclosed)	138.com ($2.2m)	–
Leicester City	Puma (Undisclosed)	King Power ($1.6m)	–
Norwich City	Errea (Undisclosed)	Aviva ($1.6m)	–
Southampton	Adidas (Undisclosed)	Veho ($1.6m)	–
Bournemouth	Cabrini (Undisclosed)	Mansion Group ($1.1m)	–

Note: Adapted from "Premier League, 2015–2016 Most Valuable Kits," by J. Tyler and M. Yesilevskiy, 2015, *ESPNFC.com*, retrieved May 2016 from http://espn.go.com/espn/feature/story/_/id/13357293/english-premier-league-most-valuable-kits-2015–2016.

2016). While certain clubs have likely always had a higher degree of brand equity, it appears as though the increased revenues brought about by commercialization have exaggerated these differences and made it so that certain clubs are "immovable" at the top of the standings.

Club-specific idiosyncrasies

While a degree of competitive imbalance appears to have coincided with the influx of commercially driven revenues, the new money, alone, is not capable of fully explaining why some teams are able to maintain an advantage over others. Indeed, the reputations and revenues that were already being realized by certain clubs far preceded the advent of the modern day EPL and Champions League. As noted by Szymanski (2015), a degree of dominance has been a feature of almost every open league football competition in the world for some time now.

> Many people believe that dominance is a relatively recent phenomenon in football, or that dominance has increased significantly over the last two decades. Commercialization, according to this sentiment, has dumped large amounts of money into the game that has corrupted the system and created a world of "haves" and "have-nots." There is no question that the amount of money in the game has increased, but in fact there is little evidence to suggest that dominance has intensified dramatically.
>
> (p. 6)

In making this claim, Szymanski goes on to highlight how the Champions League (European Cup) was won by clubs from the same number of leagues from 1964–65 to 1988–89 as it was from 1989–1990 to 2013–2014. He also notes that, barring a couple of exceptions, both the number of wins by one club and the number of different winners remained relatively steady across the two timeframes in many of Europe's top leagues. While he agrees that today's leagues are typified by an elite core of teams, he contends that football leagues have almost always been associated with dominance by a select minority.

In analyzing the apparent dominance of certain European football teams, it is natural for one to first look toward the advantages that are possessed by many of the superior clubs. These tangible and intangible benefits, whether earned over time or bought with the money of a wealthy owner, provide insights to the ways in which certain clubs have been able to establish themselves at the top of the world's game. From a more anecdotal perspective, Szymanski (2015) states that dominant clubs have traditionally benefitted from the following factors: (1) being the first-movers in a league, (2) being located in a profitable area, (3) favorable league policies, (4) the influence of an historical event or figure, or (5) some combination of the above. While each was ultimately able to achieve prominence through unique circumstances and a combination of different factors, the end result is a brand value that translates into a higher earning and spending potential.

Looking back at history, Szymanski (2015) shows that Bayern Munich was able to ride a wave of marquee player acquisitions and the construction of an Olympic stadium at the center of Bavarian culture to early success in the Bundesliga. Furthermore, the 50+1 rule that was implemented by the German league system to prevent wealthy investors from assuming sole ownership of a club has ensured that Bayern's dominance will not be challenged through financial means anytime soon. In Spain, FC Barcelona are situated at the center of Catalan influence and capitalized on the first-mover advantage of being the inaugural Spanish champion. The other dominant club in the country, Real Madrid, is situated in Spain's largest market and was the beneficiary of royal favoritism, a large stadium, and savvy managerial decisions that consistently brought some of the world's greatest players to the squad. Until recently, both clubs were also bolstered by rules that allowed them to negotiate their broadcast deals separately from the rest of La Liga (Thomas et al., 2015). Meanwhile, in France, the two clubs that have experienced the most success in recent times are PSG and Lyon. Unsurprisingly, both have rich histories and are situated in the first and third most populous French cities. In Italy, Inter Milan and Juventus are situated in two of the five largest Italian markets and have been able to build upon the levels of relevance they obtained from being the first and second league champions, respectively, in what is today known as the Serie A. In England, Manchester United stands out as the dominant club of the modern era, owing much to the success of two legendary managers in Sir Matt Busby and Sir Alex Ferguson. After winning a trio of English titles in the 1950s, the club sustained its popularity through triumph and tragedy (i.e., the 1958 Munich air disaster), endearing itself to a generation of football fans and winning two more titles in the late 1960s. When the globalization of televised sport began placing a spotlight on English football, United was able to reap the rewards of its historical popularity on a more global scale (Szymanski, 2015). From 1992–93 to 2010–2011, United won 13 EPL titles and established itself as one of the most valuable sports organizations in the world (Badenhausen, 2016).

From a more empirical perspective, there are a number of studies that have analyzed the factors posited by Szymanski (2015) in greater detail. Buraimo, Forrest, and Simmons (2007) and Buraimo and Simmons (2009a), for example, showed that long-term performance in English football was predicted to depend on market size. Clubs based in bigger markets had the potential to convert a larger fan base into higher revenues, even after accounting for the presence of other clubs in the area. Because gate receipts and television appearance funds do not have to be shared in European football, they can be used to attract premium talent with the promise of higher wages. Curran et al. (2009) cited disparities in market size as one of the earliest causes for competitive imbalance in English football. Such findings are also consistent with the earlier, theoretical propositions of El-Hodiri and Quirk (1971), whereby gate receipts are a function of the size of the market area. Approaching the dilemma from a different angle, some have even suggested that larger markets may be more attractive to star players for personal endorsement reasons (Leeds & Von Allmen, 2013), though further proof of this claim is warranted.

Stadium capacities, which represent the earning potentials of clubs via ticket sales, are also highly variable and conducive to some clubs earning more than others. Table 5.4 shows the capacities for each of the venues that played host to an EPL club during the 2016–2017 season. The difference between Manchester United's Old Trafford venue at the top and Bournemouth's Vitality Stadium at the bottom roughly equates to a 7 to 1 ratio. With capacity utilization hovering at or above 95% in recent years, it stands to reason that the clubs with the bigger venues are better poised to capitalize on the popularity of the sport and earn additional money through ticket sales. "A larger stadium – as long as utilization is maintained – can therefore provide a direct competitive advantage against rivals" (Deloitte, 2016, p. 32). In Germany, where capacity utilization was 90% in 2014–2015, a similar recommendation can be made. However, this metric stands at just 71% in Spain and France and at a comparatively meager 51% in Italy. For clubs in these leagues, simply attracting more spectators to a match can offer advantages.

Shifting the focus to historical and impactful figures, recent times have seen the advent of a new phenomenon whereby success is bought rather directly with the money of a wealthy club owner. Chelsea became one of the first clubs to achieve prominence in this way as the injections of cash provided by Russian billionaire, Roman Abramovich, allowed the EPL club to become competitive in the transfer market and on the pitch. Using a variation of the C4 to measure the concentration of transfer fees in the top four

Table 5.4 English Premier League venues and capacities (2016–2017)

Club	Venue Name	Capacity
Manchester United	Old Trafford	75,643
Arsenal	Emirates Stadium	60,260
West Ham	London Stadium	60,000
Manchester City	Etihad Stadium	55.097
Liverpool	Anfield	54,074
Sunderland	Stadium of Light	48,707
Chelsea	Stamford Bridge	41,631
Everton	Goodison Park	39,571
Tottenham	White Hart Lane	36,284
Middlesbrough	Riverside Stadium	33,746
Southampton	St. Mary's Stadium	32,384
Leicester City	King Power Stadium	32,273
Stoke City	Bet365 Stadium	27,932
West Brom	The Hawthorns	26,850
Crystal Palace	Selhurst Park	25,456
Hull City	KCOM Stadium	24,983
Watford	Vicarage Road	21,438
Burnley	Turf Moor	21,401
Swansea	Liberty Stadium	21,088
Bournemouth	Vitality Stadium	11,464

Note: Retrieved from www.transfermarkt.com.

EPL clubs from 1992–93 to 2009–2010, Tomkins et al. (2010) showed that signs of an oligopoly in the EPL became evident upon Abramovich's purchase of Chelsea ahead of the 2003–2004 season. In the first three years of his ownership, the concentration of transfer fees in the top four rose above 50% due in large part to his excessive outlays on players.

Transitioning to a more individualized assessment of spending power, Tomkins et al. (2010) also showed that the 2004–2005 season saw the biggest year-on-year rise in transfer fee concentration as the EPL's HHI value increased by 29%. This point in time happened to coincide with manager Jose Mourinho's first season in charge of Chelsea and the first full offseason in which Abramovich was able to scour the labor market for playing talent. The wealthy owner was clearly investing in an attempt to win, and in just a short matter of time he was rewarded for his expenditures. Chelsea won the EPL title three times between the 2004–2005 and 2009–2010 seasons, establishing itself as a force in the modern era of the game. Similar events unfolded with Sheikh Mansour and Manchester City. After purchasing City at the start of the 2008–2009 season, Mansour began pumping millions of dollars into player wages and transfer fees. The value of his starting 11 soon began rivaling that of Chelsea, Manchester United, and the other wealthy European clubs, and in 2011–2012, the club won its first title of the modern era.

Rules and regulations

The existing income disparities and the resulting freedom to spend differing amounts of money on players are both permitted by the unregulated and fluid nature of these open league systems. When revenues do not have to be shared and clubs are not prohibited from spending varying amounts of money on players, it is only natural for the wealthiest clubs to build on their success over time. However, it was not until 1995, a year concurring with the early stages of the modern era, that the labor market for European football players became as free and expansive as it is today. This was due to the outcome of the *Belgian Football Association v. Jean-Marc Bosman* case (hereafter referred to as *Bosman*) that granted professional football player Jean-Marc Bosman the freedom to change clubs after he had been prohibited from moving to a French club once his contract with RFC Liege, a Belgian club, had expired (Antonioni & Cubbin, 2000; Binder & Findlay, 2012; Frick, 2009). The verdict of this case changed the market for playing talent within European football by eliminating transfer fees for out-of-contract players and banning the use of quotas that limited the number of foreign, European players allowed on a team. By granting clubs the freedom to pursue the top playing talent in a variety of external territories, the Bosman ruling considerably expanded the supply of labor for European football teams. At the same time, it also put more power in the players' hands by giving them the freedom to choose the club that could offer them the best financial and playing opportunities.

The primary result of this ruling was that it signaled an exodus of the best players out of the smaller European leagues to the Big Five (Frick, 2007, 2009; Kesenne, 2007). Because most of the clubs in these smaller competitions could neither afford the high salaries nor offer the championship exposure that was being put on display by the elite, they struggled to keep hold of their star players and coaches. As noted by Frick (2009), the immediate outcome of the Bosman verdict resulted in a statistically significant 9% increase in the number of national team players signing contracts in foreign leagues. Eastern European clubs, in particular, appeared to be the main exporters to the Big Five early on, and in the Bundesliga, alone, the percentage of German players decreased from approximately 70% in 1995 to less than 50% by 2000 (Frick, 2007, 2009). Figure 5.1 shows that the trend was evident across the whole of the Big Five as the clubs in these leagues grew increasingly internationalized in the post-Bosman era (Poli, Ravenel, & Besson, 2016a). On the pitch, evidence of the talent migration was seen as the Champions League came to be dominated by the Big Five on a more consistent basis around the turn of the century (Gerrard, 2003). The Bosman ruling also helped facilitate the increase in Big Five television revenues that occurred over this time as marquee competitions like the EPL and Champions League became synonymous with global "super leagues" that showcased the world's best players (Binder & Findlay, 2012).

In theory, the opening of the labor market should have led to an increase in competitive balance within the Big Five as the increased supply of talented

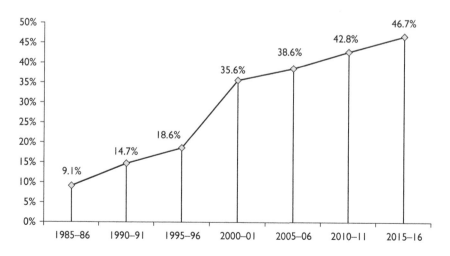

Figure 5.1 Percentage of foreign players in the Big Five (1985–1986 to 2015–2016); players were considered foreign if they were not from the same country that hosted the league

players led to a decrease in the cost of an individual unit of talent (Flores, Forrest, & Tena, 2010; Kesenne, 2007). Furthermore, it is generally understood that as talent is drawn from a larger pool the differences between the best and the worst should shrink (Gould & Halberstam, 2004; Szymanski, 2015). However, the rising financial disparities within each league and the more established pedigrees of certain teams meant that the biggest clubs still held an innate advantage over their smaller rivals when it came to securing the top talent. As noted by Poli, Ravenel, et al. (2016a) of the CIES Football Observatory, a football research center,

> The weakening of quotas in Europe has led to a multiplication of international flows. For most countries, the qualitative assessment of the exchange between players imported and players exported is henceforth negative. The main beneficiaries of the liberalization of flows are the top clubs of the most financially powerful leagues. These dominant teams can indeed concentrate talent even more strongly than in the past. This process is at the heart of the deterioration of the competitive balance in Europe.
>
> (p. 8)

Indeed, studies have shown that teams without a noticeable weak link will perform better in individual matches (Franck & Nüesch, 2010) and over the course of a season (Anderson & Sally, 2013). Further examinations have shown that the best players will tend to cluster on the best teams, and that team performance can theoretically be maximized in such situations (Vöpel, 2013). As implied above, the opening of the borders meant that the wealthy teams could now reinforce their squads at all positions with higher quality players. Furthermore, the post-Bosman elimination of the pseudo "reserve clause" that had required teams to pay a transfer fee for an out-of-contract player likely meant that smaller clubs were now enticed to sell a player for a transfer fee rather than let him walk for free at the end of his contract. Though they eventually began countering this problem by signing players to longer contracts (Feess, Frick, & Muehlheusser, 2004), this change still limited both their ability to hold onto marquee players for the long run and the amount of money they could demand at any time.

Therefore, any gains that the smaller clubs had incurred from a larger labor supply were likely negated by the decreased power they had in holding onto their own star players. Between 2010 and 2015, 68% of the transfer fees occurred within the Big Five (Poli, Besson, & Ravenel, 2015), indicating that a majority of the bigger clubs were likely buying talent from the smaller clubs in these same leagues. Perhaps, then, it is not surprising that most studies show that the Bosman ruling had a rather limited effect on competitive balance across the Big Five (Binder & Findlay, 2012; Flores et al., 2010; Haan, Koning, & Van Witteloostuijn, 2007; Kesenne, 2007).

The burgeoning effects of commercialization that were occurring at this time also make it difficult to discern the specific effects that the Bosman ruling had on performance, though its presumable contributions to the rising media revenues position it as a likely moderator.

Nonetheless, it certainly expanded the possibility for clubs to scout and hire players from larger and more obscure talent pools. As Table 5.5 reveals, numerous countries in and outside of Europe have served as talent pipelines to Big Five clubs in recent seasons (Poli, Besson, & Ravenel, 2016). While many of these countries are simply smaller European nations or traditional football hotbeds like Brazil and Argentina, there are also more obscure nations like Senegal, Colombia, and the Ivory Coast on the list. According to some, it is from these more "unfashionable" countries that clubs can purchase equally talented players for discounted prices (Kuper & Szymanski, 2012). Although it is likely that the rich clubs will eventually prize these players away if they turn out to be successful, the money made from buying a player at a discount and selling him at a premium can still represent a sizeable return on investment for a smaller club. If managed properly, these funds can then be used to improve a club or maintain its status in the top division. Even so, the tendency to maintain the status quo only further

Table 5.5 Top countries for player exports to the Big Five (2015–2016)

Country	Big Five	Other	Total
France	116	196	312
Brazil	114	355	469
Argentina	97	71	168
Spain	66	135	201
Belgium	48	51	99
Switzerland	48	17	65
Serbia	39	150	189
Netherlands	38	96	134
Portugal	36	94	130
Croatia	33	108	141
Senegal	27	44	71
Germany	26	123	149
Sweden	26	75	101
Uruguay	26	14	40
Poland	25	17	42
Austria	24	27	51
Denmark	19	58	77
Colombia	19	19	38
Italy	18	39	57
Ivory Coast	17	48	65

Notes: Adapted from Poli, Ravenel, et al. (2016a); figures accurate as of October 2016. *Other* is representative of exports to 26 top-division European leagues outside the Big Five.

shows why the Bosman's effect on competitive balance was largely seen as a wash in this setting.

More recently, another potential change has been introduced to European football that could have a noticeable effect on the labor market and competitive balance. Known as UEFA Financial Fair Play (UEFA, 2015a), this initiative was approved in 2010 and implemented for the first time in 2011 with the goals of ensuring that clubs pay their bills and meet certain break-even requirements on their balance sheets. While the intricacies of this plan are rather detailed, its basic objectives are focused on getting clubs to balance their expenses with their revenues in order to avoid an accumulation of debt. It also puts more of a restriction on owners' personal investments, which are not allowed to exceed $33.45 million over the 2015–2016 to 2017–2018 seasons. Clubs that violate these policies are subject to punishment in the form of fines or bans from UEFA competitions; however, expenditures directed to the improvement of stadia and youth academies are excluded from the break-even criteria.

Seeing as the players are the costliest item to a club, these enactments were clearly designed to deter clubs from overspending on wages and transfer fees. More specifically, they appeared to be an attempt to limit the problems that arise when clubs aspire to join the ranks of the elite and spend nearly all of their revenues on players in the pursuit of success that may or may not arrive. Because wages generally consume a majority of the new revenues that flow into a club (Deloitte, 2016), and the average transfer fee, adjusted for inflation, swelled from nearly $1 million in 1992 to approximately $7.9 million at its peak in 2008–2009 (Tomkins et al., 2010), such limitations appeared justifiable at the surface level. UEFA's findings in the 2011 Club Licensing Benchmark Report that 63% of its top division clubs were operating at a loss added further fuel to the initiative (Szymanski, 2015). The long-term sustainability of numerous clubs appeared to be at risk, and costs needed to be controlled.

However, while by UEFA's own admission, Financial Fair Play appears to have coincided with considerable improvements in club finances (UEFA, 2017), its positive impact on competitive balance remains less certain. In this respect, some experts have expressed a concern that the break-even requirements will only entrench the patterns of dominance that currently exist (Budzinski & Szymanski, 2015; Szymanski, 2015). After all, it has already been seen that clubs in each league are competing with vastly different budgets. In 2015–2016, for example, Manchester United boasted revenues of $568 million while the three EPL clubs that ended up being relegated had an average income of $119 million (Deloitte, 2016). In France, PSG's revenues, alone, were higher than the combined revenues of 14 other Ligue 1 clubs. Operating within one's "means" therefore varies according to the club that is being assessed. Furthermore, it is unclear how restrictions on the investments provided by owners will actually improve parity. In recent times, these funds have provided one of the only avenues to quick success (Tomkins et al., 2010). If not for the generous donations of Sheikh Mansour and Roman Abramovich, the EPL would have likely seen an even fewer number of champions claim the title during the early stages of the modern era. By treating these investments separately from other revenue sources, UEFA appears to be locking in the status quo for reasons that do not align with financial sustainability. "Financial injections by wealthy owners cannot be shown to damage the health of recipient football clubs," notes Szymanski (2015), "and indeed rather the opposite seems to be the case" (p. 253). Perhaps one could look to Germany for evidence of what will happen when regulations are imposed to limit the impact of owner investment. As a league that uses the 50+1 rule to keep any single investor from taking sole possession of a club, the Bundesliga has been more or less dominated by the same team (Bayern Munich) since the feature was implemented in the late 1990s.

Ultimately, the lack of clarity surrounding the implementation of Financial Fair Play has made for a difficult assessment of its initial impact on parity. In the spring of 2015, for instance, UEFA apparently "eased" the policies it had introduced following legal backlash from parties claiming that the rules restricted freedom in the European markets (Slater, 2015). Combined with a lack of transparency that overshadowed the exact requirements and punishments for the involved clubs (Müller, Joachim, & Hovemann, 2012), the initiative has remained somewhat of an enigma in football circles. Therefore, more time and clarity may be required before the full effects of this initiative on competitive balance are measurable. Nonetheless, it will likely remain a key feature of economic analyses in European football moving forward. If it does end up creating an environment where success cannot be bought with new money, then analyses focusing on strategy and innovation will become all the more important.

Strategy and efficiency

To this point, many of the factors that have contributed to clubs' revenues and subsequent successes have resided outside of their direct and current control. History and tradition, for instance, must be developed over time, and building a reputable brand is hard to do in a setting where one bad season can signal the end of a club's tenure in the top division. Similarly, first-mover advantages, while meaningful, are frequently the end result of having already achieved a certain degree of success. Additional influences such as market size, league rule changes, and governmental mandates are also uncontrollable from a managerial perspective. Even profitable actions such as building bigger stadiums and buying better players require sizeable investments with money that is not always available up front. The Financial Fair Play initiatives have also questioned the motives of bankrolling owners that purchase clubs and quickly alter their fortunes.

Nonetheless, the seemingly direct and visible relationships between money, playing talent, and success in European football lends credence to the *Moneyball* hypothesis by which teams are able to gain advantages from finding valuable playing talent for undervalued prices in the labor market (Hakes & Sauer, 2006; Lewis, 2004). The market expansion that occurred as a result of the Bosman ruling has certainly provided clubs with a plethora of regions and countries from which they can extract talent, and the growing revenues of the Big Five mean the clubs participating in these competitions are better equipped to pry players away from the clubs in smaller leagues. An element of efficiency is therefore required from teams as they strive to compete within their means. As noted by Gerrard (2014),

> Efficient teams are able to minimize the costs of playing talent and maximize the sporting performance of their playing squad. A key component in maximizing the efficiency of professional teams is the capability to identify, recruit and retain cost-effective playing talent. This represents transactional efficiency and is critical to success for teams with more restrictive resource constraints compared to some of their league rivals. Maximizing transactional efficiency is vital for small-market teams or teams operating under a financial self-sufficiency regime which still aspire to sporting success.
>
> (p. 189)

As such, identifying patterns of inefficiency in the labor market and exploiting those shortcomings can aid a less-profitable club in its quest to remain relevant. Proper methods of player valuation and development accordingly rise to the forefront as means by which clubs can achieve success without having to overspend. In essence, these techniques lend an element of strategy to a setting that has frequently been dominated by money.

Many of the analyses conducted in this area have focused on basic player variables such as experience, age, and nationality in an effort to predict transfer fees and player wages using this data. For instance, numerous studies have shown that players should be purchased in their low-to-mid-20's since performance and sell-on value take a downturn as they approach age 30 (Frick, 2007, 2011; Kuper & Szymanski, 2012; Tomkins, 2013; Tomkins et al., 2010). Others have suggested that certain nationalities will be more costly (Frick, 2011; Frick & Lehmann, 2001), and that player values will soar if they have just participated in a FIFA World Cup (Kuper & Szymanski, 2012). Similarly, costs will vary with respect to the position that a player plays, with attacking players typically commanding the highest transfer fees and goalkeepers the lowest (Anderson & Sally, 2013; Kuper & Szymanski, 2012; Tomkins et al., 2010). There also exists evidence to suggest that the more reputable a buying or selling club is, the higher the transfer fee will end up being (Dobson & Gerrard, 1999; Feess et al., 2004; Frick, 2007).

Seeing as transfer fees are an added cost to the wages that come standard with each signing, it is frequently recommended that poorer clubs focus on training techniques and the implementation of youth development plans that groom the players already in the system. As noted by former Barcelona CEO, Joan Oliver, "The problem with the football business is that usually it is managed with very, very short-term goals. After a bad year, it's very difficult not to fall in the temptation of buying a lot of people. Clubs spend irrationally and compulsively on players. And that's very difficult to restrain" (Kuper & Szymanski, 2012, p. 45). Therefore, simply having a proper strategy and plan embedded in the culture of the club can also be of value. Though such a feature may be more intangible and indiscernible to the naked eye, it is not the type of benefit that can be copied with ease. Looking for these strategies in the actions of Big Five clubs can accordingly aid in one's assessment of competition in these leagues. In seeing which clubs are able to compete with and against the odds, visualizing their strategies can help communicate why parity may or may not be present.

Conclusion

In closing, this review looked at the competitive balance analyses that had been conducted across the Big Five in the modern era and presented a series of explanations for the current status of competition in European football. As a multi-billion-dollar industry, knowledge of the factors that contribute to the rise and fall of clubs in this setting can prove beneficial to a number of parties, including owners, coaches, players, and sponsors that are looking to align with successful sports properties. In this particular examination, the influences of commercialization, club specific idiosyncrasies, rules and regulations, and strategy and efficiency were looked at in greater detail. Commercialization, for instance, was found to be contributing to the unequal earning capacities of clubs as variations in merit-based payments, stadium sizes, and commercial deals created gaps on the playing field. Some of these disparities were also the result of club-specific idiosyncrasies as varying market sizes, historical performances, and first-mover advantages exerted an impact on the competition. Changes in league and labor market policies such as the Bosman ruling, the 50+1 rule, and Financial Fair Play were also presented as factors that were capable of having an effect on the proceedings. Lastly, as a result of some or all of these aforementioned influencers, the growing gaps between the dominant clubs and the fringe competitors forced some teams to seek advantages by focusing on strategy and efficiency in lieu of raw spending power. With nearly every club finding itself in a different situation, there is no "one-size-fits-all" solution to success on the pitch, but competitive balance analyses can be useful to the extent that they outline the competitive environment and provide an avenue for examining which strategies have and have not worked.

Ultimately, the findings of this review offer researchers a number of future directions in which they can proceed should they choose to make more practically-applicable contributions to the managerial field. Strategy and efficiency, for example, can be assessed in greater detail as researchers devote more time to the study of performance metrics and financial data in European football. Accurately scouting players and teams and finding value in the labor market all represent ways in which a team up against the odds could turn the tables on the competition. Taking a closer look at more specific measures of competitive balance could also provide a benefit to league and club managers. For example, are there differences in competitive balance within the various sections of a league table? What factors are influencing competitiveness in these sectors? How likely is a club to be relegated from or promoted to a given league? Can clubs then devise strategies that protect against relegation or ensure promotion to the top-flight? These are all questions that need to be answered in greater detail. Future analyses of competitive balance in European football could certainly differentiate themselves from the collective mass of UOH and ACB studies by offering unique insights to these areas. The ever-shifting landscapes of league rules and policies also provide researchers with an opportunity to examine their effects on performance and the ways in which managers could respond to these changes. Recently devised regulations such as Financial Fair Play, for example, can become worthy sources of examination once their intricacies and effects become more transparent.

References

21st Club. (2016). *Changing the conversation*. London: CreateSpace.

Anderson, C., & Sally, D. (2013). *The numbers game: Why everything you know about soccer is wrong*. New York: Penguin.

Antonioni, P., & Cubbin, J. (2000). The Bosman ruling and the emergence of a single market in soccer talent. *European Journal of Law and Economics*, 9(2), 157–173.

Badenhausen, K. (2016, July 13). *Dallas Cowboys head the world's 50 most valuable sports teams of 2016*. Retrieved from www.forbes.com/sites/kurt badenhausen/2016/07/13/dallas-cowboys-head-the-worlds-50-most-valuable-sports-teams-of-2016/#16349853f330

Ben-Naim, E., Vazquez, F., & Redner, S. (2006). Parity and predictability of competitions. *Journal of Quantitative Analysis in Sports*, 2(4), 1–12.

Binder, J. J., & Findlay, M. (2012). The effects of the Bosman ruling on national and club teams in Europe. *Journal of Sports Economics*, 13(2), 107–129.

Bowman, R. A., Lambrinos, J., & Ashman, T. (2013). Competitive balance in the eyes of the sports fan: Prospective measures using point spreads in the NFL and NBA. *Journal of Sports Economics*, 14(5), 498–520.

Brandes, L., & Franck, E. (2007). Who made who? An empirical analysis of competitive balance in European soccer leagues. *Eastern Economic Journal*, 33(3), 379–403.

Brus, M. (2016, December 20). *Dimitri Payet hints at Arsenal transfer with champions league admission.* Retrieved from http://metro.co.uk/2016/12/20/dimitri-payet-hints-at-arsenal-transfer-with-champions-league-admission-6334432/

Budzinski, O., & Szymanski, S. (2015). Are restrictions of competition by sports associations horizontal or vertical in nature? *Journal of Competition Law and Economics, 11*(2), 409–429.

Buraimo, B., Forrest, D., & Simmons, R. (2007). Freedom of entry, market size, and competitive outcome: Evidence from English soccer. *Southern Economic Journal, 74*(1), 204–213.

Buraimo, B., & Simmons, R. (2008). Do sports fans really value uncertainty of outcome? Evidence from the English Premier League. *International Journal of Sport Finance, 3*(3), 146.

Buraimo, B., & Simmons, R. (2009a). Market size and attendance in English Premier League football. *International Journal of Sport Management and Marketing, 6*(2), 200–214.

Buraimo, B., & Simmons, R. (2009b). A tale of two audiences: Spectators, television viewers and outcome uncertainty in Spanish football. *Journal of Economics and Business, 61*(4), 326–338.

Buzzacchi, L., Szymanski, S., & Valletti, T. M. (2003). Equality of opportunity and equality of outcome: Open leagues, closed leagues and competitive balance. *Journal of Industry, Competition and Trade, 3*(3), 167–186.

Cairns, J. A. (1987). Evaluating changes in league structure: The reorganization of the Scottish Football League. *Applied Economics, 19*(2), 259–275.

Curran, J., Jennings, I., & Sedgwick, J. (2009). 'Competitive Balance' in the top level of English football, 1948–2008: An absent principle and a forgotten ideal. *The International Journal of the History of Sport, 26*(11), 1735–1747.

Deloitte. (2016). *Annual review of football finance 2016.* Retrieved from www2.deloitte.com/content/dam/Deloitte/uk/Documents/sports-business-group/deloitte-uk-annual-review-of-football-finance-2016.pdf

Demmert, H. (1973). *The economics of professional team sports.* Lexington, MA: D. C. Heath.

Depken II, C. A. (1999). Free-agency and the competitiveness of Major League Baseball. *Review of Industrial Organization, 14*(3), 205–217.

Dobson, S., & Gerrard, B. (1999). The determination of player transfer fees in English professional Soccer. *Journal of Sport Management, 13*(4), 259–279.

Dobson, S., & Goddard, J. A. (2001). *The economics of football.* Cambridge: Cambridge University Press.

El-Hodiri, M., & Quirk, J. (1971). An economic model of a professional sports league. *Journal of Political Economy, 79*(6), 1302–1319.

ESPNFC.com. (2015, June 8). *Tottenham's Hugo Lloris wants champions league football.* Retrieved from www.espnfc.us/story/2482979/spurs-goalkeeper-hugo-lloris-wants-champions-league-football

Feddersen, A., & Maennig, W. (2005). Trends in competitive balance: Is there evidence for growing imbalance in professional sport leagues? *Hamburg Contemporary Economic Discussions,* ISBN 978-3-940369-01-7.

Feess, E., Frick, B., & Muehlheusser, G. (2004). *Legal restrictions on buyout fees: Theory and evidence from European Soccer.* IZA Discussion Paper No. 1180.

Flores, R., Forrest, D., & Tena, J. D. (2010). Impact on competitive balance from allowing foreign players in a sports league: Evidence from European Soccer. *Kyklos, 63*(4), 546–557.

Forrest, D., & Simmons, R. (2002). Outcome uncertainty and attendance demand in sport: The case of English Soccer. *Journal of the Royal Statistical Society: Series D (The Statistician), 51*(2), 229–241.

Fort, R., & Maxcy, J. (2003). Competitive balance in sports leagues: An introduction. *Journal of Sports Economics, 4*(2), 154–160.

Fort, R., & Quirk, J. (1995). Cross-subsidization, incentives, and outcomes in professional team sports leagues. *Journal of Economic Literature, 33*(3), 1265–1299.

Franck, E., & Nüesch, S. (2010). The effect of talent disparity on team productivity in Soccer. *Journal of Economic Psychology, 31*(2), 218–229.

Frick, B. (2007). The football players' labor market: Empirical evidence from the major European leagues. *Scottish Journal of Political Economy, 54*(3), 422–446.

Frick, B. (2009). Globalization and factor mobility: The impact of the "Bosman-ruling" on player migration in professional Soccer. *Journal of Sports Economics, 10*(1), 88–106.

Frick, B. (2011). Performance, salaries, and contract length: empirical evidence from German Soccer. *International Journal of Sport Finance, 6*(2), 87–118.

Frick, B., & Lehmann, E. (2001). Die Kosten der externen Rekrutierung qualifizierten personals: Empirische Evidenz aus dem professionellen fußball. *Entlohnung, Arbeitsorganisation und Personalpolitische Regulierung, München und Mering: Hampp*, 243–263.

Garcia-del-Barrio, P., & Szymanski, S. (2009). Goal! Profit maximization versus win maximization in Soccer. *Review of Industrial Organization, 34*(1), 45–68.

Gerrard, B. (2003). *The impact of free agency on European professional Soccer.* Paper presented at the NASSM Conference, Ithaca, NY.

Gerrard, B. (2014). Achieving transactional efficiency in professional team sports: The theory and practice of player valuation. In J. Goddard & P. Sloane (Eds.), *Handbook on the economics of professional football* (pp. 189–202). Cheltenham, UK: Edward Elgar.

Gould, S. J., & Halberstam, D. (2004). *Triump and tragedy in Mudville: A lifelong passion for baseball.* New York: W.W. Norton.

Haan, M., Koning, R. H., & Van Witteloostuijn, A. (2007). Competitive balance in national European Soccer competitions. *Statistical Thinking in Sports*, 63–76.

Hakes, J. K., & Sauer, R. D. (2006). An economic evaluation of the Moneyball hypothesis. *The Journal of Economic Perspectives, 20*(3), 173–185.

Hall, S., Szymanski, S., & Zimbalist, A. S. (2002). Testing causality between team performance and payroll: The cases of major league baseball and English Soccer. *Journal of Sports Economics, 3*(2), 149–168.

Harris, N. (2016, May 24). *Arsenal top the premier league prize money table as they become first club to make over £100m . . . and even Aston Villa pocket £66m!* Retrieved from www.dailymail.co.uk/sport/football/article-3606538/Arsenal-Premier-League-prize-money-table-club-make-100m-Aston-Villa-pocket-66m.html

Inan, T., & Kaya, A. M. (2011). Competitive balance in Turkish Soccer. *Ekonomika a Management, 2.*

Jackson, G. (2016, May 23). *Ayew wants champions league football.* Retrieved from http://africanfootball.com/news/628964/Ayew-wants-Champions-League-football

Késenne, S. (1996). League management in professional team sports with win maximizing clubs. *European Journal for Sport Management*, 2(2), 14–22.

Késenne, S. (2000). Revenue sharing and competitive balance in professional team sports. *Journal of Sports Economics*, 1(1), 56–65.

Kesenne, S. (2007). The peculiar international economics of professional football in Europe. *Scottish Journal of Political Economy*, 54(3), 388–399.Kuper, S., & Szymanski, S. (2012). *Soccernomics: Why England loses, why Spain, Germany and Brazil win, and why the US, Japan, Australia, Turkey – and even Iraq – are destined to become the kings of the world's most popular sport*. New York: Nation.

Leeds, M., & Von Allmen, P. (2013). *The economics of sports* (5th ed.). New York: Prentice-Hall.

Lewis, M. (2004). *Moneyball: The art of winning an unfair game*. New York: W.W. Norton.

Michie, J., & Oughton, C. (2004). *Competitive balance in football: Trends and effects*. Research paper 20014. London: Football Governance Research Center.

Mourão, P. R., & Cima, C. (2015). Studying the golden generations' effects and the changes in the competitive balance of the Portuguese Soccer league. *International Journal of Sport Finance*, 10(1), 42.

Müller, J. C., Joachim, L., & Hovemann, G. (2012). The financial fair play regulations of UEFA: An adequate concept to ensure the long-term viability and sustainability of European club football? *International Journal of Sport Finance*, 7(2), 117.

Neale, W. C. (1964). The peculiar economics of professional sports. *The Quarterly Journal of Economics*, 78(1), 1–14.

Noll, R. G. (1974). Government and the sports business. In R. G. Noll (Ed.), *Studies in the regulation of economic activity*. Washington, DC: The Brookings Institution.

Noll, R. G. (1988). Professional basketball. *Stanford University Studies in Industrial Economics*, Working Paper No. 144.

Peel, D. A., & Thomas, D. A. (1988). Outcome uncertainty and the demand for football: An analysis of match attendances in the English football league. *Scottish Journal of Political Economy*, 35(3), 242–249.

Peel, D. A., & Thomas, D. A. (1992). The demand for football: Some evidence on outcome uncertainty. *Empirical Economics*, 17(2), 323–331.

Penn, R., & Berridge, D. (2016). The dynamics of quadropoly: League position in English football between 1888 and 2010. *The International Journal of the History of Sport*, 33(3), 325–340.

Poli, R., Besson, R., & Ravenel, L. (2015). *Mapping transfer fees in football*. Retrieved from www.football-observatory.com/IMG/sites/b5wp/2015/119/en/

Poli, R., Besson, R., & Ravenel, L. (2016). *Exporting countries: Brazil and France head the table*. Retrieved from www.football- observatory.com/IMG/sites/b5wp/2016/167/en/

Poli, R., Ravenel, L., & Besson, R. (2016a). *Foreign players in football teams*. Retrieved from www.football-observatory.com/IMG/sites/mr/mr12/en/

Premier League. (2015). *Premier league awards UK live broadcast rights for 2016/17 to 2018/19* [Press release]. Retrieved from www.premierleague.com/en-gb/news/news/2014-15/feb/100215-premier-league-uk-live-broadcasting-rights-announced.html

Quirk, J. P., & Fort, R. D. (1992). *Pay dirt: The business of professional team sports*. Princeton, NJ: Princeton University.

Rottenberg, S. (1956). The baseball players' labor market. *Journal of Political Economy, 64*(3), 242–258.

Schmidt, M. B., & Berri, D. J. (2001). Competitive balance and attendance the case of major league baseball. *Journal of Sports Economics, 2*(2), 145–167.

Scully, G. W. (1989). *The business of major league baseball.* Chicago, IL: University of Chicago Press.

Slater, M. (2015, May 18). *Michel Platini: UEFA to 'ease' financial fair play rules.* Retrieved from www.bbc.com/sport/football/32784375

Sloane, P. J. (1976). Restriction of competition in professional team sports. *Bulletin of Economic Research, 28*(1), 3–22.

Szymanski, S. (2001). Income inequality, competitive balance and the attractiveness of team sports: Some evidence and a natural experiment from English Soccer. *The Economic Journal, 111*(469), 69–84.

Szymanski, S. (2015). *Money and Soccer: A soccernomics guide.* New York: Nation Books.

Thomas, L., Duckworth, R., & Gonzalez, F. (2015, June 11). *La Liga's media rights: The new law that prompted suspension of spanish football.* Retrieved from www.lawinsport.com/blog/squire-patton-boggs/item/la-liga-s-media-rights-the-new-law-that-prompted-suspension-of-spanish-football

Tomkins, P. (2013). *These turbulent times: Liverpool FC's search for success.* London: GPRF.

Tomkins, P., Riley, G., & Fulcher, G. (2010). *Pay as you play: The true price of success in the Premier league Era.* London: GPRF.

Tyler, J. (2015, August 12). *The premier league's most valuable kits, 2015–16.* Retrieved from www.espn.com/espn/story/_/id/13424241/premier-league-most-valuable-kits-2015-16

UEFA. (2015a). *Financial fair play: All you need to know.* Retrieved from www.uefa.com/community/news/newsid=2064391.html

UEFA. (2015b). *UEFA welcomes European Court of Justice ruling on financial fair play* [Press release]. Retrieved from www.uefa.org/mediaservices/newsid=2267061.html

UEFA. (2016). *2016/17 Champions league revenue distribution* [Press release]. Retrieved from www.uefa.com/uefachampionsleague/news/newsid=2398575.html

UEFA. (2017). *European club football's financial turnaround* [Press release]. Retrieved from www.uefa.org/protecting-the-game/club-licensing-and-financial-fair-play/news/newsid=2435355.html

Vöpel, H. (2013). *A Zidane clustering theorem: Why top players tend to play in one team and how the competitive balance can be restored.* HWWI Research Paper I-3.

Zimbalist, A. S. (2002). *Competitive balance in sports leagues: An introduction.* Thousand Oaks, CA: Sage.

Zimbalist, A. S. (2003). Competitive balance conundrums response to fort and Maxcy's comment. *Journal of Sports Economics, 4*(2), 161–163

Chapter 6

Competitive balance in the Chinese soccer league

Jie Xu, Scott Tainsky, Liang Wei, and Natalie L. Smith

Introduction

Sport leagues across the globe often seek out competitive balance due to its presumed predictive influence on consumer demand (Dittmore & Crow, 2010). Despite the Chinese Football Association's long-standing goal to create a league recognized among the best in the world, it has been plagued with both scandal and possible competitive balance issues. To achieve international attention, for years teams have invested considerable sums in numerous star coaches and players including Marcello Lippi, Alessandro Diamanti, Dai Lin and Wang Dalei, among others. Of late, player transfer spending among Chinese teams exceeds even the most lucrative ones in Europe. Case in point, during the most recent transfer window, Chinese teams outspent Barclay's Premier League (England) teams 311 to 253 million Euros, culminating in Jiangsu Suning's 50 million Euros purchase of Alex Teixeira (The National, 2016).

Although CSL policy restricts the number of foreign players on each team (i.e., five per team), and the maximum number of foreign players on the pitch (i.e., four per team), no restrictions govern the salary of foreign players. Nevertheless, the league has built only modest popularity within China and is recognized internationally more for corruption – including illegal betting, on-pitch violence, and match fixing – than quality football. As a point of reference, the International Federation of Football History and Statistics ranked the CSL as the 34th best league in the world in 2013 (IFFHS, 2014), a considerable rise from its 2012 ranking (70th), but still trailing both neighboring S. Korea (23rd) and Japan (30th).

To provide a brief history, since 2004 the top football league in China has been known as the CSL. The league was rebranded from the Chinese Football Association Jia-A League, which itself represented the highest-level professional football competition from 1994–2003. The CSL began with 12 teams in 2004, growing since that time to its current roster of 16 teams. The CSL is an open league whose schedule follows a traditional double round robin format. Similar to the most prestigious leagues in Europe with respect to the UEFA Champions League, the top three finishing teams in CSL as well as the winner of the Chinese FA Cup earn berths in the lucrative Asian Football Championship Champions League.

Beyond the aforementioned notorious international distinctions, Chinese scholars have questioned whether the league may also be plagued by competitive balance issues (e.g., Chen, 2013; Zhang, Zhang, & Wang, 2010). Indeed, the relatively young league has already experienced its share of dynasties, with Dalian Shide (previously Dalian Wanda) winning eight of ten titles from 1994–2005 (the 2003 title was vacated by Shanghai Shenhua following its match-fixing scandal), Shandong Luneng winning in 1999 and three times from 2006–2010, and Guangzhou Evergrande three-peating from 2011–2013. Furthermore, although Shanghai Shenhua has won only one title, it has been runner up a remarkable eight times.

In response to the importance ascribed by scholars and league managers alike as to the competitive balance (hereafter CB) of sports leagues generally and the CSL specifically, in this research, we measure CB of the CSL since its inception in 1994 using several of the most popular metrics in the previous literature. We compare the CSL to a number of the most successful European leagues using these metrics, examining how various competing preferences may exert influence in opposite directions as it relate to league balance. To preface some of our speculation regarding league balance expanded on in the Discussion, both products of China's rich history and tradition, national pride may drive the domestic league in the direction of competitive imbalance in order to benefit the league's top teams in international club competition. By contrast, intragroup harmony may induce more balance, as the notion of a harmonious culture emphasizes the balance within the society, nature and humanity.

This chapter proceeds as follows. In the next section, we review the related work on CB and particularly that on Chinese professional sports. The following section details our data and approach to measuring CB for the CSL. We then detail the results and comparisons to top European football leagues. In the penultimate section, we explore how China's traditional cultural values maybe related to league balance. Conclusions are presented in the final section.

Competitive balance

Sport scholars have created a number of metrics to account for different dimensions of balance (for a comprehensive review, please see Fort & Maxcy, 2003; Lenten, 2015). Both Western and Chinese scholars have calculated and discussed CB across a range of professional sports leagues. Table 6.1 shows a broad summary of the empirical analyses of CB in Western football leagues, while Table 6.2 lists the studies have been conducted on Chinese sports. The previous research highlights a precedent of using the standard deviation of winning percentages and the Competitive Balance Ratios as among the most commonly used measures in the research.

Table 6.1 CB analyses of Western football leagues

Paper	League	Measure
Brandes and Franck (2007)	German 1.Bundesliga	ISD
	English Premier League	CR5
	English football league championship	HHI
	Italian Serie A	
	Italian Serie B	
	French Ligue 1	
Cain and Haddock (2006)	Major League Baseball	ISD
	English Football league	
Fort (2007)	English Football League	RSD
Goossens (2006)	European football leagues	RSD, Gini, CBR, Relative entropy, HHI, Strength Index, Surprise Index
Koning (2000)	Dutch football	CR
Owen and King (2013)	English Premier League	RSD
		ASD*
Owen (2012)	English Premier League	RSD

Previous studies have compared the CSL to Western professional sports leagues in terms of CB; however, these studies have methodological flaws. Specifically, many of the CB metrics used in CSL analyses do not match up precisely with the measures as they are defined in the CB literature familiar to Western scholars. For example, Chen (2013) first calculated the CSL's actualized standard deviation of win percent (ASD) and idealized standard deviation of win percent (ISD), and then calculated the relative standard deviation of win percent (RSD). However, although the author references Fort and Quirk (1995), the ISD formula utilized differs from theirs and does not account for draws. Curiously, the author also employs an RSD formula generated for a two-point system when three points in the table are awarded for a CSL win. Similarly He, Zhang, and Wu's (2009) comparison of the CSL, English Premier League, and NBA aims to compare different sports altogether (i.e., football and basketball) and employing different ranking systems (i.e., win percentage versus points awarded for wins). It is therefore necessary to calculate CSL's CB across several metrics and over the duration of the league's existence to begin to answer whether balance is indeed a league issue, in what ways league balance manifests, and to subsequently make appropriate comparisons to the values of other major football leagues. Moreover, multiple measures targeting different aspects of league balance have the capacity to illuminate comparative issues across leagues.

Table 6.2 CB analyses of Chinese professional sport leagues

Author	League	Season	Measure
Bai (2012)	CBA, NBA, and European professional basketball	2006–2011	ASD, ISD, RSD, HHI C5, C5CBI
Chen (2013)	CSL	2010–2012	ASD, ISD, RSD, HHI
He (2005)	CBA, Jia A	2003–2004	Win% for each team, and using X-square to test the average win% of top 4, middle 4 and last 4 teams for 2003–2004 season
He, Zhang, and Wu (2009)	NBA, English Premier League, CSL	2004–2008	ASD, CBR
Huang (2007)	CBA	1995–2007	ASD, ISD, RSD, HHI, Top K Ranking
Sun, Du, Wang, and Yang (2010)	CBA and NBA	2000–2010	RSD
Yan (2013)	CBA	1995–2012	ASD, ISD, RSD, HHI
Zhang, Zhang, and Wang (2010)	CSL	1998–1999	Kendall's Rank Correlation Coefficient
Zhao and Wang (2012)	CSL, Premier League, La Liga, Bundesliga, Serie A, Ligue 1	2007–2012	C5, C5ICB, HHI, HICB

Notes: Top K ranking in Huang (2007) applies Goossen's (2006) measure. Huang used the total number of teams among the top three in four seasons.

CBR: as developed by Humphreys (2002).

C5:C5 = total points of top 5 teams/total points of all teams in the league, and C5ICB:,

$C5ICB = \dfrac{C5}{5/N} * 100$, N is the total number of teams in one league.

CBA: Chinese Basketball Association.

National pride and harmony

National pride is discussed as an important basis for the staging of mega-events and competing in international sports for the Chinese people. For example, Heslop, Nadeau, and O'Reilly (2010) argued that there is "a tradition of national pride and an East Asian culture characterized by the importance of 'face'" (p. 417). Furthermore, they contended that national pride likely plays a significant role in the vast support of Chinese fans for Chinese hopefuls in international sport competitions (Heslop et al., 2010). This has not, to date, transcended international competition to professional club sport in spite of strong Chinese ambition to create a well-respected national football league. Like Table Tennis and other sports beloved by Chinese fans, the CSL has not regularly experienced the same fervor as the Olympics and other international sports competitions, nor has it reached the stability of national club leagues in Europe or the Americas.

A notable exception to the relative disinterest in professional sports spectatorship took place in 2013 when CSL champions Guangdong Evergrande competed with FC Seoul in the Asian Football Confederation Champions League Final. More than 120 million Chinese spectators viewed the second leg of the final on television, the largest football audience on CCTV-5 over the past decade (which includes FIFA World Cup and Olympic games; AFC, 2013), thus displaying the tremendous potential of the league should it adequately capture the attention of the Chinese viewing public.

Given the undeniable nationalistic sentiment of Chinese fans, a traditional collectivist approach to the CSL would organize the league to create conditions where a super-team or super-teams could emerge to represent China in international club competition. If there is a strong nationalistic drive in fashioning league policy, this could result in a large concentration of talent accumulation (and, by extension, winning) in the teams that represent China and the CSL in international club matches.

Harmony is also an important concept in Chinese traditional culture. Originating from Taoism, which advocates that human beings should live in harmony with nature, the cosmos and the universe, harmony also emphasizes the fundamental principles of nature, society, and humanity (Low, 2011). Several classical statements on harmony are considered to be the core of Chinese traditional culture. For example, Chinese people believe that "harmony grows profit" (Low, 2011, p. 114). Also the Chinese traditional culture dictates interpersonal conflicts should be avoided if they "disturb the harmony between person and environment or among person" (Chen, 2001). The centrality of harmony among the Chinese notwithstanding, it has not been studied as a criterion of sports competition policy. If harmony is indeed a critical factor in the creation of policy or even simply the milieu among individuals competing in the league, then individuals and teams competing in Chinese sports may desire to increase the quality of harmony with one another. One indicator of increased harmony may be a high level of CB across all teams in the CSL.

Method

The data set utilized in this study was collected from the official website of the CSL, which includes all game records from 1994–2013. This study is restricted in its focus on within-season balance, for which there are a number of potential measurements. We have utilized several among the most popular CB measurements, specifically selecting those that will allow comparisons to other major football leagues and distinguish the possible effects of national pride and harmony. Here we emphasize that this is not intended to rule out rival hypotheses, rather solely to quantify the CB and introduce possible explanations related to culture. The measures include the ASD, ISD and RSD, and the concentration ratio (CR).

ASD is the ex post value of teams' winning in a single season and is a natural measurement of competitive balance (Owen, 2010). We follow Owen and King (2013) in calculating ASD as

$$ASD = \sqrt{\sum_{i=1}^{N} (p_i - \bar{p})^2 / (N-1)},$$

in which p_i = points for team i/ the maximum possible points total attainable by team i in a given season. $\bar{p}$ is the league's mean points ratio and N is the number of teams in the league.

The ISD utilized in this research uses Owen's (2012) formula because the CSL awards three points for a win. The equation used to calculate ISD is

$$ISD = \sqrt{\left[\frac{(1-d)(d+9)}{4} \right] / 9G}$$

(Owen, 2012, p. 89), where d is the proportion of draws, and G is the number of games in a given season.

RSD is typically calculated by ASD/ISD (e.g., Fort, 2007), however this leads to values below unity as shown by Owen and King (2013). As Goossens (2006) argued, this implies "a competition that is more equal than when the league is perfectly balanced" (p. 87). Thus, we also use RSD*(=RSD/RSD^{ub}) and ASD*(=ASD/ASD^{ub}) as is common to the recent studies of CB (e.g., Owen, 2010; Owen, 2012; Owen & King, 2013) and the upper bound as defined by Owen (2010, p. 39) $RSD^{ub} = \dfrac{ASD^{ub}}{ISD}$.

The concentration ratio utilized here is that as defined by Koning (2000) and Haan, Koning and van Wittelostuijn (2002). As stated by Koning (2000), "the concentration ratio is not a measure of competitive balance in the whole competition; it applies to the quality of the top teams" (p. 426). If CR is high, then the top teams did not lose many points to weaker teams. Typically winning success of the top teams have been taken as

$$CR_t^n = \frac{\sum_{I=1}^{n} P_{it}}{n * W * (2 * N - n - 1)},$$

where N is the number of teams in season t, W is the number of points awarded for a win, P_{it} is the number of points accumulated by the ith team in season t, n represents the top n teams, with five serving as the most common quantity of teams representing the top.

Results

The CSL results are shown in Table 6.3 and discussed as follows. The Ratio of Standard Deviation (RSD) for each season from 1994–2013 is depicted in Figure 6.1. The RSD result shows that the most imbalanced season is 2008. Very few seasons (e.g., 1999, 2005, and 2008) result in an RSD higher than 2, but most seasons are above 1.5. The exceptions – the most balanced seasons – are 1994, 2004, 2009, 2010, and 2012. There is no clear pattern of the league becoming more or less balanced, although the seasonal balance appears to have become more volatile since the rebranding of the league in 2004. The pattern of RSD* is similar with that of the traditional RSD. RSD* tells us that the most imbalanced season is 2005 and the most balanced season 2009. Still no clear trend of more or less balance over the entirety of the league's existence emerges in Figure 6.1.

The concentration ratio places more emphasis on how top teams perform relative to others in the league. From Figure 6.2, we see the top five teams

Table 6.3 Competitive balance of the CSL

Year	ASD	ISD	RSD	RSD*	CR5	CR3
1994	0.0971	0.0909	1.0681	0.3095	0.5000	0.4778
1995	0.1479	0.0923	1.6027	0.4713	0.7333	0.7222
1996	0.1383	0.0853	1.6215	0.4406	0.6815	0.6667
1997	0.1360	0.0886	1.5347	0.4335	0.6778	0.6944
1998	0.1257	0.0827	1.5201	0.4052	0.6667	0.6944
1999	0.1666	0.0808	2.0617	0.5372	0.6606	0.6481
2000	0.1322	0.0839	1.5761	0.4263	0.7000	0.6944
2001	0.1634	0.0871	1.8762	0.5270	0.7333	0.6898
2002	0.1312	0.0814	1.6127	0.4252	0.6889	0.6880
2003	0.1390	0.0816	1.7027	0.4503	0.7000	0.6923
2004	0.0977	0.0882	1.1077	0.3112	0.6370	0.6111
2005	0.1944	0.0857	2.2690	0.6268	0.7909	0.7870
2006	0.1576	0.0806	1.9550	0.5107	0.7250	0.7265
2007	0.1299	0.0791	1.6429	0.4210	0.6861	0.6709
2008	0.1765	0.0772	2.2862	0.5744	0.7462	0.7222
2009	0.0732	0.0763	0.9588	0.2382	0.6128	0.5913
2010	0.1020	0.0761	1.3393	0.3318	0.6538	0.6389
2011	0.1259	0.0779	1.6172	0.4097	0.6795	0.6786
2012	0.0926	0.0774	1.1961	0.3013	0.6385	0.6349
2013	0.1508	0.0785	1.9213	0.4907	0.6974	0.7421

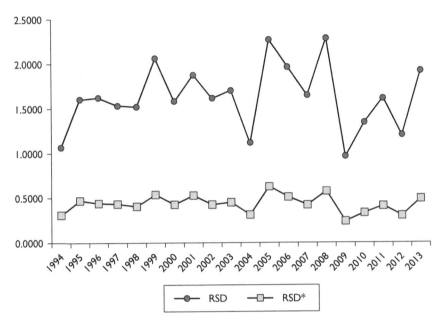

Figure 6.1 RSD and RSD* of the CSL 1994–2013

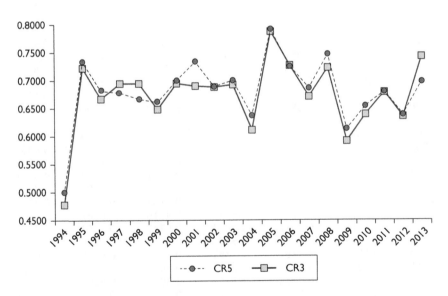

Figure 6.2 CRs of the CSL 1994–2013

in each year captured around 70% of the number of points that they could obtain. CR5 was at a low in 1994 (50%), and peaked in 2005 at around 80%. Like the RSD and RSD*, CR5 remained fairly consistent until 2004 whereupon the seasonal measure became less stable, although not as much as the RSD.

Because the top three teams of the league are promoted to play in the AFC Champions League, we also calculated the CR3 for each season. The pattern and values of CR3 are similar to the CR5 in most seasons, with the top three teams capturing around 70% of the available points. CR3 was also at a low at the beginning of the time series (around 48%) and peaked in 2005 (around 79%).

Discussion

Comparisons of CB measures for the CSL

It is evident that the same general patterns emerge across the three measurements (see Figure 6.3). There is no clear increasing or decreasing trend of competitive balance, although the values are less stable during the most

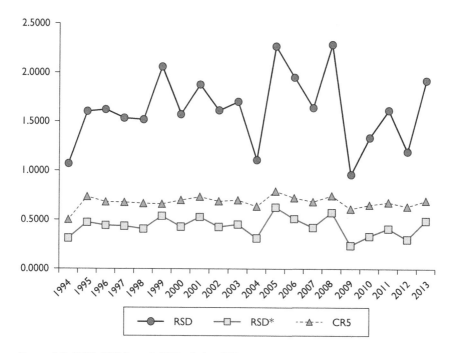

Figure 6.3 RSD, RSD*, and CR5 of the CSL

recent decade, from 2004–2013. The two most imbalanced seasons during this period are 2005 and 2008. The most balanced season prior to the reorganization is 1994, and the most balanced season following reorganization is 2009. Observing individual seasons across the three measures, some interesting findings materialize. In 1999, CR5 shows a relatively balanced league, while RSD and RSD* paint a different picture. The opposite is true in 2000 when the RSD shows a relative balanced league while CR5 describes imbalance.

Most notably, across all three measurements, 1994 and 2004 are the two most balanced seasons. It is clear that the league began as a balanced league and returned to such with the CSL rebranding. Upon reflection, this pattern is expected according to product life cycle theory in combination with the value of harmony. Rebranding is used to promote the product's growth when product life cycle enters into the decline period (Berry, 1988). Essentially, 1994 is also a "rebranding" year during the development process of Chinese Super League, since, although the league's inauguration had been announced earlier, 1994 marked the season of full implementation. As with most products, in the beginning there is an increase in communication across "departments," in this case teams (Klepper, 1996). This increase in communication could influence the relative balance in 1994 and 2004.

While some rebranding strategies fail due to a lack of stakeholder buy-in (Miller & Merrilees, 2013), the values of Chinese culture discussed in this chapter may have played a role in the buy-in for a league branding and rebranding. The peaks of balance could therefore be both a reflection of the increased communication that occurs at the beginning of a product's life cycle (Klepper, 1996) due to an increase of shared practice, as well as the desire to be harmonious in those interactions based on Chinese cultural traditions.

Besides these two seasons of birth and rebirth, the most balanced season was 2009. This however may be an anomaly due to scandal rather than a reflection of product life cycle or cultural norms around harmony. In 2009 Chendu Blades and Guangzhou GPC were paneled because of bribery. Were it not for this scandal, two different franchises, Hangzhou Greentown and Chongqing Lifan, would have been relegated.

Comparison to major UEFA leagues

In this section the CB of European football leagues is compared to that of the CSL. The top four leagues according to UEFA coefficients, namely the German Bundesliga, English Premier League, Italia Serie A, and French Ligue 1, were selected to compare with the CSL. With the exception of 1999, 2005 and 2008, the CSL has been among the most balanced leagues based on the RSD (Table 6.4; Figure 6.4). As the RSD measures the relative balance across all teams, this would provide some suggestion that harmony

Table 6.4 RSD comparison of European football leagues and the CSL

Year	German Bundesliga	English Premier League	Italia Serie A	French Ligue 1	CSL
1994	1.9824	1.9616	1.9834	1.5991	1.0681
1995	1.4041	1.8767	1.8422	1.4980	1.6027
1996	1.6069	1.5449	1.6379	1.7607	1.6215
1997	1.2957	1.5312	2.0981	1.5680	1.5347
1998	1.8450	1.7833	1.5932	1.8024	1.5201
1999	1.7418	1.9692	2.0198	1.0618	2.0617
2000	1.3154	1.7379	1.9017	1.3508	1.5761
2001	1.9296	2.0758	1.9880	1.3908	1.8762
2002	1.4452	1.8724	1.9092	1.5113	1.6127
2003	1.8335	1.9102	2.3144	1.7346	1.7027
2004	1.7715	2.1574	1.8041	1.3527	1.1077
2005	1.9277	2.2290	2.0800	1.7434	2.2690
2006	1.5993	1.9620	2.0778	1.3457	1.9550
2007	1.7066	2.4508	1.9822	1.6489	1.6429
2008	1.8892	2.2536	1.9170	1.8680	2.2862
2009	1.7748	2.3285	1.8360	1.8661	0.9588
2010	1.5923	1.6166	1.8517	1.5371	1.3393
2011	1.9835	2.1413	1.8733	1.8208	1.6172
2012	2.0947	2.2426	2.1106	1.6922	1.1961
2013	2.2071	2.3119	2.3767	2.0291	1.9213

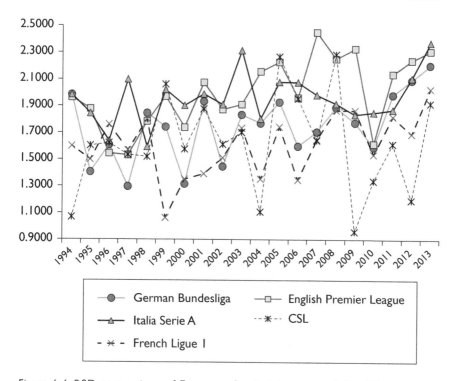

Figure 6.4 RSD comparison of European football leagues and the CSL

across teams may play a role in Chinese league competitiveness. Although it is beyond the intended scope of this research, this perhaps explains part of UEFA's motivation for Financial Fair Play – as competitive imbalance within leagues widens, it could hinder maximizing consumer interest across the leagues, although the exact influence on CB is up for debate (Sass, 2014).

Besides the comparison of RSD, we also examine the concentration ratio (CR5 and CR3) comparison of European football leagues and the CSL (Tables 6.5 & 6.6; Figure 6.5; CR5 figure available upon request of the authors). It is unclear precisely which league is most balanced over the past two decades. Of particular interest to this study, the CSL's concentration ratios show different patterns than the RSD, mostly before 2007. The CSL's CRs stand out as high among the five football leagues in 1995–1997, 2000, 2002, and 2005–2006.

While an increase in communication along with an emphasis on harmony may have produced more CB in the CSL after 2004, the rebrand process, much like the birth of the product (i.e. CSL in 1994), would result in growth (Day, 1981; Kunkel, Funk & King, 2014). However, because the sub-brands (i.e. teams) have their own unique identity and capacities, this may result in an uneven success for each sub-brand (Kunkel, Funk & King, 2014). This could explain the volatility in competitive balance in the 2005 season.

Table 6.5 CR5 comparison of European football leagues and the CSL

Year	German Bundesliga	English Premier League	Italia Serie A	French Ligue 1	CSL
1994	0.7244	0.7035	0.7067	0.6588	0.5000
1995	0.6356	0.7000	0.6978	0.6588	0.7333
1996	0.7044	0.6667	0.6578	0.6569	0.6815
1997	0.6511	0.6706	0.7178	0.6844	0.6778
1998	0.7044	0.6980	0.6756	0.7267	0.6667
1999	0.6844	0.7157	0.7111	0.6267	0.6606
2000	0.6578	0.6922	0.7200	0.6667	0.7000
2001	0.7311	0.7471	0.7089	0.6733	0.7333
2002	0.6711	0.7078	0.6978	0.6431	0.6889
2003	0.7267	0.7059	0.7533	0.7020	0.7000
2004	0.7000	0.7333	0.7059	0.6255	0.6370
2005	0.7244	0.7608	0.6059	0.6569	0.7909
2006	0.7000	0.7216	0.6922	0.6216	0.7250
2007	0.6978	0.7765	0.7235	0.6549	0.6861
2008	0.7200	0.7725	0.7216	0.6980	0.7462
2009	0.6933	0.7510	0.7137	0.7059	0.6128
2010	0.7244	0.6902	0.7059	0.6392	0.6538
2011	0.7378	0.7490	0.6882	0.7059	0.6795
2012	0.7289	0.7588	0.7314	0.6824	0.6385
2013	0.7689	0.7902	0.7647	0.7255	0.6974

Table 6.6 CR3 comparison of European football leagues and the CSL

Year	German Bundesliga	English Premier League	Italia Serie A	French Ligue I	CSL
1994	0.7049	0.7056	0.6910	0.6636	0.4778
1995	0.6354	0.7130	0.6840	0.6420	0.7222
1996	0.7049	0.6512	0.6493	0.6481	0.6667
1997	0.6563	0.6790	0.7188	0.6771	0.6944
1998	0.7049	0.7160	0.6771	0.7153	0.6944
1999	0.7118	0.7191	0.7083	0.6215	0.6481
2000	0.6354	0.6759	0.7535	0.6632	0.6944
2001	0.7188	0.7531	0.7292	0.6563	0.6898
2002	0.6667	0.7099	0.6875	0.6173	0.6880
2003	0.7188	0.7531	0.7708	0.7099	0.6923
2004	0.6910	0.7870	0.7315	0.6451	0.6111
2005	0.7396	0.7901	0.6265	0.6636	0.7870
2006	0.7083	0.7407	0.7222	0.6265	0.7265
2007	0.7153	0.7870	0.7377	0.6667	0.6709
2008	0.6944	0.7994	0.7160	0.7037	0.7222
2009	0.6806	0.7593	0.7160	0.6821	0.5913
2010	0.7222	0.6852	0.7037	0.6420	0.6389
2011	0.7569	0.7654	0.7037	0.7253	0.6786
2012	0.7708	0.7469	0.7315	0.6821	0.6349
2013	0.7813	0.7778	0.8179	0.7407	0.7421

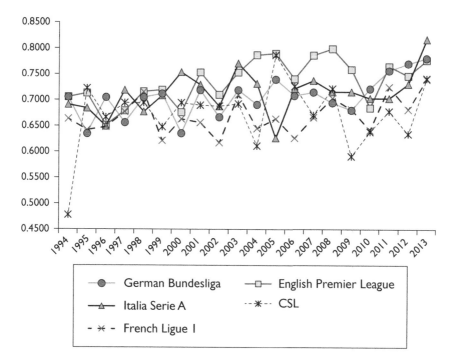

Figure 6.5 CR3 comparison of European football leagues and the CSL

National pride, although a central characteristic of Chinese culture, it is not one exclusive to this culture. This may partially explain the relatively middling CR ranking over time. From the tables and figures, it is apparent that the English Premier League regularly showed higher CR values, especially after 1999. Since that time, and particularly from 2005–2012, the traditional English Big Four teams (i.e., Liverpool, Manchester United, Chelsea, and Arsenal) and of late Manchester City have consistently turned in good performances. Thus, although national pride may well impact the concentration of winning among top teams, it does not translate into a clear impact on CR relative to other leagues.

Conclusion

The purpose of this study was to analyze the CSL with specific reference to how the concepts of national pride and harmony may influence the league's competitive balance. This study provides insights into these concepts via two within-season balance metrics utilized in studying the CSL and is precise in employing the metrics that are familiar to CB scholars.

CR5 analyzes the concentration of winning at the top of the league within each season. Although convention dictated our measurement of the top five teams' winning, a more practical measure for the study of the CSL is that of the top three teams, those who earn the opportunity to play in the Asia Football League games. In comparison to top European leagues it seems that the CSL can enact policy to strengthen its top teams to become more competitive in international club competitions without being conspicuous as having manipulated this to a point of CB concern.

The RSD looks at the whole league and not solely the top teams relative to all others. In this respects the CSL appears to be among the more balanced leagues. A potential explanation is that the culture of harmony is fairly influential on league balance. That the CSL is comparable to the very successful UEFA leagues explored in this preliminary investigation suggests that CB may not be the issue some Chinese scholars and officials project it to be in hindering the league's international reputation.

Figure 6.6 shows very similar patterns between the CB metrics pre- and post-establishment of the league and rebrand. Notably, and conceding that it is not the primary endeavor of this work to rule out rival hypotheses, the culture of harmony may greatly influence league policy at the time of establishment and reorganization, where it seems non-coincidental that balance is greatest at these points in time. This may indicate the significance of harmony to league members, however imbalance grows as the league develops and moves from these moments of intensive regulation. Future research may build on the comparisons made in this research and endeavor to discover qualitatively the extent to which league officials consider the various forms of balance associated with their league objectives.

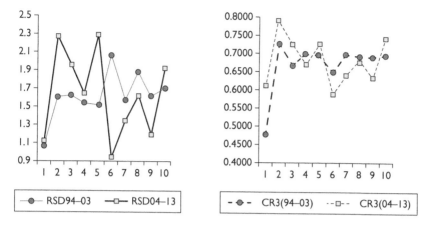

Figure 6.6 Comparison within the CSL pre- and post-reorganization

Acknowledgments

We are indebted to Leif Brandes and Brian Mills for their helpful comments on the manuscript.

References

AFC. *ACL Final attracts record TV viewers*. Retrieved on March 16, 2014, from www.the-afc.com/en/about-afc/afc-departments/marketing/27198-acl-tvrecord-131 113.html

Bai, P. (2012). *Contrasting the competitive balance CBA, NBA, and Euro league* (Master's thesis). Retrieved from China Masters' Theses Full-test Database.

Berry, N. C. (1988). Revitalizing brands. *Journal of Consumer Marketing*, *5*(3), 15–20.

Brandes, L., & Franck, E. (2007). Who made who? An empirical analysis of competitive balance in European football leagues. *Eastern Economic Journal*, *33*(3), 379–403.

Cain, L. P., & Haddock, D. D. (2006). Research notes, measuring parity: trying into the idealized standard deviation. *Journal of Sports Economics*, *7*, 330–340.

Chen, K. (2013). Research of the competitive balance in Chinese super league. *Journal of Guangzhou Sport University*, *33*(4), 28–30.

Chen, Y. (2001). Chinese values, health and nursing. *Journal of Advanced Nursing*, *36*(2), 270–273.

Day, G. S. (1981). The product life cycle: Analysis and application issues. *Journal of Marketing*, *45*(4), 60–67.

Dittmore, S. W., & Crow, C. M. (2010). The influence of the Bowl Championship Series on competitive balance in college football. *Journal of Applied Sport Management: Research That Matters*, *2*(1), 7–19.

Fort, R. (2007). Comments on "measuring parity". *Journal of Sports Economics*, 8(6), 642–651.

Fort, R., & Maxcy, J. (2003). Competitive balance in sports leagues: An introduction. *Journal of Sport Economics*, 4, 154–160.

Fort, R., & Quirt, J. (1995). Cross-subsidization, incentives, and outcomes in professional team sports leagues. *Journal of Economic Literature*, 38(3), 1265–1299.

Goossens, K. (2006). Competitive balance in European football: Comparison by adapting measures and national measure of seasonal imbalance and top 3. *Rivista di Diritto ed Economia dello Sport*, 2, 77–122.

Haan, M., Koning, R., & van Witteloostuijn, A. (2002). *Market forces in European football*. Research Report 02F18, SOM, University of Groningen.

He, B. (2005). Research on balance of competition of the professional basketball. *Journal of Beijing Sport University*, 28(7), 990–992, 994.

He, W., Zhang, B., & Wu, Y. (2009). The measurement and analysis of competitive balance in professional team sports leagues. *China Sport Science*, 29(12), 12–18.

Heslop, L. A., Nadeau, J., & O'Reilly, N. (2010). China and the Olympics: Views of the insiders and outsiders. *International Marketing Review*, 27(4), 404–433.

Huang, G. (2007). The competitive balance in Chinese professional basket league matches. *Journal of TUS*, 22(5), 437–440.

IFFHS. (2014, January 29). *The strongest national league of the world*. Retrieved from www.iffhs.de/the-strongest-national-league-of-the-world/

Klepper, S. (1996). Entry, exit, growth, and innovation over the product life cycle. *The American Economic Review*, 86(3), 562–583.

Koning, R. H. (2000). Balance in competition in Dutch football. *The Statistician*, 49(3), 419–431.

Kunkel, T., Funk, D., & King, C. (2014). Developing a conceptual understanding of consumer-based league brand associations. *Journal of Sport Management*, 28(1), 49–67.Lenten, L. J. A. (2015). Measurement of competitive balance in conference and divisional tournament design. *Journal of Sports Economics*, 16, 3–25.

Low, K. C. P. (2011). Confucianism versus Taoism. *Conflict Resolution & Negotiation*, 4, 111–127.

Miller, D., & Merrilees, B. (2013). Rebuilding community corporate brands: A total stakeholder involvement approach. *Journal of Business Research*, 66(2), 172–179.

The National. (2016). *Chinese super league spent more during winter transfer window than English premier league*. Retrieved on March 30, 2016, from www.thenational.ae/sport/transfer-talk/chinese-super-league-spent-more-during-winter-transfer-window-than-english-premier-leagueOwen, P. D. (2010). Limitations of the relative standard deviation of win percentages for measuring competitive balance in sports leagues. *Economics Letters*, 109, 38–41.

Owen, P. D. (2012). Measuring parity in sports leagues with draws: Further comments. *Journal of Sports Economics*, 13(1), 85–95.

Owen, P. D., & King, N. (2013). *Competitive balance measures in sports leagues: The effects of variation in season length*. Economics Discussion Papers No. 1309. University of Otago. Retrieved from http://hdl.handle.net/10523/4151

Sass, M. (2014). Glory hunters, sugar daddies, and long-term competitive balance under UEFA financial fair play. *Journal of Sports Economics*. doi:10.1177/1527002514526412

Sun, R., Du, J., Wang, Z., & Yang, B. (2010). Comparative study on the "competitive balance" of CBA and NBA in recent ten years. *Journal of Wuyi University*, *29*(5), 93–97.

Yan, X. (2013). *The research on competitive balance of CBA* (Master's thesis). Retrieved from China Masters' Theses Full-test Database.

Zhang, B., Zhang, L., & Wang, Y. (2010). Dynamic competitive balance of China football association super league. *Journal of Shenyang Sport University*, *29*(6), 121–124, 133.

Zhao, J., & Wang, L. (2012). Competitive equilibrium of five European football leagues and the enlightenment to CSL. *Journal of Chengdu Sport University*, *38*(9), 55–57.

Section II

Marketing perspectives

Chapter 7

Psychographic profiling and segmenting Major Indoor Soccer League fans

Glaucio Scremin and Su Liu

Introduction

Football is a global sport. The game is played and consumed in all parts of the world. The 3.2 billion viewers who watched the 2014 FIFA men's World Cup ("2014 FIFA World Cup Brazil – Television Audience Report," 2015), the 265 million people – about 4% of the world population – who actively play football ("265 million playing football," 2007), and the Fédération Internationale de Football Association's (FIFA) higher country membership than that of the United Nations (FIFA: Six facts about world football's governing body, 2011) illustrate the ubiquity of football around the world. The global appeal of football is due, at least in part, to its simplicity, accessibility, and adaptability. The game of football has 17 simple rules, many of which (e.g., number of players, player's equipment, the ball) can be adapted to fit diverse environmental and playing conditions. Football can be played nearly anywhere using almost any round object as a ball – asphalt streets as a pitch, trash cans as goal posts, and thread socks bundled together as a ball.

Football comes in different shapes and sizes. The traditional and most popular version of the game – 11 versus 11 players on an outdoor grass field – is the dominant form, but it is far from being the only one. The traditional form of football imposes environmental, field, and space constraints that limit the practice of the game. To circumvent those constraints, many variations of the game of football organically surfaced overtime (e.g., futsal, beach football, street football, five-a-side, and indoor football). The rapid and exponential growth of two of these variants of football – futsal and beach football – led FIFA to recognize, sanction, and organize world tournaments for futsal since 1988 and for beach football since 2005. Futsal grew to be the most popular variant of football. The game evolved in cities where space was limited and where environmental conditions prevented traditional football from being played year round. Futsal is an indoor version of football played on a smaller, hard-surface field with a smaller goal and ball and five players on each side. The game is played in two fast-paced 20 minute halves packed with action, goals, and displays of skill.

The indoor football popularized in the United States was a version of football done the "the American way." Professional indoor football is played on synthetic turf on an oblong field in the shape and size of ice hockey rink with six players on each side. The game is divided in four 15-minute quarters. Walls instead of lines delimit the field of play. The walls keep the ball from going out of bounds and players can play off the walls thus making for a fast paced and exciting game. In some indoor football leagues, the game is scored on a point system. Goals have different point values depending on the distance where they are scored. For instance, goals scored on or beyond a 45-foot-arc are worth three points (Major Indoor Soccer League Rules of the Game 2002–2003). Indoor football incorporated many elements of more popular and traditional American sports (e.g., ice hockey's power play, basketball's three-point line, and multi-point scoring system) in an effort to appeal to American audiences, used to high scoring and fast-paced sports (Holroyd, 2010).

Indoor football grew in the mid-1970s, when the premier American outdoor professional football league, the NASL, organized the first large scale professional indoor football tournament. NASL leaders saw indoor football as an opportunity to increase fan's overall interest in football and generate additional revenue streams during the winter months, when outdoor football was unfeasible, but players were still under contract. In its 1975 inaugural season, the NASL indoor tournament was a success, both on and off the field, with average game attendance among its 16 teams of 9,000 fans (Holroyd, 2010). While NASL indoor league averaged game attendance dropped to 4,869 fans per game by the 1979–80 season, many teams continued to draw crowds of over 10,000 to their games, and some teams (e.g., Memphis and Atlanta) regularly attracted more fans to their indoor than their outdoor games (Litterer, 2010; Holroyd, 2010).

The success of the NASL indoor football league led to the creation of rival indoor professional football leagues. By the early 1980s, two leagues – the Super Soccer League, the Major Indoor Soccer League (MISL) – had entered the professional indoor football market. The MISL boosted the popularity of indoor football. In its first few seasons, the MISL average game attendance grew to 8,000 a game, and some clubs, such as St. Louis Steamers and Kansas City Comets, regularly outdrew their NBA and NHL competition (Litterer, 2010). When the NASL folded in 1984, the MISL became and remained the highest level of professional football in the United States until the inaugural MLS season in 1996 (Moore, 2016). Developing a version of football in the mold of more popular American professional team sports was a vital but not the only strategy used to attract audiences to indoor football. To increase the entertainment value of the game, leagues such as the MISL pioneered creative product extensions and promotional strategies. Professional indoor football teams hosted post game concerts, offered souvenir giveaways, and ran themed game day promotions to attract spectators to their games. Cheerleaders, extravagant mascots, music, and live artistic performances, and other gam theatrics entertained spectators during games. In some cases, those game theatrics generated more publicity for the indoor football than the quality of play on the field (Moore, 2016; Holroyd, 2010).

Despite the early success in creating a version of football palatable to American audiences and enhancing the entertainment value of the game with creative product extensions and promotional strategies, professional indoor football teams and leagues struggled to remain viable. In a saturated sports and entertainment marketplace, professional indoor football teams compete for the attention and dollars of consumers not only among themselves but also with other sports and with other forms of entertainment. Further, as a niche sport, professional indoor football receives limited media attention and fails to appeal to large audiences and big time sponsors, all of which limit its competitive power (Greenwell, Greenhalgh, & Stover, 2013).

To better package and deliver the professional indoor football product to consumers, a clear understanding of why people consume indoor football is essential.

Uncovering the motives behind sport consumption is no easy task. First, there are numerous reasons why sport spectators follow and consume sport (e.g., entertainment, vicarious achievement, social interaction). Moreover, some motives are more salient than others in directing and shaping sport consumption behavior. For example, Zorzou et al. (2014) found that self-identity, information, socialization, financial reasons and escape were the most important factors in explaining game attendance in Greek professional football. Karakaya, Yannopoulos, and Kefalaki (2016) found that supporting the team or athlete, entertainment, interest in football, and bonding with friends as the most important reasons for attending Greek professional football games. Second, sport spectators vary in their degree of fanship ranging from mere spectators to loyal fans. It is unknown which factors or combination thereof account for the difference in fanship behavior. Third, there are several factors that mediate and moderate the relationship between sport consumption motives and behavior. For example, the involvement and team identification constructs have been purported to link motivation antecedents to sport consumption behaviors such as game attendance (Funk & James, 2004; Funk, Ridinger, & Moorman, 2004).

Researchers in sociology, social psychology, marketing, and sport management have used different theoretical models (e.g., social identity theory, attitude theory) to further our understanding of sport fan behavior (e.g., Funk & Pastore, 2000, Heere & James, 2007a). Studies of sport team identification and sport fan motivation led to the discovery of relationships between team identification, psychological well-being, and self-esteem (e.g., Wann, 2006). In sport management, Funk and Pastore (2000) used contemporary attitude theory to study fan loyalty. These authors conceptualized fan loyalty in terms of underlying attitude properties (e.g., importance, knowledge, extremity, certainty) and its strength-related consequences (e.g., resistance and behavior). Funk and colleagues (2001, 2002, and 2003) tested how well several motivational variables explained the level of spectator support among women's professional football and basketball.

The purpose of this study was to test the proposition that team identity mediates the relationship between sport fan motives and team loyalty in professional indoor football fans. Secondarily, this investigation sought to uncover whether selected personal and social-situational factors have a moderating role in the relationships between professional indoor football fan motives and team identity and between team identity and team loyalty (Figure 7.1). From a practical perspective, creating sport fan loyalty and identification profiles based on their motives for sport consumption may prove very fruitful for sport marketers. Sport consumer profiles based solely on socio-demographic parameters (e.g., age, gender, socioeconomic status) are limited in scope in that not all consumers within a specific demographic have the same wants and needs. An alternative approach is to segment sport fans based on their motives for sport consumption and their level of team identification and loyalty. Thus, sport marketers could develop promotional and advertising campaigns targeted specifically to a given segment of sport fans with the same motivations for sport consumption and with similar levels of team identification and loyalty.

Review of literature

Motives of sport fans

Sport products and services provide consumers with a wide range of hedonic consumption motives. Hedonic motives relate to the experiential, subjective, and emotional nature of consumer choices. The escape, excitement, entertainment value, social interaction opportunities, and vicarious achievement associated with sport consumption are examples of hedonic motives. Sports consumers are also motivated by utilitarian reasons – instrumental, objective, and tangible benefits offered by sport products and services (Funk & James, 2006) (Funk, 2006). The price of admission to a sporting event as well as the convenience and accessibility of sport facilities are examples of utilitarian motives (Ross, 2007).

Stress and stimulation seeking motives include but are not limited to escape, excitement, and drama. For instance, attending a professional indoor football game may be motivated by a diversion from one's day-to-day routines. On the other hand, someone else may find that a professional indoor football game is not an escape from everyday life but that it provides quality and affordable entertainment. Achievement seeking motivations pertain to the vicarious achievement some sport fans attain through their connection with a sport's team. This psychological need is inherently

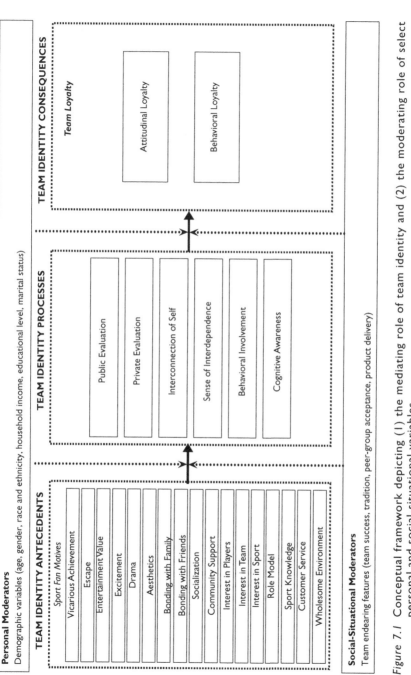

Personal Moderators
Demographic variables (age, gender, race and ethnicity, household income, educational level, marital status)

TEAM IDENTITY ANTECEDENTS

Sport Fan Motives

Vicarious Achievement
Escape
Entertainment Value
Excitement
Drama
Aesthetics
Bonding with Family
Bonding with Friends
Socialization
Community Support
Interest in Players
Interest in Team
Interest in Sport
Role Model
Sport Knowledge
Customer Service
Wholesome Environment

TEAM IDENTITY PROCESSES

Public Evaluation
Private Evaluation
Interconnection of Self
Sense of Interdependence
Behavioral Involvement
Cognitive Awareness

TEAM IDENTITY CONSEQUENCES

Team Loyalty

Attitudinal Loyalty

Behavioral Loyalty

Social-Situational Moderators
Team endearing features (team success, tradition, peer-group acceptance, product delivery)

Figure 7.1 Conceptual framework depicting (1) the mediating role of team identity and (2) the moderating role of select personal and social-situational variables

tied with the concept of basking in reflected glory (Cialdini et al., 1976). Social interaction motives deal with one's interest in socializing with family, friends, and other sport fans at games and other team related functions. Altogether these motivation categories encompass the social and psychological needs of sport consumers. In an effort to quantify the motives of sport consumers, researchers have developed numerous scales to measure sport consumption motivation.

Over the past decade the motives behind sport fanship have received considerable attention from sport management researchers (e.g., James & Ridinger, 2002; Mahony et al., 2002 Trail & James, 2001; Funk, Mahony, Nakazawa, & Hirakawa, 2001). These researchers have not only furthered our understanding of the motives of sport fans but also provided us with valid and reliable scales to assess their motives (e.g., Sport Interest Inventory, Motivation Scale for Sport Consumption). Beyond identifying the motives of sport fans, sport management researchers have also used the motives of sport fans to try to explain the level of sport interest (e.g., Funk & James, 2006), fan involvement (Funk, Ridinger, & Moorman, 2004), and team identity (e.g., Fink, Trail, & Anderson, 2003). For instance, Funk, Mahony, and Ridinger (2002b) showed that five motivational factors explained 54% of the variance in spectator support for women's professional football. Fink, Trail, and Anderson (2002) found that the sport fan motives explained 72% of the variance in team identification (Fink, Trail, & Anderson, 2002). Nonetheless, team identity was measured as a one-dimensional variable and thus failed to capture the true scope of the team identity construct (Heere & James, 2007a).

Sport management researchers also investigated whether sport fan motives differ according to gender (e.g., Fink, Trail, & Anderson, 2002; James & Ridinger, 2002; Wann, Schrader, & Wilsen, 1999), race and ethnicity (e.g., Armstrong, 1999; Bilyeu & Wann, 2002), age (e.g., Wann, 1995; Wann, Schrader, & Wilsen, 1999), type of sport (e.g., James & Ridinger, 2002; Robinson & Trail, 2005), economic factors (Pan, Gabert, McGaugh, & Branvold, 1997), and other environmental factors (Fink, Trail, & Anderson, 2002). Specifically, Wann, Schrader, and Wilsen (1999) report that while men scored higher in motivational items related to self-esteem, eustress, and aesthetic, women scored higher than men in family motivation items. James and Ridinger (2002) found additional gender differences in the motives of sport fans related to achievement, empathy, and knowledge. Over the years, an effort has been made to assess and measure consumer's interests, attitudes, and beliefs associated with the consumption of sport products. Several scales were developed but most of them have not been constructed under sound psychometrical grounds. Nevertheless, these research endeavors constitute the first attempts to uncover and operationalize the underlying motivational variables behind sport consumption.

Team identity

The concept of team identity can be understood as a form of group identity. One is thought to be identified with a group when one acknowledges that he or she is member of the group and attaches emotional significance to that membership (Tajfel, 1978). In this context, team identity is a part of one's self-concept that is based on his or her knowledge of belonging to a sport team and the emotional significance he or she attaches to that membership (Heere & James, 2007b). People are all members of different social groups. These groups can be generally classified as demographic categories (e.g., geographic, gender-based) and membership organizations (e.g., religious, political). One's relationship with his or her social groups and the worth he or she places on those relationships serve as the foundation for the social capital theory (Putnam, 2000). The theory of Social Capital posits that the collection of social groups we belong to, form communities that are part of larger social networks. Fans of sport team can be considered a social group and as such are a significant source of group identity. Thus, based on the social capital theory sport fans can also be viewed as a community that is part of a larger social network representing other social groups. For example, the fans of national teams (e.g., football, rugby) identify with their teams because of a geographic connection. The notion that sport teams not only serve as source of group identity but provide a symbolic representation of other communities was put forward by Heere and James (2007b). In their proposed model, Heere and James contend that external group identities (i.e., demographic categories and membership organizations) are antecedents of team identity. The influence of external group identities onto team identity has not been empirically tested, however.

Theoretical framework

Because of their purported link to behavior, several investigators have correlated motives for sport consumption with behavior measures. Several conceptual frameworks were put forth as an attempt to explain the role of sport consumer motivations in shaping and predicting behavior. Of particular interest for this investigation are the Fan Attitude Network (FAN) model (Funk & James, 2004) and the Psychological Continuum Model (PCM) (Funk & James, 2001; 2006).

The Fan Attitude Network model

Funk and James (2004) proposed a conceptual model to advance our understanding of attitude formation relative to sport teams. Funk and James called this model the FAN model. The FAN model proposes that through a process of internalization attitudes are formed and then changed. The

FAN model advances a process through which the fulfillment of dispositional needs serves as a catalyst for the internalization of a sport team. The internalization process culminates in a sport identity that mediates the formation of the structural property of attitude importance, which in turn influences the formation of additional structural attitude properties that subsequently impact attitude consequences such as fan loyalty. From this model, the researchers proposed two lines of research. The first deals with how dispositional needs interact with endearing characteristics of behavior formation. For instance, they contend that the relationship between dispositional needs and endearing characteristics may also provide a means to examine how motivation drives a fan's sport identity with a given team and how it may change over his/her lifetime. The second deals with how internalization can be used to understand how individuals form attitudes toward sport teams. Accordingly, investigating the influence of socializing agents on initial awareness of a sport team could also provide a better understanding of the impact of situational features on attitude formation and change. The conceptual considerations and future study recommendations made by Funk and James were adopted in this investigation. In Funk and James's conceptual model of attitude formation and change, sport identity plays a mediating role. The moderating role of endearing features is also proposed. In the current investigation, motivations for sport consumption (a component of the dispositional needs variable proposed by Funk and James) would be correlated with team identity and team loyalty (a type of attitudinal consequence) measures. The moderating role of selected endearing features was also examined.

The psychological continuum model

Beginning with the work of Cialdini et al. (1976), the research on sport spectators and fans has been grounded in a multi-disciplinary approach drawing from more established disciplines of sociology, psychology, consumer behavior, and marketing. From that point on, understanding the relationship between spectators or fans and sport teams have continued to be a topic of much interest (Wann et al., 1999). Nevertheless, it was not until Funk and James in 2001 that a theoretical framework was develop to guide understanding of the "underlying social-psychological process accounting for an individual's shift from initial awareness of a sport or team to subsequent allegiance" (Funk & James, 2001, p. 120). Funk and James (2001) conceived a theoretical framework to try to explain the psychological connections that fans experience with sports teams. In developing their model, they argued for the need of a theoretical framework that could guide our understanding of the underlying social-psychological process accounting for an individual's shift from initial awareness of a sport or team to subsequent allegiance as well as a need for existence of a model that would differentiate sport spectators from fans. Funk and James proposed that the PCM could specify the general parameters in which a relationship between an individual, sport, or athlete is mediated. They further conceptualized that these parameters operate in a continuum. The initial parameter, awareness, denotes when an individual first learns that certain sports, and/or teams exist, but does not have a specific favorite. The second parameter, attraction, indicates when an individual acknowledges having a favorite team or favorite sport based upon various social-psychological and demographic-based motives. On the third parameter, attachment, a psychological connection begins to crystallize, creating various degrees of association between the individual and the sport object (e.g., a favorite team). Attachment represents the degree or strength of association based upon the perceived importance attached to physical and psychological features associated with a team or sport. The fourth parameter, allegiance, an individual has become a loyal (or committed) fan of the sport or team. Allegiance results in influential attitudes that produce consistent and durable behavior, including consumer behavior. The utility of the PCM lies on the fact that it provides an initial framework for understanding and examining sport-related research in the context of an individual's psychological connection to sport and exploring the temporal process through which that connection moves. The authors further assert that although the PCM offers general parameters in which a relationship between an individual and a sport or team can be characterized, understanding how movement among and between these boundaries is mediated is not fully understood and future research needs to address these issues (Funk & James, 2001).

Funk and James (2006) revised the PCM to account for the inputs, processes, and outputs of each stage of psychological connection. Unlike previously, this time Funk and James tested portions of the model, which provided partial support for the model propositions. One of such propositions was the role of team identification as a mediating variable within the process of fan allegiance (i.e., loyalty) formation. However, Funk and James operationalized team identity as a one-dimensional variable and thus failed to capture the full array of connections between the team identity dimensions and other variables (e.g., dispositional needs). For instance, Funk and James (2001) proposed a comprehensive theoretical framework to explain an individual's psychological connection to sport. The PCM was developed as a vertical continuum and attempts to describe the increasing levels of commitment of sport spectators. Starting at the bottom level with awareness and moving up the ladder to attraction, attachment and allegiance, they provided the first integrated theoretical framework in the area of sport fan behavior.

Funk and James (2006) revised the PCM and tested some of its underlying assumptions. Although the authors found empirical support for the mediational role of attachment process, other parts of the model remain untested. One of such untested areas is the role of team identification in the development of fan loyalty. In Funk and James's revised PCM, team identification was proposed as an outcome of the attachment process and assessed as a one-dimensional variable. Recent work has suggested, however, that team identification is a multi-dimensional variable that may be linked to sport consumption behavior (Heere & James, 2007b, Funk & James, 2004). The revised model predicts among other things that team identity is an outcome variable of the attachment process and those dispositional needs are an input variable of level two outcomes. As with the FAN model discussed above, the model being proposed for this study can be understood within the framework of the revised PCM and that when tested can offer further support for proposed relationships of the revised PCM.

Method

Participants and procedures

A fan intercept method was used to survey spectators at two professional indoor football teams in the northeast region of the United States. Everyone who passed through the arena gates and appeared eighteen and older was approached and asked to participate in the study. Two research assistants were stationed one hour before each game at each entrance of the arenas where the games took place. Researchers were trained to politely approach game spectators and ask them to complete a questionnaire. The questionnaire contained a cover letter explaining the purpose of the study and instructions. For their participation, fans were given the option to enter in a draw to win a $100 gift certificate. Questionnaires were collected during the game breaks by the members of the research team or dropped off by the spectators at a research table located inside the arena concourse. The survey questionnaire contained a total of 106 items. Each item was presented in random order in a seven-point response format ranging from "7 = strongly agree" to "1 = strongly disagree."

Instrumentation

The Sport Interest Inventory (SII) was used to assess the motives of professional indoor football fans. In its last version, the SII contained eighteen unique sport fan motives. These eighteen motives include: (1) interest in sport, (2) interest in players, (3) bonding with family, (4) bonding with friends, (5) socialization, (6) drama, (7) interest in team, (8) community support, (9) supporting women's opportunity in sport, (10) role model, (11) aesthetics, (12) customer service, (13) excitement, (14) entertainment value, (15) sport knowledge, (16) vicarious achievement, (17) wholesome environment, and (18) escape. The SII is a 54-item scale that has been used and validated in different sport settings (e.g., professional men's and women's football, professional women's basketball). The SII showed good reliability with each variable's Cronbach alpha ranging from .75 to .93. Confirmatory Factor Analysis showed that the SII was a valid instrument for measuring eighteen unique motives related to sport consumer interest. Goodness-of-fit indices supported the SII measurement model's discriminant and convergent validities ($\chi2$ = 1686.45, df = 1,224, RMSEA = 0.05, SMRM = 0.05). Multiple linear regression analyses revealed that the eighteen motives assessed by the SII explained 48% of the variance in sport spectator interest in professional women's basketball (Funk, Ridinger, & Moorman, 2003). As presented above, the SII possesses good psychometric properties and it is an appropriate tool to assess the motives for sport consumption of sport fans and spectators. For this investigation, the supporting women's opportunity in sport factor was dropped because data was collected from a men's professional indoor football league.

Team identity was assessed in this investigation using the Team *ID scale developed by Heere and James (2007a). The Team*ID scale was developed based on the work of Ashmore, Deaux, and McLaughlin-Volpe (2004) and conceptualized as a multidimensional psycho-social construct. The Team*ID scale is six-dimensional construct of team identity. The six dimensions are: (1) public evaluation, (2) private evaluation, (3) interconnection of self, (4) sense of interdependence, (5) cognitive awareness, and (6) behavioral involvement. Heere and James reported that the overall fit of the six-dimensional model was acceptable ($\chi2$ = 296.19, df = 174; RMSEA = .067, ECVI = 2.646, NFI = .862, TLI = .924, CFI =.937, IFI = .938, GFI = .847) indicating that the team identity is a multi-dimensional construct (Heere & James, 2007a). In addition, the scale showed good convergent validity with all AVE scores exceeding the cutoff of .50. Moreover, all six Team*ID dimensions showed statistically significant correlations with the Psychological Commitment Scale (Kwon & Trail, 2003) and four out of the six Team*ID dimensions, cognitive awareness, public and private evaluation, and behavioral involvement, showed statistically significant correlations with the self-regard dimension of Collective-Self Esteem scale (Luhtanen & Crocker, 1992). These results indicate that the Team*ID possesses good criterion validity. Fourth, the Team*ID scale showed good internal consistency as the Cronbach's alpha for each team identity dimension fell between .77 and .87. Last, the average variance extracted (AVE) values for behavioral involvement, private and public evaluation were higher than the squared correlations between the other constructs, indicating good discriminant validity.

Team loyalty is purported as a consequence of team identity in this study. And like team identity, team loyalty has been conceptualized as a multi-dimensional construct. Namely, fan loyalty has been presented as having attitudinal and behavioral components (Funk & James, 2006). The attitudinal component of fan loyalty "reflects an individual's psychological commitment to a sport team and explains why a team is valued and considered meaningful" (Funk & James, 2006, p. 197). Psychological commitment in turn has been operationalized as the attitude property of resistance to change. Gladden and Funk (2001) develop a scale with four items to measure the attitudinal component of brand loyalty and reported a Cronbach alpha value of .75, which were adopted for this investigation. Behavioral loyalty reflects several sport consumer behavior-related measures. These measures include (1) frequency of game attendance, media consumption, and team merchandise, (2) proportion, (3) duration, (4) intensity of use, purchase, and/or participation associated with a sport's team, and (5) probability of brand use overtime (Iwasaki & Havitz, 2004). All five measures of behavioral loyalty were incorporated in this investigation.

Several socio-situational, demographic, and personal variables were hypothesized to moderate the relationship between team identity antecedents and its related consequences. Five social-situational factors highlighting team endearing features were tested. These five factors are: (1) peer group acceptance, (2) product delivery, (3) tradition, (4) team success, and (5) wholesome environment. Factors one through four were taken from Gladden and Funk's (2002) Team Association Model (TAS). All four variables have been used in several different studies (e.g., Funk & James, 2006; Gladden & Funk, 2001, 2002) and have shown good internal consistency measures (i.e., Cronbach alphas above the .70 benchmark). The personal moderators included the demographic variables of gender, age, ethnic background, marital status, income, and education level.

Data analyses

A confirmatory factor analysis (CFA) was conducted to test how the proposed theoretical model fit the sample data; a two-step approach, first described by James, Muliak, and Brett (1982), was used. This two-step approach is preferred over a one-step modeling approach where both the measurement and structural methods are modeled simultaneously. It is so because it prevents interpretational confounding and makes it easier to locate the source of misspecification in the case of a poorly fitted model (Kline, 2005, p. 216–217). Jöreskog and Sörbom, (1996) further stated that "the testing of the structural model may be meaningless unless it is first established that the measurement model holds. If the chosen indicators for a construct do not [truly] measure that construct, the specified theory must be modified [or the model respecified] before it can be tested. Therefore, the measurement model must be tested before the structural relationships are tested" (p. 113). The two-step approach involves the analysis of two conceptually distinct latent variable models: a measurement and a structural model (Schumacker & Lomax, 2004, p. 209). Starting with the measurement model, a model containing only indicators and their proposed latent variables is specified, identified, and tested to determine how well it fits the data (Kline, 2005). If the initial measurement model is acceptable, the second step (i.e., the evaluation of the structural model) can proceed. If the model is not acceptable respecification needs to ensue.

The estimation method used in this investigation was the Maximum Likelihood (ML) estimation method. The ML method is the most common method in SEM and the default in most of the SEM software packages including AMOS 7.0. The ML derives parameter estimates that maximize the changes that the observed covariances are similar to those of the implied covariance matrix. The ML method assumes that (1) indicator variables are normally distributed, (2) observations are independent, (3) the sample size is large, and (4) the model is correctly specified (Kline, 2005; Schumacker & Lomax, 2004). When ordinal level data is used, like in the case of this investigation, the ML method may not be robust (Schumacker & Lomax, 2004, p. 68). However, as explained above, when the ordinal categories are five or more and no significant deviations from normality assumption exist, the effects of ordinal level data on parametric statistics are negligible (Johnson & Creech, 1983; Zumbo & Zimmerman, 1993). Another assumption of the ML estimation method – multivariate normality – was not met in this investigation. Kline (2005) proposed several different ways for dealing with the lack of multivariate normality. Some of these strategies include using: (1) data transformation techniques, (2) a corrected normal theory method, (3) an estimation method that does not assume multivariate (e.g., ADF, WLS), (4) normal theory method with nonparametric bootstrapping, and (5) parcels instead of individual items.

Two approaches were used to deal with the lack of multivariate normality in this study. The first was a corrected normal theory method using the Bollen-Stine bootstrap method available in AMOS 7.0. The Bollen-Stine bootstrap offers a corrected p-value for the chi-square goodness-of-fit statistic in nonnormal datasets (Byrne, 2001). The second was to use the ML estimation method procedure with nonparametric bootstrapping available in AMOS 7.0. Bootstrapping is a resampling procedure that draws several random subsamples based on the original sample (Byrne, 2001). This procedure creates an empirical sampling distribution, as opposed to a normal distribution. The model's parameters, standard errors, and test statistics are then based in the empirical sampling distributions from the large numbers of simulated subsamples generated (Kline, 2005, p. 197). The major advantage of bootstrapping is that for nonnormal distributions, it yields parameter estimates that are less biased than those of ML estimates with no bootstrapping (Nevitt & Hancock, 2001).

Following the two-step approach for the validation of both the measurement and full structural models, using the model fit criteria described above, the test of mediation ensued. To test the mediating effect of team identity onto the relation between sport fan motives and team loyalty two alternative and nested models were evaluated (Bentler & Chou, 1987; Bollen, 1989). The first is the full model, which contains structural paths connecting sport fan motives to team identity and team loyalty as well as a structural path connecting team identity to team loyalty. The second is the restricted model, which the structural path connecting sport fan motives and team loyalty was constrained to zero. A likelihood ratio test was used to examine whether the chi-square differences between the two nested models were statistically significant at the $p < 0.05$ level. For one degree of freedom, a chi-square change equal or greater than 3.84 yields a statistically significant result. Medium splits were used to classify socio-situational variables (peer group acceptance, tradition, team success, and product delivery) into high and low scores. The models for the different conditions (e.g., low versus high scores in tradition) were then tested against each other for structural invariance. The test for structural invariance involved first testing a baseline unconstrained model. This original model was then compared to the models for the different conditions, which had structural paths constrained (Schumacker & Lomax, 2004).

Results

From the total of 1,259 questionnaires (770 in the first game and 489 in the second) distributed to spectators, 486 were returned with no missing items (316 in the first game and 190 in the second). The usable questionnaires yielded a response rate of 38.6%. Table 7.1 shows the range of scores along with the means and SDs for all the 17 sport fan motive variables

Table 7.1 Descriptive statistics for sport fan motives (N = 476)

Variable	Range	M	SD
Vicarious Achievement	1 to 7	4.75	1.66
Escape	1 to 7	4.91	1.59
Community Support	1 to 7	4.89	1.52
Sport Knowledge	1.67 to 7	5.41	1.33
Drama	1.33 to 7	5.74	1.15
Excitement	1 to 7	5.89	1
Interest in Players	1 to 7	3.7	1.68
Bonding with Friends	1 to 7	5.09	1.47
Role Model	1 to 7	5.81	1.1
Entertainment Value	1.67 to 7	5.87	1.05
Aesthetics	1 to 7	5.09	1.4
Socialization	1 to 7	4.62	1.56
Interest in Team	1 to 7	5.7	1.17
Bonding with Family	1 to 7	5.66	1.33
Customer Service	1 to 7	5.53	1.2
Interest in Sport	1 to 7	4.54	1.7
Wholesome Environment	1.33 to 7	5.91	1.09

used in this study. Table 7.1 data are presented as item parcels (i.e., the average of the items that are purported to measure each variable). Concerning which motives were most attractive to professional indoor football spectators, Wholesome Environment (M = 5.91 ± 1.09), Excitement (M = 5.89 ± 1.00), and Entertainment Value (M = 5.87 ± 1.05) showed the highest averages. In contrast, Interest in Players (M = 3.70 ± 1.68), Interest in Sport (M = 4.54 ± 1.70), and Socialization (M = 4.62 ± 1.56), exhibited the lowest average scores.

The range of values along with the means and standard deviations for all the six team identity processes and team loyalty variables are depicted on Table 7.2. The Private evaluation team identity facet had the highest average values (M = 5.58 ± 1.19) among the six team identity processes, while Sense of Interdependence had the lowest average values (M = 3.16 ± 1.94). The behavioral loyalty items, although measured in a one-to-seven scale, were not rated by strongly disagree to the strongly agree items. For example, the duration behavioral loyalty item was assessed by asking spectators how long they have been a fan of their respective team, and measured in years. Professional indoor football spectators had been fans of their teams on average between three and four years (M = 4.67 ± 2.18). Similarly, the intensity behavioral loyalty item was assessed by asking spectators how many hours a week they spend reading, listening, watching, and/or participating in team-related activities. Results showed that spectators spend less than one hour a week reading, listening, watching and/or participating in team related activities a week. In addition, spectators indicated that they would attend between four and six games next season (i.e., probability of brand use). Additionally, respondent fans did not seem to agree that being a fan provides a vehicle for social approval (M = 3.87 ± 1.81). In contrast, respondents seem to think that the organization satisfy their need for entertainment

Table 7.2 Descriptive statistics for team identity processes and team loyalty variables

Variable	Range	M	SD
Team Identity Processes			
Public Evaluation	1.33 to 7	5.49	1.11
Private Evaluation	1 to 7	5.58	1.19
Interconnection of Self	1 to 7	3.52	1.88
Sense of Interdependence	1 to 7	3.16	1.94
Behavioral Involvement	1 to 7	4.23	1.76
Cognitive Awareness	1 to 7	4.55	1.69
Team Loyalty – Behavioral			
Proportion of Participation	2 to 7	4.73	1.44
Duration	1 to 7	4.67	2.18
Probability of Brand Use	1 to 7	3.57	1.93
Intensity	1 to 7	2.59	1.54
Frequency	1 to 7	2.92	1.90
Team Loyalty – Attitudinal	1 to 7	5.00	1.65

(M = 6.12 ± 0.95). Table 7.3 also shows that Wave/KiXX fans are aware of their team's successes and tradition.

Measurement and structural model fit

To evaluate model fit, a two-step approach was taken. First, the measurement model was evaluated and after it showed an acceptable fit the structural model was tested. Information on how the models were specified, identified, estimated, tested, and modified is presented next. Both measurement and structural models were specified according to the latest theoretical assessment of how the model constructs are related to one another. A description of each construct along with an explanation of how they are related to one another was explained in chapter II. Model identification deals with number of model parameters that are fixed, free, or constrained (Schumacker & Lomax, 2004). The measurement model had 568 possible parameters to be estimated. The number of distinct parameters in the model was 462 (56 factor loadings, 300 covariances among indicator variables, and 106 measurement error variances). There are 106 fixed-factor loading parameters in the measurement model. Because the number of possible parameters (568) is greater than the number of distinct parameters in the model (462) the model is over- identified. The AMOS 7.0 ML estimation method was used along with a corrected normal theory – the Bollen-Stine bootstrap method, which was also available in AMOS 7.0. To minimize parameter estimation bias associated with nonnormal data, an ML estimation method procedure with nonparametric bootstrapping was also used. The measurement model was then tested yielding an acceptable fit.

The CFA of the measurement model showed that the sample data collected were a good fit for the proposed theoretical model. Inspection of the goodness-of-fit indices revealed favorable results ($\chi2$ = 6351.29, df = 2859, Bollen-Stine p < .001; CMIN/DF = 2.22). The chi-square fit index was statistically significant at the p < .001 level even with the Bollen-Stine corrected normal method. This finding implies a poor model fit. Interpreting model fit based solely on the chi-square fit index is problematic, however. The chi-square interpretation can be misleading because of (1) the larger the sample size (> 200) the greater the chances of obtaining a statistically significant chi-square; and (2) the chi-square fit index is very sensitive to nonnormal

Table 7.3 Descriptive statistics for social-situational moderator variables

Variable	Range	M	SD
Tradition	2.33 to 7	5.65	1.36
Product Delivery	I to 7	6.12	0.95
Team Success	I to 7	5.23	1.35
Peer Group Acceptance	I to 7	3.78	1.81

distributions. Dividing the chi-square by the *df* can attenuate the chi-square dependence on sample size. The relative chi-square, CMIN/*df* = 2.22, falls within the acceptable range (i.e., 1 to 3) for a good model fit (Kline, 2005).

Following Hu and Bentler's (1998) recommendation in addition to the chi-square fit index, the root mean square error of approximation (RMSEA) and the standardized root mean residual (SRMR) were also evaluated. The RMSEA value was .051 with a 90% confidence interval of .049-.052. The .051 RMSEA value is below the .06 cutoff value suggested by Hu and Bentler's (1999) for a close model fit. The other goodness-of-fix index, SRMR was .054. This value is below the .08 cutoff value also suggested by Hu and Bentler's (1999) for a good model fit. The parameter estimates show that all observed variables (i.e., survey items) had a statistically significant correlation at the $p < .01$ level with their corresponding indicator variables. The standardized factor loadings were moderate ranging from a high of .87 to a low of .41. A few items, however, were below the .70 benchmark (BLPPar, BLD, CS3, WE2, AL2, BI1, PuE3, CmS1, CmS2, CmS3, IT1, Ex3, D2, and D1) were deleted and are not depicted in the model. Altogether, the discriminant validity tests, the goodness-of-fit indices, and the model parameter estimates indicate that the measurement model fits the data well. Therefore, according to the two-step approach to model testing the good fit of the measurement model allows for the next step – the testing of the structural model.

The structural model had 327 possible parameters to be estimated. The number of distinct parameters in the model was 190 (81 factor loadings, 109 measurement and residual error variances). There are 137 fixed-factor loading parameters in the measurement model. Because the number of possible parameters (327) is greater than the number of distinct parameters in the model (190) the model is over-identified. The CFA of the structural model showed that the sample data collected had a mediocre fit for the proposed theoretical model. Inspection of the goodness-of-fit indices revealed ambiguous results ($\chi2$ = 8801.16; *df* = 3131; Bollen- Stine $p < .001$; CMIN/*df* = 2.81; RMSEA = .062 (.060-.063); SRMR = .092). While the RMSEA is a just about at the cutoff level for an acceptable model fit, the SRMR is above the .08 benchmark (Hu & Bentler, 1999). Based on the mediocre model fit indices a decision was made to modify the model in an attempt to achieve a better model fit. The first modification made was to drop the scale items that possessed item-to-total correlations below .50. There were seven items (D2, CmS1, CS3, WE2, AL4, BLPPar, BLD) with item-to-total correlations below .50. The second modification was to drop the indicator variables that had standardized structural coefficients below .50. Interest in player, and drama were in that situation and were dropped from analysis. The last modification was based on the Modification Indices (MIs) suggested by AMOS 7.0. Based on those suggestions the residual parameter of public evaluation was allowed to correlate with the team identity residual. The residual of the interconnection of self was also allowed to correlate with the residual from sense of interdependence.

Table 7.4 Comparison of model fit indices between the original and modified structural models

Fit Indices	Original Model	Modified Model
χ2	8801.16	6087.9
Df	3131	2250
P	< .001	< .001
CMIN/df	2.81	2.71
SRMR	0.0927	0.0846
RMSEA	0.062	0.060
CFI	0.78	0.83
AIC	9181.16	6417.9
BIC	9972.59	7105.2

The structural model with those modifications was run and the results are presented in Table 7.4. There was a noticeable improvement in the modified structural model. The RMSEA, SRMR, AIC, BIC, and CMIN/df were all lower indicating an improvement in the model. The CFI increased from .78 to .83 – also indicative of an improvement in the model. The tests of mediation and moderation were conducted using the modified structural model. Figure 7.2 shows the structural coefficients for all latent variables in the modified-restricted model. All latent paths except the path connecting sport fan motives to team loyalty were statistically significant at $p < .01$ level. In addition, all R-squared values were statistically significant at $p < .01$ level. R-squared values ranged from a low of .19 for public evaluation to a high of .96 for attitudinal loyalty. These results indicate that each latent variable is well represented by its underlying observed variables (i.e., survey items) and that each first order latent variable explains a moderate proportion of variance on its corresponding second-order latent variable.

Mediational hypothesis results

Upon validation of the measurement and structural models, the test of mediation ensued. The structural model with unrestricted paths was tested against an alternative nested model where the path from sport fan motives to team loyalty was restricted. A likelihood ratio test between the two models showed that restriction of the sport fan motives → team loyalty path did not significantly alter the model (Table 7.5). In addition to lack of significant improvement of the restricted model, the path connection sport fan motives to team loyalty was highly insignificant $p = .49$ (Figure 7.3). These two findings support the research hypothesis that team identity mediates the relation between sport fan motives and team loyalty. All values presented in Figure 7.3, expect the β coefficient of the unrestricted model liking Sport Fan Motives and Team Loyalty ($p = .49$), are statistically significant at $p < .01$ level.

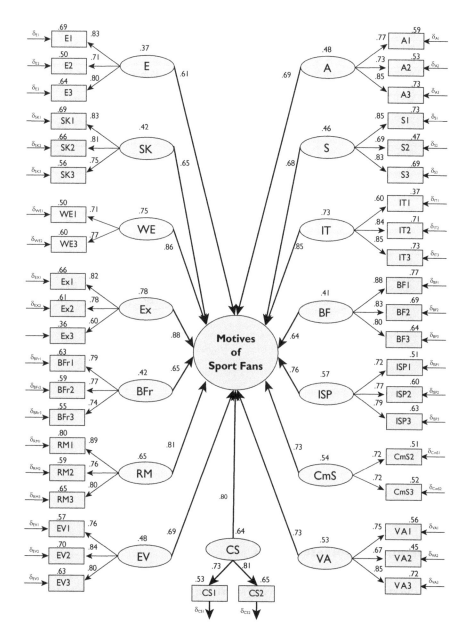

Figure 7.2 Path model of measurement and structural β coefficients and the R-squared associated with each observable and latent variable: modified model

Note: All values presented in Figure 7.2 are statistically significant at *p* < .01 level.

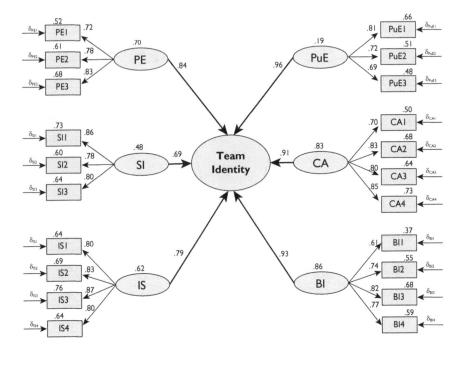

Figure 7.2 (Continued)

Moderation hypotheses results

To test whether selected demographic and social-situation variables moderated the structural relation between sport fan motives and team identity and between team identity and team loyalty a test of structural invariance was performed. A simultaneous group analysis of the restricted structural model was done. First, a simultaneous group analysis was conducted in which the path between sport fan motives and team identity was not constrained. The chi-square statistic for this analysis was noted. Second, a simultaneous group analysis was done in which the path between sport fan motives and team identity was constrained. The chi-square value for this analysis was

Table 7.5 Comparison of model fit indices between the unrestricted and restricted structural models

Fit Indices	Restricted Model	Unrestricted Model
χ2	6087.9	6087.5
Df	2250	2249
P	< .001	< .001
CMIN/DF	2.71	2.71
SRMR	0.0846	.0842
RMSEA	0.060	.060
CFI	0.83	.83
AIC	6417.9	6419.5
BIC	7105.2	7105.0
LR test $\chi^{2\,res} - \chi^{2\,un} = .4, < 3.84\ for\ 1\ df > .05$		

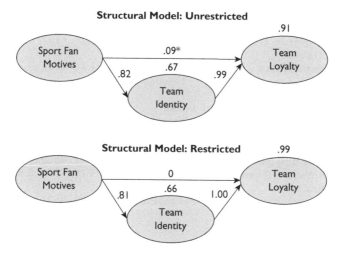

Structural Model: Unrestricted

Structural Model: Restricted

Figure 7.3 Structural path model of second-order latent variables depicting the β coefficients and the R-squared values associated with each latent variable: unrestricted versus restricted models

also noted. The difference between chi-square values was then computed. If the difference between the two values was greater than 3.84 (p = .05 with a single degree of freedom), the path between sport fan motives and team identity was deemed to be different across both groups – thus, suggesting that the particular variable did moderate the relationship between sport fan motives and team identity. The results presented in Table 7.6 show that there was statistically significant effect of age, marital status, and income on the structural path between sport fan motives and team identity. Product delivery had a statistically significant effect on the structural path between team identity and team loyalty.

Table 7.6 Tests of structural invariance for all proposed moderating effects

Model Description	Comparative Model	χ^2	df	$\Delta\chi^2$	Δdf	p
Gender baseline		9362.40	4500	–	–	–
Sport Fan Motives → TI structural path constrained	Gender baseline	9363.87	4501	1.47	1	ns
TI → TL structural path constrained	Gender baseline	9364.68	4501	2.28	1	ns
Age baseline		9548.36	4500	–	–	–
Sport Fan Motives → TI structural path constrained	Age baseline	9554.83	4501	6.47	1	.05
TI → TL structural path constrained	Age baseline	9548.50	4501	0.14	1	ns
Education baseline		9515.13	4500		–	–
Sport Fan Motives → TI structural path constrained	Education baseline	9516.04	4501	0.91	1	ns
TI → TL structural path constrained	Education baseline	9516.06	4501	0.93	1	ns
Marital Status baseline		9423.97	4500	–	–	–
Sport Fan Motives → TI structural path constrained	Marital Status baseline	9428.29	4501	4.32	1	.05
TI → TL structural path constrained	Marital Status baseline	9424.21	4501	0.24	1	ns
Income baseline		8897.51	4500	–	–	–
Sport Fan Motives → TI structural path constrained	Income baseline	8901.33	4501	3.82	1	.05
TI → TL structural path constrained	Income baseline	8897.70	4501	0.19	1	ns
Product Delivery (PD) baseline		9293.11	4500	–	–	
Sport Fan Motives → TI structural path constrained	PD baseline	9293.79	4501	0.68	1	ns
TI → TL structural path constrained	PD baseline	9297.38	4501	4.27	1	.05
Peer Group Acceptance (PGA) baseline		8927.88	4500	–	–	
Sport Fan Motives → TI structural path constrained	PGA baseline	8928.58	4501	0.70	1	ns
TI → TL structural path constrained	PGA baseline	8928.77	4501	0.89	1	ns
Team Success (TS) baseline		9292.19	4500	–	–	
Sport Fan Motives → TI structural path constrained	TS baseline	9292.19	4501	0.00	1	ns
TI → TL structural path constrained	TS baseline	9292.31	4501	0.12	1	ns
Tradition baseline		9482.93	4500	–	–	
Sport Fan Motives → TI structural path constrained	Tradition baseline	9484.17	4501	1.24	1	ns
TI → TL structural path constrained	Tradition baseline	9483.50	4501	0.57	1	ns
Sport Fan Motives → TI structural path constrained	Team baseline	9764.18	4501	0.82	1	ns
TI → TL structural path constrained	Team baseline	9764.55	4501	1.19	1	ns

To provide further support for the moderating role of demographic and socio-situational variables a critical ratio for differences test was conducted. The results are presented in Table 7.7. The data from the critical ratio for differences test support the results from the test of structural invariance except for the effect of income. Results show that the structural path coefficient of the two age and marital status conditions was statistically and

Table 7.7 Standardized (β) and unstandardized (B) path coefficients as well as critical ratio for differences for all proposed moderating effects

Variable	Sport Fan Motives → Team Identity			Team Identity → Team Loyalty		
	β	B	Critical Ratio for differences	β	B	Critical Ratio for differences
Gender			−1.20			1.51
Men (n = 235)	.86	1.03		.99	1.06	
Women (n = 230)	.82	.78		1.01	1.32	
Age			2.19*			.38
Younger than 44 (n = 298)	.79	.78		1.03	1.12	
Older than 45 (n = 171)	.82	1.30		.96	1.18	
Marital Status			−1.96*			−.49
Married (n = 264)	.78	1.18		1.00	1.24	
Not-married (n = 202)	.84	.78		.99	1.15	
Education Level			−0.95			.95
College or more (n = 287)	.78	1.00		1.02	1.06	
Some college or less (n = 177)	.84	.83		.97	1.23	
Income			−1.62			−.43
$ 80,000 or more (n = 172)	.76	1.11		.98	1.29	
$ 79,000 or less (n = 162)	.82	.67		.98	1.19	
Peer Group Acceptance			0.82			−.94
High (n = 226)	.83	.81		.96	1.30	
Low (n = 218)	.74	.97		1.05	1.12	
Product Delivery			−0.83			−2.04*
High (n = 235)	.85	.71		.93	1.43	
Low (n = 241)	.65	.59		.99	.94	
Team Success			−.07			−1.03
High (n = 234)	.85	.93		.96	1.39	
Low (n = 242)	.63	.91		.98	1.15	
Tradition			−1.14			−.76
High (n = 237)	.87	.91		.92	1.16	
Low (n = 239)	.65	.71		1.02	1.01	
Team			−.94			−1.07
Wave (n = 285)	.87	.96		.99	1.07	
KiXX (n = 191)	.73	.8		.99	1.26	

* $p < .05$.

significantly different for the path between sport fan motives and team identity. The structural path coefficient between the two product delivery conditions was found to be statistically and significantly different for the path between team identity and team loyalty. Altogether the results presented in Tables 7.6 and 7.7 support the finding that age marital status, and income moderate the relation between sport fan motives and team identity. Product delivery was found to moderate the relation between team identity and team loyalty. No evidence was found to support the moderating role of all other socio-situational and demographic variables.

Discussion

The most important finding of this study was the mediating role of team identity in the relation between sport fan motives and team loyalty. The LR test showed that there was no improvement in the model with the addition of a path between sport fan motives and team loyalty. Moreover, both the b and β coefficients associated with the path between sport fan motives and team loyalty were not statistically significant. The mediating role of team identity in the development of team loyalty had been proposed on theoretical grounds by other sport management researchers (e.g., Funk & James, 2004; Heere & James, 2007a, b). This theoretical proposition had not been empirically tested, however. The results of this study confirm the suspicions of sport management researchers and help to solidify the role of team identity in the development of team loyalty.

Another significant finding of this study was that income and tradition moderated the relation between sport fan motives and team identity and that age as well as product delivery moderated the relation between team identity and team loyalty. The finding that income and tradition moderated the relation between sport fan motives and team identity seems to suggest that fans with a household income less than $79,000 and fans who are more aware of the team traditions identify more strongly with the team. By the same token, the relation between team identity and team loyalty is likely to be stronger in fans who are below 44 years of age and believe that the organization can satisfy their needs for entertainment. The moderating of role of demographic and socio-situational variables has not been widely investigated in sport management literature involving the constructs of motivation, identity, and loyalty. Fink, Trail, and Anderson (2002) study was one of a few studies that took such an approach. They studied the moderating role of gender in the relation between motives of sport fans and team identification. Contrary to this study, they found that gender moderated the motives to identity connection. More specifically, Fink, Trail, and Anderson found that while vicarious achievement explained the most variance in team identification for both men and women, for women it explained 55% versus only 20% in men. Moreover, they found that there was a significant and positive correlation between the knowledge motive and team identification for men but not for women.

The last significant finding of this study was that the motives of sport fans vary significantly according to their level of team identity and loyalty. All but the drama motive of highly identified and loyal fans were significantly higher than those of moderately and not identified and loyal fans. These findings are difficult to interpret in light of what sport management researchers know and understand about the behavior of sport fans. For example, Funk and colleagues (2001, 2002, and 2004) found that not all SII variables significantly predicted and/or explained the level of sport spectator support. Similarly, Fink, Trail, and Anderson (2003) found that only the motives of vicarious achievement, aesthetics, drama, and social interaction significantly explained a percentage of variance in team identification. These seemingly contradictory results seem to be a function of statistical versus practical significance. For example, the entertainment motive mean score for highly identified fans was 6.17 versus a 5.62 for moderate, and 5.29 for not identified fans. While statistically significant, this small difference may not be meaningful. That is the equivalent of a somewhat agree versus an agree rating on a seven-point scale. On the other hand, the achievement motive mean score for highly identified fans was 5.82 versus a 4.53 for moderate, and 3.68 for not identified fans. This difference can be argued to have both statistical and practical significance. The average score of 5.82 is close to an agree rating versus the average score of 3.68, which is between a somewhat disagree and neutral rating.

Conclusions

The results of this study offer sport management practitioner's insight regarding the level of team identification and loyalty and which set of variables motivate indoor football fans. This information may prove useful in the development of marketing strategies geared toward a specific segment of fans. Contrary to the segmenting consumers based solely on demographic information the results of this study offer insight into the motivations of sport fans – a psychographic variable. The results of this study indicate that the motives of sport fans vary according to their level of identification and loyalty to the organization. Moreover, the data supporting the notion that that team identity mediates the relation between sport fan motives and team loyalty suggest to practitioners that marketing strategies that tap into the different points of identification with the team may prove useful in the maturity process to fan loyalty.

Based on the 80/20 rule of consumer behavior, about 80% of a company's business comes from about 20% of its consumers. This 20% consumer sector is likely to be made of the most loyal and identified group of consumers. As such, it is vital to learn about what motivates these loyal indoor football fans so that marketing efforts can be geared toward meeting their wants and needs. Understanding what motivates loyal and identified indoor football fans is an important piece of the consumer behavior puzzle. For instance, if loyal fans are motivated by the achievement motive then sport marketers can develop promotional strategies that tap into a fans' sense of achievement through their connection with a sports team.

The consumer escalator notion posits that consumption behavior is a process starting at a stage when consumers are not aware of a given product/service going to the next stage when they become aware of the product/service and then moving to increasing levels of consumption until they become heavy product/service users. The results of this investigation offer insight about the motives of sport fans who are at different escalator stages of consumption. For example, highly identified and loyal fans were significantly more motivated to follow a team because of the sense of achievement provided by their connection with that team. Therefore, using the vicarious achievement motive to build marketing strategies around it can assist in meeting fans needs and prevent them from falling off the escalator. On the other hand, it would be unwise to try to motivate unidentified and not-loyal fans with messages related to a sense of achievement. Unidentified and not-loyal, in the case of this investigation, are more motivated to follow a team because they see their games as exciting, dramatic, entertaining, and because the players serve as role model to young kids. Creating marketing strategies to meet these motivational needs would not necessarily move unidentified and not-loyal fans up the escalator but could keep them as light consumers until they develop a stronger connection with the team.

Last, based on the finding that team identity mediates the relation between sport fan motives and team loyalty it would be wise for indoor football marketers to create as many points of identification with a team as possible. This study did not focus on points of identification but others have. For example, Heere and James (2007b) proposed that external group identities, which include demographic categories (i.e., gender, geographic based) and membership organizations (i.e., corporate, university affiliation) may influence one's level of team identification. As such, sport marketers should create attachment opportunities between the team and these external group identities to maximize the chances for fan identification. A strategy used by almost all professional sport teams is to affiliate their organization with a specific geographic location (e.g., city, state). This strategy creates an immediate point of identification between residents of a specific geographic region and the city's or state's team.

References

Armstrong, K. L. (1999). A quest for a market: A profile of the consumers of a professional women's basketball team and the marketing implications. *Women in Sport and Physical Activity Journal, 8,* 103–126.

Ashmore, R. D., Deaux, K., & McLaughlin-Volpe, T. (2004). An organizing framework for collective identity: articulation and significance of multidimensionality. *Psychological Bulletin*, *130*(1), 80–114.

Bilyeu, J. K., & Wann, D. L. (2002). An investigation of racial differences in sport fan motivation. *International Sports Journal*, *6*(2), 93.

Bentler, P. M., & Chou, C. P. (1987). Practical issues in structural modeling. *Sociological Methods & Research*, *16*, 78–117.

Bollen, K. A. (1989). *Structural equations with latent variables*. New York: Wiley-Blackwell.

Byrne, B. M. (2001). Structural equation modeling with AMOS: Basic concepts, applications, and programming.

Cialdini, R. B., Borden, R. J., Thorne, A., Walker, M. R., Freeman, S., & Sloan, L. R. (1976). Basking in reflected glory: Three football field studies. *Journal of Personality and Social Psychology*, *34*, 366–375.

Cronbach, L. J. (1951). Coefficient alpha and the internal structure of tests. *Psychometrika*, *16*, 297–334.

Dimmock, J. A., Groove, J. R., & Eklund, R. C. (2005). Reconceptualizing team identification: New dimensions and their relationship to intergroup bias. *Group Dynamics: Theory, Research, and Practice*, *9*(2), 75–86.

Eagly, A. H., & Chaiken, S. (1993). *The psychology of attitudes*. Fort Worth, TX: Harcourt, Brace & Jovanovich.

Fink, J. S., Trail, G. T., & Anderson, D. F. (2002). An examination of team identification: Which motives are most salient to its existence? *International Sports Journal*, *6*, 195–207.

Fisher, R. J. (1998). Group-derived consumption: The role of similarity and attractiveness in identification with a favorite sports team. *Advances in Consumer Research*, *25*, 283–290.

Fornell, C., & Larcker, D. F. (1981). Evaluating structural equation models with unobservable and measurement error. *Journal of Marketing Research*, *18*(1), 39-80.

Fournier, S. (1998). Consumers and their brands: Developing relationship theory in consumer research. *Journal of Consumer Research*, *24*, 343–373.

Funk, D. C., & James, J. D. (2001). The psychological continuum model: A conceptual framework for understanding an individual's psychological connection to sport. *Sport Management Review*, *4*, 119–150.

Funk, D. C., & James, J. D. (2004). The fan attitude network (FAN) model: exploring attitude formation and change among sport consumers. *Sport Management Review*, *7*, 1–26.

Funk, D. C., & James, J. D. (2006). Consumer loyalty: the meaning of attachment in the development of sport team allegiance. *Journal of Sport Management*, *20*, 189–217.

Funk, D. C., Mahony, D. F., Nakazawa, M., & Hirakawa, S. (2001). Development of the Sports Interest Inventory (SII): Implications for measuring unique consumer motives at sporting events. *International Journal of Sports Marketing & Sponsorship*, *3*, 291–316.

Funk, D. C., Mahony, D. F., & Ridinger, L. (2002a). Characterizing consumer motivation as individual difference factors: Augmenting the Sport Interest Inventory (SII) to explain level of spectator support. *Sport Marketing Quarterly*, *11*, 33–43.

Funk, D. C., Mahony, D. F., & Ridinger, L. L. (2002b). Understanding consumer support: extending the Sports Interest Inventory to examine individual differences among women's professional sport consumer. *Sport Management Review*, 6, 1–32.

Funk, D. C., & Pastore, D. L. (2000). Equating attitudes to allegiance: The usefulness of selected attitudinal information in segmenting loyalty to professional sports teams. *Sport Marketing Quarterly*, 9(4), 175–184.

Funk, D. C., Ridinger, L. L., & Moorman, A. M. (2003). Understanding consumer support: Extending the Sports Interest Inventory to examine individual differences among women's professional sport consumers. *Sport Management Review*, 6, 1–32.

Funk, D. C., Ridinger, L. L., & Moorman, A. M. (2004). Exploring the origins of involvement: Understanding the relationship between consumer motives and involvement with professional teams. *Leisure Sciences*, 26, 35–61.

Gantz, W., & Wenner, L. A. (1991). Men, women, and sports: Audience experiences and effects. *Journal of Broadcasting & Electronic Media*, 35, 233–243.

Garbarino, E., & Johnson, M. S. (1999). The different roles of satisfaction, trust, and commitment in customer relationships. *Journal of Marketing*, 63, 70–87.

Gerbing, D. W., & Anderson, J. C. (1993). Testing structural equation modeling. In K. A. Bollen & J. S. Lond (Eds.), *Monte Carlo evaluations of goodness-of-fit indices for structural equation models* (pp. 1–9). Newbury Park, CA: Sage.

Gladden, J. M., & Funk, D. C. (2001). Understanding brand loyalty in professional sport: Examining the link between brand association and brand loyalty. *International Journal of Sports Marketing & Sponsorship*, 3, 67–94.

Gladden, J. M., & Funk, D. C. (2002). Developing an understanding of brand associations in team sports: empirical evidence from consumers of professional sport. *Journal of Sport Management*, 16, 54–81.

Gladden, J. M., & Milne, G. R. (1999). Examining the importance of brand equity in professional sports. *Sport Marketing Quarterly*, 8(1), 21–29.

Gorsuch, L. R. (1983). *Factor analysis* (2nd ed.). Hillsdale, NJ: Lawrence Erlbaum.

Greenwell, C., Greenhalgh, G., & Stover, N. (2013). Understanding spectator expectations: an analysis of niche sports. *International Journal of Sport Management and Marketing*, 13(3/4), 144–157.

Heere, B., & James, J. D. (2007a). Stepping outside the lines: Developing a multidimensional team identity scale based on Social Identity Theory. *Sport Management Review*, 10(6), 65–91.

Heere, B., & James, J. D. (2007b). Sports teams and their communities: examining the influence of external group identities on team identity. *Journal of Sport Management*, 21, 319–337.

Holroyd, S. (2010). History of indoor soccer in the USA. Retrieved May 03, 2017, from http://www.rsssf.com/usadave/usindoor.html

Hu, L., & Bentler, P. M. (1998). Fit indices in covariance structure modeling: Sensitivity to underparameterized model specifications. *Psychological Methods*, 3, 424–453.

Hu, L., & Bentler, P. M. (1999). Cut-off criteria for fit indexes in covariance structure analysis: Conventional criteria versus new alternatives. *Structural Equation Modeling*, 6, 1–56.

Iwasaki, Y., & Havitz, M. E. (2004). Examining the relationships between leisure involvement, psychological commitment and loyalty to a recreation agency. *Journal of Leisure Research*, 36(1), 45–72.

Jaccard, J., & Choi, K. W. (1996). *LISREL approaches to interaction effects in multiple regression*. Thousand Oaks, CA: Sage.

James, J. D., & Ridinger, L. L. (2002). Female and male sport fans: a comparison of sport consumption motives. *Journal of Sport Behavior, 25*, 260–278.

James, L. R., Muliak, S. A., & Bret, J. M. (1982). *Causal analysis: Assumptions, models, and data*. Los Angeles: Sage.

Johnson, D. R., & Creech, J. C. (1983). Ordinal measures in multiple indicator models: A simulation study of categorization error. *American Sociological Review, 48*, 398–407.

Jöreskog, K., & Sörbom, D. (1996). Structural equation modeling with the SIMPLIS command language. Chicago, IL: Scientific Software International.

Kahle, L. R., Kambara, K. M., & Rose, G. (1996). A functional model of fan attendance motivations for college football. *Sport Marketing Quarterly, 5*(4), 51–60.

Karakaya, F., Yannopoulos, P., & Kefalaki, M. (2016). Factors impacting the decision to attend Soccer games: An exploratory study. *Sport, Business and Management: An International Journal, 6*(3), 320–340.

Kline, B. R. (2005). *Principles and practice of structural equation modeling*. New York: Guilford.

Kwon, H., & Trail, G. (2003). A reexamination of the construct and concurrent validity of the Psychological Commitment to Team scale. *Sport Marketing Quarterly, 12*(2), 88–93.

Litterer, D. (2010, May 30). *A history of USA indoor Soccer*. Retrieved November 1, 2016, from The American Soccer History Archives. http://homepages.sover.net/~spectrum/indooroverview.html

Luhtanen, R., & Crocker, J. (1992). A collective self-esteem scale: self-evaluation of one's social identity. *Personality and Social Psychological Bulletin, 18*(3), 302–318.

Mahony, D. F., & Moorman, A. M. (2000). The relationship between the attitudes of professional sport fans and their intentions to watch televised games. *Sport Marketing Quarterly, 9*, 131–139.

Mahony, D. F., Nakazawa, M., Funk, D. C., James, J. D., & Gladden, J. M. (2002). Motivational factors influencing the behavior of J. league spectators. *Sport Management Review, 5*(1), 1–24.

Mahony, D. F., Nakazawa, M., Funk, D. C., James, J. D., & Gladden, J. M. (2002). Motivational factors influencing the behavior of J. League spectators. *Sport Management Review, 5*, 1–24.

Major Indoor Soccer League rules of the game 2002–2003. Retrieved in 2002 from www.kicksfan.com/downloads/rulebook/mislrules02.pdf

Moore, N. (2016, November 1). Major indoor soccer: The hype of the U.S.' one-time biggest league remembered. *FourFourTwo*. Retrieved May 11, 2017, from www.fourfourtwo.com/us/features/major-indoor-soccer-hype-us-one-time-biggest-league-remembered

Nevitt, J., & Hancock, G. R. (2001). Performance of bootstrapping approaches to model test statistics and parameter standard error estimation in structural equation modeling. *Structural Equation Modeling, 8*, 353–377.

Pan, D. W., Gabert, T. E., McGaugh, E. C., & Branvold, S. E. (1997). Factors and differential demographic effects on purchases of season tickets for intercollegiate basketball games. *Journal of Sport Behavior, 20*(4), 447.

Putnam, R. D. (2000). Bowling alone: America's declining social capital. In Culture and politics (pp. 223-234). Palgrave Macmillan US.

Robinson, M. J., & Trail, G. T. (2005). Relationships among spectator gender, motives, points of attachment, and sport preference. *Journal of Sport Management, 19*(1), 58–80.

Ross, S. D. (2007). Segmenting sport fans using brand associations: A cluster analysis. *Sport Marketing Quarterly, 16*(1), 15–24.

Schumacker, E. R., & Lomax, G. R. (2004). *Beginner's guide to structural equation modeling.* Mahwah, NJ: Lawrence Erlbaum.

Tajfel, H. (1978). *Differentiation between social groups: Studies in the social psychology of intergroup relations.* London: Academic.

Trail, G. T., Fink, J. S., & Anderson, D. F. (2003). Sport spectator consumption behavior. *Sport Marketing Quarterly, 12*(1), 8–17.

Trail, G. T., & James, J. D. (2001). The motivation scale for sport consumption: Assessment of scale's psychometric properties. *Journal of Sport Behavior, 24*(1), 108–127.Trail, G. T., Robinson, M., Gillentine, A., & Dick, R. (2003). Motives and points of attachment: Fans versus spectators in intercollegiate athletics. *Sport Marketing Quarterly, 12,* 217–227.

Wann, D. L. (1995). Preliminary motivation of the sport fan motivation scale. *Journal of Sport and Social Issues, 19,* 377–396.

Wann, D. L. (2006). Examining the potential causal relationship between sport team identification and psychological well-being. *Journal of Sport Behavior, 29*(1), 79–95.

Wann, D. L., & Branscombe, N. R. (1993). Sports fans: Measuring degree of identification with their team. *International Journal of Sports Psychology, 24,* 1–17.

Wann, D. L., Drewer, K. R., & Royalty, J. L. (1999, Summer). Sport fan motivation: relationships with team identification and emotional reactions to sporting events. *International Sports Journal, 3,* 8–18.

Zorzou, A., Zorzou, J., Laios, A., Bebetsos, E., Kobodietas, D., & Apostolidis, N. (2014). Motivations, attitudes and behavioral intentions of Soccer games spectators. *Journal of Physical Education and Sport, 14*(4), 507–513.

Wann, D., Schrader, M., & Wilsen, A. (1999). Sport fan motivation: Questionnaire validation, comparisons by sport, and relationship to athletic motivation. Journal of Sport Behavior, 22(1), 114.

Zumbo, B. D., & Zimmerman, D. W. (1993). Is the selection of statistical methods governed by level of measurement? *Canadian Psychology, 34,* 390–400.

Chapter 8

When the beautiful game turns ugly

Fan experiences of perceived match fixing in football

Adriano M. Lamberti and Craig Hyatt

Introduction

On March 5th, 2013, a controversial decision in a prominent match brought an ugly issue to the forefront of football[1] fans' collective consciousness. On that night, storied clubs Manchester United FC and Real Madrid CF were competing in the advanced stages of the prestigious UEFA Champions League tournament. Just before the hour mark of the match, Turkish referee Cüneyt Çakir left an indelible mark on the game – and its worldwide audience – by dismissing a player for what most would deem a marginal infraction. As a result of the red card, prominent Manchester United player Luís Carlos Almeida da Cunha (who goes by the name Nani) was sent off, leaving his team to complete the game with one less player than their opponent. Adding to the controversy was Çakir's alleged involvement in fixing matches in his native Republic of Turkey (Gold, 2011; Hurriyet Daily News, 2013).

The phenomenon at the core of the controversy is match fixing in sport, which is an occurrence involving a match being played to a completely or partially pre-determined result for a host of motivations – typically financial gain (Forrest, 2012) – that threatens to rob sport of its essence and spirit (Adcroft & Teckman, 2008; Smith, 2011). This particular case drew the ire of many worldwide, so much so that more than 185 people *paid* to express their opinion in an online petition to hold Çakir accountable for his actions (iPetitions, 2013). In addition, social networking site Twitter was inundated with messages from users expressing displeasure in the hours after the suspicious call. The match in question is just one of many known or speculated cases of match fixing that has plagued football internationally (cf. Hill, 2010b; Longman, 2015; Maennig, 2005; McNamee, 2013; Smith, 2011).

Match fixing is beginning to draw worldwide attention from high-ranking delegates. In a March 2011 decree, then-IOC president Dr. Jacques Rogge spoke to the loss of credibility sport and its leagues risk by being implicated in match rigging scandals: "there are already countries where football com-petitions are no longer credible and where the public has very clearly lost interest in that sport" (Boniface et al., 2011, p. 4). It is this notion of dimin-ished interest in the sport that we aimed to explore. As fans' consump-tion of sport is a large financial contributor to leagues and their teams, their loss of interest and lessened consumption could be devastating to the global sport market. Additionally, any phenomenon that undermines the integrity of sport is a worthy topic of investigation in order to better under-stand prevention, detection and image recovery methods. Focusing on the Manchester-Madrid match has merit considering the high-profile nature of the match, as the UEFA Champions League is one of the most prestigious tournaments in what can be argued is the world's most popular sport (Alegi, 2010; Brahmana, 2011; Palacios-Huerta, 2004; Smith, 2001).

Football match fixing is receiving extensive attention in Europe and abroad. A Europol investigation of nearly 700 matches in 30 countries (Canadian Broadcasting Corporation, 2013) and a 124-page *European Affairs* report specifically on the topic (European Commission, 2012) are testaments to this statement. Recent events indicate match fixing is mak-ing its way to the Americas. The February 2013 news of Canadian Soccer League matches being fixed (Hill 2010a; Rycroft, 2013) as well as current reports of a 2015 Gold Cup match between Panama and Mexico being fixed (Longman, 2015) support this notion. Despite the ubiquity of match fixing in football, and the global multitude of fanatics who claim football as their favorite sport, little work has been completed on the nexus between match fixing and fandom (Buraimo, personal communication, March 22, 2013). The present study intended to bridge this gap.

The objective of the current research was to better understand the lived experiences of highly identified football fans living through this era of foot-ball match fixing, by employing in-depth, interpretive, semi-structured interviews aimed to address the following research questions:

1   What has it been like to live through this era of match fixing in football?
2   How has perceived match fixing affected your fandom, if at all?
3   What changes must be undertaken for trust/belief to be restored in the sport?

Social media website Twitter played an integral role as participants were recruited based on posts pertaining to match fixing submitted to the website during and soon after the aforementioned UEFA Champions League match.

We will first examine the pertinent literature on both sport fandom and match fixing, then explain our methods and data analysis strategies. Next, the findings generated from the 12 interviews are presented as 13 themes organized under three broader categories. We conclude with a dis-cussion of the research implications, limitations, and directions for future research.

Review of literature

Beginning in the late twentieth century, scholars began developing theories to understand and/or predict the feelings, thoughts, and behaviors of sport fans using a wide range of psychological, sociological, or marketing-based concepts (cf. Cialdini et al., 1976; Melnick, 1993; Mullin, Hardy, & Sutton, 1993; Sutton, McDonald, Milne, & Cimperman, 1997; Wann & Branscombe, 1993). Starting in the early twenty-first century, more attention was given to developing models to classify fans into different categories based on their levels of psychological commitment and/or the frequency of their behaviors directed towards their favorite sport and/or team (Funk & James, 2001; Giulianotti, 2002). One model was the PCM, which classified fans into one of four levels based solely on their psychological commitment to their favorite sport or team (Funk & James, 2001). The awareness stage is first, where people know a sport or team exists but have no real connection. At the second stage of attraction, a psychological bond between the person and sport/team forms. Individuals consider themselves a fan, but the bond might be weak. Only at the third stage of attachment can a fan be considered highly identified, as the psychological bond has become strong and long-lasting. Finally, at the allegiance stage, identification is so strong that it commonly affects cognition preventing fans from "thinking straight" (Funk & James, 2001).

Giulianotti (2002) developed his own model (Figure 8.1), categorizing football fans into one of four groups based not only on psychological

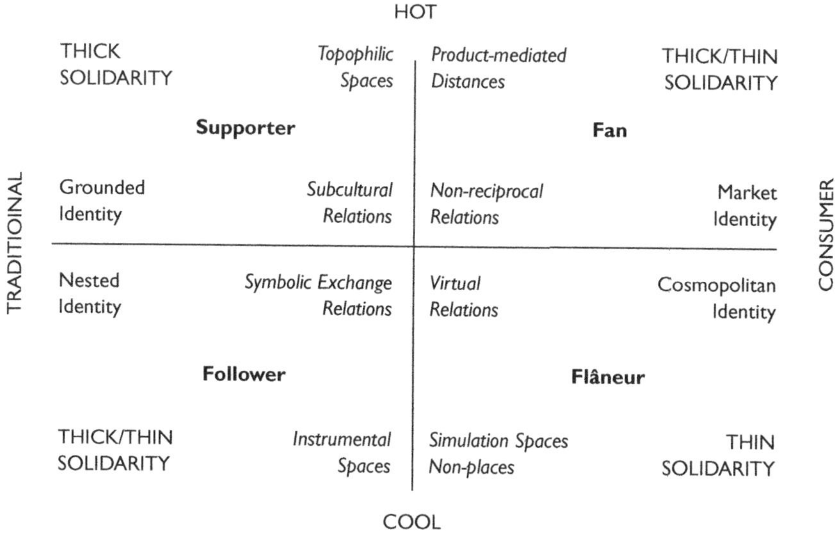

Figure 8.1 Contemporary spectator identities

Source: Giulianotti, R. (2002). Supporters, followers, fans and flâneurs: A taxonomy of spectator identities in football. *Journal of Sport & Social Issues, 26*(1), 31.

commitment, but also on behaviors directed towards their favorite team. The four spectator categories are supported by two opposing spectrums: hot – cool and traditional – consumer. This creates four quadrants into which spectators may be classified: traditional – hot, traditional – cool, consumer – hot, consumer – cool. The traditional – consumer axis measures an individual's investment (be it time, financial, and/or emotional) in a specific club while the "the hot – cool vertical axis reflects the different degrees to which the club is central to the individual's project of self – formation" (Giulianotti, 2002, p. 31). Hot forms of loyalty stress a deep kind of fan identification and solidarity with the team while cool forms represent the contrary. Giulianotti's (2002) model blends psychology-based theories focusing on commitment (Funk & James, 2001) and marketing-based theories of fan behavior (Mullin et al., 1993).

Sport fandom deescalation

Despite calls from Funk and James (2001) as well as Mullin, Hardy, and Sutton (2007) for studies on how fandom could wane, fandom deescalation research is limited. Research on this issue suggests greed, labor disputes, time constraints, fantasy sport participation, losing, geographical displacement, the loss of certain players, franchise relocation, increased violence, team or league mismanagement, and the media are all factors that could weaken the team-fan bond (Drayer, Shapiro, Dwyer, Morse, & White, 2010; Fink, Parker, Brett, & Higgins, 2009; Hyatt, 2007; Hyatt & Foster, 2015; Lewis, 2001; Smith et al., 1981; Wann, Tucker, & Schrader, 1996). To the best of our knowledge, there have been no studies specifically designed to determine if match fixing can cause fandom deescalation.

Match fixing in sport

A fixed match has occurred when a match is played to a completely or partially pre-determined result, violating the rules of the game and, often, the law (Forrest, 2012). Match fixing can occur in two forms, either non-betting or betting-related. Non-betting instances transpire when matches are thrown to achieve a sporting advantage – such as when sumo wrestlers, who have already qualified to advance, purposely lose to help their opponent also qualify (Duggan & Levitt, 2002). Betting-related match fixing occurs when matches are thrown to achieve economic gain, such as jockeys passing insider information to bookmakers (Maennig, 2005). Instances of betting-related match fixing have become more prevalent than its non-betting counterpart. Gorse and Chadwick (2011) analyzed known cases of match fixing from 2000–2010 and determined 33 of 57 (57.89%) reported cases were betting-related. Match fixing in sport appears to be most common in football as nearly three-quarters (21/30 or 70%) of reported match fixing cases in Gorse and Chadwick's (2011) 2000–2010 sample involved football matches. Please note these are *known* cases of match fixing – there is little doubt more football match fixing goes undetected (European Commission, 2012; Smith, 2011). Regarding types of fixes, Boniface et al. (2011) state, "the most typical and common form of corruption in football involves a number of players who come onto the field with the aim of deliberately conceding goals" (p. 16). While purposely conceding goals is one way to fix a match, it is not the only method as bribing referees is also common (Gorse & Chadwick, 2011; Hill, 2010b; Maennig, 2005).

Match fixing in football

Despite the prevalence of match fixing in the world's most popular sport, a scant amount of literature exists pertaining specifically to match fixing and football, save for Boeri and Severgnini (2008), Buraimo, Migali, and Simmons (2015), European Commission (2012), Forrest (2012), Hill (2010a, 2010b), Mazanov, Tenero, Connor, and Sharpe (2012), Preston and Szymanski (2003), and Smith (2011). Boeri and Severgnini (2008) wrote about match fixing in football when studying the significance of media perception in the wake of the 2006 Serie A *Calciopoli* scandal. This scandal resulted in a lifetime ban for Juventus managing director Luciano Moggi as well as significant fines and relegation to Serie B, amongst other sanctions, for historic Italian club Juventus (Boeri & Severgnini, 2008; Buraimo et al., 2015). As this chapter was prognostic and judicial in nature, there was minimal mention of fandom. Similarly, Mazanov et al. (2012) investigated the impact of the same Italian scandal on investor valuation of sport by examining changes in share prices. They concluded share prices increased suggesting that scandal *increased* perceived team values. While these findings were intriguing, no interviews with fans or investors were conducted to explain these happenings, leaving one to speculate as to why changes occurred. Meanwhile, investigative journalist Hill (2010a) analyzed the inner workings of various worldwide high-profile football fixes (including FIFA World Cup matches) without emphasizing fandom. Smith (2011) – like Boeri and Severgnini (2008) and Hill (2010a) – authored little in terms of match fixing impacting consumers or fans. Rather, Smith (2011) reviewed football match fixing and offered suggestions to combat corruption.

Forrest (2012) writes of the economic threat betting-related corruption may impose on world football, with limited hints to how fans may feel. Forrest (2012) believes betting-related corruption "is a potential threat to the football industry to the extent that it may deter fans, sponsors and broadcasters from purchasing the product" (p. 99). Outside of this quotation, fandom went unmentioned. In contrast, Preston and Szymanski (2003) feel there is a negligible impact on fandom as "there certainly does not seem to be any clear evidence that scandals related to cheating have reduced interest" (p. 621). The authors believed highly identified fanatics – who may no longer be thinking logically in accordance with Funk and James' (2001) PCM – can preserve belief in their own team by placing the blame of cheating on their opponent (Preston & Szymanski, 2003). Buraimo et al. (2015) investigated consumer – or fan – response to corruption. The authors examined consumer reactions to the 2006 Italian Serie A match rigging indignity by analyzing pre- and post-scandal attendance figures. Buraimo et al. (2015) uncovered a substantial drop in attendance numbers of punished teams, but could only speculate on the cause as no fans were interviewed.

Lastly, Hill (2010b) examined Europe's most corrupt football leagues. This study provided a closer focus on football supporters than his earlier mentioned work. Hill (2010b) interviewed some 220 people, predominantly players, referees, sport officials, journalists, and corrupters. However, one fan interview was particularly insightful, as an Asian football fan claimed the Singaporean league has "too much bribery" (p. 233), deeming the games a "waste of money!" (p. 233). This Singaporean fan now supports Liverpool of the English Premier League (EPL), showing fan migration is possible when presented with a perceived non-corrupt alternative (Hill, 2010b).

Despite a lack of comprehensive attention given to the link between match fixing and fandom in academia, literature exists that acknowledges the relationship. In addition, football's global followers, the prevalence of match fixing in the sport as well as other authors flirting with the subject matter (namely Buraimo et al., 2015; Hill, 2010b) are all factors that suggest this topic is a worthwhile pursuit. Additionally, Smith's (2011) claim that "the very essence of sport is that competition is fair; its attraction to spectators is the unpredictability of its outcome" (p. 2), is supported by Gorse and Chadwick (2011), who felt the uncertainty inherent in sport gives it its unpredictable joy. Forrest and Simmons (2003) build on these sentiments by suggesting fans may be disenchanted by the charade and refuse to attend live events because a "loss of confidence in the integrity of competition will lessen the attractiveness of the spectacle and, consequently, lower attendance" (p. 607).

The concepts of consumer reaction when faced with match fixing corruption (Buraimo et al., 2015) and spectator attraction dwindling (Forrest & Simmons, 2003; Gorse & Chadwick, 2011; Smith, 2011) are where this study was launched. The purpose of this qualitative, interpretive study was to better understand the lived experiences of football supporters living through this era of match fixing. We now shift focus to the research methodology.

Method

In-depth, semi-structured interviews were the foundation of data collection. The objective of these lengthy interviews was to understand the lived experiences of devoted (or formerly devoted) football supporters living through this era of match fixing in the sport. Semi-structured interviews capture the participants' own words, giving them power and control over the interview's direction (Crotty, 1998; Liamputtong, 2009). As the researchers subscribe to an interpretive paradigm underpinning, one where there are no single objective truths (Kvale & Brinkmann, 2009), semi-structured interviews using open-ended questions fit nicely with this research project. They afforded interviewees the opportunity to express their views on match fixing – views shaped by the context of their personal life-world, history, and experiences (Crotty, 1998; Kvale & Brinkmann, 2009; Sveinson & Hoeber, 2016).

The sample

In order that they would be likely to provide the rich, thick descriptions required to address the research questions, participants needed to both be current or former highly identified football fans and be aware of match fixing in the sport. Consequently, the perceived fix surrounding the high-profile UEFA Champions League match of March 5th, 2013 between Manchester United and Real Madrid provided an opportunity for the purposive, criterion-based sampling of such a group. This method, ubiquitous in qualitative research, uses small-scale samples chosen because they meet prescribed criteria (Crotty, 1998; Kvale & Brinkmann, 2009; Liamputtong, 2009). The lead researcher searched Twitter for any posts (known as "tweets") from the day of the match or the following day that not only mentioned match fixing, but also referred to that specific game. English-language tweets from 283 unique individuals met these criteria. To expand the recruitment pool, those who retweeted (forwarding other people's tweets to one's Twitter followers – typically indicating agreement with the original tweet) these tweets were also recruited, adding 109 people to the pool of potential participants. Because this project became the master's thesis for the lead author, much time was needed to not only design the project, but also gain approval from the supervising committee and our university's institutional review board. As such, attempts by the lead author to contact the 392 potential participants were not made until a year had passed after the game in question had been played. At that time, 20 people were unable to be contacted, as either their Twitter account had become inactive or they had blocked contact with the study's account (@MatchFixStudy). The 372 individuals contacted for an interview received either a personal invitation via Twitter's direct messaging feature or were messaged publically on their timeline. To clarify, direct messages can only be sent to users who follow your account. If the contactee followed our account, this direct message was sent: "In March you expressed opinions on match fixing in a ManU-Madrid game. I'd like to interview you for my Masters thesis. Reply if interested." If our account was not reciprocated with a follow back, a similar message was sent to the user via their timeline. Of these 372, 40 (10.75%) indicated interest and were sent both an invitational email outlining the study's purpose as well as the informed consent form. Of those 40 interested in participating, 19 agreed on a date and time for an interview with 12 (3.23%) actually following through by completing an interview with the lead author. Just before commencing the interview, the adult participants (11 of the 12) verbally gave informed consent and completed a short demographic questionnaire (see Appendix A for a demographic breakdown). For the lone interviewee under 18, his mother consented by signing a scanned copy of the form.

Participants had to both have knowledge of match fixing and be (or once have been) a highly identified fan. While we felt confident the interview process would confirm the former (all 12 mentioned match fixing on Twitter), it would take the interview process to confirm the latter. After each interview's completion, we felt confident all 12 were – or once were – at least on the third of four floors of the PCM, as each conveyed anecdotes of what the sport meant to them and could express the centrality it harbored in their lives. According to Funk and James (2001), centrality becomes important to individuals who have developed an attachment to a sport and/or a team. Some participants went a step further by displaying levels of loyalty at the allegiance stage, characterized by attitudinal or psychological importance (Gladden & Funk, 2002), biased cognition (e.g., placing blame on referees, not their teams' players), resistance to change (e.g., fandom would *never* waver), as well as season ticket ownership (Funk & James, 2001). With reference to Giulianotti's (2002) taxonomy of contemporary spectator identities, we concluded each participant was (or once was) on the "hot" end of the spectrum as they displayed signs of thick solidarity to their team and/or the sport of football.

The interviews

The interview guide (Appendix B) contained questions designed to elicit a rich, thick description of how they understood the nexus of football fandom and perceived match fixing. While the guide provided enough structure to ensure the three research questions were addressed, the interviews typically also consisted of many unscripted questions or prompts that came about naturally as the conversation unfolded. These spontaneous statements helped enhance data trustworthiness, as most were clarifying and/or rapport-building in nature.

Although the participants lived worldwide, the lead author conducted face-to-face interviews in real-time by using either Skype or FaceTime video conferencing software. All interviews were audio recorded and later transcribed verbatim by the lead author. At this point, each participant was sent a copy of his or her transcript as a member check (whereby each was asked to verify the interview's accuracy), thus enhancing the data's authenticity, credibility, and trustworthiness (Crotty, 1998; Liamputtong, 2009). Seven of the dozen participants replied with clarification to their transcripts, while five did not respond to member checking efforts. Every participant had the opportunity to reply to member checking before data analysis commenced.

Data analyses

Thematic analysis involves searching across a data set to find repeated patterns or meanings (Braun & Clarke, 2006). In accordance with Liamputtong (2009), the transcripts were analyzed thematically with stimulating wording garnering more attention. From this point, the researchers performed "initial and axial coding in order to deconstruct data, put them into codes, and find links between them" (Liamputtong, 2009, p. 285). Initial coding is the first pass through that opens the data to in-depth views and theoretical categorization, while axial coding takes it a step further by "examining the codes at a more conceptual level" (Liamputtong, 2009, p. 217). In terms of the current study, 13 themes were found that directly addressed the three research questions – three with the first question, four with the second, and six themes under the final question (see Appendix C for each participant's thematic contribution). The 13 themes are presented below.

Research findings

Fan attitudes and emotions during the match fixing era

Regarding the first research question, the fans' interviews revealed three themes: skepticism with respect to football's purity, the possibility of media cover-ups, and the possibility of favoritism towards one of the two competing teams.

Skepticism

Manchester United (of the EPL) season ticket holder Jamie argued match fixing has undoubtedly seeped into the English game in the past. After discussing former elite goalkeeper Bruce Grobbelaar – who was implicated in a match fixing scandal in 1994 – Jamie described his nagging feeling that the EPL is not free of illegal betting corruption:

> They must try it. They must be! And you see it in different sports, you know? What are we – 25 years of it, or 20 years of the [English] Premier League? You know, 20 years have gone by and you sort of think in the back of your mind, "there must've been a game that was fixed." You know, there must've been! If it's happened in other countries, why not – what's so special about England? Why has England not?

Cover-ups

Five interviewees mentioned the media's involvement in football match fixing. When discussing the 2006 Italian Serie A scandal, Phil from London, UK retorted with, "but you see, that's just the thing. It's the way the media goes, they protect things, you know? They made it seem like it's just in Italy." Both Sam and Lucy wondered if media outlets are being paid hush money. Lucy succinctly chimed in with, "Maybe the bigger leagues have the money to pay people off to keep them quiet?"

A degree of skepticism leading to a damaged reputation and the belief that media cover-ups may be occurring are potentially destructive forces that can negatively impact fandom. In addition to the above opinions, some interviewees also expressed perceptions of favoritism.

Favoritism

Randy, Julian, Ricky, and Bobby shared similar sentiments in regards to preferential treatment for certain "darling" teams that may or may not be linked to match fixing. In a quotation representative of the views of these four, Manchester United fan Ricky shared his English discriminatory and Spanish favored opinions:

> So there always seems to be some sort of favoritism – or maybe it's just perceived favoritism for the non-English based, or should I say non-British based [teams] because the Scottish and Welsh teams don't get any favors either . . . And just some of the decisions come up – seems to be favored towards Spanish teams and I think the Italian teams also had a run at some stage as well. So, when the [Nani red card] decision happened it just seemed to be the wrong decision from a refereeing point of view.

He subsequently explained:

> Until then, we've [Manchester United] gotten the advantage. We'd have taken the win gladly. But you always want to know that you've competed fairly. And the two darlings in Europe at the moment are probably Real Madrid and Barcelona and it just seems to me they get the run of the green more than anyone else.

When expressing their attitudes and emotions, the participants used negatively toned language and expressed feelings of cynicism and contempt; but has this dark cloud hanging over football altered their fandom? Possible fandom fluctuations will be discussed next.

Impacts on fandom

Unchanged

Half of the participants definitively deemed their fandom was not affected negatively despite their match fixing knowledge. In fact, Jim claimed his fanaticism increased since becoming aware of match rigging. When asked about corruption's impact on his fandom he said, "not really, not much impact on the game." When prompted to elaborate, Jim explained:

> Yeah, I'm watching a lot of football now, since that point [learning of match fixing] started. I'm watching a lot more but also because it doesn't happen that often and you don't notice that much from match fixing. I think it happens more in lower divisions and in the East Europe. Not really in the big competitions.

It should be noted that Jim was the youngest interviewee and, as such, is in a different stage in life or family cycle than most of the others. It is possible Jim has not developed the faculties to engage in the complex process of consumer decision making alluded to by Mullin et al. (1993), who suggest decision making involves several environmental and individual factors. Environmental influences include – but are not limited to – significant others, cultural norms and values, market behavior of sport firms, as well as class, race, or gender relations that may be more central to older people than teenagers. Meanwhile individual factors like self-concept, stage in life or family cycle, learning, motivation, and perception may also be age-sensitive (Mullin et al., 1993). These notions will be elaborated upon in the Deescalating section below.

Randy, Julian, Jamie, Bobby, and Trevor were the others who suggested their awareness of football match fixing has not had an impact on their fandom. Bobby even claimed he would remain a fan if he learned every football game was fixed:

> I love the game. I mean, even if every single game was match fixed I probably wouldn't enjoy it as much but I still want to watch football, you know? I still want to watch the skills of the players so I'd still be a fan.

All six contributors to this theme helped strengthen Preston and Szymanski's (2003) assertion that "[i]t is not clear how much cheating has to occur before interest in the sport starts to suffer, but there certainly does not seem to be any clear evidence that scandals related to cheating have reduced interest" (p. 620). As a counterpoint, the themes that follow illustrate that match fixing scandals have the ability to hinder fandom and tarnish the game.

Minimal

The three interviewees who populated this theme are undoubtedly fans who still support football. In the researchers' judgment, however, they showed signs of dithering in their answers compared to the definitive replies provided by those in the Unchanged theme. Sarah expressed her opinion with some hesitation and a few pauses to contemplate her answers, "[Long pause] I don't think it has because [pauses] you know, with so much stuff happening you always kind of sort of expect the next bad news to be around the corner." Cory's offering was similar to Sarah's, "I don't think it has had too much of a negative effect. You know, it's definitely frustrating, I think the confirmed ones are, you know?" To round out this theme, Phil opined:

> I mean I still play. I still love the sport . . . when I see something wrong in the game and I see the ref[eree] ruining the game obviously the ref[eree] can ruin it with just a red card but when it's something that doesn't seem right that really can dent my love for the game. What I'm saying is it's all down to greed . . . that's spoiling it for those who love the game for the game.

A key differentiating factor between the Unchanged and the Minimal themes was the conviction with which respondents answered the "how – if at all – has match fixing in football impacted your fandom?" question. As a reiteration, it should be mentioned that all three are still attached to the sport. The differentiation is in the possibility of accepting change to their fandom. To clarify, those in the Unchanged theme definitively stated their fandom had not changed, demonstrating a resistance to change typical of the PCM's allegiance level (Funk & James, 2001). Sarah, Cory, and especially Phil, however, showed an acceptance to potential fandom change in using terms like *I don't think*, whereas the Unchanged participants spoke in convincing language, such as *it hasn't*. In relation to Giulianotti's (2002) model, these three would be plotted lower on the hot axis than their Unchanged counterparts as their solidarity could be seen as thick but with thinning potential. This is noteworthy for fandom literature as these once allegiant fanatics are showing potential for disengagement from their sport of interest (Giulianotti, 2002).

Deescalating

Both Ricky and Lucy communicated feelings of disappointment resulting from the realization that football is not as pure as they once believed it to be leading to a deescalation in their fandom. As Ricky eloquently worded it:

> I think it kills the whole romanticism around it, you know? It's [pauses] when I spoke about finding a football in a park and kicking it around,

that's probably as pure as it gets. There's no money involved, there's nothing else.

He would later add:

> Because it's [match fixing] there and what that does long term is it kills the passion for watching the game and for following – I suppose – the bigger dealings around the game the bigger events like the World Cups and the championships, etcetera. I don't think it kills the passion on the ground, because those supporters will still go out and kick the ball around. But it definitely kills the commercialization because it's – you know, would I pay to go see a match where there's a chance of match fixing? No!

Lucy – who "just feels the whole game is corrupt" – shared similar feelings of deescalating fandom and disillusionment as Ricky:

> I think it's something, if you know something is fixed there's no point really in watching it because it's just cheating. I can't be bothered with these things like that, you know? So I don't really take much interest anymore.

It is worth noting that both Ricky (early 40's) and Lucy (mid-50's) were two of the three oldest interviewees. As such, they are in the advanced stages of their family and life cycle in accordance with Mullin et al. (1993). In comparison to teenager Jim, for instance, there is a distinct change in perceived levels of fandom. Jim claimed his football consumption has increased, ironically, since learning about match fixing, while Ricky and Lucy are showing signs of disengaging possibly due to their ability to navigate through the complex process of consumer decision making (Mullin et al., 1993). For example, Ricky and Lucy are married and have children, whereas Jim is a single teenager living with his parents. As such, Ricky and Lucy are in an advanced stage in their life and family cycles that may lead to different perceptions, motivations and attitudes towards topics discussed in this study. Mullin et al. (1993) add to the life cycle discussion by mentioning life stage transitions, which "may have a profound effect on our sport involvement and commitment" (p. 71) as our values and identities change over time. In their study of former fans, Hyatt and Foster (2015) echo the ideas of Mullin et al. (1993), as they found that moving through various life stages could negatively affect fandom levels.

It is also likely Ricky and Lucy are turning away for reasons postulated by Forrest (2012) who wrote "a competition that is perceived to be a charade may be shunned" (p. 99) which may explain their feelings. They also appear to be moving downward – or deescalating – with reference to Funk and James's (2001) PCM, as they have both lost interest in the commercialized Big league spectacle. Ricky and Lucy are now turning their love for the game to the grassroots level – its purest form. While Ricky and Lucy have already begun the deescalation process, there were other informants who hypothesized scenarios in which they, too, would notice a decline in their football fanaticism, as discussed next.

Projected

The final topic under the Impacts on Fandom category is predictive. Seven respondents provided insight into how match fixing *may* negatively impact their fandom in the future. Their answers fall under three rationales – if the plight intensifies, if their team was involved, or if a major scandal occurred.

Randy and Phil both prognosticated that their fandom would take a negative hit if this current trend of match fixing continues or intensifies. As Randy stated:

> Well I could definitively see it change if more revelations came out. If more ref[eree]s or [laughs] people from the gambling syndicates or whatever came out or even the management of the teams and said this had happened in such and such match.

Julian and Sarah's fandom would change if one of their favorite teams – Portuguese outfit Benfica and EPL club Arsenal, respectively – were involved in match fixing. Julian uttered:

> It would probably change if Benfica or Portugal was in the final of the World Cup or Champions League and you find out that game was fixed. And the team I was cheering for got robbed. Because even, let's say Portugal is now the World Cup champion because of the fixing, it's not the same because you don't get that glory of watching the victory and partying in the street when that happened.

If another match fixing scandal broke, it would have to be one of large magnitude to dissuade Sam and Cory's fandom. As Cory explained:

> If there's a major, major scandal. I think it would have to be something unbelievable like a World Cup Final, a Champions League Final or something of tremendous magnitude. Not even just tremendous magnitude but, like, showing that probably most of the top European teams were involved.

It should be noted that the above scenarios were hypothetical, where the interviewees envisioned an occurrence whereby their fandom could potentially lessen.

Issues and suggested changes to improve the game's perception

All study participants were knowledgeable and self-identified football fans. As well-informed fans, however, they knew football needs repair. The themes in this category are a combination of issues plaguing the game and suggestions to counter these issues.

Transparency

Greater transparency was mentioned frequently. Nearly half of the participants alluded to governmental and/or administrative transparency. When discussing an investigation of fixed matches in her native South Africa during the lead up to the 2010 FIFA World Cup, Sarah noted:

> Well the frustrating thing is with the Bafana [South Africa's national football team] games, at the moment, is the government was meant to launch an inquiry – sort of their own commission of inquiry beyond FIFA's investigation. And the government had just said, "no, sorry, we're not going to do that!" And that's worse for me than the actual fixing, because it's the government's responsibility in part to ensure that the game's clean and the fans can confidently feel that their game is clean.

Referees

Five participants discussed referees. Both Randy and Julian agreed that football referees have far too much power compared to other sports. Below Randy compares football and basketball referees' authority:

> It seems to me that maybe it would be much easier to fix the outcome of a football game than almost any [other] sport. And that the referee has really outside influence . . . I'm a basketball fan and people complain when the referee makes a foul call in a basketball game, which is, as you know, nothing but a free throw of a game where you could score over 100 points. It's like, the [football] referees giving away a red card which actually removes a player and not allowing him to be replaced, which I think is unique in sport. Or awarding a penalty kick, which is about as close as you can come to just simply giving a goal.

Cory, Trevor, and Ricky offered suggestions to help fix the perceived issues currently surrounding football refereeing. As a way of combatting the questionable integrity of referees, Ricky suggested a ranking system to remove the guesswork in officiating crew assignments:

> So I think there are a few lessons you can take from other sports. But I think FIFA's really got to step it up – they've got to reach a decision

and say "we don't accept this at all, and we're going to show that we're above it" do whatever they need to do. So, if it means the top ref[eree] is an English ref[eree] and he's got to referee a game between Manchester United and Real Madrid, nobody is going to question it because he is the top ref[eree], you know what I mean? And his officials are the top officials and at the same time, they have to provide in-match assistance to him. So, if it looks like that decision or one of those decisions that could be argued [pauses] he should have enough time to bounce it off the other officials that are there. They're all wired up these days now in any case so it'll take a 10- to 15-second discussion for him to get that right.

Consequences

Stricter penalties for known offenders were an emergent view expressed by a quarter of the participants. All three discussed Juventus' punishments, as Cory illustrates:

> I think also it really depends on the football association's diligence too. They need to come down and crack down hard on anyone involved in match fixing. And I know the person at the top of Juventus at the time of the Italian scandal . . . was banned for life . . . and I think it's got to be life bans for everyone that if they were involved in it. It's got to. It kind of has to be no nonsense, you know? Just crack the whip on everyone!

In keeping with the Juventus scandal as the gauge all other punishments should be measured against, Trevor weighed in. After deeming a match fixing player or team as "unsupportable" that they "don't deserve second chances with something like that [match fixing]" and those involved should experience "criminal proceedings" he went on to note:

> Just as a punishment, you're on about this Juventus director and he won't be allowed to play – won't be involved in football again. I think anybody in any league who is involved in match fixing should never be allowed anywhere near football again.

Technology

FIFA has been notoriously slow to adjust to modern technology, having just implemented goal line technology for the first time at a World Cup in 2014 (Psiuk, Seidl, Strauß, & Bernhard, 2014). In the following discussion, Julian presents a thought-provoking argument for why football governing bodies like UEFA and FIFA may be hesitating to implement more technological measures to aid officials:

I'm not saying that game specifically, but just like the game of football so whenever you see that you're like "whoa, what is the motive? He missed that so blatantly!" And also why is football so neglecting going to modern technology to make calls easier? Is that because it'll be harder to prove, for the ref[eree]s to fix these matches? If Man United could challenge the play . . . and see that Nani didn't even touch him and reverse the red card . . . Just now [at the 2014 World Cup] they're introducing goal line technology!

Sam draws inspiration from other sports in his recommendation to improve the beautiful game:

I'm a big supporter of technology in football. I think they should have video evidence to be able to recall back. It wouldn't take them long, they use it in rugby all the time; they use it in sports like tennis. Just a quick review system; a manager could just get one review a game and he can review an incident.

Gambling

Ricky, Jamie, and Cory discussed their concerns surrounding the illegal betting culture in football and how the key to eliminating match fixing might involve examining who is placing bets and from where. Two of the three specifically referenced Asian betting syndicates corrupting cricket, as Jamie pointed out:

This just happened in cricket, because there were a few cricket matches that were fixed in England a couple of years ago. The reason they got found out was because people in the Far East – in India and Asia – were betting heavily on the three no balls in an over.

Jamie went on to describe the unlikelihood of three balls in a cricket over and how these fixers were caught with a combination of suspicious betting on that occurrence and an impressive monitoring systems in place in English cricket. Naturally, Jamie recommended world football adopt a similar monitoring system. According to Smith (2011), this monitoring system is slowly being implemented as many sport-governing bodies – not necessarily in football – have agreed to assist in detection and reporting of suspicious betting activity. Despite these efforts, Cory's belief that ". . . it's a tough thing to tackle. It's admirable that people are even investigating it, but – it's definitely a tough problem to tackle" segues well into the next theme as a sense of "what can you do?" has overcome football fans.

Helplessness

In an unfortunate reality, Julian, Jamie, and Sarah voiced their concerns in the form of helplessness against match rigging corruption. Sarah, who has lived through match fixing scandals as a fan of cricket and football, bellowed, "after seeing it [match fixing] you wish they would all go to jail, you feel like your hands are tied, I guess, because there's so little you [fans] could do about it."

These three have developed a "what can be done?" attitude regarding football match fixing. However, they could still be considered fans – especially Julian and Jamie. Their words illustrate they are acutely aware of the match fixing plight, understand combatting it is a daunting task, but still remain fanatics.

Implications

Our results suggest three major implications – two from an applied perspective and one theoretical. As this study was international, we will first examine the practical implications from a European and international perspective, then a North American one, before addressing Funk and James's (2001) PCM.

While there were four North Americans in our sample, the fandom of all 12 was focused primarily on both European club teams and national teams playing in international competition. Within this context, we heard fans desire efforts be made to ensure football's integrity, which included harsh punishments for fixers. European and international football administrators would be wise to hire integrity officers and implement educational programs to help keep football pure. Efforts are underway in other sports – particularly cricket and tennis (European Commission, 2012) – to monitor betting irregularities and educate athletes but greater efforts are needed in football. A movement is afoot to combat match fixing through criminal legislation and Sportradar's sport betting integrity education programs (European Commission, 2012; Smith, 2011). While this is positive, none of our 12 informants were aware of such actions. To better preserve football's image and reduce further tarnishing, these efforts should be better marketed. Fans who are becoming disillusioned with the sport – as two participants were – may be interested to know anti-corruption methods are in place as it may prevent them from ceasing their fandom. Should anti-corruption initiatives not completely eradicate match fixing, our participants insisted on harsh action for fixers. Interviewees hoped for severe punishment – as proposed by Maennig (2002) – for future fixers including three informants who insisted on similar criminal actions as those outlined in European Commission (2012) and Smith (2011). Letting fixers off easy would be a public relations nightmare and the game will have to work especially hard to recover its image in the face of another scandal.

While none of the 12 said their primary allegiance was to a team in North America's MLS, our findings are noteworthy to a league still gaining popularity. In terms of spectatorship, football falls well behind the North American "major four" of American football, baseball, basketball and hockey (Carlin, 2010). As such, MLS is still considered a second-tier league (Peterman & Suntornpithug, 2013). Therefore, it is important that North American football leagues retain as many fans as possible. Having two of the 12 highly committed fans start deescalating illustrates that another match fixing scandal could have potentially destructive effects on peripheral fans. Consequently, MLS could benefit greatly from introducing integrity officers. No such position exists in MLS, which is surprising considering the Canadian Soccer Association's recent appointment of an integrity officer (Squizzato, 2014). If MLS is to safeguard their integrity and retain fans, they must proactively fight match fixing. Given what some interviewees expressed, a scandal would be enough to shake the foundation of a second-tier league and turn off casual followers. As Wang, Zhang, and Tsuji (2011) explain in relation to an upstart Chinese baseball league, match fixing and gambling scandals tarnished the league's image and "hurt fans' belief in game authenticity" (p. 349). It is conceivable MLS could suffer the same fate should it experience a match fixing controversy. MLS administrators should look to Europe where, despite the game's popularity being undeniably strong, they have begun to implement anti-match fixing methods.

Another implication drawn from the current study is uncovering another manner for decreased fandom in relation to the PCM (Funk & James, 2001). While the PCM is influential and cited often in sport fandom literature (de Groot & Robinson, 2008; Lock & Filo, 2012; Spaaij & Anderson, 2010), downward movement through it has been understudied. Match fixing is a phenomenon that could result in committed fans beginning to reduce their connection to a team and/or a sport. Referring specifically to the two deescalating and disillusioned participants, they are beginning to disassociate from a sport they once loved, thus beginning a downward movement through the PCM (Funk & James, 2001).

Limitations and directions for future research

The sample was limited to those who not only have a Twitter account, but also used that account to comment (in English) on match fixing during a brief timeframe while referencing a specific game. As well, participants had to have access to the Internet and videoconferencing software to participate. As such, millions of football fans worldwide who may have had their thoughts, feelings, and behaviors impacted by perceived match rigging were not heard.

We felt confident that all 12 participants were, or once were, in the PCM's top two stages (Funk & James, 2001). Consequently, the opinions of casual football fans were not heard. It is possible perceived match fixing would have more of a negative impact on less highly identified fans. Future studies should include people across all four PCM stages.

Sport fandom is not a static phenomenon. It is not only couched in the context of a person's present situation, but also evolves over time as a person's life-world changes. Considering seven of our 12 participants suggested match fixing might have an impact on their future fandom, researchers should study fans longitudinally to better understand which factors affect fandom over time.

Conclusion

The researchers found that negativity shrouds today's fans of the beautiful game, with a tarnished reputation and feelings of skepticism chief amongst current attitudes. Despite this negativity, our participants illustrated that the psychological bond is difficult to break, even when facing uncertainty and controversy. The strength of their bond lends support to Funk and James's (2001) descriptions of allegiant fans as well as Giulianotti's (2002) traditional-hot spectator. The researchers, however, also uncovered that sporting scandals, regardless of the current strength of the bond, can potentially move supporters down the PCM (Funk & James, 2001). Seven participants who projected their fandom being negatively impacted if match fixing continued in football, as well as the two informants beginning to deescalate, enlightened this notion.

The variation in fan responses – unaffected, slight affect, deescalating and potential for change – suggests this study was worthwhile to pursue and build upon. It also extended academic dialogue on corruption and consumerism in sport while demonstrating a practical need for integrity officers to protect the image of football while safeguarding against future indignities. Second-tier sport leagues with developing, yet fragile, fan bases should actively fight corruption, as losing precious supporters could be devastating. Our findings provide important implications for sport governing bodies and sport stakeholders, especially those who believe in upholding sport's purity.

Note

1 In North America, the sport is almost exclusively referred to as soccer; however, in Europe, it goes by football. Also, the game is typically called a match played by clubs (not teams). The authors and interviewees use all these words interchangeably and hope the reader comprehends when any of these terms are used.

References

Adcroft, A., & Teckman, J. (2008). Theories, concepts and the rugby World Cup: Using management to understand sport. *Management Decision*, 46(4), 600–625.

Alegi, P. (2010). *African Soccerscapes: How a continent changed the world's game.* Athens, OH: Ohio University Press.

Boeri, T., & Severgnini, B. (2008). *The Italian job: Match rigging, career concerns and media concentration in Serie A* (No. 3745). IZA discussion papers. Retrieved from http://hdl.handle.net/10419/35480

Boniface, P., Lacarriere, S., Verschuuren, P., Tuaillon, A., Forrest, D., Icard, M. J, Meyer, J-P., & Wang, X. (2011). Sport betting and corruption: How to preserve the integrity of sport. *SportAccord*. Retrieved from www.sportaccord.com/multime dia/docs/2012/02/2012_-_IRIS_-_Etude_Paris_sportifs_et_corruption_-_ENG.pdf

Brahmana, R. K. (2011). The euphoria effect of UEFA champions league final on Asian stock market. *International Journal of Economics and Finance, 3*(1), 178–187.

Braun, V., & Clarke, V. (2006). Using thematic analysis in psychology. *Qualitative Research in Psychology, 3*(2), 77–101.

Buraimo, B. (2013, March 22). Personal communication.

Buraimo, B., Migali, G., & Simmons, R. (2015). An analysis of consumer response to corruption: Italy's *Calciopoli* Scandal. *Oxford Bulletin of Economics and Statistics, 78*(1), 22–41. doi:10.1111/obes.12094

Canadian Broadcasting Corporation. (2013, February 4). Match fixing probe uncovers 680 suspicious soccer games. *CBC Sports*. Retrieved from www.cbc.ca/sports/ soccer /match fixing-probe-uncovers-680-suspicious-soccer-games-1.1390194

Carlin, J. (2010, June 14). The global game. *Time, 175*(23), 60–71.

Cialdini, R. B., Borden, R. J., Thorne, A., Walker, M. R., Freeman, S., & Sloan, L. R. (1976). Basking in reflected glory: Three (football) field studies. *Journal of Personality and Social Psychology, 34*(3), 366–375.

Crotty, M. (1998). *The foundations of social research: Meaning and perspective in the research process.* London: Sage.

de Groot, R., & Robinson, T. (2008). Sport fan attachment and the Psychological Continuum Model: A case study of an Australian football league fan. *Leisure/ Loisir, 32*(1), 117–138.

Drayer, J., Shapiro, S. L, Dwyer, B., Morse, A. L., & White, J. (2010). The effects of fantasy football participation on NFL consumption: A qualitative analysis. *Sport Management Review, 13*(2), 129–141. doi:10.1016/j.smr.2009.02.001

Duggan, M., & Levitt, S. D. (2002). Winning isn't everything: Corruption in sumo wrestling. *American Economic Review, 92*(5), 1594–1605.

European Commission. (2012, March). *A mapping of criminal law provisions in EU 27.* Retrieved from http://ec.europa.eu/sport/library/studies/ study-sports-fraud-final-version_en.pdf

Fink, J. S., Parker, H. M., Brett, M., & Higgins, J. (2009). Off-field behavior of athletes and team identification: Using social identity theory and balance theory to explain fan reactions. *Journal of Sport Management, 23*, 142–155.

Forrest, D. (2012). The threat to football from betting-related corruption. *International Journal of Sport Finance, 7*(2), 99–116.

Forrest, D., & Simmons, R. (2003). Sport and gambling. *Oxford Review of Economic Policy, 19*(4), 598–611.

Funk, D. C., & James, J. (2001). The Psychological Continuum Model: A conceptual framework for understanding an individual's psychological connection to sport. *Sport Management Review, 4*(2), 119–150.

Giulianotti, R. (2002). Supporters, followers, fans, and flâneurs: A taxonomy of spectator identities in football. *Journal of Sport & Social Issues*, 26(1), 25–46.

Gladden, J. M., & Funk, D. C. (2002). Developing an understanding of brand associations in team sport: Empirical evidence from consumers of professional sport. *Journal of Sport Management*, 16(1), 54–81.

Gold, D. (2011, July 8). Turkish Football Federation implicated in match fixing scandal as Fenerbahce risk relegation. *Inside World Football*. Retrieved from www.insideworldfootball.com/worldfootball/europe/9429-turkish-football-federation-implicated-in-match fixing-scandal-as-fenerbahce-risk-relegation

Gorse, S., & Chadwick, S. (2011). The prevalence of corruption in international sport – a statistical analysis. *Consultancy Report for the Remote Gambling Association*. Retrieved from www.rga.eu.com/data/files/Press2/corruption_report. pdfHill, D. (2010a). *The fix: Soccer and organized crime*. Toronto, ON: McClelland & Stewart.

Hill, D. (2010b). A critical mass of corruption: Why some football leagues have more match fixing than others. *International Journal of Sports Marketing & Sponsorship*, 11(3), 221–235.

Hurriyet Daily News. (2013, July 5). Match fixing accusations center on Fener officials. *Hurriyet Daily News*. Retrieved from www.hurriyetdailynews.com/default. aspx?pageid=438&n=matchfixing-accusation-center-on-fener-officials-2011–07–05

Hyatt, C. G. (2007). Who do I root for now? The impact of franchise relocation on the loyal fans left behind: A case study of Hartford Whalers fans, *Journal of Sport Behavior*, 30(1), 1–20.

Hyatt, C. G., & Foster, W. M. (2015). Using identity work theory to understand the deescalation of fandom: A study of former fans of National Hockey league teams. *Journal of Sport Management*, 29(4), 443–460. doi:http://dx.doi.org/10.1123/jsm.2013-0327

iPetitions. (2013). Hold referee Cüneyt Çakir accountable. *iPetitions.com*. Retrieved from www.ipetitions.com/petition/banrefereecuneytcakir/signatures

Kvale, S., & Brinkmann, S. (2009). *InterViews: Learning the craft of qualitative research interviewing* (2nd ed.). Thousand Oaks, CA: Sage.

Lewis, M. (2001). Franchise relocation and fan allegiance. *Journal of Sport & Social Issues*, 25(1), 6–19. doi:10.1177/0193723501251002

Liamputtong, P. (2009). *Qualitative research methods* (3rd ed.). New York: Oxford University Press.

Lock, D., & Filo, K. (2012). The downside of being irrelevant and aloof: Exploring why individuals do not attend sport. *Sport Management Review*, 15(2), 187–199.

Longman, J. (2015, July 24). Gold cup match fixed, Panama official says. *NYTimes. com*. Retrieved from www.nytimes.com/2015/07/25/sports/soccer/gold-cup-match-fixed-panama-official-says.html?_r=0

Maennig, W. (2002). On the economics of doping and corruption in international sports. *Journal of Sports Economics*, 3(1), 61–89.

Maennig, W. (2005). Corruption in international sports and sport management: Forms, tendencies, extent and countermeasures. *European Sport Management Quarterly*, 5(2), 187–225.

Mazanov, J., Tenero, G. L., Connor, J., & Sharpe, K. (2012). Scandal + football = a better share price. *Sport, Business and Management: An International Journal*, 2(2), 92–114.

McNamee, M. (2013). The integrity of sport: Unregulated gambling, match fixing and corruption. *Sport, Ethics & Philosophy*, *7*(2), 173–174.

Melnick, M. J. (1993). Searching for sociability in the stands: A theory of sports spectating. *Journal of Sport Management*, *7*(1), 44–60.

Mullin, B. J., Hardy, S., & Sutton, W. A. (1993). *Sport marketing*. Champaign, IL: Human Kinetics.

Mullin, B. J., Hardy, S., & Sutton, W. A. (2007). *Sport marketing* (3rd ed.). Champaign, IL: Human Kinetics.

Palacios-Huerta, I. (2004). Structural changes during a century of the world's most popular sport. *Statistical Methods & Applications*, *13*(2), 241–258.

Peterman, R., & Suntornpithug, N. (2013). Investigating the impact of economic uncertainties on attendance of premier league Soccer in the United Kingdom and major league Soccer in the United States. *Journal of Applied Business and Economics*, *14*(3), 16–23.

Preston, I., & Szymanski, S. (2003). Cheating in contests. *Oxford Review of Economic Policy*, *19*(4), 612–624.

Psiuk, R., Seidl, T., Strauß, W., & Bernhard, J. (2014). Analysis of goal line technology from the perspective of an electromagnetic field based approach. *Procedia Engineering*, *72*, 279–284.

Rycroft, B. (2013, January 31). CSA cuts ties with Canadian Soccer league. *CBC Sports*. Retrieved from www.cbc.ca/sports-content/soccer/opinion/2013/01/csa-cuts-ties-with-canadian-soccer-league.html

Smith, A. (2011). All bets are off: Match fixing in sport – some recent developments. *Entertainment & Sports Law Journal*, *9*(1), 1–10.

Smith, G. J., Patterson, B., Williams, T., & Hogg, J. (1981). A profile of the deeply committed male sports fan. *Arena Review*, *5*(2), 26–44.

Smith, J. (2001). An introduction to the archaeology and conservation of football stadia. *Industrial Archaeology Review*, *23*(1), 55–66.

Spaaij, R., & Anderson, A. (2010). Psychosocial influences on children's identification with sports teams: A case study of Australian Rules football supporters. *Journal of Sociology*, *46*(3), 299–315.

Squizzato, D. (2014, May 30). Canadian Soccer Association launches initiatives to help prevent match fixing. *MLSSoccer.com*. Retrieved from www.mlssoccer.com/news/article/2014/05/30/canadian-soccer-association-launches-initiatives-help-prevent-match fixing

Sutton, W. A., McDonald, M. A., Milne, G. R., & Cimperman, J. (1997). Creating and fostering fan identification in professional sports. *Sport Marketing Quarterly*, *6*, 15–22.

Sveinson, K., & Hoeber, L. (2016). Female sport fans' experiences of marginalization and empowerment. *Journal of Sport Management*, *30*(1), doi:http://dx.doi.org/10.1123/jsm.2014-0221

Wang, R. T., Zhang, J. J., & Tsuji, Y. (2011). Examining fan motives and loyalty for the Chinese professional baseball league of Taiwan. *Sport Management Review*, *14*(4), 347–360.

Wann, D. L., & Branscombe, N. R. (1993). Sports fans: Measuring degree of identification with their team. *International Journal of Sport Psychology*, *24*(1), 1–17.

Wann, D. L., Tucker, K. B., & Schrader, M. P. (1996). An exploratory examination of the factors influencing the origination, continuation, and cessation of identification with sports teams. *Perceptual and Motor Skills*, *82*, 995–1001.

Appendix A

Participant profile summary

Pseudonym	Gender	Age	Supports	Residence	(Re)Tweet	Occupation
Randy	Male	Early 40's	English clubs and USA	Suburban Cleveland, Ohio, USA	Tweet	Freelance political writer
Julian	Male	Early 30's	Benfica and Portugal	Suburban Toronto, Ontario, Canada	Tweet	Bank operations analyst
Ricky	Male	Early 40's	Manchester United	Johannesburg, South Africa	Tweet	Software sales director
Jamie	Male	Late 20's	Manchester United	Manchester, England	Tweet	Employment consultant
Bobby	Male	Early 20's	AC Milan and Italy	Boston, Massachusetts, USA	Tweet	Professional footballer
Sarah	Female	Mid 20's	Arsenal and South Africa	Cape Town, South Africa	Tweet	Journalist
Jim	Male	Teen	Ajax, Chelsea and Netherlands	Almelo, Netherlands	Retweet	Student
Sam	Male	Early 20's	Manchester United	Leeds, England	Tweet	Student
Lucy	Female	Mid 50's	Manchester United	North Wales, Wales	Retweet	Unemployed
Cory	Male	Early 20's	Manchester United and USA	Suburban New York City, New York, USA	Retweet	Unemployed
Trevor	Male	Teen	Manchester United	Birmingham, England	Retweet	Student
Phil	Male	Mid 20's	Manchester United	London, England	Tweet	Rehabilitation officer

Detailed breakdown:

- Male-to-female ratio – 10:2
- Average age – 28.8 years
- Continental representation – Europe: 6, North America: 4, Africa: 2
- Tweet-to-retweet ratio – 8:4

Interview guide

1 Tell me about your first experience with the game of football.
2 Could you explain how the sport made you feel?
3 Do you support one of Manchester United or Real Madrid? If no, which club do you root for?
4 When did you first become aware of the match fixing phenomenon?

- [Give Forrest (2012) definition about predetermined result]

5 What is your knowledge of the match fixing phenomenon now?

- [Remind and discuss interviewee of their March 2013 tweet]

6 If possible, could you take me back to that day and describe your emotions?
7 How, if at all, has match fixing in football impacted your fandom?
8 [Depending on answer] What would need to be done for your fandom to return to pre-match fixing levels? **OR** Do you envision your fandom changing at all if this current trend continues?
9 Is there anything else you would like to discuss about match fixing?

Participant theme contribution summary

	Category #1			Category #2							Category #3		
	Skepti-cism	Cover-ups	Favorit-ism	Unchanged	Mini-mal	Deescalat-ing	Pro-jected	Transpar-ency	Refer-ees	Conse-quences	Technol-ogy	Gam-bling	Helpless-ness	
Randy	X	X	X	X			X		X					6
Julian	X	X	X	X			X		X				X	7
Ricky	X		X					X	X		X	X		6
Jamie	X					X						X	X	4
Bobby	X		X	X			X							4
Sarah	X			X			X	X					X	5
Jim	X			X	X									2
Sam		X					X			X	X			4
Lucy		X				X								2
Cory	X				X		X	X	X	X		X		7
Trevor	X			X				X	X	X				5
Phil		X			X		X	X						4
	8	5	4	6	3	2	7	5	5	3	2	3	3	

Category #1: Fan Attitudes and Emotions during Match Fixing Era
Category #2: Impacts on Fandom
Category #3: Issues and Suggested Changes to Improve the Game's Perception

Chapter 9

Videographic analysis of "Weird Guys"

What do relationships mean to football fans?

Herbert Woratschek, Chris Horbel, and Bastian Popp

Introduction

Sport is a massive and still growing industry and football (in this chapter "football" refers to European football, i.e., soccer) is perhaps one of the great phenomena in terms of attraction to people of every age, gender, and nationality. The behavior of sport spectators has received huge attention in the academic sport management literature (e.g., Bristow & Sebastian, 2001; Doyle, Kunkel, & Funk, 2013; Funk & James, 2001; Funk, Lock, Karg, & Pritchard, 2016; Laverie & Arnett, 2000; Palmer & Thompson, 2007; Tapp, 2004; Theodorakis, Koustelios, Robinson, & Barlas, 2009; Trail, Anderson, & Fink, 2003; Trail, James, Kwon, Anderson, & Robinson, 2016; Trail & Kim, 2011; Trail, Robinson, & Kim, 2008; Wann, Grieve, Zapalac, & Pease, 2008). The commercial, cultural, and even political impact of football demonstrates the important role that sport plays in contemporary life. It is also widely accepted that "the most powerful organizing forces in modern life are the activities and associated personal relationships that people undertake to give their lives meaning" (Schouten & McAlexander, 1995, p. 43). Being a loyal fan to a particular football team is undoubtedly a highly meaningful activity for football fans (Tapp, 2004). Nevertheless, the factors that provide meaning to them and their complex relationships are not yet completely decoded. Fans may derive meaning from a variety of aspects including the club brand itself, the history of the club, and superstar players (Brandes, Franck, & Nuesch, 2008; Gladden & Funk, 2001; Lucifora & Simmons, 2003). However, the empirical investigation of sport fan behavior clearly shows that most of the activities connected with fandom, e.g., watching a game in a stadium, traveling to away games of the team, or discussing team performance over a drink in a bar, are undertaken in a group. Hence, the social aspect seems to be an important part of the experience. How else could it be explained that people meet at large public places or in bars and pubs to watch sport games at a big screen instead of watching it on TV in the comfort of their homes?

This book chapter is intended to add to the existing literature by taking a closer look at the social relationships of football fans. Social relationships are the culture that evolves between two or more people (McCall, 1970; Wood, 1982). They build on strong bonds that emerge from the interaction between individuals as they act according to common accepted norms and rules. We contribute to a better understanding of how these relationships provide meaning to football fans and, thus, affect their behavior and loyalty to a team. Because of the explorative nature of the research, an ethnographic approach using data from filmed observations of and depth interviews with football fans in Germany was applied. Fans, who follow their teams to away games were chosen for the analysis, because it was assumed they are the most loyal and engaged fans. The remainder of the chapter is organized as follows. We will start with an overview on the related literature. This is followed by an illumination on the research framework and the research setting. We will explain the research methodology used whereby the focus will be on videography as a research method because it has not yet been widely used in sport marketing. Afterwards, the most important themes drawn from interviews and observation are presented and discussed in light of the existing literature. Finally, the concluding sections point out the implications of this study for understanding the social relationships of football fans and the consequences for their relationship to a team. A complementary video which illustrates some interviews and observations can be made available by the authors upon email request.

Review of literature

The literature review is divided into two parts. The first subsection will provide a summary of sport marketing and sport economics literature regarding fan behavior. In particular, we will have a look on loyalty and motives of sport fans and spectators. Second, as a theoretical foundation for investigating the meaning of social relationships to football fans, we will provide some general ideas of the research associated with cultural meanings, subcultures of consumption, and brand communities that are discussed in marketing and consumer research.

Whereas sport economics and sport management literature are focused on studying the peculiarities of sport fan behavior and their implications for management and economic success, the mentioned research on subcultures and communities is focused on the meaning of group activities for consumers. So, we attempt to integrate the findings of sport management and sport economics literature on the one hand and marketing and consumer behavior research on the other to increase our understanding of the meaning of social relationships for football fans and the consequences for their behavior.

Fan motives and fan loyalty

A good deal of previous research on sport spectator behavior has been conducted in the area of team sports. Two main streams of research can be identified that have used different approaches in increasing our understanding of sport fan behavior. On the one hand, most of the research from the field of sport economics is based upon the assumption that the primary reason for sport interest is the so-called competitive balance (Schmidt & Berri, 2001; Vrooman, 1995). This research tradition (Rottenberg, 1956) is based on the assumption that sport series where the capabilities of the teams are almost equally distributed, attract more spectators than unbalanced sport series (Knowles, Sherony, & Haupert, 1992; Schmidt & Berri, 2001). Consequently, the more uncertain the outcome of a game, the more interesting it is for spectators, and the more people go to the stadium or watch it on TV. But, other research shows that spectators actually may prefer unequally distributed capabilities (Peel & Thomas, 1992). Hence, research from the field of sport economics provides inconsistent results concerning the influence of competitive balance on game attendance and fan loyalty. Consequently, we believe that the perspective of the outcome of the game as the dominating motivational factor of spectators attending sport events is too narrow to describe fan behavior.

Another view on sport fan behavior is provided in the sport marketing literature. In this stream of research, fan loyalty and identification with the team are regarded as the main determinants of fan behavior. Within the field of fan loyalty, both behavioral and attitudinal loyalty have been investigated, e.g., game attendance (Laverie & Arnett, 2000), merchandise purchase (Derbaix, Decrop, & Cabossart, 2002), and self-perception of being a fan (Tapp, 2004). The popularity of fan loyalty in research is probably mainly due to the fact that loyalty of sport fans appears sometimes dysfunctional, especially when it is even increasing the worse the team is performing (Bristow & Sebastian, 2001). Hence, in contrast to the assumptions in sport economic literature, satisfaction with the outcome of the game appears to have little link to loyalty, at least for some of the sport fans (Yoshida, Heere, & Gordon, 2015).

In addition, loyalty of sport fans is fascinating because "loyalty is important to them in a way that it is not to consumers in most consumer sectors (how many shoppers will sing 'loyal customers' as they make their weekly trip to Asda?)" (Tapp, 2004, p. 204). Therefore, loyalty to a team is a highly meaningful concept for sport fans. While Parker and Stuart (1997) point out that exclusive loyalty to a team is the norm, and that loyalty is not affected by team success at all, other authors state that loyalty of sport fans cannot be taken for granted. They emphasize that different types of sport fans show different loyalty and different behavior depending on the team's success (Tapp, 2004). Based on the work of Dick and Basu (1994), Tapp (2004) identified five football supporter categories based on their attitudinal and behavioral loyalty to a team. In his four-year study on British Premier League football fans, he found a sizeable segment of "fanatics," i.e. highly committed fans who actively and consciously expressed their loyalty to the club and in whose lives the football club played an important role. The segment of "collectors" were also highly committed fans who additionally intensively bought merchandise items and club memorabilia. Another segment were "repertoire fans" who not only watched the games of their favorite teams, but frequently also games of other teams. On the lower end of the spectrum, Tapp (2004) found two segments of spectators who attended the games of the team only occasionally. Whereas "committed casuals" saw themselves as very loyal and were attitudinally highly committed, the group of "carefree casuals" was only interested in watching an interesting football game from time to time, no matter which team was playing. The reactions of these five segments on the team's success are certainly very different. Whereas fanatics will still be loyal to the team even when success is missing, casual supporters might cease to watch the games in such a situation. These different reactions are described by Cialdini et al. (1976) as BIRGing (Basking in Reflected Glory) and CORFing (Cutting Off Reflected Failure) behavior and have been found to vary across different types of sport fans (Madrigal, 1995; Sloan, 1989). Wann and Branscombe (1990) found that individuals high in team identification were more likely to BIRG after a victory and less likely to CORF after defeat. Those fans are likely to support their team even when they drop down the league, and satisfaction with the outcome of a game is not linked to their loyalty (Tapp, 2004).

In addition to the study of different supporter segments there is a substantial literature on hooliganism, which examines the socio-cultural backgrounds of hooligans and their impact on other fans as well as on society (Frosdick & Marsh, 2005; Hahn, Pilz, Stollenwerk, & Weis, 1988; Pilz, Albrecht, & Gabler, 1987; Pilz et al., 2006; Van Hiel, Hautman, Cornelis, & De Clercq, 2007). Motives of sport spectators are another important area of research related to sport fan behavior (Trail, Anderson, & Fink, 2000; Wann, 1995; Wann et al., 2008). Motives of sport fans have an effect on fan behavior because they do not only directly influence their expectations of game outcomes, but also indirectly, through identification with the team (Trail et al., 2003). Hence, motives of sport fans also influence their loyalty to a team. Wann (1995) developed a sport fan motivation scale (SFMS) including the eight motivational factors escape, economic (i.e., gambling), eustress (i.e., positive arousal), self-esteem, group affiliation, entertainment, family, and aesthetics. Based upon this scale and an extensive literature review, Trail et al. (2000) proposed nine different motives that explain why individuals attend sport events or why they are sport fans. The motives include vicarious achievement, acquisition of knowledge, aesthetics, social interaction, drama/excitement, escape (relation), family, physical attractiveness of participants, and quality of physical skill of the participants. While these motives are considered as general motives of sport fans, we assume that different motives influence the behavior of the various fan segments. Therefore, our study focused on the particular group of fans who travel to away games of their teams, since we assume that they have very special characteristics and motivations.

Furthermore, this study seeks to test the suitability of a service-dominant logic perspective on value creation in sport as it is provided in the Sport Value Framework (Woratschek, Horbel, & Popp, 2014). This perspective contrasts traditional sport economic and sport management approaches which are based on a goods-dominant logic (Chelladurai, 2013). According to this traditional logic, sport organizations and firms create value by producing and selling sport goods, for example sport events that are understood as products. In contrast, the perspective of service-dominant logic (Vargo & Lusch, 2004) suggests that sport organizations, firms, athletes, spectators, fans, and other actors collaboratively create value (Woratschek et al., 2014). According to the Sport Value Framework (SVF), sport events are not considered as goods or products, but "as platforms that actors can use to co-create value in their business and leisure activities" (Woratschek et al., 2014, p. 21). Relationships between fans, spectators, athletes, sport organizations, and other actors influence the value derived from sport events. Therefore, we assume that SVF is a more appropriate framework to analyze sport events than the traditional perspective on sport events as products. However, there is still lack of empirical evidence for the adequacy of SVF. Nevertheless, actors' motives are decisive for participation in sport events. Moreover, they govern their relationships and behavior before, during and after a sport event and hence, their value co-creation with others. The meaning of relationships with other fans can be interpreted as one indicator of value co-created through sport events.

Cultures of consumption

Various theoretical perspectives have been developed that emphasize the experiences, identities, social dynamics, and cultural meanings associated with consumption (Arnould & Thompson, 2005). In the 1980s, some authors (Belk, 1986, 1987; Holbrook, 1987) still claimed that research of consumption and consumer behavior should be free of a managerial perspective. However, subsequent developments such as relationship marketing "have brought consumer meanings to the centre of managerial concerns" (Arnould & Thompson, 2005, p. 870). Understanding consumer behavior is essential to developing successful marketing strategies. Many of the early consumer behavior studies have tried to illuminate how cognition, perceptions or traits of individuals influence their consumption behavior. Since the 1990s, more and more studies have introduced the concept of community in order to gain a better understanding of communal consumption (Cova, 1997). Most of these studies are based on Maffesoli's (1996) thoughts on neotribalism, which he describes as the consumers' response to the isolating conditions of modern societies. These conditions lead to the development of communities or tribes, which are networks of people "held together through shared emotions, styles of life, new moral beliefs, senses of injustice and consumption practices" (Cova, 1997, p. 301). Consumer researchers have investigated this phenomenon of consumers pursuing common consumption interests and thereby sharing consciousness, rituals, traditions, and symbols (Arnould & Thompson, 2005; Muniz & O'Guinn, 2001). Various labels have been used for these communities: subculture of consumption (Schouten & McAlexander, 1995), consumption world (Holt, 1995), consumption microculture (Thompson & Troester, 2002), and culture of consumption (Kozinets, 2001). One specific kind of these communities are brand communities. Muniz and O'Guinn (2001, p. 412) define them as "a specialized, non-geographically bound community, based on a structured set of social relationships among admirers of a brand." The study of such brand communities has received increasing attention because it could be shown that inter-customer relationships have important influence on customer loyalty to a brand (Holt, 1995; McAlexander, Schouten, & Koenig, 2002; Muniz & O'Guinn, 2001).

Early research mainly studied the phenomenon of brand communities in prototypical examples of cars (e.g., *Jeep*, *Saab*, *Hummer* as in Muniz and O'Guinn (2001); McAlexander, Schouten, and Koenig (2002); Algesheimer, Dholakia, and Herrmann (2005); Bagozzi and Dholakia (2006); Luedicke (2006)), motorcycles (e.g., *Harley-Davidson* as in McAlexander, Schouten, and Koenig (2002); *Ducati* as in Marzocchi, Morandin, & Bergami (2013)) and computers (*Apple* as in Muniz and O'Guinn (2001); Muniz and Schau (2005)) and investigated characteristics of brand community members. The studies reveal that a brand community is characterized by consciousness of kind, shared rituals and traditions and a sense of moral responsibility (Muniz & O'Guinn, 2001). The members of a brand community strongly identify with their group as well as the brand (Bagozzi & Dholakia, 2006; O'Guinn & Muniz, 2005). Thus, according to the social identity theory (Tajfel, 1978; Turner, 1982), the individuals possess a social identity which in conjunction with the individual's personal identity constitutes the consumer's self-concept. This social psychological theory of group membership, group processes, and intergroup relations stresses the importance of social relationships among the group members (Hogg & Michell, 1996). In addition, members of a brand community often consciously distance themselves from other brands, which is referred to as oppositional brand loyalty (Muniz & O'Guinn, 2001; Thompson & Sinha, 2008). Organized events, so called brandfests (McAlexander & Schouten, 1998; Solomon, 2003) can help brand community members both to convene and socialize and to strengthen their identification with the brand. Such activities are very effective as Schouten, McAlexander, and Koenig (2007) proved with their brand community study on transcendent customer experiences regarding the importance of flow and/or peak experiences.

A prominent example of a brand community is the Harley Owners Group (HOG), whose members share the usage or interest in Harley-Davidson motorcycles. The HOG was initiated in 1983 by Harley-Davidson to help organize chapters and allow for greater interaction between members of the Harley-Davidson brand community. The consciousness of kind is facilitated by restricting the membership to owners of Harley-Davidson motorcycles. Shared rituals and traditions are encouraged by rallies and brandfests and the moral responsibility is ensured by rules governing the membership and the members' commitment to the HOG culture.

Inter-customer relationships are also a key concern of tribal marketing, which emphasizes the contribution of products or services to establishing and/or reinforcing bonds between individuals. It has been found that consumer tribes are capable of collective action and their members are often even advocates of the product or service they support (Cova & Cova, 2002). Similar effects have been studied in the field of organizational identification, which can be seen as an extension of group identification (Elsbach, 1999). Organizational identification has been defined as "the degree to which a person defines him or herself as having the same attributes that he or she believes define the organization" (Dutton, Dukerich, & Harquail, 1994). Organizational identification has been shown to increase members' loyalty to the organization, their promotion of the organization and willingness to contribute to it financially, as well as their engagement in extra-role behaviors (Adler & Adler, 1988; Mael & Ashforth, 1992; O'Reilly & Chatman, 1986). Identification is considered as favorable because identifiers align organizational outcomes with their own (Pratt, 1998). However, similar to the oppositional brand loyalty of brand community members, it is possible to disidentify with an organization, thus expressing a negative organizational relationship (Elsbach, 1999; Foster & Hyatt, 2007). Regardless of the form of identification, theoretical and empirical research suggests the importance of this construct for consumers or fans.

Quantitative studies in emerging research on sport-linked consumer behavior and brand communities support that fan community attachment increases game attendance frequency (Yoshida et al., 2015). Moreover, membership in a consumption community has been shown to affect attendance, purchase, and word-of-mouth intentions (Hedlund, 2014). Insightful qualitative research also investigated the interaction of sport team-related brand communities in the online environment (Healy & McDonagh, 2013;

Pongsakornrungsilp & Schroeder, 2011). However, knowledge about the meaning of relationships for the multifaceted groups of football fans is still limited. We therefore now turn to an overview of the research framework and the setting in which we will shed further light into this issue.

Research framework

For the primary research undertaken, it was decided to focus on a group of very loyal and committed fans. It was felt that within our ethnographic research approach these fans would best be able to express their feelings both, towards their favorite team and the social relationships that are associated to their fan identity. Funk and James (2001) categorize these extremely loyal fans into the allegiance stage of their Psychological Continuum Model and point out that this group of fans is unlikely to stop being loyal to their club. Nevertheless, it is particularly interesting and valuable to study this group of fans in more detail for several reasons. First, these fans are loyal to the club even if the team is not successful, thus, unlike other sources of revenue (e.g. sponsoring, merchandising, broadcasting rights), the loyal fans constitute the steady base of a club. Hence, for club management, it is imperative to understand the factors underlying their loyalty in order to ensure their commitment in the future. In addition, this "hard core" of fans represents a significant factor for attracting other fans, since they root for the team and are mainly responsible for the atmosphere in the stadium, which attracts occasional or first time spectators (Uhrich & Königstorfer, 2009). In addition, members of fan communities recruit new fans and spectators by recommending the club to friends who want to take part in the group or even feel squeezed into it (Algesheimer et al., 2005).

The group of fans that was selected for our study are 'fan tourists.' As fan tourism, we define a specific form of both sport tourism (Standeven & DeKnop, 1999) and event tourism (Getz, 1997), where a passive engagement in competitive sport as supporter or spectator (Turco, Riley, & Swart, 2002) is the main reason for traveling. In other words, a fan tourist is a fan who travels to watch an away game of a team. The characteristics of these fans are probably very similar to the segment of "fanatics" described by Tapp (2004). However, as we employed the actual travel behavior to away games to identify the segment of fan tourists, we used another term in order to avoid confusion with Tapp's (2004) typology of fans. In our study, many fan tourists told us that they travel to each out-of-town game of their team, which means every second weekend during an eight-month season. As this is both very time-consuming and costly, you might say that these people are "Weird Guys." They dedicate most of their time and money to their favourite team and they are proud to be 'special' because they go to the extremes for their club. They document their distinctiveness by counting the number of games they have attended or the number of kilometres they have travelled to see the games of their team and present their 'records' publicly on their fan clothes.

Based on our literature review on brand communities we believe that fans showing such high levels of commitment and behavioral loyalty to a team, like the fan tourists in our study, have a lot in common with members of (sub)cultures of consumption (Kozinets, 2001; Schouten & McAlexander, 1995) or brand communities (McAlexander et al., 2002; Muniz & O'Guinn, 2001). We will therefore use the findings from brand community and consumption subcultures research and compare them to our findings on fan tourists. We will pay particular attention to the social relationships of the fans and their meanings. Based upon that, we will have a closer look at how these relationships affect fan behavior, most importantly, their loyalty to the team. This leads us to our overall research questions that will guide our study:

1   What do social relationships mean to football fans?
2   How do social relationships affect fan behavior and loyalty to a team?
3   Is the SVF a more appropriate framework to analyze relationships among fans than the traditional goods-dominant logic in sport management?

Methodology

In this study, we collaborated with three clubs of the first, second, and third German football league. Several reasons accounted for the selection of a qualitative approach to our research. First of all, a high degree of trust between researcher and respondent is necessary in order to discuss and understand why football is such an important part of the self of a fan. Further, our literature review showed that the factors that influence football fans' behavior and loyalty are very complex. So, it was doubted that it would be possible to integrate all these aspects in a standardised questionnaire without asking too much of the participants. In addition, most of the existing studies on sport fan behavior had been undertaken in other team sports (basketball, Laverie and Arnett (2000); baseball, Bristow and Sebastian (2001)), and/or another cultural environment (e.g., in the United States as in Trail et al. (2003), or in the United Kingdom, as in Tapp (2004)). For these reasons, it was felt that not all of the earlier findings might be relevant within our research setting, but additional motives and behaviors of the fans might play a role. In particular, it should be avoided that important aspects that are relevant for the behavior of football fans were missing in the survey.

Ethnographic field work was conducted at home games and away games of the cooperating teams. In addition, data were collected in fan busses or fan trains, which were used by the fans to travel to away games. The study consists of two major elements: (1) face-to-face depth interviews conducted directly before or after home and away games, mainly in front of the stadiums or in fan busses and fan trains, and (2) observations in stadiums, fan busses and trains, and in front of stadiums. Observed events and depth interviews were recorded with a digital video camcorder. This method, which is also referred to as videography is "a form of visual anthropology encompassing the collection, analysis, and presentation of visual data" (Kozinets & Belk, 2006, pp. 318–319). Video-based data collection and analysis was chosen for several reasons. Most important, it enabled us to "capture the subtle temporal, social, and spatial dimensions" (Kozinets & Belk, 2006, p. 320) of the football fans' behavior. In particular, it provides for the analysis of emotional expressions and body language (Belk & Kozinets, 2005). This was important, because football fans' behavior and body language, e.g., singing battle chants, is special for this particular group and an expression of their loyalty. However, the inclusion of interpretations of mimic, facial expressions, gestures, or vocal alterations of the informants in the analysis was limited to very obvious aspects in order to avoid misinterpretations. Further, videos allow observing and documenting peoples' behavioral interactions, for example with other fans. These are expressions of their relationships to other people and therefore of particular interest for our study. Finally, we agree with Belk and Kozinets (2005) that videotaped data enable to present a multi-sensory set of materials to an audience. This has several advantages. Intersubjective reliability of qualitative data analysis increases, as those who are interested can easily be presented with the data collected. In contrast to other forms of data presentation, the audience is able to not only gain a cognitive understanding, but also an emotional understanding of the data collected (Belk & Kozinets, 2005).

Field work took place from February until May 2005. Within this period 86 depth interviews with football fans were conducted and about 2:45 hours of observations were videotaped. Participants in our study were not only fans from the three collaborating clubs, but also fans from other clubs who were the opponents of the teams in the games we visited. As a result, fans from nine German football clubs participated in the study. The interviews were of varying duration: videotaped interviews ranged from five to 40 minutes. Male informants constituted nearly 90% of the sample and participants were aged between 15 and 65.

We analyzed the videotaped materials using content analytic techniques (Krippendorff, 2004). Especially, the videotaped observations and interviews were coded and analyzed following qualitative content analysis (Kohlbacher, 2005; Mayring, 2000). Two researchers participated in the interpretive process. In a first step, both researchers independently sighted the film footage and inductively determined categories relevant for our research questions. Thereafter, the coders compared and discussed the categories in an iterative process until the themes presented in the following section were derived. In a next step, the two researchers derived sequences within the videos and assigned them to the categories. Measures of intercoder reliability were calculated in order to increase the probability of intersubjective replicability of the results. For all steps, values of the percentage of agreement and Perreault and Leigh's (1989) reliability index I_r exceeded the suggested threshold of .80. At the end of the data analysis, we translated parts of the interviews into English and cut a subtitled video for the presentation of our research. We now turn to the themes drawn from interviews and observations.

Results

Identification

As suggested by previous research on sport fan behavior, strong identification with the team is most important to many fans and one of the major driving forces for their behavior. But why does identification with the club mean so much to the fans? One of our informants answered as follows:

M68: We are simply Nuremberg fans, and a Nuremberg fan is a Nuremberg fan, once you have been a Nuremberg fan you are always a Nuremberg fan.

Another fan said:

M41: Actually, every game is positive, whether you win or lose, you are just committed to the club – and that is what is most important to me.

For some fans, identification with the club also comes with local patriotism:

M20: I am a fan of Darmstadt by conviction. Darmstadt fans are their own people anyway – either you are a fan or you're not. And if you are a fan you are a fan with body and soul. And as a person with strong local bonds [being a fan of] this sports club comes with the territory.

Brand communities and (sub)cultures of consumption are typical sources of identity for their members (Kozinets, 2001; Muniz & O'Guinn, 2001). This obvious analogy can serve as a first indicator, that the community of highly committed football fans can be analyzed using theories from brand communities and (sub)cultures of consumption.

In addition to the quotes from the interviews with the participants, videography showed that identification with a team is to a great extent emotionally driven. Delivering information about the emotional state of the informants, which can, for example, be drawn from their body language, pitch of the voice, and intonation is one of the powerful advantages of this method. For example, one male fan expressed his deep loyalty to his favorite club, Darmstadt 98, by wearing a jacket with patches he had collected over the years. He could tell the story of each of them and explain their meaning to him. His emotions became obvious when he was talking with a big smile about happy memories, e.g. winning in an important local derby. You could see his excitement when he was telling about the events in a particularly thrilling game. He then spoke faster and faster and used a lot of hand gestures to emphasize his explanations, which nearly made them visible before our eyes. On the other hand, telling us about sad experiences, e.g., his team getting relegated to the third league or his own unemployment, he spoke slower, his voice much lower, and with his body bowed down.

Social relationships

In the interviews, we found that establishing and maintaining social relationships to other fans are essential parts of being a loyal fan of a football club. Therefore, it is not surprising that many fans have been brought to a football stadium by relatives or acquaintances for the first time:

M12: It starts with your friends. I am part of a circle of friends. These friends go to the 98ers. So, I am doing what my friends are doing. This is the first step.

Being a part of a larger group is also an important motivation:

M67: It makes you getting closer to the others. At home, in front of a TV, you sit alone, or together with one, two, or sometimes ten other people. But, in the stadium, there are 2,000, 3,000, or 4,000 other fans [of your club] at an away game, at a home game even 20,000 or 30,000 – that unites with the other fans.

For many fans, it is also important to use the time they spend in the stadium or in a fan bus or fan train to maintain their existing social relationships and get together with their friends:

M23: It means, many of your social contacts are related to it. These are people you can't meet every day because of your job, but, at the weekends you have time. You meet there. It is the environment where you can meet your friends. And that is very important.
M20: That is the reason why we go there: because we always meet our whole circle of friends there. Besides the mere game, being together with your friends is the main reason to go there.

Particularly at trips to away games, fans appreciate that they always meet many friends:

M31: The special thing about away games is, you meet more people you know than at home games. At away games there are always the same people. I really meet more people at away games, no matter where we go, than at home games.

Being together with the other fans can also be a family substitute:

M43: Hansa Rostock – and then you are there, and you travel to away games and that is like a family.

Of course, fans also like celebrating parties in the stadiums, the busses, or trains:

M48: We have fun together, we party together.

In our study, a number of observations of these celebrations have been made and videotaped. Again, the videos expressed the emotions and vibes involved in the parties and proved that the fan tourists' behavior is similar to that of members of (sub)cultures of consumption. One impression of the fans celebrating in the train is shown in Figure 9.1.

Figure 9.1 Social relationships – celebration in the fan train

On the other hand, besides meeting friends and acquaintances, there is also the opportunity to meet new people at football games, particularly at away games. So, both establishing new social relationships and keeping up with existing ones is valued by the fans:

M32:   You meet a lot of football friends you would not have met in front of the stadium. It is a good way to mingle with people. And I like that time and time again.

F06:   What really fascinates me und what I did not know before is that [I get the chance] to mingle with people I usually never would have met.

Fans who go to many away games of their team often mention another interesting group of people they build relationships with: they even build friendships with fans of other teams and games against these teams belong to the highlights of the season. Hence, football seems to provide the "linking value" that is proposed by the advocates of tribal marketing (Cova, 1997). Football games, and especially common travels to away games, are platforms where people can meet and social relationships can be developed and maintained. By remaining loyal to the other fans, loyalty to the club is built. Reducing social isolation and building personal relationships to others is a theme which has also been found in other studies of (sub)cultures of consumption which again supports the assumption that highly loyal football fans can be characterized as a (sub)culture of consumption (Kozinets, 2002).

Distancing from occasional spectators

Fan tourists also see themselves as a special group within the broader community of football fans and spectators. They characterize themselves as the 'hard core' of fans and appreciate to be 'special':

M43:   Yes, because the hard core travels along. And that the hard core is present. That is the bottom line because at home, people like to show up with their family simply because they want to see a football game; whoever comes along here – to Nuremberg – of course comes here because he is a die-hard Rostock fan.

F03:   Only the hard core takes part in it, and not only those people are along, who merely go to one good game per season, but instead those people, who are interested in it and go along often.

For some fans, this relatively small community of "hardcore" fans, who always travel to away games, and the common interest they have, supporting the club, is the center of their lives:

M24:   If the hard core, what I really can't and don't want to imagine, would not stick together any longer, I probably would not watch every game.

It is very important, that if you go to football games like us you need your group, your environment.

Fan tourists who regularly travel to away games not only perceive themselves as 'hard-core' fans and like to be special. They are even proud of being 'extreme.' A 65-year-old male informant has already traveled many hundred thousands of kilometers to see games of his team.

M32: Well, football-traveling record, I am proud of it, you know, I already travelled many hundred thousands of kilometres. This week, I wrote up a record of the distances and came up with 760.000 kilometres – counting all games – all compulsory games.

In addition, traveling to away games is prestigious and can even lead to achieving a higher status within the fan community:

M36: Of course, a fan who always travels everywhere and goes to his limit for the club claims a certain, higher rank for himself.
INTERVIEWER: Farther distances are more interesting?
M38: Of course; actually, they are more interesting – the less people that come along from Stuttgart, the more interesting it is . . . because not everyone went along and because we can be proud of it or because we travelled quite far.

Distancing from others is a theme which has also been found essential for brand communities (Muniz & O'Guinn, 2001) and other (sub)cultures of consumption (Kozinets, 2002). Muniz and O'Guinn (2001, p. 418) even see consciousness of kind as "the most important element of community". They found similar comments of brand community members who referred to themselves as being 'different' or 'special' in comparison to other brand users.

Rituals

Rituals play an important role for football fans. Most obvious, battle chants and merchandising items are an integral part of football fan culture. More and more, football fans even rehearse whole choreographies to present in the stadium:

M36: At the one hand, it is a gift of the fans, that means from us to the other fans and of course, primarily to the team. And in the end, it is a fantastic feeling if you get it right to make such a big choreography work.

Battle chants are organized in the stadium, very often by one person who acts as a conductor and sometimes even like a drill sergeant. Our videos very powerfully show the emotions involved in the battle chants and choreographies, because noises, people movements, and body language are depicted. One of these rituals, showing fans in the stadium supporting their team directed by two of them standing in front of the others is shown in Figure 9.2. Rituals are typically centered on the shared experience with the team, i.e. the games of the team:

M45: The team just feels that in a certain moment – whether someone is there or not. Now when three hundred fans are somewhere or a thousand fans are in a stadium, and you root a little – I think that the team does notice that.

M35: That is definitely what I think – that it definitely – that it helps the club when people are along who root for them, particularly in the out-of-town stadium.

Besides battle chants and other rituals associated with the support of the team, there is also the same course of activities undertaken before, during and after each game that unites the fans:

M22: For home games, you leave forty-five minutes ahead of time and then arrive and drink two or three beers and are pleased and watch the game.

Figure 9.2 Rituals – organized battle chants in the stadium

M24: In a home game you meet three hours ahead of time, get everything set up, carry the things into the stand and so forth.

Rituals are also an analogy with brand communities and (sub)cultures of consumption. Rituals serve as a means to maintain the culture of the community (Muniz & O'Guinn, 2001). Other members of the community can be identified because of the rituals they carry out, they support cohesion between the fans of one team, they support the expression of feelings, and they have symbolic meanings to the fans (Derbaix et al., 2002; Kozinets, 2001).

Escape

Being a football fan and even more traveling to away games of the team for some fans functions as a means to break out from roles they play in everyday life:

M46: It is possible to put yourself into a completely different role, I mean, by wearing these outfits, no one would believe that I am going back to work for the Deutsche Bank tomorrow again.

Sometimes, it is not only an escape from everyday role models, but also from other difficulties in life, for example, unemployment and frustration:

M12: Even if this club – and that's what I believe – even if this club should be relegated to the Amateur League, I would go there time and time again. Because I am – I have to put it like this – like four million others, I am out of work. I'm at home all day long – during the whole week. You go to the Darmstadt 98 games because that is the only thing you are left with, yes – you are practically living it out.

This quotation from a 38-year-old unemployed fan already gives an impression of his frustration with his personal situation. However, the videotape of this interview carries his emotions and feelings in a much more explicit way. Another informant even expresses that in his role as football fan he is able to compensate a lack of self-confidence:

M46: Now I'm 5 feet 2 inches tall, I usually get picked on. People step to the side, you let your beard grow for five weeks, you walk through the streets, you are perceived differently, you approach people differently . . . and – it's amazing, you sit in the urban railway and can be a bit of a bully, without being one.

A confession like this could only be articulated in a setting where the informant was feeling comfortable and trusted in the interviewer. In this particular

Figure 9.3 Escape – fans in fan outfits arriving at the train station

situation the informant was even a little bit excited because it was right before the game. The relaxed atmosphere, which is very obvious on the videotape, because he is also joking around with a friend, enabled him to talk freely about his feelings, what he would probably not have done in a laboratory setting.

Figure 9.3 shows fans at an away game of their team arriving at the train station. Although arriving at opponents' territory, they feel powerful as can be noticed by studying their body language. Living out other roles has also been found to be an important element of (sub)cultures of consumption. For example, "Burning Man offers its participants a social arena where they are encouraged to experimentally express and re-create their identities . . ." (Kozinets, 2002, p. 30). Also, for *Star Trek* fans, the whole *Star Trek* world serves as a utopian refuge (Kozinets, 2001).

Discussion

Although activities of sport fans are mainly group activities and social inter-action obviously is an important part of the experience, these aspects are barely discussed in-depth in the literature on sport fan behavior. There-fore, this ethnographic study analysed some of the articulations and behav-iors of a specific group of football fans, who we label "fan tourists." The focus of our study was on the meanings of social relationships to this group of football fans. In particular, we were interested in learning more about the impact of social relationships on fan behavior and on their loyalty to the team. The analysis of the data collected was based upon the theory of subcultures and brand communities where the social and inter-subjective aspects of consumer behavior are discussed (e.g., Cova, 1997; Kozinets, 2001; McAlexander et al., 2002; Muniz & O'Guinn, 2001; Schouten & McAlexander, 1995).

Evident throughout the articulations of the study participants are a num-ber of analogies with (sub)cultures of consumption and brand communities which illustrate what relationships mean to football fans. Like (sub)cultures of consumption or brand communities which are formed around one par-ticular object, e.g., *Star Trek* (Kozinets, 2001), or a product or service brand, e.g., *Harley Davidson* (Schouten & McAlexander, 1995), fan tourists can be described as a community formed around a particular sports club brand. Such communities typically provide a basis for identification for their mem-bers and influence the community members' relationships and the meanings derived (Algesheimer et al., 2005). Whereas identification with the team and valuing the opportunity to establish and maintain social relationships are to some degree true for all football fans, one theme was mainly articulated by fan tourists: they characterized themselves as being 'special' because they go to the extremes to support their team. Hereby, they differentiate between 'true' members of the community and those who are not. This "conscious-ness of kind," where members "note a critical demarcation between users of their brand and users of other brands" (Muniz & O'Guinn, 2001, p. 418) has also been found a characteristic of brand communities. Sharing rituals is also an element that can be found in (sub)cultures of consumption. Whether it is "burning the man" (Kozinets, 2002, p. 21) at the Burning Man Festival, greeting the drivers of the same car brand by beeping or flashing the lights (Muniz & O'Guinn, 2001), or singing battle chants in a football stadium; all these rituals represent social processes by which the meanings of the com-munity are built and shared. Within the community of football fans, people are able to escape from everyday life and their usual role models. (Sub)cul-tures of consumption and brand communities are likewise used for escapes from those behaviors that are permissible in everyday society to more radi-cal types of self-expression (Kozinets, 2002). Our findings therefore contrib-ute to emergent research on sport fans relationships that draw on a brand community perspective. In particular, Katz and Heere (2013) studied the formation of a new brand community and illuminate how particular social networks develop within the overall community. We further complement Grant, Heere, and Dickson's (2011) research on brand community markers in the context of newly established sport teams, in which the authors studied whether managers of newly established New Zealand professional sports teams utilize group experience, organizational history, ritual/traditions, and physical facility in their branding strategies.

In our study on fan tourists, identification with the team clearly was one of the major themes articulated by participants. Football brings together people who very often share no other connection than an interest in the club and in football in general, as they come from very different social backgrounds. Football gives the opportunity for context-rich interaction and for sharing meaningful consumption experiences in various contexts such as stadiums, public screening areas, and bars (Horbel, Popp, Woratschek, & Wilson, 2016). Sharing experiences in these contexts strengthens interpersonal ties among the fans. Hence, the notion that the relationship of the fans to the club alone serves as a repository for meaning overlooks other relationships that supply significant value to fans (McAlexander et al., 2002). These social relationships clearly affect fan behavior and loyalty towards a team. In particular, the relationships with other fans play an important role for the loyalty to the club, because by being loyal to other fans, loyalty to the club is strengthened at the same time. Hence, in contrast to sport economic literature that sees constructs like competitive balance or the uncertainty of the outcome of the game, i.e. the quality of the games, as major forces driving fan attendance at sport games, "the link is more important than the thing" (Cova, 1997, p. 314).

In order to ensure loyalty of their fans, football clubs therefore have to care for opportunities that function as linking places where bonds between individuals can be established and/or reinforced. Football stadiums and, even more so, fan busses and fan trains, are "linking places" (Cova, 1997, p. 313) that support the construction and maintenance of social relationships. These relationships are highly valued by the fans, and sometimes they are even the main reason to watch a game. Therefore, fans do not value sport events as products, but they use sport events as platforms to meet others to establish new and maintain existing social relationships. Hence, the social ties have a substantial impact on the loyalty to the team and value is not only derived by the fans but also by their team. Value is co-created for all actors at the sport event. We therefore argue that sport organizations can provide a platform for value creation, but value is not solely being created by them. Value is always co-created by actors such as the fan tourists who use the platform provided by the sport organization. Our research on the group of fan tourists thus supports the notion of the SVF as a valuable framework for analysis of the relationships of sport fans. Fans do not consume value which is provided by sport organizations and firms, but they co-create value through social relationships by using the sport event as a platform. As a consequence, SVF is a more appropriate framework than traditional approaches to explain relationships among fans. Following

SVF and complementary approaches, fan tourists are members of a specific brand community showing characteristics of subcultures (e.g., rituals) and using platforms provided by sport organisations to co-create value through social ties. This interpretation is very different from traditional perspectives where sport events are regarded as products. SVF leads to a deeper understanding of the behavior of social actors at sport events, respectively the behavior of fan tourists before, during, and after a sport event.

Conclusions

This chapter contributes to the existing literature by analysing the meaning of social relationships for football fans and how they affect their behaviors and loyalty to a team. It can be observed that sport fans love to take part in group activities, e.g., watching games in stadiums, bars, or other public places and traveling to away games in a group. Group affiliation is discussed as a motive of attending sport events and becoming a fan. However, the meanings of social relationships to the fans and their impact on behavior are hardly discussed in the literature on sport fans. Furthermore, an adequate framework leading to a deeper understanding how different approaches are linked to each other was missed. With our study, we tried to fill this gap by building on brand community and subcultures of consumption research and discussing our primary data on sport fans in light of SVF with a focus on the social relationships between the members of the sport brand community.

An ethnographic approach using videography was applied. For the investigation of this particular research question videography proved to have some very powerful advantages. Most noteworthy, it enabled us to gather information about the emotions of the informants by analyzing their body language, pitch of the voice, or intonation. The conclusion of this work is that sport fan loyalty to a team is much more complex than is suggested by only looking at the relationship between a fan and the team. Studies on game attendance from the field of sport economics, which are focused on the uncertainty of the outcome of the game as main driver of sport fan behavior do not only deliver inconsistent results, but also overlook other factors that have probably a more substantial influence on fan loyalty. The fan is part of a whole network of relationships that all provide meaning to him or her and also to his or her relationship to the team. Consequently, a holistic approach like SVF is necessary when looking at fan loyalty.

We were able to show that football fans form communities similar to those discussed in brand community and subcultures of consumption research. This has important management implications. If you realize that football fans build a brand community, you also need to realize that their relationships among each other might be even more important and meaningful to them than their relationship to the club. The relationships between the fans cannot directly be influenced by managers. Sport club managers therefore must find ways to contribute to the process of community building by creating a context that facilitates fan interaction. The opportunity to establish and maintain relationships to other fans accounts considerably to fan loyalty. These indirect measures of relationship building can be even more powerful than direct approaches to the fans, e.g., sending a regular newsletter. The benefits from high levels of fan loyalty are many and diverse. Loyal fans are less likely to cease watching the games in a period of lacking performance; they are motivated to function as advocates, thereby supporting the extension of the fan base, they constitute a strong market for merchandising products and they are emotionally involved with the team, which leads to a desire to contribute to the team's success. In order to be able to provide linking places, a deeper understanding of the fans is necessary.

The findings of this study are subject to limitations that must be noted. Our research has inherent methodological limitations. Some of the drawbacks are associated with the use of videography. Participants' reactions on the video camera were diverse. While the sample mainly comprises of people who had no negative emotions about being filmed with some of them having been almost magically attracted by the sight of the camera, others might have felt uncomfortable to be videotaped. Recordings in fan busses and trains were constrained by the limited space and shakes of the means of transportation, so that in some cases not all advantages of the video could be used. Our research touches on the issue that football clubs should provide linking places for the establishment of social ties between fans. For the future, it would be valuable to examine, for example, how such opportunities can be created around a sport event. However, our study is limited to relationships of fan tourists. SVF stand to reason that value is always co-created by many different actors. Therefore, it is important for future research to extend the analyses of social ties of other social actors like athletes, coaches, managers, security staff, service providers, and many more. Finally, our research is limited to the real-world interaction among fan tourists. Future studies therefore should address how the use of social and other digital media influences the offline relationships among fan tourists in particular and sport fans in general.

References

Adler, P., & Adler, P. (1988). Intense loyalty in organizations: A case study of college athletics. *Administrative Science Quarterly*, *33*(3), 401–417.

Algesheimer, R., Dholakia, U. M., & Herrmann, A. (2005). The social influence of brand community: Evidence from European car clubs. *Journal of Marketing*, *69*(3), 19–34.

Arnould, E. J., & Thompson, C. J. (2005). Consumer Culture Theory (CCT): Twenty years of research. *Journal of Consumer Research*, *31*(4), 868–882.

Bagozzi, R. P., & Dholakia, U. M. (2006). Antecedents and purchase consequences of customer participation in small group brand communities. *International Journal of Research in Marketing, 23*(1), 45–61.

Belk, R. W. (1986). What should ACR want to be when it grows up? In R. J. Lutz (Ed.), *Advances in consumer research, Vol. 13* (pp. 423–424). Provo: Association for Consumer Research.

Belk, R. W. (1987). Happy thought. In M. Wallendorf & P. Anderson (Eds.), *Advances in consumer research, Vol. 14* (pp. 1–4). Provo, UT: Association for Consumer Research.

Belk, R. W., & Kozinets, R. V. (2005). Videography in marketing and consumer research. *Qualitative Market Research: An International Journal, 8*(2), 128–141.

Brandes, L., Franck, E., & Nuesch, S. (2008). Local heroes and superstars: An empirical analysis of star attraction in German Soccer. *Journal of Sports Economics, 9*(3), 266–286.

Bristow, D. N., & Sebastian, R. J. (2001). Holy cow! Wait 'til next year! A closer look at the brand loyalty of Chicago Cubs baseball fans. *Journal of Consumer Marketing, 18*(3), 256–275.

Chelladurai, P. (2013). A personal journey in theorizing in sport management. *Sport Management Review, 16*(1), 22–28.

Cialdini, R. B., Borden, R. J., Thorne, A., Walker, M. R., Freeman, S., & Sloan, L. R. (1976). Basking in Reflected Glory – three (football) field studies. *Journal of Personality and Social Psychology, 34*(3), 366–375.

Cova, B. (1997). Community and consumption: Towards a definition of the "linking value" of product or services. *European Journal of Marketing, 31*(3–4), 297–316.

Cova, B., & Cova, V. (2002). Tribal marketing: The tribalisation of society and its impact on the conduct of marketing. *European Journal of Marketing, 36*(5/6), 595–620.

Derbaix, C., Decrop, A., & Cabossart, O. (2002). Colors and scarves: The Symbolic Consumption of material possessions by Soccer fans. *Advances in Consumer Research, 29*, 511–518.

Dick, A. S., & Basu, K. (1994). Customer Loyalty: Toward an integrated conceptual framework. *Journal of Academy of Marketing Science, 22*(2), 99–113.

Doyle, J. P., Kunkel, T., & Funk, D. C. (2013). Sports spectator segmentation: Examining the differing psychological connections among spectators of leagues and teams. *International Journal of Sports Marketing and Sponsorship, 14*(2), 20–36.

Dutton, J. E., Dukerich, J. M., & Harquail, C. V. (1994). Organizational images and member identification. *Administrative Science Quarterly, 39*(34), 239–263.

Elsbach, K. D. (1999). An expanded model of organizational identification. *Research in Organizational Behavior, 21*, 163–200.

Foster, W., & Hyatt, C. (2007). I despise them! I detest them! Franchise relocation and the expanded model of organizational identification. *Journal of Sport Management, 21*(2), 194–212.

Frosdick, S., & Marsh, P. E. (2005). *Football hooliganism*. Cullompton, UK: Willan.

Funk, D. C., & James, J. (2001). The psychological continuum model: A conceptual framework for understanding an individuals psychological connection to sport. *Sport Management Review, 4*(2), 119–150.

Funk, D. C., Lock, D., Karg, A., & Pritchard, M. (2016). Sport consumer behavior research: Improving our game. *Journal of Sport Management, 30*(2).

Getz, D. (1997). *Event management & event tourism*. New York: Cognizant Communication.

Gladden, J. M., & Funk, D. C. (2001). Understanding Brand loyalty in professional sport: Examining the Link between brand associations and brand loyalty. *International Journal of Sports Marketing and Sponsorship*, 3(1), 67–94.

Grant, N., Heere, B., & Dickson, G. (2011). New sport teams and the development of brand community. *European Sport Management Quarterly*, 11(1), 35–54.

Hahn, E., Pilz, G. A., Stollenwerk, H. J., & Weis, K. (1988). *Fanverhalten, massenmedien und gewalt im sport*. Schorndorf, Germany: Hofmann.

Healy, J. C., & McDonagh, P. (2013). Consumer roles in brand culture and value co-creation in virtual communities. *Journal of Business Research*, 66(9), 1528–1540.

Hedlund, D. P. (2014). Creating value through membership and participation in sport fan consumption communities. *European Sport Management Quarterly*, 14(1), 50–71.

Hogg, M. K., & Michell, P. C. N. (1996). Identity, self and consumption: A conceptual framework. *Journal of Marketing Management*, 12(7), 629–644.

Holbrook, M. B. (1987). What Is consumer research? *Journal of Consumer Research*, 14(1), 128–132.

Holt, D. B. (1995). How consumers consume: A typology of consumption practices. *Journal of Consumer Research*, 22(6), 1–16.

Horbel, C., Popp, B., Woratschek, H., & Wilson, B. (2016). How context shapes value co-creation: Spectator experience of sport events. *The Service Industries Journal*, 36(11–12), 510–531.

Katz, M., & Heere, B. (2013). Leaders and followers: An Exploration of the notion of scale-free networks within a new brand community. *Journal of Sport Management*, 27(4), 271–287.

Knowles, G., Sherony, K., & Haupert, M. (1992). The demand for major league baseball: A test of the uncertainty of outcome hypothesis. *American Economist*, 36(2), 72–80.

Kohlbacher, F. (2005). The use of qualitative content analysis in case study research. *Forum Qualitative Sozialforschung/Forum: Qualitative Social Research*, 7(1), Art. 21.

Kozinets, R. V. (2001). Utopian enterprise: Articulating the meanings of Star Trek's culture of consumption. *Journal of Consumer Research*, 28(1), 67–68.

Kozinets, R. V. (2002). Can consumers escape the market? Emancipatory illuminations from Burning Man. *Journal of Consumer Research*, 29(1), 20–38.

Kozinets, R. V., & Belk, R. W. (2006). Videography. In V. Jupp (Ed.), *Sage dictionary of social research methods* (pp. 318–320). London, England: Sage.

Krippendorff, K. (2004). *Content analysis: An introduction to its methodology* (Vol. 2). Thousand Oaks, CA: Sage.

Laverie, D. A., & Arnett, D. B. (2000). Factors affecting fan attendance: The influence of identity salience and satisfaction. *Journal of Leisure Research*, 32(2), 225–246.

Lucifora, C., & Simmons, R. (2003). Superstar effects in sport: Evidence from Italian Soccer. *Journal of Sports Economics*, 4(1), 35–55.

Luedicke, M. K. (2006). Brand community under fire: The role of social environments for the Hummer brand community. *Advances in Consumer Research*, 33, 486–493.

Madrigal, R. (1995). Cognitive and affective determinants of fan satisfaction with sporting event attendance. *Journal of Leisure Research, 27*(3), 205–227.

Mael, F. A., & Ashforth, B. E. (1992). Alumni and their alma mater: A partial test of the reformulated model of organizational identification. *Journal of Organizational Behavior, 13*(2), 103–123.

Maffesoli, M. (1996). *The time of the tribes – the decline of individualism in mass society*. London: Sage.

Marzocchi, G., Morandin, G., & Bergami, M. (2013). Brand communities: Loyal to the community or to the brand? *European Journal of Marketing, 47*(1/2), 93–114.

Mayring, P. (2000). Qualitative content analysis. Forum Qualitative Sozialforschung/ Forum: *Qualitative Social Research, 1*(2), Art. 20.

McAlexander, J. H., & Schouten, J. W. (1998). Brandfests: Servicescapes for the cultivation of customer commitment. In J. F. Sherry (Ed.), *Servicescapes: The concept of place in contemporary markets* (pp. 377–402). Newbury Park, CA: Sage.

McAlexander, J. H., Schouten, J. W., & Koenig, H. F. (2002). Building brand community. *Journal of Marketing, 66*(1), 38–54.

McCall, G. (1970). The Social organization of relationships. In G. McCall, M. McCall, N. Denzin, G. Suttles, & S. Kurth (Eds.), *Social relationships* (pp. 3–34). Chicago, IL: Aldine.

Muniz, A. M., & O'Guinn, T. C. (2001). Brand community. *Journal of Consumer Research, 27*(4), 412–432.

Muniz, A. M., & Schau, H. J. (2005). Religiosity in the abandoned Apple Newton brand community. *Journal of Consumer Research, 31*(4), 737–747.

O'Guinn, T. C., & Muniz, A. M. (2005). Communal consumption and the brand. In D. G. Mick & S. Ratneshwar (Eds.), *Inside Consumption: perspectives on consumer motives, goals and desires* (pp. 252–272). London: Routledge.

O'Reilly, C., & Chatman, J. (1986). Organizational commitment and psychological attachment: the effects of compliance, identification, and internalization on prosocial behavior. *Journal of Applied Psychology, 71*(3), 492–499.

Palmer, C., & Thompson, K. (2007). The paradoxes of football spectatorship: On field and online expressions of social capital among the 'Grog Squad'. *Sociology of Sport Journal, 24*(2), 187–205.

Parker, K., & Stuart, T. (1997). The West Ham Syndrome. *Journal of the Market Research Society, 39*(3), 509–517.

Peel, D. A., & Thomas, D. A. (1992). The demand for football: Some evidence on outcome uncertainty. *Empirical Economics, 17*(2), 323–331.

Perreault, W. D., Jr., & Leigh, L. E. (1989). Reliability of nominal data based on qualitative judgements. *Journal of Marketing Research, 26*(2), 135–148.

Pilz, G. A., Albrecht, D., & Gabler, H. (1987). *Sport und gewalt*. Schorndorf, Germany: Hofmann.

Pilz, G. A., Behn, S., Klose, A., Schwenzer, V., Steffan, W., & Wölki, F. (2006). *Wandlungen des Zuschauerverhaltens im Profifußball*. Schorndorf, Germany: Hofmann.

Pongsakornrungsilp, S., & Schroeder, J. E. (2011). Understanding value co-creation in a co-consuming brand community. *Marketing Theory, 11*(3), 303–324.

Pratt, M. G. (1998). To be or not to be? Central questions in organizational identification. In D. A. Whetten & P. C. Godfrey (Eds.), *Identity in organizations: Building theory through conversations* (pp. 171–207). Thousand Oaks, CA: Sage.

Rottenberg, S. (1956). The Baseball player's labor-market. *Journal of Political Economy, 64*(3), 242–258.

Schmidt, M. B., & Berri, D. J. (2001). Competitive balance and attendance – the case of major league baseball. *Journal of Sports Economics, 2*(2), 145–167.

Schouten, J. W., & McAlexander, J. H. (1995). Subcultures of consumption: An ethnography of the new bikers. *Journal of Consumer Research, 22*(6), 43–61.

Schouten, J. W., McAlexander, J. H., & Koenig, H. (2007). Transcendent customer experience and brand community. *Journal of the Academy of Marketing Science, 35*(3), 357–368.Sloan, L. R. (1989). The motives of sports fans. In J. H. Goldstein (Ed.), *Sports, games, and play: Social & psychological viewpoints* (Vol. 2). Hollsdale, NJ: Lawrence Erlbaum Associates.

Solomon, M. R. (2003). *Conquering consumerspace marketing strategies for a branded world.* New York: AMACOM.

Standeven, J., & DeKnop, P. (1999). *Sport tourism.* Champaign, IL: Human Kinetics.

Tajfel, H. (1978). The achievement of group differentiation. In H. Tajfel (Ed.), *Differentiation between social groups: Studies in the social psychology of intergroup relations* (pp. 77–98). London: Academic.

Tapp, A. (2004). The loyalty of football fans – we'll support you evermore? *The Journal of Database Marketing & Customer Strategy Management, 11*(3), 225–246.

Theodorakis, N. D., Koustelios, A., Robinson, L., & Barlas, A. (2009). Moderating role of team identification on the relationship between service quality and repurchase intentions among spectators of professional sports. *Managing Service Quality: An International Journal, 19*(4), 456–473.

Thompson, C. J., & Troester, M. (2002). Consumer value systems in the age of postmodern fragmentation: The case of the natural health microculture. *Journal of Consumer Research, 28*(4), 550–571.

Thompson, S. A., & Sinha, R. K. (2008). Brand communities and new product adoption: The influence and limits of oppositional loyalty. *Journal of Marketing, 72*(6), 65–80.

Trail, G. T., Anderson, D. F., & Fink, J. S. (2000). A theoretical model of sport spectator consumption behavior. *International Journal of Sport Management, 1*(3), 154–180.

Trail, G. T., Anderson, D. F., & Fink, J. S. (2003). Sport spectator consumption behavior. *Sport Marketing Quarterly, 12*(1), 8–17.

Trail, G. T., James, J. D., Kwon, H., Anderson, D., & Robinson, M. J. (2016). An examination of Oliver's product loyalty framework. *International Journal of Sports Marketing and Sponsorship, 17*(2), 94–109.

Trail, G. T., & Kim, Y. K. (2011). Factors influencing spectator sports consumption: NCAA women's college basketball. *International Journal of Sports Marketing & Sponsorship, 13*(1), 60–82.

Trail, G. T., Robinson, M. J., & Kim, Y. K. (2008). Sport consumer behavior: A test for group differences on structural constraints. *Sport Marketing Quarterly, 17*(4), 190–200.

Turco, D. M., Riley, R., & Swart, K. (2002). *Sport tourism.* Morgantown, WV: FIT.

Turner, J. C. (1982). Towards a cognitive redefinition of the social group. In H. Tajfel (Ed.), *Social identity and intergroup relations* (pp. 15–40). Cambridge: Cambridge University Press.

Uhrich, S., & Königstorfer, J. (2009). Effects of atmosphere at major sports events: A perspective from environmental psychology. *International Journal of Sports Marketing & Sponsorship, 10*(4), 325–342.

Van Hiel, A., Hautman, L., Cornelis, I., & De Clercq, B. (2007). Football hooliganism: Comparing self-awareness and social identity theory explanations. *Journal of Community & Applied Social Psychology, 17*(3), 169–186.

Vargo, S. L., & Lusch, R. F. (2004). Evolving to a New dominant logic for marketing. *Journal of Marketing, 68*(1), 1–17.

Vrooman, J. (1995). A general theory of professional sports leagues. *Southern Economic Journal, 61*(4), 971–990.

Wann, D. L. (1995). Preliminary validation of the sport fan motivation scale. *Journal of Sport and Social Issues, 19*(1), 377–397.

Wann, D. L., & Branscombe, N. R. (1990). Die-hard and fair weather fans: Effects of identification on BIRGing and CORFing tendencies. *Journal of Sports and Social Issues, 14*(2), 103–117.

Wann, D. L., Grieve, F. G., Zapalac, R. K., & Pease, D. G. (2008). Motivational profiles of sport fans of different sports. *Sport Marketing Quarterly, 17*(1), 6–19.

Wood, J. T. (1982). Communication and relational culture: Bases for the study of human relationships. *Communication Quarterly, 30*(2), 75–84.

Woratschek, H., Horbel, C., & Popp, B. (2014). The sport value framework: A new fundamental logic for analyses in sport management. *European Sport Management Quarterly, 14*(1), 6–24.

Yoshida, M., Heere, B., & Gordon, B. (2015). Predicting behavioral loyalty through community: Why other fans are more important than our own intentions, our satisfaction, and the team itself. *Journal of Sport Management, 29*(3), 318–333.

Chapter 10

Comparison of marketing approaches in men's and women's football events

Dana Ellis and Becca Leopkey

Introduction

As research in the area of sport event marketing has evolved, much attention has been paid to the marketing and sponsorship approaches of mega-sport events (e.g., Giannoulakis, Stotlar, & Chatziefstathiou, 2008; Séguin & O'Reilly, 2008). However, less attention has been focused on examining marketing in large-scale sporting events. For the purpose of this study, a large-scale sporting event is one that receives international and/or national media coverage due to the caliber of competition and attracts more than 1,000 spectators (Emery, 2001). Essentially, a large-scale event is conceptualized as smaller in size and scope than a mega-event but still having significant impact on the host community, national or international appeal, and great importance for involved athletes. In general, there has been a move towards developing a greater understanding of the nature, management, and outcomes of non-mega events but the focus has, so far, been limited to such areas as social outcomes, economics, tourism, and the impact on sport participation (Taks, Chalip, & Green, 2015). Despite the still considerable scale and importance of these events, to date, most marketing-related research on large-scale events has focused on event brand creation (e.g., Parent & Séguin, 2008) and the opportunity for destination marketing and brand building (e.g., Chalip, 2004). The strategies and challenges of marketing and sponsorship within these events have yet to be examined in a comprehensive manner.

Furthermore, when surveying research on marketing and women's sport, there are surprisingly few studies and those that exist seem to focus on professional sport (e.g., Lough & Irwin, 2001; Zhang et al., 2003). When looking specifically at large-scale women's events, much of the literature focuses on media portrayals (e.g., Christopherson, Janning, & McConnell, 2002); however, Hallmann (2012) examined how images of women's football at the 2011 World Cup impacted interest in attending matches. There have been no studies that specifically examine the marketing of a large-scale women's sporting event. Women's sport continues to grow each year around the world. This is particularity true in the case of football where FIFA has set a goal to see 45 million girls involved in football worldwide by the 2019 Women's World Cup (WWC) (FIFA, 2016a). Most recently, the 2015 WWC broke all-time viewing records with over 764 million in-home television viewers and more than 86 million mobile or digital viewers, making it second only to the Men's World Cup in terms of broadcast viewing numbers for FIFA tournaments (FIFA, 2015a). Furthermore, the 2015 WWC set a new total attendance record with 1,353,506 spectators enjoying the event; this figure also makes it second only to the Men's World Cup in terms of attendance at FIFA tournaments (FIFA, 2015b). With such growth and popularity comes a need for a more engaged understanding of the associated business realities, such as the marketing of women's sport in general and women's large-scale sporting events in particular.

This study aims to fill the gaps identified above, and with this in mind, the purpose of this study is to increase our understanding of marketing in large-scale events by seeking to discern the similarities and differences in marketing approaches between men's and women's large-scale, single sport events. In order to fulfill this purpose, two case studies have been developed (Yin, 2013) examining the 2007 U20 FIFA World Cup Canada (U20WC) and the FIFA Women WWC 2015.

Review of literature

Literature in the area of event management and marketing covers a wide variety of topics from how event stakeholders can be identified, categorized, and managed in an effort to increase the recognition and successful management of event stakeholder interests (Getz, Andersson, & Larson, 2007) to what issues organizing committee's and event stakeholders have to manage during the process (Parent, 2008) and general event management policies and practices (Aisbett & Hoye, 2015). For this study, however, the area of event marketing is most pertinent and will be discussed in further detail below.

Event marketing and sponsorship

The event marketing and sponsorship literature focuses on three main areas of inquiry event sponsorship, event consumers, and event brands. While many studies do touch on more than one of these areas, such as research that examines how consumer's perception of sponsor-event fit impacts consumer behaviors (Koo, Quarterman, & Flynn, 2006), for the purpose of this literature review they will be discussed as individual areas of inquiry. The first area, event sponsorship, is arguably a separate topic in its own right with various areas of concentration within the topic. One frequently examined concentration in this area asks if there is a measurable return on investment

(ROI) (through brand equity, awareness, recognition etc.) for event sponsors (Cornwell, Roy, & Steinard, 2001; Coughlan & Mules, 2001; O'Reilly, Lyberger, McCarthy, Séguin, & Nadeau, 2008). The measurement of ROI for sponsors of mega-events has found that while intent to purchase seems to be relatively low (O'Reilly et al., 2008), properly conducted sponsorship agreements can lead to differentiation and brand equity (Cornwell et al., 2001). Specifically through avoiding clutter, leveraging and integrating the sponsorship into marketing and communications plans have been shown to produce moderately high returns on awareness (Coughlan & Mules, 2001).

Another area of concentration with in event sponsorship involves the examination of how sponsorship interacts with brand image transfer between a mega-event and a sponsor (e.g., Grohs & Reisinger, 2005; Gwinner, Larson, & Swanson, 2009; Novais & Arcodia, 2013). Gwinner (1997) has been a leader in this area and presented an early framework for image creation and transfer in event sponsorship. He suggested that there are not only many factors that impact the event image (event type, event characteristics, and individual factors) but also several moderating variables that impact the transfer of that event image to a sponsor's brand image (Gwinner, 1997). In a follow-up study, Gwinner and Eaton (1999) examined the degree of image transfer between an event and a sponsor based on sponsorship activity. They found that image transfer took place on both sides of a sponsorship relationship. This image transfer was argued to be a key in realizing brand positioning goals and was strengthened by the extent of fit between the sponsor and the sponsee. With this in mind, they suggested that events seeking sponsorship differentiate themselves in the market by investigating and promoting their own unique brand image (Gwinner & Eaton, 1999).

More recently, Gwinner et al. (2009) continued to refine this area of study by examining the degree to which team identification and fit between the event and sponsor brand effects image transfer finding the greater the level of team identification and the stronger the fit, the greater the image transfer. Alternatively in their enquiry of Gwinner and Eaton (1999), Kwon, Ratneshwar, and Kim (2015) supported the finding that brand sponsorship enhanced image similarity between sponsor and sponsee brands, and that functional similarity between the two was a moderating factor of that image transfer but rejected the idea that image-based similarity between the two brands was a moderating factor. Finally, a broader area of concentration in the event sponsorship literature deals with the theme of Olympic sponsorship in particular. Articles widely examining the topic (e.g., Brown, 2002; Giannoulakis et al., 2008), those examining specifics like sponsor activation (Papadimitriou & Apostolopoulou, 2009), sponsor motivations (e.g., Apostolopoulou & Papadimitriou, 2004), and Olympic sponsorship value (Miyazaki & Morgan, 2001) and sub-areas like ambush marketing (e.g., Preuss, Gemeinder, & Séguin, 2008) contribute to this concentration.

While the research on event brands has been sparse in comparison with the other noted areas, it is still an important part of understanding research in event marketing. To date, researchers have focused mainly on brand creation and management. Studies have asked what factors impact the ability of an organizing committee to effectively and efficiently build and manage an event's image, identity, or brand (Parent & Foreman, 2007; Parent & Séguin, 2008). Several factors are recognized as being essential to help the organizing committee build a successful event brand/image/identity. Certain qualities such as networking skills are important for those in leadership positions, while the context (i.e., regional setting) and timing of the event will also have an impact. Additionally, the nature of the event in regards to existing images and the governing body identity and the management and communication of the brand are also presented as important (Parent & Foreman, 2007; Parent & Séguin, 2008). This understanding of event brand creation has also been further extended through an examination of recurring event brand creation to account for the importance of the organization's core values, induced event experiences (i.e., event member experiences), reciprocal media relationships, and an expanded notion of the nature of the event (Parent, Eskerud, & Hanstad, 2012).

Marketing of women's sport and events

When examining research on marketing and women's sport there are surprisingly few studies when compared with the vast number discussing primarily male sporting contexts. With that said, there are some examples of articles that examine the marketing and sponsorship of women's sport in general and women's events in particular. Looking at the marketing of women's sport in general, Jowdy and McDonald (2003) provided a case study on the use of interactive fan festivals by the Women's United Soccer Association. While this League no longer exists, the authors noted that this type of relationship marketing can be key for leagues that are trying to build their brand and consumer base, as it allows marketers to highlight the direct engagement between teams, players, and management and the fans that can be offered by smaller or newer Leagues. Other marketing research has focused on understanding the consumers of women's sport (e.g., Funk, Ridinger, & Moorman, 2003; Zhang et al., 2003) and the sponsorship of women's sport (e.g., Lough & Irwin, 2001; Shaw & Amis, 2001; Sparks & Westgate, 2002). For instance, Lough and Irwin (2001) compared sponsorship objectives between U.S women's sport and "traditional" sport sponsorship and found that there are few differences between the two sport settings with only a slightly greater focus on image and awareness as opposed to sales-based objectives for sponsor's involved with women's sport.

When looking specifically at large-scale women's sporting events we find similar topics of interest to those identified above for women's sport in general: consumers, sponsorship, and specific marketing strategies. With respect to consumers there seems to be a focus on understanding what drives their interest in women's sport events (e.g., Funk, Mahoney, Naka-zawa, & Hirakawa, 2001; Hallman, 2012; Preuss, Woratschek, & Durch-holz, 2008). Funk et al. (2001) looked at consumer motives for attending the 1999 WWC and found that those that were most pertinent were: interest (in the sport of football or in a specific team), event excitement, the support of women's sport, aesthetics, and vicarious achievement. Also looking at fan interest in the WWC, this time the 2011 WWC, Hallman (2012) sought to better understand and differentiate between how various key drivers related to the image of women's football and the image of the World Cup would impact interest in the event. In general she noted that the image of the WWC was perceived more favourably than the image of women's football but both were associated with positive characteristics and, in the case of the WWC, the overall image has a meaningful impact on interest in attending games (Hallman, 2012). The results also showed that while age influenced the per-ceived image and positive purchase intentions for both the event and the sport, gender was found to impact only the perceived image of the World Cup while having no impact on the image of the sport or on purchase inten-tions (Hallman, 2012).

For both the sponsorship and specific marketing strategies of women's sport events, there is very little research to draw on. However, in this case, we will still draw on the existing research given the limited attention in the literature to the area of women's events. In the area of sponsorship, one of the only studies comes from Lough (1996), who investigated the sponsorship of women's sport events and organizations together. Among her key conclu-sions were observations that the sponsorship of women's events is more realistic for large corporations (based on level of risk and available capital), that women's sport may offer more value to a sponsor, and that increased competition in the sponsorship marketing, event crowds, and media cover-age will positively impact women's sport sponsorship (Lough, 1996). With respect to specific marketing strategies, Bell and Blakey (2010) highlighted the use of a social marketing approach during the 2005 European Women's Football Championship. They argued that the approach should be seen as a valuable strategy: "particularly when there are multiple objectives, levels and stages of change to consider" (Bell & Blakey, 2010, p. 170). While these studies have provided the valuable glimpse into the marketing of women's sport events much work remains to be done, and the present study hopes to be a first step in this direction.

Method

A case study was developed to help the researchers focus on the hosting of two large-scale FIFA events. The method was selected for this research project as it allows researchers to develop a deeper understanding of a social phenomenon (Yin, 2013). Case study analysis has been deemed an appropriate method of inquiry for settings where the researchers have no control over the situation (Yin, 2013). In an effort to develop cross-setting conclusions two settings were reviewed in depth: the FIFA U20WC Canada 2007 and the FIFA WWC Canada 2015. These settings were selected based on their important roles in sport event hosting history in Canada. More specifically, they have both broken national records in terms of size and scope. In addition, several stakeholders, including host cities, organizing committee members, and sponsors, remained the same in both settings. Additional details regarding the case settings are reviewed in the next section. Data collection consisted of the accumulation of publically available documents of significance from both events dealing with marketing topics. The case settings were then constructed from a content analysis of these official documents, archival materials, blogs, government documents, web site information and newspaper clippings. Approximately 90 documents were amassed.

Data analysis was conducted in a collaborative fashion but with on researcher assuming the role of primary coder, particularly during the first phase of open coding. Following this effort the authors engaged in peer debriefing to ensure a higher level of trustworthiness (Guba, 1981). After the first step of open coding (Corley & Gioia, 2004) where the authors used descriptive codes (Miles, Huberman, & Saldaña, 2014) to identify emergent and reoccurring themes related to marketing and sponsorship within the data. This was done with the help of qualitative data analysis software ATLAS.ti for OsX (version 1.0.3). Next, axial coding was completed to further explore the relational aspects between the coded data (Corley & Gioia, 2004) in the two settings. Resulting themes were then deliberated between the researchers and arranged according to the four key themes across which the marketing approaches of the two events were comparable: (1) marketing planning and implementation, (2) sponsorship approach, (3) brand identity, and (4) marketing legacies. As a last step, the authors revisited the data to engage in selective-coding looking for representative examples of the analysis and identified themes (Jones, 2015).

The case settings

FIFA U-20 World Cup Canada 2007

The FIFA U20WC tournament has been around since the late '70s, with the first edition of the event taking place in Tunisia in 1977. It is now regularly hosted every two years. This event is the 2nd largest sport event under the FIFA brand. For approximately three weeks over 750 athletes from 24 different countries play in a total of 52 matches. The 2007 edition was hosted in Canada. Planning took place over a three-year period following the 2015 host selection on August 10, 2004. The tournament took place across the country with games hosted in six different cities: (1) Victoria, British Columbia, (2) Burnaby, British Columbia, (3) Edmonton, Alberta, (4) Toronto, Ontario, (5) Ottawa, Ontario, and (6) Montreal, Québec. The U20WC broke several national sport event hosting records at the time including both Canadian single-sport and FIFA U20WC attendance numbers. In total, over 1,195,239 total spectators enjoyed the event (Canadian Soccer Association, 2007). Approximately 73% of tickets were sold with four cities (Victoria, Burnaby, Toronto, and Ottawa) selling out to 95% of their capacity (Canadian Soccer Association, 2007). Many fans also watched from home. Numbers indicated a cumulative worldwide television audience of 469.5 million with over 8.7 million in Canada alone (Canadian Soccer Association, 2007).

FIFA Women's World Cup Canada 2015

The WWC is a newer event under the FIFA umbrella with the first edition taking place in China in 1991. Similar to the FIFA World Cup, it is hosted every four years in a new country around the world. Part of the responsibilities for the hosts of the WWC is to host the Women's U-20 World Cup in the year leading up to the bigger event, allowing the U-20 Women's event to serve as a test event. Canada won the right to host the 2015 WWC in 2011 when their only competitor, Zimbabwe, pulled out of the running. Six cities across six different Canadian provinces in five different time zones saw some tournament action: (1) Vancouver, British Columbia, (2) Edmonton, Alberta, (3) Winnipeg, Manitoba, (4) Ottawa, Ontario, (5) Montreal, Québec, and (6) Moncton, New Brunswick. In total, 24 teams battled each other in 52 matches for the right to become the 2015 WWC champions. Similarly to the U20WC, the 2015 WWC set several records at the time including the Canadian attendance record with an audience of 1,353,506 cumulative spectators (the largest for any FIFA competition besides the FIFA World Cup) (FIFA.com, 2015). The television audiences were also impressive. A total of 45 million people around the world watched the final match with Fox capturing their biggest audience ever for a football match in the United States.

Results

Results suggested there were four key emergent themes across which the marketing approaches of the two events were comparable (1) marketing planning and implementation, (2) sponsorship approach, (3) brand identity, and (4) marketing legacies. A description of each theme and the specific key categories of comparisons identified within each of these themes are outlined in Table 10.1 and discussed in more detail below.

Table 10.1 Emergent themes and categories of comparison in marketing approaches between the U20WC and the WWC 2015

Theme	Description	Key Categories of Comparison
Marketing planning and implementation	Factors related to how the National Organizing Committee and/or FIFA went about building awareness and selling the event to consumers. Discussion of: the objectives of the National Organizing Committee and/or FIFA with respect to the selling and success of this event.	1. Nation branding 2. Target markets 3. Experiential promotions strategy
Sponsorship approach	Factors related to how the organizers undertook the task of selling, servicing, and leveraging/ activating sponsorships with respect to each event. Discussion of: perceived success in sponsorship sales and activation, how sponsor's leveraged/ activated their association, the impact of scandals on sponsorship, the perceived objectives of sponsors associated with the event, the presence of ambush marketing, criticism of sponsors or the sponsorship program.	1. Success 2. Supplementary marketing 3. Leveraging and activation 4. Criticism
Brand identity	What the NOC and/or FIFA hope to project as what the brand represents. Includes discussion of: brand positioning in the market, messaging, and slogans related to the event and the sport.	1. Message type 2. Message focus
Marketing legacies	Factors related to the perception of how what was learned or gained from the marketing and sponsorship programs these events can/will be used to improve the overall marketing capacity of football in Canada.	

Marketing planning and implementation

The first theme that emerged as a clear area of comparison between the U20WC and the WWC was within the planning and implementation of marketing programs. Broadly this refers to factors relating to how the National Organizing Committee (NOC) and/or FIFA went about building awareness and selling the event to consumers. Three, more specific, key categories of comparison then emerged within this theme: (1) nation branding, (2) target markets, and (3) experiential promotions strategy.

Nation branding

Nation branding refers to the creation or shaping of a country's international image with respect to such features as prestige and corporate capacity with a view towards positively impacting areas such as tourism, business investment, and international relations within that country (Grix & Houlihan, 2014; Nauright, 2013). At the U20WC, there was an understanding of the role the marketing of the tournament could, and perhaps should, play as part of nation branding. When discussing the success of the event Colin Linford, Chairman of the NOC, noted the impact for the country saying: "it also presents a wonderful opportunity to promote our country to the world" (Canada Soccer, 2007a, p. 4). Likewise when discussing the hosting of the final game in Toronto, Mayor David Miller recognized the potential importance for an individual city noting: "this is a fantastic opportunity to showcase our incredible city to the world" (Canada Soccer, 2006, p. 9) while Edmonton's Ron Gilbertson, president and CEO of Edmonton Economic Development similarly noted: "from our standpoint, the direct immediate impact is important and the long-term impact of reinforcing Edmonton as an attractive place that does a really good job of hosting events and just gets our name on an international stage, that's very positive as well" (Howland-Morris, 2007). The use and discussion of mega and large-scale sporting events for nation (or city) branding purposes is certainly not uncommon (cf., Grix & Houlihan, 2014; Knott, Fyall, & Jones, 2015; Nauright, 2013) and seemingly the NOC for the U20WC understood this as part of their marketing strategy tournament.

For the WWC, when examining the data available from the NOC and FIFA there was no obvious discussion of the impact, potential, intended, or perceived, on nation branding from the event. This suggests that the event was not necessarily viewed as a way for the Canada to market itself to the rest of the world and as a result the planning and implementation of marketing strategies were likely undertaken with a mostly internal (i.e. within Canada or perhaps North America) perspective and national-level objectives.

Target markets

This category refers to the particular groups of consumers that were the focus of the marketing and promotional strategies for each event. For the U20 World Cup it is suggested that identifying those with a significant involvement in football was key to the defined target markets. The organizing committee categorized two of their three main target markets as football evangelists and football enthusiasts, while also directly targeting ethnic communities (Canadian Soccer Association, 2007). For instance it was noted in the *FIFA U-20 2007 Final Report* (2007) that when Portugal was confirmed as a Toronto-based team the organizing committee placed ads in three local Portuguese language publications: the *Toronto Sol Portuguese, Toronto Post Milenio* and *Soccer 360* Magazine to speak directly to the football supporters in that community. This "ethnic community ticket sales strategy" (p. 10) was identified among the key success factors for the tournament. While not specifically gender defined, it could be argued that these categories arguably tend to be made of up mostly young male individuals.

Conversely for the WWC, the key target markets can be understood to be girls, women, and (upper-income) football families (Schum, 2015). Much discussion about the event focused on the inclusion of family events, be it the fan zones or the Trophy Tour, while families and the football community were specifically targeted in the wide variety of community outreach initiatives undertaken as part of event promotion (Canada Soccer, 2015). Exemplifying the specific targeting of young female football players, the final stop on the Trophy Tour provided the opportunity for two local female football clubs, Fusion FC and Richmond Girls Soccer Club, to have their picture taken with the trophy and play a mini game at the celebrations (FIFA, 2015c). Furthermore, the use of a group of strong Canadian female event ambassadors, including a former star player (Kara Lang) and Twitter Executive (Kristine Stewart), by the NOC demonstrated the desire to reach out directly to a female audience.

Experiential promotions strategy

Experiential promotions strategies can be understood simply as marketing strategies that involve the creation of different types of experiences for the consumer to enjoy (Schmitt, 2000). When examining the marketing of the U20WC event it is clear that such promotions were an important part of the organizing committee's marketing strategy. A key part of the strategy seemed to be geared around building word of mouth through guerilla style promotions and viral exposure. Specifically, as part of their 360-degree integrated multi-media plan, they noted word of mouth/events/street teams and outdoor activities as two key facets. More specifically they undertook promotions such as ticket crawls, in-bar/pub action teams, a Toronto Event Outdoor spectacular, a guerilla style inflatable football initiative, and street based stunts to "create a sense of urgency, excitement, and anticipation for the event" (Canadian Soccer Association, 2007, p. 65).

Many of the experiential promotions appear to be targeted to younger male audiences. For instance, in the *Edmonton, Toronto*, and *Ottawa Sun* newspapers, Sun Shine girls (Canadian newspaper pin-ups) wearing the Canadian team shirt and the shirts of other participating countries, were featured in the lead up to the tournament, while advertisements for the event focused on rock and sport stations such as 102.1 the Edge and in Toronto and Rock 101 in Vancouver. Additionally bars and pubs were seemingly a main target for promotions with in bar/pub action teams and in-bar poster campaign in all six host cities (Canadian Soccer Association, 2007). This is in keeping with the observation above that while the target markets for the U20WC were not identified as gender specific, both their description and the promotional strategies used arguably seem to cater to male audiences.

Like the U20WC, there was a focus on experiential promotions at the WWC, in fact it was noted that there was more than 445 community outreach activities held to promote the WWC (Canada Soccer, 2015). Where they differed however was in style. The experiential promotions used around the WWC were perceived to be less aggressive in style. For instance, a big part of the promotion of the WWC came from the Coca Cola Trophy Tour, which offered a chance for families to come out and see the trophy in an effort to build both excitement and connection to the event. The tour was the first of its kind, covering 6126 kilometers across 12 Canadian cities and welcoming 50,000 people (Canada Soccer, 2015). At each stop, there was a Fan Experience zone where visitors could participate in such activities as the Coca-Cola Ultimate Goalie (a virtual game), or they could record a cheer for their team with the Video Celebration activity. Coca-Cola also gave away limited edition aluminum bottles of Coca-Cola products with commemorative designs relating to the six Canadian host cities (Dipardo, 2015). Similarly, in Vancouver, there was a fan zone outside of the venue that offered such activities as an interactive women's locker room exhibit, sponsor activations, live entertainment, big screens to watch the games on, and the chance to meet some of the athletes (Vancity Buzz, 2015). The fan zone was promoted as highly family oriented. It was specifically noted that the fan zone seemed to offer: "has the food and alcohol that adults seek, without the rowdy bar scene baggage that often comes with it" (Kassouf, 2015, p. 9). It was highlighted as a place for parents to get involved in the atmosphere and excitement while still being able to bring their young children who they might not want to take into the stadium. Once again, there is a clear connection between the chosen target markets and the style of experiential marketing campaigns undertaken leading to the similar but still varied approaches taken by the two events.

Sponsorship approach

The second theme that emerged as a clear area of comparison between the U20WC and the WWC was the approach taken to sponsorship. This refers to how the organizers undertook the task of selling, servicing, and leveraging/activating sponsorships for each event. Overall four key categories of comparison then emerged from within this theme: (1) success, (2) supplementary marketing, (3) leveraging and activation, and (4) criticism.

Success

The sponsorship programs for both the U20WC and the WWC were built within the FIFA sponsorship structure. As a result each event was automatically associated with the FIFA Partners. A FIFA Partner is the premier level of sponsorship within FIFA and any company that is a FIFA Partner has access to all FIFA properties and events around the globe (FIFA, 2016b). At any given time it consists of a group of six to eight global corporations that reportedly pay between $25 and $50 million per year for the sponsorship rights (Smith, 2014). During the U20WC, there were five FIFA Partners that could leverage their association with the event (Adidas, Coca-Cola, Emirates Airlines, Hyundai, and Sony). There was also five FIFA Partners during the WWC (Adidas, Coca-Cola, Gazprom, Hyundai/Kia, and Visa) with some overlap and some differences from the U20WC. In addition to the FIFA Partners both the U20WC and the WWC can be considered a moderate success in national sponsorship sales. In both cases, organizers sought to sign six National Supporters (national sponsors). The U20WC was able to sign four National Supporters: BMO financial group (insurance), Bell Media (media and telecommunications), Winners (retail), and Europe's Best (frozen vegetables) (FIFA, 2007). The WWC was not quite as successful and ended up with three National Supporters: Bell Media (media and telecommunications), Labatt (alcoholic beverages), and Trend Micro (IT security) (FIFA, 2015d).

Supplementary marketing

In this context, supplementary marketing refers to the marketing and sponsorship activities that, while linked, are not directly associated with U20WC and WWC tournament sponsorship and marketing. Around the U20WC, integration with other related sponsorship and advertising in the host country was evident mainly in the substantial participation of Soccer Canada (SC) partners in leveraging around the event. By using the hype provided by the event to bring greater recognition to their contributions to football in Canada, they arguably participated in coattail ambush marketing (Chadwick & Burton, 2011). While ambush marketing is generally frowned upon, the argument can be made that perhaps there is a co-creation of value in such circumstance as opposed to a detrimental effect, as the U20WC would also seem to potentially benefit from such publicity (Séguin, Rodrigue, O'Reilly, & MacIntosh, 2013). For instance, the Canadian Egg Marketing Agency signed a sponsorship deal for eggs to be the official nutritional partner of Soccer Canada near the beginning of the U20WC event. They built off this indirect connection to the event by involving Craig Forrest, the

Honorary Chair of the U20 WC tournament, in their announcement of the sponsorship and conducting football themed campaigns such as the *Score with Eggs* in-store promotion during the event (CEMA, 2007). Similarly, Canada Soccer and National Team sponsor Nutella ran a promotion in the lead up to the U20WC called the *Cheer for Team Canada Nutella Contest*. The winners of this contest were given the opportunity to travel to Toronto for the week before the tournament, train with the Canadian U20WC team, participate in a photo and autograph session with the players, and receive a U20WC tournament program and other souvenirs (Canada Soccer, 2007c).

For the WWC, there were also examples of coattail ambushing by both SC partners and individual player/team partners. For example, linking to the 11 teams in the tournament they sponsored, Nike developed an interactive space called the *Nike Underground* showcasing their latest technology and allowing for people to participate in a pick-up game (Danforth, 2015). Linking to their SC partnership Canadian Tire also took advantage of the attention around the WWC by developing a football-themed version of its *We all play for Canada* campaign that backs the importance of play for Canadian kids. Using Canadian football star Christine Sinclair, a television ad and online Instagram video were released to coincide with the WWC using the slogan *Wanna Play* and imagery of fans cheering her on alongside Canada Soccer and Canadian Tire logos (Powell, 2015).

In addition to coattail ambushing there was also a large amount of interest in the sale of broadcast advertising during the WWC, particularly in the United States, with Fox selling more than $17 million USD in advertising to 20 companies, more than three times the amount sold for the 2011 WWC (Harwell, 2015). Again looking to the United States, it was interesting to note that WWC partnerships in non-traditional sponsorship categories were deemed a great success in both Fox broadcast advertising as well as United States Soccer Federation sponsorship. Specifically, this increased interest seemed to stem from companies that did not have a historical involvement with football, but rather arguably focused on the link to a female target audience (Advertising Age, 2015; Harwell, 2015). For instance, American football star Alex Morgan was at the center of a campaign by feminine care product company Tampax where she starred in a video series giving advice to young girls learned from her sporting success (Walgrove, 2015).

Leveraging and activation

As it will be discussed here leveraging and activation is defined as "the marketing activities a company conducts to promote its sponsorship. Money spent on activation is over and above the rights fee paid to the sponsored property" (IEG, 2016, p. 1). Leveraging is considered a vital requirement for the mutually beneficial success of any sponsorship program (O'Keefe, Titlebaum, & Hill, 2009). For the U20WC, there appears to have been activation by sponsors across various diverse platforms and the sponsor acti- vation strategies were noted as being critical success factors for the tourna- ment (Canadian Soccer Association, 2007). With the exception of Emirates Airlines all FIFA Partners and National Sponsor for the U20WC participated in fan zones to varying degrees. Adidas, Hyundai, and the Bank of Mon- treal had the greatest involvement with 23 total fan zone activations across Canada, while Coca-Cola and Bell Media were involved, but only in a sin- gle activation each (Canadian Soccer Association, 2007). At these fan zones visitors had the opportunity to participate in activities such as test drives (Hyundai), skills areas (Adidas), mascot meet and greets (Europe's Best), and have their picture taken with the trophy (Sony) (Canada NewsWire, 2007; Canadian Soccer Association, 2007). FIFA Partners in particular also lever- aged their association by focusing on youth involvement at the games. Adidas sponsored a Fair Play Flag Bearers program, Sony sponsored the FIFA Flag Bearers, and Coca-Cola was responsible for the Ball Kids and National Flag Bearers programs (Canadian Soccer Association, 2007). From the event per- spective sponsor activation seems to have consisted mainly of including event sponsor logos on pre-event advertising such as posters, post cards, emails, billboards, bus shelters, and print advertising and on field boards and around the stadiums during the tournament (Canadian Soccer Association, 2007).

For the WWC, there was also some activation across similar diverse plat- forms. As already noted, Coca-Cola, alongside Bell Media, was involved in the first ever FIFA WWC Trophy Tour across Canada. At each stop along the way there was product giveaways, contests, chances to meet the mascot, freestyle demonstrations, a replica locker room and winner's tunnel, and more (Coca-Cola Company, 2015; Dipardo, 2015). One thing to note in this area was that there seemed to be some evidence of a lack of follow- through on the part of Adidas in particular. *Marketing Week* noted that Adidas claimed they would be "the most visible and talked about brand at the tournament" promoting their #bethedifference campaign (Milling- ton, 2015, p. 13), and yet, in the immediate lead up to the event, it was noted that "Adidas' website showed no mention of their association with the Women's World Cup, a visibility level that would be deemed unthink- able a week away from their male counterparts' tournament, for which they created 3,000 images and 300 videos" (Armstrong, as cited in Millington, 2015, p. 18). The shoe and apparel company publicly said they were going to activate across multiple platforms and in many different ways, but their efforts were minimal and during the event their association was barely vis- ible to anyone not attending a game or the Vancouver fan zone.

Criticism

A key difference between the men's and the women's event is evident in the level of criticism directed at the marketing and sponsorship activities of the organizers and sponsors. There was no evidence of direct criticism of the marketing of the men's tournament, while alternatively the women's tournament attracted criticism in many areas with criticism of both sponsors and organizers. It is also important to note that all of this criticism was put forth in the context of a more general critique of the approach to marketing and sponsorship of women's sports in general rather than just a specific critique of the WWC.

For sponsors, it was noted that the tournament felt like a lost opportunity (Millington, 2015; Schum, 2015; Walgrove, 2015). Sponsors were criticized for their lack of engagement with the event, both on the ground and in the digital sphere (Schum, 2015; Walgrove, 2015). A marketing professional who experienced games in both Montreal and Ottawa remarked, "what I saw (in addition to two fantastic games) was one huge missed opportunity; an opportunity to be part of a movement, capture the passion of a mission, and reach an extremely engaged and high-income demographic [. . .] the fans were there, the passion was there. The sponsors, not so much" (Schum, 2015, p. 5). There was also a more general critique of the fact that the marketing blitzes and mega-deals for the players and the event seemed to be specifically lacking (Harwell, 2015).

Organizers were likewise criticised for not offering significant opportunities for fan experiences (particularly those without tickets) and sponsor engagement during the tournament. For instance, not all fan zones were open to the public for the whole tournament. Only the fan zone in Vancouver was open to the pubic every day, and only Vancouver included activations from every sponsor. In Winnipeg and Montreal, fan zones were only open on match days, while in Moncton, fan zones were open to the public, but only for three days and with very few activations. Fan zones in both Edmonton and Ottawa were only available for those attending the matches (FIFA, 2015e; Vancity Buzz, 2015). A more ideological complaint came from Carrie Serwetnyk who was the first female inductee to the Canadian Soccer Hall of Fame and is the current Director of Equal Play. She argued that while the marketing messages of the tournament promoted the building of equality and role of the event in promoting women's sport, the reality is that message is hypocritical given that the event only really serves to bring the level of inequality to the surface through issues such as player treatment and the playing surface debate. She stated, "they [the NOC] will ensure the public knows the television ratings are high, that many bums in seats are sold and a legacy of equity changes are unfolding, but we only have to look as far as the national team family and see that hypocrisy and hype outweighs the heroics" (Serwetnyk, 2015, p. 8).

Brand identity

The third theme that emerged as a clear area of comparison between the U20WC and the WWC was brand identity. Brand identity refers to the "set of associations that the brand strategist aspires to create or maintain" (Aaker & Joachimsthaler, 2000, p. 43). In this case it refers to what the NOC and/or FIFA intended the brand to represent through their branding and marketing activities. Overall, two key categories of comparison emerged from within this theme: (1) message type and (2) message focus.

Message type

The U20WC was the first major FIFA event to be held in Canada, and the key messaging around the event was very simple and straightforward, focusing on the obvious key message of the fact it was a major event and sticking with the same message type through all promotional stages. Imagery used in official poster campaigns drove home this point with obvious but impactful illustrations. On the other hand, it could be argued that the messaging around the WWC was more involved and nuanced. This is to say the message was more socially reflective in nature and was less overt in official promotional imagery. For instance, the U20WC poster image of a giant football ball hurtling towards various the host cities sends an unmistakable message, while the WWC official poster represents a much more symbolic representation of the event's brand identity. This can be demonstrated by the following official explanation of the poster's imagery:

> With its warm colours, the poster's football and sun icon expresses positivity and ambition. The cascading shapes, meanwhile, evoke Canada's breathtaking landscapes, expansive skies, towering mountains, rich green forests, vast lakes, powerful rivers and dynamic cityscapes. Together, this iconic imagery flows as the hair from a woman's head, her proud expression exuding confidence, determination and freedom.
>
> (Canada Soccer, 2015, p. 19)

Message focus

The simplest and mostly singular message related to the U20WC was that size matters, and this event was going to be huge. The concept of the event being big was linked to many different aspects of the event and played out in marketing materials. The event was defined as huge with respect to the fact that football is the biggest game in the world, the event was the biggest single sport event in Canada to date, the U20WC boasts some of the biggest stars in world football as alumni of the event, and it hosts the next group of biggest and brightest stars of the football world.

With this in mind the main advertising thrust of the event was the three part *it's gonna be huge* campaign that was supplemented by phrasing such as *the world's biggest game is here* and *be huge* (Canadian Soccer Association, 2007). These slogans found their way onto posters and other marketing materials and plays on this theme were frequently used in news releases discussing the progress of event planning and ticket sales. One such example is a Canada Soccer news release sent during the event titled: *Beyond Huge! Canada officially sets a FIFA U-20 World Cup Attendance Record* (Canada Soccer, 2007b).

As noted in the discussion of message type, the types of messages put forth by the marketing team for the WWC were more socially reflective. In particular, the messages focused on highlighting the positive values (empowerment, freedom, positivity, ambition, determination, etc.) they felt were linked to the tournament, the position of players as positive role models and the positive social impacts of hosting the tournament. The official slogan of the tournament was *to a greater goal* which denotes the perception that the social impacts of the tournament are as important as what is happening on the field. The NOC defined its meaning as:

> the best of on- field performance and a unique victory for all, beginning with girls and women [. . .] what every individual, team, or nation was fighting for, and what each fan supported [. . .] it also embodies[s] the hopes and dreams of many and a turning point for women's sport.
>
> (Canada Soccer, 2015, p. 14)

These ideas were also reflected back to them in the statements made by sponsors discussing their reason for being involved. For instance, Trend Micro's CEO Eva Chen stated:

> Trend Micro's corporate culture aligns with the official slogan of the FIFA Women's World Cup Canada 2015 – "To a greater goal." We firmly believe that this isn't just a tournament, but a celebration of the talents and abilities of world class female athletes. Inspiring and empowering women to achieve their dreams is important to me, as well as our team as a whole.
>
> (FIFA, 2015d)

It some cases, it was even noted that given the ongoing scandal at FIFA, the Women's World Cup offered "an opportunity for women's football to shine some light onto the game that perhaps has lost a little bit of its moral compass" (Quinn & De Vynck, 2015, p. 8).

Some similarity to the U20WC also came from the focus on the breadth of the tournament across Canada represented in the marketing by the guiding concept of *coast to coast*. Alongside the social focus of the brand identity, the characteristics of Canada helped define the eight elements comprising the official look of the tournament: coast; sky, ice, and cityscape; ambition and mountains; modernity and urbanism; pride and honor; water, ocean, and inspiration; celebration and fans; and passion and innovation (Canada Soccer, 2015).

One important distinction between the brand identity and of the U20WC and the WWC was related to the gendered nature of some of the WWC identity, both implicit and explicit. Implicitly, it was noted that, at times, players were referred to as the biggest stars of the "women's game." By qualifying the statement as the so-called women's game, it arguably suggests they are not on even footing with the best in the game (football), which is the best male football player. They are defined as among the best women football players in the world as opposed to just the best football players in the world. A more explicit example can be found in the identity assigned to the tournament mascot, Shuéme. The mascot is described as:

> Imagined and created to reflect the esteem Canadians hold for the women's game, Shuéme is every inch the sporty, elegant owl-about-town. With colours that symbolise peace and fair play, and with stylish hair that exudes self-confidence and pride, Shuéme's flowing contours suggest grace under pressure, while her wings and tail ensure precise control and agility.
>
> (Canada Soccer, 2014, p. 5)

By highlighting her stylish hair, flowing contours, and grace under pressure, the description at times represents an idealized femininity which does little to move the perception of women's sport forward and place it alongside the men's game.

Marketing legacies

The fourth and final theme that emerged as an area of comparison between the U20WC and the WWC was the perceived marketing legacy for sport of football in Canada. While legacy has been recognized as a key part of any event and has been examined in many forms (cf. Girginov & Hills, 2008; Kasimati & Dawson, 2009; Minnaert, 2012), the concept of marketing legacy has been virtually ignored. In this study, marketing legacy refers to the perception of how what was learned or gained from the marketing and sponsorship programs these events can/will be used to improve the overall marketing capacity of football in Canada. While marketing legacy was not something that was overtly noted by either event, discussions around what each tournament and sponsor hoped to accomplish can give some indication of the perceived marketing legacies and there is some difference to be noted in overall focus. For the U20WC, it appeared organizers recognized the opportunity to use the event to stimulate greater long-term sponsor investment in Canadian football at the amateur and professional levels. One of the overall outcomes of hosting the event was the building of a national football stadium in Toronto to house Toronto FC, the first Canadian MLS team. This offered a new opportunity for the involvement of sponsors in professional football in Canada. Similarly, tournament sponsors appeared to view an investment in the U20WC as a stepping-stone to greater support and recognition within the game of football. The BMO Financial Group for example specifically noted that "this tournament is going to be something special, drawing a wide audience from across Canada and around the world. Our participation gives us the chance to [. . .] establish ourselves as a strong supporter of football in Canada" (BMO Financial Group, 2007, p. 2). It was also noted that the number of sponsors involved with SC increased directly as a result of the hosting of the U20WC and the impact of a new MLS team in the city. Colin Linford, Chairman of the NOC and then President of Canada Soccer, argued that:

> Toronto FC and the Under20 World Cup have raised football's profile in Canada, and have in turn helped the CSA [Canada Soccer] secure more sponsorships this year than ever before [. . .] You've got the chance (to secure sponsorships) and I believe this is the year we can do some of those things.
>
> (Campbell, 2007, p. C2)

It could also be argued that such a marketing legacy from the U20WC would also have helped with sponsorship success at the WWC.

For the WWC, the marketing legacy focus was somewhat different. While there is little doubt that organizers still sought to increase corporate involvement in the sport of football in Canada, it is suggested that their focus on growing the game in Canada and around the world also helps stimulate the growth of a new and valuable generation of consumers through an increase in participation. FIFA noted that their *Live your Goals* program implemented through the event, first and foremost sought "to encourage girls and women to participate in football" (Canada Soccer, 2015, p. 84) while Soccer Canada declared that they "are committed to the growth of women's football both in Canada and internationally and anticipate that this event [the WWC] will be another successful FIFA competition that will have a lasting impact on the sport in this country" (Canada Soccer, 2011, p. 2). It was also stated that "by contributing over 112,000 volunteer hours, volunteers played an important role in establishing a meaningful legacy for sport and women's football in Canada" (Canada Soccer, 2015, p. 60) and arguably an increase in volunteers within the sector can accomplish many of the same consumer based legacies as an increasing number of participants. From the perspective of Canada Soccer, these outcomes mean a new generation of participants in their sport while from the sponsor's perspective this means a new generation of highly engaged potential consumers. While these consumer outcomes are perhaps not an intended legacy goal of FIFA of the NOC, it is arguably an important unintended legacy.

Discussion and implications

The overall results arguably suggest that marketing and sponsorship within the two events were the same, yet different. While they had much in common there were also notable differences in strategy, implementation, and focus. This is similar to what Lough and Irwin (2001) noted when looking at women's sport sponsorship objectives. With that in mind this discussion will highlight some key findings and implications from the analysis and comparison, particularity for the marketing of women's sport events.

Nation branding

While nation branding was not the focus of this analysis, results did raise an interesting implication related to the concept. It can be suggested that such a focus on national branding is often viewed as a key part of the strategic legacy of an event (cf. Grix & Houlihan 2014; Knott et al., 2015); with this in mind, the absence of such a goal is also potentially a point of interest. Findings from this study suggested that while nation branding was discussed in the context of the men's event, the U20WC, there was no mention of such a goal for the WWC. As these two events both had an international media reach through television and the Internet, it raises questions about the different role women's events may be perceived as playing in a national event strategy. Perhaps this in an indication that those in leadership positions currently see an event like the WWC as an event which offers purely social advantages such as increased participation or the creation of prominent female role models, and this offers the key message for brands to associate themselves with. If this is the case, those seeking to advance the marketing and sponsorship potential of women's events perhaps need to expand the understanding of what opportunities exist within women's sport in general and women's international large-scale events in particular.

Experiential promotions

Once again in their use of experiential marketing strategies the two events demonstrated a same but different approach. While they both concentrated their attention on the use of these strategies, they did so with a unique focus and varied implementation. As Jowdy and McDonald (2003) noted, such a strategy can not only engage fans in meaningful activities during the event (short-term), but can also be used to provide long-term benefits such as a lasting brand image and increased interest in the sport/event. In the case of large-scale events like the WWC and the U20WC such outcomes could serve to provide a lasting positive impact for various groups including female football players (participants), FIFA (the associated international federation), sponsors, and SC (the national governing body). This suggests that an experiential promotions strategy could be one way to help ensure short-term and long-term benefits for a variety of key stakeholder groups.

Research also suggests that the inclusion of staged brand experiences as part of sponsorship activation can help increase the effectiveness of sponsorship, specifically top of mind awareness, brand recall, affective brand experiences, and, in some cases, brand attitude (Fransen, Rompay, & Muntinga, 2013). While those in charge of marketing for the individual events seemed to recognize the value of using experiential promotions to drive ticket sales and build anticipation, the criticism of fan zones, particularly at the WWC, suggest that sponsors of these events should be paying more attention to consumer's experiences, not just at the game but also for those who are not attending a match if they hope to improve the effectiveness of their activation strategy. Similarly, those in charge of marketing the event should perhaps ensure they are paying as much attention to the consumer brand experiences they create at and around the matches as in the lead up to the event if they hope to offer sponsors a recognizable ROI and fans a memorable experience with long-term benefits.

Knowledge transfer

The finding that marketing and sponsorship for the U20WC and WWC were similar in many ways but also unique indicates both learnings and growth in marketing capabilities from the first event to the second. In both cases there was evidence of the use of an experiential promotions strategy that allowed the events to generate word-of-mouth and build anticipation in the lead up to the event by directly engaging potential consumers. Furthermore, there seemed to be a level of professional advancement in key messaging. The brand identity of the WWC appeared to be more involved and nuanced, with greater details, more symbolic attributes, and a deeper meaning. While it may be related to the nature of each event, it seemed as though the organizing committee for the WWC was somewhat more sophisticated in their approach, suggesting the experience of the hosting the U20WC positively impacted their core competences in marketing and sponsorship. Similarly, it can be argued that the U20WC ticket sales success, brought about using experiential marketing, may have influenced the choices of those planning marketing strategy for the WWC. While it is not clear if these links were an outcome of a formal transfer of knowledge program or an informal transfer of knowledge resulting from fact that many of the same stakeholders (individuals and organizations) were involved in both events, there seems to be evidence that the NOCs of these events shared learnings and strategy. Examining the informal transfer of knowledge, the importance of previous event experience among organizers as a key facet of knowledge transfer has been previously discussed in the literature with respect to the Olympic Games (cf., Parent, MacDonald, & Goulet, 2014). It is suggested that this should be a consideration when coordinating a central NOC and, in a case where the event takes place in multiple locations, the various Local Organizing Committees. The sport event industry in any country and within any sport could be advantaged by the extension of the concept of Olympic nomads (Girginov & Olsen, 2013) to the more general idea of event nomads and a realization of the knowledge value of these individuals.

This study also suggests that there could similar advantages to be realized by formal transfers of knowledge not just within the same event, but also between different events, of similar size and circumstances. With this in mind and as suggested by Halbwirth and Toohey (2001), both governing bodies, such as Canada Soccer in this case, and large-scale events should develop formal knowledge management programs to aid in future marketing success and build event hosting capacity in a country's sport community.

Strategy and opportunity of marketing women's sport events

The results of this study also offer interesting implications for the marketing strategy and opportunity of women's sporting events. During the analysis, there was an indication that despite progress and some level of success in marketing the WWC, there was still criticism and room for growth. It is suggested that in order to continue moving forward those responsible for marketing women's events must overcome a sense of deterministic apathy towards generating sponsorship revenue for such events. There is a sense that some feel less media attention and fewer spectators mean that sponsors have less interest in women's events because they don't offer a significant ROI. This may result in them not pushing to seek more from sponsors or to think creatively about how the property can best be marketed, both to sponsors and the public. With this in mind, it would seem there is also a need to market their own product to those in charge of women's events before their commercial value can be fully realized. Gwinner (1997) has suggested that companies need to consider more than just the number of eyeballs that will reach a sponsor's signage when considering sponsorship value, and this would seem especially true in the case of women's sport events. Both sponsors and event marketers need to look beyond eyeballs and focus on what would appear to be numerous advantages of an association with women's sport and sporting events. In this respect, it can be argued that the WWC, and events like it, serve as an opportunity criticize the corporate community and sport industry for perceived lack of sponsor contribution to, and engagement in, women's events (e.g., Millington, 2015) and to draw attention to the unique and valuable attributes of women's events, hopefully stimulating change as a result. Some of the key attributes of women's events that could be emphasized by those in charge of marketing women's events are (1) the uncluttered sponsorship environment, (2) positive messaging and role models, and (3) access to female consumers. As sponsorship has increasingly become an integral part of firms' marketing promotions mix the sponsorship environment around mega-events have become cluttered. This sponsorship clutter can negatively impact both the recognition and recall of sponsors (Cornwell & Relyea, 2000). If an organization is seeking a link to a sport event property and yet wants to escape the normally cluttered market associated with most mega-events, perhaps a women's event can offer this opportunity. Positive messaging and role models are so important because as Gwinner et al. (2009, p. 9) note: "image matters." Sport events offer the opportunity to foster image transfer between the event and its sponsor, and so the image of the event is often as important as other attributes, such as television audience and signage (Gwinner et al., 2009). Particularly in a sport that has recently been rocked by scandal at the highest levels, events like the WWC and the female athletes who star on the field and off provide a valuable link to positive messages and role models that companies should take advantage of. Lastly, Warner (2005) notes that female consumers are the most significant consumer segment in the American marketplace, and so it could be argued that any sport event that offers a unique opportunity to build connection and affinity with this market should hold great potential value for sponsors. While there are still recognized barriers to women consuming women's sport (Farrell, Fink, & Fields, 2011), the WWC seemed to focus much of its marketing on families and the women who participate in football in Canada. This implies that such an event can offer access to that key consumer market: women. If those in charge of marketing women's events can make sponsors aware of the opportunity for an uncluttered marketplace, that offers positive messaging, and access to a key consumer segment and sponsor can see the positives in activating these associations, perhaps they can generate more positive results and lessen the criticism that still, rightly, plagues their efforts in women's sport events.

A last point of interest related to the marketing strategy and opportunity of women's sporting events is the indication that when seeking sponsorship, it is perhaps productive to think outside of the box when it comes to potential sponsors. There was evidence of some success for WWC sponsorships when linked to sponsors with a unique target market fit. Perhaps marketers should seek non-traditional sponsorship groups in order to provide a better match with the distinctive values of an event (O'Reilly & Seguin, 2013). While fit has long been understood and studied as a key element of sponsorship success (Cornwell, Weeks, & Roy, 2005), the need to not just seek fit, but to move beyond the usual and seek out a unique fit might be one way to not only advance sponsorship of women's events, but sponsorship in general.

Gender

While an in-depth sociological analysis of how gender may have impacted the suggested differences between the U20WC and the WWC was beyond the scope of this chapter, comparison of the events did give rise to some problematic gender divisions. The two most obvious issues were the use of qualifiers when discussing the athletes (i.e., world-class female athletes) and an official description of the mascot Shuéme that seemed to place an emphasis on idealized feminine aesthetics. This suggests that while women's sport has made great strides in recent years there is much still to be done. Women's sport in general, and large-scale women's sporting events in particular, require continued vigilance, activism, education, and the increased involvement of women in leadership and decision-making roles if they are to continue to make progress in closing the still significant gender gap.

Limitations and future research

Given the timing of the tournament, which took place just weeks after the 2015 police raids on FIFA headquarters and the arrest of several FIFA members, consideration must be taken with respect to the potential impact of this scandal. Such negative publicity may have influenced the approach of some sponsors. FIFA's well-publicized issues may have discouraged sponsors from actively leveraging their sponsorship to its greatest advantage to avoid being too closely associated to FIFA at that time. With that said, by the time these issues exploded, sponsors would likely have already invested much time and money in a planned activation program that would have been unproductive to cancel. Furthermore, FIFA's problems, while not as overt, had long been a news item, and it is unlikely sponsors would have chosen to focus their message on FIFA as an organization even before the bad publicity arose. Sponsors executing a well-conceptualized campaign linking to football and the social message of the tournament, rather than FIFA itself, would be unlikely to cancel them at the last minute to avoid any association with the organization.

It is also important to note that these case studies involve just two events in one country. While such an approach can add to our understanding of the complex differences among men's and women's large scale sporting events (Yin, 2013), comparisons in other countries and among other events should be undertaken to increase depth and generalizability of the results outside of this context. In the future, it will also be interesting to include further comparison with large-scale, multi-sport events that include both male and female athletes to develop an understanding of the similarities and differences evident in those events and to gain a greater understanding of the marketing of large-scale sporting events as a whole. Further research into this area can also advance our understanding by including alternative methods and areas of analysis. Interviews with key stakeholder of these events would offer the opportunity to continue the analysis, to triangulate findings, and perhaps to move beyond the purely descriptive.

Finally, a more in-depth gender analysis of key messages and differences would also advance literature in the area. There has recently been a call to continuing expanding the "theorizing of gender and gendering of theory in the field of marketing and consumer research" (Arsel, Eräranta, & Moisander, 2015, p. 1553), and using a more sociological lens to analyze comparisons, such as that discussed in this chapter, could contribute to such a call.

Conclusion

In conclusion, this study has sought to increase our understanding of marketing in large-scale events by seeking to discern the similarities and differences in marketing approaches between men's and women's large-scale, single sport events. Such research helps to fill a gap in the event management literature, which lacks both a comprehensive understanding of the strategies and challenges of marketing and sponsorship within large-scale events and a more specific understanding of the marketing of women's sport in general, and women's large-scale sporting events in particular. Four main bases for comparison between marketing in men's and women's events emerged from the analysis and have framed this study: (1) marketing planning and implementation, (2) sponsorship approach, (3) brand identity, and (4) marketing legacies. Overall, it was noted that across these areas of comparison the marketing and sponsorship of men's and women's large-scale events were the same, but different. The importance of experiential marketing promotions in all types of large-scale events, and the need to increase the focus on engaging fans specifically at women's events was noted. Furthermore, the number of similarities between men's and women's events suggested they should be thought of as a vital source of marketing and sponsorship knowledge for each other. The use of both formal and informal knowledge transfer processes between such events within a country can perhaps help ensure their success. Finally, while there were many similarities, there were also noted differences. Most specifically, the missed opportunities of the WWC were highlighted, and suggestions to help move the marketing of women's large-scale events forward were provided. While there is still much to examine in this area, this chapter offers a new perspective that incorporates findings from both men's and women's events and helps advance towards a greater understanding of marketing and sponsorship of large-scale sporting events.

References

Aaker, A., & Joachimsthaler, E. (2000). *Brand leadership*. New York: Simon and Schuster.

Advertising Age. (2015, May 28). FIFA woes not scaring sponsors off Fox's women's world cup package inventory being gobbled up by auto, insurance and fast-food brands. *Advertising Age* [online]. Retrieved October 5, 2015, from http://adage. com/article/ media/fox /298798/

Aisbett, L., & Hoye, R. (2015). Human resource management practices to support sport event volunteers. *Asia Pacific Journal of Human Resources, 53*(3), 351–369.

Apostolopoulou, A., & Papadimitriou, D. (2004). Welcome home: Motivations and objectives of the 2004 Grand National Olympic sponsors. *Sport Marketing Quarterly, 13*(4), 180–192.

Arsel, Z., Eräranta, K., & Moisander, J. (2015). Introduction: Theorising gender and gendering theory in marketing and consumer research. *Journal of Marketing Management, 31*(15–16), 1553–1558.

Bell, B., & Blakey, P. (2010). Do boys and girls go out to play? Women's football and social marketing at EURO 2005. *International Journal of Sport Management and Marketing, 7*(3–4), 156–172.

BMO Financial Group. (2007). *BMO insurance named as an official national supporter of FIFA U-20 world cup.* Retrieved October 20, 2015, from www.newswire.ca/news-releases/bmo-insurance-named-as-an-official-national-supporter-of-fifa-u-20-world-cup-533805801.html

Brown, G. (2002). Taking the pulse of Olympic sponsorship. *Event Management, 7*(3), 187–196.

Campbell, M. (2007, May 25). Nykamp dunks hoops for soccer: Former basketball executive beats out 110 applicants for top CSA position. *Toronto Star* [online]. Retrieved October 20, 2015, from http://search.proquest.com/docview/439210147?accountid=12005

Canada NewsWire. (2007, June 19). *Media alert/photo opportunity – Sony and best buy kick off "score with sony" week and give Canadian Soccer fans a chance to see the FIFA U-20 World Cup trophy.* Retrieved October 19, 2015, from http://search.proquest.com/docview/455470317?accountid=12005

Canada Soccer. (2006, January 26). *It's final – Toronto to host the FIFA U-20 world cup championship game.* Retrieved October 5, 2015, from www.canadasoccer.com/it-s-final-toronto-to-host-fifa-u-20-world-cup-championship-game-p147198

Canada Soccer. (2007a, July 2). *A Canada day record: 1,000,000 spectators and counting.* Retrieved October 5, 2015, from www.canadasoccer.com/a-canada-day-record-1-000-000-spectators-and-counting-p146976

Canada Soccer. (2007b, July 19). *Beyond huge! Canada officially sets FIFA U-20 world cup attendance record.* Retrieved July 15, 2015, from www.canadasoccer.com/beyond-huge-canada-officially-sets-fifa-u-20-world-cup-attendance-record-p146960

Canada Soccer. (2007c, June 26). *NUTELLA contest winners practice with the men's U-20 squad.* Retrieved July 17, 2015, from www.canadasoccer.com/nutella-contest-winners-practice-with-the-men-s-u-20-squad-p146982

Canada Soccer. (2011, March 3). *Canada to welcome the world and its game in 2015.* Retrieved October 20, 2015, from www.canadasoccer.com/canada-to-welcome-the-world-and-its-game-in-2015-p145594

Canada Soccer. (2014). *FIFA women's world cup Canada 2015™ unveils official mascot.* Retrieved July 31, 2015, from www.canadasoccer.com/fifa-women-s-world-cup-canada-2015-unveils-official-mascot-p156513

Canada Soccer. (2015). *FIFA women's world cup Canada 2015 review.* Retrieved November 12, 2015, from http://issuu.com/canadasoccer/docs/2015_fwwc_canada2015_pdf /1?e=18596573/32190146

Canadian Soccer Association. (2007). *FIFA U-20 2007 final report.* Ottawa, ON: Canadian Soccer Association.

CEMA. (2007). *Canadian egg marketing agency annual report 2007.* Retrieved June 13, 2016, from www.eggfarmers.ca/wp-content/uploads/2014/10/CEMA_Annual_Report _2007.pdf

Chadwick, S., & Burton, N. (2011). The evolving sophistication of ambush marketing: A typology of strategies. *Thunderbird International Business Review, 53*(6), 709–719.

Chalip, L. (2004). Beyond Impact: A general model for sport event leverage. In B.W. Richie & D. Adair (Eds.), *Sport tourism: Interrelationships, impacts and issues* (pp. 226–252). North York, ON: Channel View.

Christopherson, N., Janning, M., & McConnell, E. D. (2002). Two kicks forward, one kick back: A content analysis of media discourses on the 1999 women's world cup Soccer championship. *Sociology of Sport Journal, 19*(2), 170–188.

Coca-Cola Company. (2015, February 19). *First-ever FIFA women's world cup trophy tour to visit 12 Canadian cities.* Retrieved October 5, 2015, from www.coca-colacompany.com/coca-cola-unbottled/first-ever-fifa-womens-world-cup-trophy-tour-to-visit-12-canadian-cities

Corley, K. G., & Gioia, D. A. (2004). Identity ambiguity and change in the wake of a corporate spin-off. *Administrative Science Quarterly, 49,* 173–208.

Cornwell, T. B., & Relyea, G. E. (2000). Understanding long-term effects of sports sponsorship: Role of experience, involvement, enthusiasm and clutter. *International Journal of Sports Marketing and Sponsorship, 2*(2), 39–55.

Cornwell, T. B., Roy, D. P., & Steinard II, E. A. (2001). Exploring managers' perceptions of the impact of sponsorship on brand equity. *Journal of Advertising, 30*(2), 41–51.

Cornwell, T. B., Weeks, C. S., & Roy, D. P. (2005). Sponsorship-linked marketing: Opening the black box. *Journal of Advertising, 34*(2), 21–42.

Coughlan, D., & Mules, T. (2001). Sponsorship awareness and recognition at Canberra's Floriade festival. *Event Management, 7*(1), 1–9.

Danforth, C. (2015, June 21). *Nike unveils "The Nike underground" space in Vancouver for FIFA women's world cup.* Retrieved October 5, 2015, from www.notey.com/@highsnobiety_unofficial/external/4864582/nike-unveils-%E2%80%9Cthe-nike-underground%E2%80%9D-space-in-vancouver-for-fifa-women%E2%80%99s-world-cup.html

Dipardo, M. (2015, May, 7). Coke celebrates FIFA Women's World Cup with trophy tour. *Marketing Magazine* [online]. Retrieved June 1, 2015, from www.marketingmag.ca/brands/coke-celebrates-fifa-womens-world-cup-with-trophy-tour-145507

Emery, P. R. (2001). Bidding to host a major sports event. In C. Gratton & I. P. Henry (Eds.), *Sport in the city: The role of sport in economic and social regeneration* (pp. 90–108). London, England: Routledge.

Farrell, A., Fink, J. S., & Fields, S. (2011). Women's sport spectatorship: An exploration of men's influence. *Journal of Sport Management, 25*(3), 190–201.

FIFA. (2007, May 25). *FIFA announces four national supporters for FIFA U-20 world cup Canada.* Retrieved October 5, 2015, from www.fifa.com/u20worldcup/news/y=2007/m=5/news=fifa-announces-four-national-supporters-for-fifa-world-cup-canada-129174.html

FIFA. (2015a, December 17). *Record breaking FIFA women's world cup tops 750 million TV viewers*. Retrieved April 14, 2016, from www.fifa.com/womensworldcup/news/y=2015/m=12/news=record-breaking-fifa-women-s-world-cup-tops-750-million-tv-viewers-2745963.html

FIFA. (2015b, November 5). *FIFA tournaments deliver big economic boost in Canada*. Retrieved April 14, 2016, from www.fifa.com/womens-football/news/y=2015/m=11/news=fifa-tournaments-deliver-Bigeconomic-boost-in-canada-2730259.html

FIFA. (2015c, June 1). *Trophy tour comes to a spectacular end*. Retrieved October 5, 2015, from, www.fifa.com/fifa-tournaments/news/y=2015/m=6/news=trophy-tour-comes-to-a-spectacular-end-2614763.html

FIFA. (2015d, February 17). *Canada 2015 welcomes trend micro as national supporter*. Retrieved October 5, 2015, from www.fifa.com/womensworldcup/news/y=2015/m=2/news=canada-2015-welcomes-trend-micro-as-national-supporter-2524858.html

FIFA. (2015e). *FIFA women's world cup Canada 2015 fan zone locations*. Retrieved April 14, 2015, from http://resources.fifa.com/mm/document/tournament/competition/02/60/70/ 66/fwwcfanzonelocationsen_neutral.pdf

FIFA. (2016a, April 13). *Women's football continues to go global*. Retrieved April 14, 2016, from www.fifa.com/womens-football/news/y=2016/m=4/news=women-s-football-continues-to-go-global-2780793.html

FIFA. (2016b). *FIFA world cup sponsorship strategy*. Retrieved June 1, 2016 from, www.fifa.com/about-fifa/marketing/sponsorship/

FIFA.com. (2015). *Key figures from the FIFA women's world cup Canada 2015*. Retrieved from www.fifa.com/womensworldcup/news/y=2015/ m=7/news=key-figures-from-the-fifa-women-s-world-cup-canada-2015tm-2661648.html

Fransen, M. L., Rompay, T. J. V., & Muntinga, D. G. (2013). Increasing sponsorship effectiveness through brand experience. *International Journal of Sports Marketing and Sponsorship*, 14(2), 37–50.

Funk, D. C., Mahony, D. F., Nakazawa, M., & Hirakawa, S. (2001). Development of the sport interest inventory (SII): Implications for measuring unique consumer motives at team sporting events. *International Journal of Sports Marketing and Sponsorship*, 3(3), 38–63.

Funk, D. C., Ridinger, L. L., & Moorman, A. M. (2003). Understanding consumer support: Extending the Sport Interest Inventory (SII) to examine individual differences among women's professional sport consumers. *Sport Management Review*, 6(1), 1–31.

Getz, D., Andersson, T., & Larson, M. (2007). Festival stakeholder roles: Concepts and case studies. *Event Management*, 10(2), 103–122.

Giannoulakis, C., Stotlar, D., & Chatziefstathiou, D. (2008). Olympic sponsorship: Evolution, challenges and impact on the olympic movement. *International Journal of Sports Marketing & Sponsorship*, 9(4), 256–270.

Girginov, V., & Hills, L. (2008). A sustainable sports legacy: Creating a link between the London olympics and sports participation. *The International Journal of the History of Sport*, 25(14), 2091–2116.

Girginov, V., & Olsen, N. (2013). Chapter 5: A temporary organisation within a high-velocity environment. In V. Girginov (Ed.), *Handbook of the London 2012 olympic and paralympic games: Volume two: Celebrating the games* (pp. 71–83). London: Routledge.

Grix, J., & Houlihan, B. (2014). Sports mega – events as part of a nation's soft power strategy: The cases of Germany (2006) and the UK (2012). *The British Journal of Politics & International Relations*, 16(4), 572–596.

Grohs, R., & Reisinger, H. (2005). Image transfer in sports sponsorships: An assessment of moderating effects. *International Journal of Sports Marketing and Sponsorship*, 7(1), 36–42.

Guba, E. G. (1981). Criteria for assessing the trustworthiness of naturalistic inquiries. *Educational Technology Research and Development*, 29(2), 75–91.

Gwinner, K. (1997). A model of image creation and image transfer in event sponsorship. *International Marketing Review*, 14(3), 145–158.

Gwinner, K. P., & Eaton, J. (1999). Building brand image Through event sponsorship: The role of image transfer. *Journal of Advertising*, 28(4), 47–57.

Gwinner, K. P., Larson, B. V., & Swanson, S. R. (2009). Image transfer in corporate event sponsorship: Assessing the impact of team identification and event-sponsor fit. *International Journal of Management and Marketing Research*, 2(1), 1–15.

Halbwirth, S., & Toohey, K. (2001). The olympic games and knowledge management: A case study of the Sydney organising committee of the Olympic Games. *European Sport Management Quarterly*, 1(2), 91–111.

Hallmann, K. (2012). The impact of perceived images of women's Soccer and the world cup 2011 on interest in attending matches, *Sport Management Review*, 15(1), 33–42.

Harwell, D. (2015, July 6). Why hardly anyone sponsored the most watched Soccer match in U.S. history. *The Washington Post* [online]. Retrieved October 5, 2015, from www.washingtonpost.com/news/wonk/wp/2015/07/06/the-sad-gender-econo mics-of-the-womens-world-cup/

Howland-Morris, A. (2007, July 24). Soccer provides kick to economy: FIFA tournament was worthy venture right across Canada. *Edmonton Journal* [online]. Retrieved October 19, 2015, from http://search.proquest.com/docview/253461 226?accountid=12005

IEG, (2016). *IEG lexicon and glossary*. Retrieved June 1, 2016, from www.sponsor ship.com/Resources/IEG-Lexicon-and-Glossary.aspx

Jones, I. (2015). *Research methods for sports studies* (3rd ed.). New York: Routledge.

Jowdy, E., & McDonald, M. (2003). Relationship marketing and interactive fan festivals: The Women's United Soccer Association's 'Soccer Sensation. *International Journal of Sport Marketing & Sponsorship*, 4(4), 295–311.

Kasimati, E., & Dawson, P. (2009). Assessing the impact of the 2004 olympic games on the Greek economy: A small macroeconometric model. *Economic Modelling*, 26(1), 139–146.

Kassouf, J. (2015, June 16). Americans invade Vancouver, a city fit for the World Cup. *Equalizer Soccer*. Retrieved June 19, 2015, from http://equalizersoc cer.com/2015/06/16/vancouver-womens-world-cup-fan-zone-uswnt-american-outlaws/

Knott, B., Fyall, A., & Jones, I. (2015). The nation branding opportunities provided by a sport mega-event: South Africa and the 2010 FIFA World Cup. *Journal of Destination Marketing & Management*, 4(1), 46–56.

Koo, G-Y., Quarterman, J., & Flynn, L. (2006). Effect of perceived sport event and sponsor image fit on consumers' cognition, affect, and behavioral intentions. *Sport Marketing Quarterly*, 15(2), 80–90.

Kwon, E., Ratneshwar, S., & Kim, E. (2015). Brand image congruence through sponsorship of sporting events: A reinquiry of Gwinner and Eaton (1999). *Journal of Advertising*, *45*(1), 130–138.

Lough, N. L. (1996). Factors affecting corporate sponsorship of women's sport. *Sport Marketing Quarterly*, *5*(2), 11–19.

Lough, N. L., & Irwin, R. L. (2001). A comparative analysis of sponsorship objectives for U.S. Women's sport and traditional sport sponsorship. *Sport Marketing Quarterly*, *10*(4), 202–211.

Miles, M. B., Huberman, A. M., & Saldaña, J. (2014). *Qualitative data analysis: A methods sourcebook* (3rd ed.). Thousand Oaks, CA: Sage.

Millington, A. (2015, June 11). Women's world cup shows how brands are underserving women's sport. *Marketing Week*. Retrieved from www.marketingweek.com/ 2015/06/11/womens-world-cup-shows-how-brands-are-underserving-womens-sport/

Minnaert, L. (2012). An olympic legacy for all? The non-infrastructural outcomes of the Olympic Games for socially excluded groups (Atlanta 1996 – Beijing 2008). *Tourism Management*, *33*(2), 361–370.

Miyazaki, A. D., & Morgan, A. G. (2001). Assessing the market value of sponsoring: Corporate olympic sponsorships. *Journal of Advertising Research*, *41*(1), 9–15.

Nauright, J. (2013, Winter). Selling nations to the world through sports: Megaevents and nation branding as global diplomacy. *Public Diplomacy Magazine*, *9* (winter), 22–27.

Novais, M., & Arcodia, C. (2013). Measuring the effects of event sponsorship: Theoretical frameworks and image transfer models. *Journal of Travel & Tourism Marketing*, *30*(4), 308–334.

O'Keefe, R., Titlebaum, P., & Hill, C. (2009). Sponsorship activation: Turning money spent into money earned. *Journal of Sponsorship*, *3*(1), 43–53.

O'Reilly, N., Lyberger, M., McCarthy, L., Séguin, B., & Nadeau, J. (2008). Megaspecial-event promotions and intent to purchase: A longitudinal analysis of the super bowl. *Journal of Sport Management*, *22*(4), 392–409.

O'Reilly, N., & Seguin, B. (2013). *Sport marketing: A Canadian perspective* (2nd ed.). Toronto, ON: Nelson Education.

Papadimitriou, D., & Apostolopoulou, A. (2009). Olympic sponsorship activation and the creation of competitive advantage. *Journal of Promotion Management*, *15*(1–2), 90–117.

Parent, M. M. (2008). Evolution and issue patterns for major sporting event organizing committees and their stakeholders. *Journal of Sport Management*, *22*(2), 135–164.

Parent, M. M., Eskerud, L., & Hanstad, D. V. (2012). Brand creation in international recurring sports events. *Sport Management Review*, *15*(2), 145–159.

Parent, M. M., & Foreman, P. O. (2007). Organizational image and identity management in large-scale sporting events. *Journal of Sport Management*, *21*(1), 15–40.

Parent, M. M., MacDonald, D., & Goulet, G. (2014). The theory and practice of knowledge management and transfer: The case of the Olympic Games. *Sport Management Review*, *17*(2), 205–218.

Parent, M. M., & Séguin, B. (2008). Toward a model of brand creation for international large-scale sporting events: The impact of leadership, context and nature of the event. *Journal of Sport Management*, *22*(5), 526–549.

Powell, C. (2015, June 8). Canadian tire gets playful in new campaign. *Marketing Magazine* [online]. Retrieved June 23, 2015, from www.marketingmag.ca/brands/canadian-tire-gets-playful-in-new-campaign-148600

Preuss, H., Gemeinder, K., & Séguin, B. (2008). Ambush marketing in China: Counterbalancing Olympic sponsorship efforts. *Asian Business & Management*, 7(2), 243–263.

Preuss, H., Woratschek, H., & Durchholz, C. (2008, September). *Image-analysis and sponsoring-fit on woman Soccer in Germany – empirical findings of a representative survey among six German world cup cities in 2011.* Presented at the 16th European Association of Sport Management Conference, Heidelberg, GER. Abstract Retrieved from www.easm.net/download/2008/69899d52a5106afb3c2b 36fef34c8c41.pdf

Quinn, G., & De Vynck, G. (2015, June 4). Women's World Cup set to open amid FIFA bribe scandal. *Bloomberg* [online]. Retrieved October 5, 2015, from www.bloomberg.com/news/articles/2015-06-04/women-s-world-cup-set-to-open-amid-fifa-bribe-scandal

Schmitt, B. H. (2000). *Experiential marketing: How to get customers to sense, feel, think, act, relate.* New York: Simon and Schuster.

Schum, C. (2015, July 2). *The missed opportunities of the women's world cup.* Retrieved August 14, 2015, from www.porternovelli.com/intelligence/2015/07/02/the-missed-opportunities-of-the-womens-world-cup/

Séguin, B., & O'Reilly, N. J. (2008). The olympic brand, ambush marketing and clutter. *International Journal of Sport Management and Marketing*, 4(1), 62–84.

Séguin, B., Rodrigue, F., O'Reilly, N., & MacIntosh, E. (2013). *Ambush marketing: Value co-creation or co-destruction.* Paper presented at the 21st European Association of Sport Management Conference, Istanbul, Turkey. Abstract Retrieved from www.easm.net/download/2013/AMBUSH%20MARKETING.pdf

Serwetnyk, C. (June 26, 2015). Carrie Serwetnyk: For their own goal. *Vancouver Sun* [online]. Retrieved October 5, 2015, from www.vancouversun.com/touch/story.html?id=11166621

Shaw, S., & Amis, J. (2001). Image and investment: Sponsorship and women's' sport. *Journal of Sport Management*, 3, 219–246.

Smith, C. (2014, June 12). The biggest sponsors of Brazil's 2014 World Cup spend big to engage with fans. *Forbes* [Online]. Retrieved June 1, 2016, from www.forbes.com/sites/chrissmith/2014/06/12/the-biggest-sponsors-of-brazils-2014-world-cup/#26682b8b15e5

Sparks, R., & Westgate, M. (2002). Broad-based and targeted sponsorship strategies in Canadian women's ice hockey. *International Journal of Sports Marketing and Sponsorship*, 4(1), 48–73.

Taks, M., Chalip, L., & Green, B. C. (2015). Impacts and strategic outcomes from non-mega sport events for local communities. *European Sport Management Quarterly*, 15(1), 1–6.

Vancity Buzz. (2015). *Celebrate Soccer at the free Vancouver FIFA fan zone for the women's world cup 2015.* Retrieved October 5, 2015, from www.vancitybuzz.com /2015/06/free-fifa-fan-zone-vancouver-womens-world-cup/

Walgrove, A. (2015, June 24). *Why the women's world cup is a missed opportunity for brands.* Retrieved October 5, 2015, from https://contently.com/strategist/2015/06/24/why-the-womens-world-cup-is-a-missed-opportunity-for-brands/

Warner, F. (2005). *The power of the purse: How smart businesses are adapting to the world's most important consumers – women*. Upper Saddle River, NJ: Prentice Hall.

Yin, R. (2013). *Case study research: Design and methods* (4th ed.). Thousand Oaks, CA: Sage.

Zhang, J. J., Pennington-Gray, L., Connaughton, D. P., Braunstein, J. R., Ellis, M. H., Lam, E. T., & Williamson, D. (2003). Understanding women's professional basketball game spectators: Sociodemographics, game consumption and entertainment options. *Sport Marketing Quarterly, 12*(4), 228–243.

Chapter 11

The equalizer

Feminist themes in NWSL club marketing

Chris Henderson, Becca Leopkey, and James J. Zhang

Introduction

Conceived in the second half of 2012 and beginning play in 2013, the National Women's Soccer League (NWSL) is the third attempt in the United States at a professional women's football league in the country. While there were a multitude of factors that contributed to the demise of the Women's United Soccer Association (WUSA) and Women's Professional Soccer (WPS) over the past decade, financial mismanagement and a lack of marketing nous were chief amongst the culprits (Dure, 2013; Grainey, 2012). As has been the case with other women's sport leagues, viability has been difficult to come by, creating an unstable business environment (Grainey, 2012).

Puzzlingly, participation in women's football has flourished among youths, enjoying booming participation numbers for the last quarter century, while the United States' Women's National Team (USWNT) has consistently drawn the attention of both major sponsors and spectators (Lisi, 2013). This disconnect has created a situation where players for the USWNT have often been able to collect lucrative endorsements and healthy salaries from U.S. Soccer but have toiled in obscurity for unstable club leagues in the U.S.

While the USWNT's rise to fame in 1999 and subsequent revival in fortunes in the summers of 2011 and 2012 captured media and fan attention, research into the rise of the team has been anecdotal and scattered. Christopherson, Janning, and McConnell's (2002) research was the most high profile study conducted on the rise of the USWNT during the 1999 FIFA WWC, but it dwelled on thematic analysis of media coverage of the event instead of how the team and the event was marketed and sold by event organizers. Subsequent examinations have been virtually non-existent, which seems unfathomable given the team's rise back into the spotlight within the past half decade.

Though much research was undertaken over a decade ago, there have been numerous instances of feminist-themed research into women's football worldwide (e.g., Knoppers & Anthonissen, 2003; Martinez, 2008; Scraton, Fasting, Pfister, & Bunuel, 1999). Some issues involving the intertwining of feminist theory and women's football that researchers have examined have included a continuing inequity in resources and coverage between men's and women's football, the use of sexualization and an ideal of heteronormative femininity to sell women's football, and the stigmatization of those who participate but don't fit that heteronormative mold (Caudwell, 1999; Cox & Thompson, 2004). While the internet has opened up the women's game for consumption and discussion by increasingly devoted fanbases, research into the game along feminist theoretical lines has not kept pace with this growth nor with the continuing evolution of how the game is sold, presented, and consumed.

This is especially true of professional women's leagues in the United States, where research into marketing practices and connections with feminist themes have gone unexamined through the birth and death of the WUSA and WPS, as well as through the first three years of the NWSL. Early examinations of the NWSL have been anecdotal, looking at marketing in terms of dollars and cents while ignoring the rationale and greater themes of marketing decisions from the teams and the league (Dure, 2013). Feminist enquiries into other women's sport have laid the groundwork for explanations of successes and failures as well as offering cogent policy recommendations to ease stakeholders towards prosperity. Similar research into the NWSL could do the same, highlighting how the nascent league is succeeding, as well as steps it can take to improve its fortunes.

Therefore, the purpose of this study is to examine and explain the marketing of the clubs of the NWSL and the league as a whole through feminist themes, using five of the league's clubs to better understand how they have used these feminist themes in their marketing. Feminist themes have been used to dissect and critique societal inequities, including within sport, to minimize and eliminate these differences. This study identifies three feminist themes common in marketing of women's sport, and the roles those themes have played in the marketing of the NWSL, specifically: the effects of an inequity of rules, resources, and coverage on marketing; the embracing of motherhood, family values, and role models while shunning the "other"; and the use of ideal heteronormative femininity to construct consumption communities.

This chapter first provides a brief look at feminist theory, gender theory, and gender barriers and their relation to sport. Next, a more specific framework built around three major feminist themes that have been common in the marketing of sport is briefly discussed. This is followed by details of the study's findings on the use of feminist themes in marketing by NWSL clubs, as well as a discussion to contextualize the findings with previous literature and research into the marketing of women's football through feminist themes. Finally, concluding thoughts, managerial implications, and potential future directions for research are provided.

Feminism in sport

Definitions of feminism have been deconstructed and constructed for decades while branching out into gender theory. The growth of feminism over the past half-century has been built on a foundation of what feminism actually means, with the concept often meaning something different entirely to two different people who declare themselves feminists (McRobbie, 2009). This has made it hard to define "feminism" as a single construct, but Birrell (2000) argues that this debate has helped empower feminism as a strong, deep theory. Feminism has been divided into three distinct "waves" by scholars, each in a distinct time period and with its own political and social reality.

First-wave feminism largely applied to the cause of women's suffrage, emerging at the heart of the industrial revolution during a surge of liberalized politics (Heywood, 1997; Madsen, 2000). Second-wave feminism largely took hold in the 1970s and 1980s with a premise of sex and gender being distinct (Butler, 1993). However, second-wave feminism came under heavy criticism for homogenizing the experience of women into a one-size-fits-all mold, while ignoring factors such as race, sexuality, and class in molding the experience of different women (Evans, 1995).

The 1990s brought third-wave feminism to the fore, with Judith Butler, among other things, seeking to bring the above complicating factors into focus when examining the struggles of women in achieving equality. Many third-wave feminists had become disenchanted with a perception of gains towards equality being tilted to white, middle-class women, while minority groups still suffered (Caudwell, 2011). This line of inquiry notes that oppression does not just come from men but from racism, homophobia, and income inequality that cuts across gender lines and condemns both men and women as contributing to struggles.

Feminist viewpoints have argued that the sport industry ascribes to strict binary gender classification, promoting an intractable sense of male superiority (Shaw, 2006). Messner (2002) notes that male dominance is upheld by a "gender regime of sport," where power brokers "maintain and promote male hegemony in sport" (p. 65). In Messner's eyes, equity between the genders in sport is actively resisted by rigid institutions that stonewall with separate and unequal rules, gaps in funding, and a stark difference in opportunity.

At the same time, feminist theory's primary goal of equality has been felt through policy that has leveled the playing field for sport in general and, specifically, women's football. Worldwide, but especially in North America and Europe, women's football players have benefitted from legislation that has offered more opportunity, including Title IX in the United States (Caudwell, 2011).

Gender theory

Gender can be seen as a central facet on feminism and feminist studies (Caudwell, 2011). Caudwell notes that to the regular person, gender often "denotes biological differences between women and men" (p. 331–332). However, Butler (1990) has argued that gender is not inscribed on us but socially constructed by performing gender, in effect 'doing' masculinity and femininity. Butler (1993) claims that "the regulatory norms of 'sex' work in a performative fashion to constitute the materiality of bodies," through "reiterative and citational practice" (p. 2).

Roth and Basow (2004) claim that "sexed bodies are constructed through the activities we do continually, often without conscious thought" (p. 246). Beyond this construction, the differences in masculinity and femininity have been emphasized, with the construction and perpetuation of the former being lauded by the hegemony, while the construction and perpetuation of the latter has been seen as "lesser" by hegemonic forces. This dichotomy is reflected throughout the building blocks of society daily.

Many feminists have argued that traditional heteronormative constructions of femininity have served to perpetuate inequality and denote the bodies of those not conforming as illegitimate (Butler, 1993). These feminists have argued this framework of heteronormative femininity has been erected by a patriarchally obsessed society, with men in positions of power using popular culture such as movies, television, and the internet to empower a picture of what a "desirable" woman looks like: young, thin, white, heterosexual, and voluptuous (Gill, 2007). This image is then disseminated daily to the population at large and used to sell products to women now under pressure to "do" heteronormative femininity with these products, helping them conform to this pervasive standard as a pathway to success, creating a consumption community (Goldman, 1992).

One area of society that has served as a pedestal to exalt the superiority/inferiority male/female dichotomy is sport (Connell & Messerschmidt, 2005). Bryson (1987) claims the masculine hegemony underpinning sport has "negative evaluations of women's capacities" deep within it (p. 350). Messner (1992) notes sport has historically been used as a male preserve, where males can bond with each other, friend-to-friend, father-to-son, as well as establish their masculinity and distance themselves from the unwanted stigma of "being feminine." The creation of these "female-free zones" allows men to create affirming identities separate from the looked down upon "feminine" identity (Fields, 2006).

Theoretical framework

The following section offers a brief overview into three predominant feminist marketing themes that have featured into women's sport and women's football marketing in the past and which still play an important role in current marketing of women's football. The presented themes have been found in previous examinations of the relationship between feminism and sport (Burstyn, 1999; Caudwell, 1999; Kane & Lenskyj, 1996; Messner, 2002) and their absence in examinations of women's football contexts in the United States may be obscuring potential explanations of marketing failures and successes and strategies of NWSL clubs, as well as those of leagues before.

Inequity of rules, resources, and coverage

Historically, women have been subject to pernicious myths meant to discourage them from taking part in athletic endeavors. Tacitly, social barriers were erected to separate women from sport, disenfranchising them, while men were glamorized instead of ostracized. De Varona (2004) identified common myths used as barriers to participation in sport (e.g., participating in sport will make women unfeminine and could harm their reproductive organs resulting in the inability to produce children, and women athletes will never be as popular as male athletes; therefore, they will not attract audiences large enough to make women's sport financially profitable).

Participation in sports at youth and college levels skyrocketed as many of the myths concerning female participation in sports were debunked. In particular, De Varona (2004) found that women's participation in sport had positive side effects attached to it including, for example, females who participate in sport are less likely to abuse drugs, suffer from depression, and/ or engage in self-destructive behavior. The profligation of these facts has depowered many of the myths that had kept women from the game, bridging the participation gap between boys and girls which had developed as a consequence of those myths.

When myths did not work, those in power moved to limit opportunity. A study conducted by Scraton et al. (1999) in England found that many young women claimed they were not allowed to play football at school, instead being diverted into "sex-appropriate" activities. Limiting opportunity also meant making players jump through enormous financial hoops to fund opportunities to play. In New Zealand, players ran marathons, held car washes, and even went into pubs to kiss patrons for handouts to raise the money needed for tournament travel, with fundraising being "part and parcel of being a female football player" (Cox & Thompson, 2004, p. 215). Globally, even elite female players have had to take part-time jobs just to make ends meet, as player pay was perilously low, even for international competitions.

Beyond myth making and myth breaking and financial constraints, sometimes governing bodies were loath to treat men and women's players equally. In a paternalistic and condescending move, FIFA ruled that matches at the first WWC would only last 80 minutes instead of the customary ninety in men's games, because of a belief that "women did not have the stamina to play a full ninety minutes like men" (Lisi, 2013, p. 2). It would not be the last time FIFA meddled with notions of equality in the rulebook, as the organizing body briefly gave credence to an idea for the 1999 FIFA WWC that the ball should be slightly deflated so that it would not "hurt" the players (Longman, 2001).

The USWNT found itself underfunded and seen as an afterthought in its early years. The team's annual budget during those formative years was a paltry $175,000 (Lisi, 2013). It was a difficult existence, with players unable to obtain more lucrative full-time jobs outside of football, knowing employers would not wait when they were away with the USWNT (Grainey, 2012).

Media coverage in those early days for the USWNT was also largely absent. Fortunato (2000) stated that the media has a strong influence on how events, organizations, and individuals are perceived by the public. Coverage of the U.S. men's national team outstripped that of its female counterpart for decades, with only highlights being shown of the USWNT's 1996 Summer Olympic win. The USWNT wouldn't receive a big media push until the 1999 WWC, where every game was broadcast by ABC and two ESPN networks (De Varona, 2004). A media not used to covering women's sports outside of the Olympic Games was slow to respond, but in newspapers that did cover the tournament, WWC storylines dominated the sports pages during the summer, while an increasingly enthralled nation tuned in, with forty million viewers watching on television (Longman, 1999).

While the public still seemed engaged with the exploits of the USWNT after the 1999 WWC, the team still struggled with equality in recognition from their own federation. Men's national team accomplishments were still listed above the women's World Cup win in publications, while highlights of the USWNT's triumph were also curiously absent from end of year retrospectives. They were slights that were to continue for over a decade until the team's return to the limelight in the summer of 2011 (Grainey, 2012).

Embracing motherhood, family values, and role models

While sociological factors propping up the rise in popularity of youth football as a whole in the United States as well as in the popularity of the USWNT has been written about in great length, recent changes to the narrative have gone unexamined within professional women's football. Whereas previous authors (e.g., Knoppers & Anthonissen, 2003; Martinez, 2008) have noted how "middle America" ideals have been cherished in football circles in America, they have noted how behavior deviating from a traditionally feminine, heterosexual norm has been shunned, ignored, and ostracized. Recently, homophobia has been confronted and countered by many within women's football, through players, officials, and fans. These new steps have gone largely ignored in research, with this study seeking to build on previous narratives with new developments.

Cultivating a wholesome, "All-American" image for the USWNT has been key for marketing purposes for a decade and a half, beginning with the 1999 WWC that vaulted the team to fame. The USWNT were described by some as a "safe-sexy picture of bouncy femininity" (Longman, 2001, p. 41). It was theorized that part of the marketing success of the WWC came about from its perpetuation of "a particularly narrow definition of feminism – one that excludes variation in terms of race, class, and sexual orientation" (Christopherson et al., 2002, p. 172).

Homophobia has been described as a powerful political weapon of sexism, with the label of being a lesbian used as a marker to "define the boundaries of acceptable female behavior in a patriarchal culture" (Griffin, 2002, p. 194). Those who admitted homosexuality and who refused to conform to those boundaries saw endorsement opportunities vanish (Longman, 2001). Festle (1996) claims that male sexuality in sport goes unexamined as sport confirms their masculinity, but that sport calls into question women's "heterosexual femininity."

Kane and Lenskyj (1996) argue that "homophobic representations of female athletes, most notably the symbolic erasure of women who participate in sports traditionally considered a male preserve, play a central role in perpetuating male sporting hegemony" (p. 200). Being called a lesbian, especially in sport, has been seen as being the victim of an act of intimidation, with some women in sport feeling sensitive and vulnerable to the use of the term, as much of women's sport has been stereotyped by many as a 'lesbian activity' (Grainey, 2012).

Homophobia still lingered over women's football in the U.S. despite its growing popularity. Some claimed that the necessity of presenting women athletes as heterosexual had little to do with football and more with a prevailing air of homophobia permeating much of American sport (Griffin, 1998; Hargreaves, 2000). For much of the twentieth century, sports figures denied the existence of lesbianism by underlining heterosexual normality, specifically the existence of motherhood, boyfriends, husbands, and babies (Longman, 2001). Marketing and media coverage of the USWNT diverged from implications of homosexuality, using sex appeal to promote women's empowerment and in being good role models (Christopherson et al., 2002). Such decisions were also undertaken in the general promotion of the 1999 WWC.

The USWNT was not portrayed as "less feminine, or more lesbian, than non-athletes," a portrayal which Lipsyte (1999) framed as being "normal," proper role models for young girls who also happen to form a very lucrative consumption community. Lipsyte (1999) also posited that it was necessary for the team to dispel any notion of homosexuality that often was used to stifle women athletes if they were to successfully market themselves.

Joy Fawcett and Carla Overbeck were fawned over by the press as "true football moms," raising kids while trying to play football (Grainey, 2012). The media's tactics of "trumpeting the football-mom angle" came under fire from feminists though, as they argued that that narrative "reinforced the notion that a woman must be heterosexual and attractive to be a successful and accepted athlete" (Longman, 2001, p. 139).

It has been said that the simultaneous portrayal of the USWNT as "tough, strong, and muscular" while also being "nice, feminine, American women" was attractive to the general public (Christopherson et al., 2002, p. 182). The latter appealed to families, while the former played upon a theme of female empowerment appealing to many women. The above also argued that the media may not have just been playing towards attracting families and women though, as they also controlled the message, celebrating "individual achievements within a group-oriented heterosexual, middle and upper-class white context" that assuaged male fears of a potential upheaval in the hierarchal order while simultaneously "[appealing] to the hopes of women" (p. 184).

A theme of camaraderie and togetherness resonated in the marketing and presentation of the USWNT before and during the 1999 FIFA WWC, most prominently shown in Nike's "I Will Have Two Fillings" television advertisement, where USWNT players get matching fillings as a show of unity. It was an ad that resonated with the public and became a famous ad for this generation of football fan (Longman, 2001). These themes were repeated in media coverage and marketing, generating a narrative that increased the team's popularity and contributed to the team's status as role models.

The campaign may have fit into a narrative of "stereotypically feminine qualities," such as "selflessness, modesty, and desire for harmony" that some argue helped the team's surge in popularity, though some stated that those traits are not associated with a theme of empowerment (Christopherson et al., 2002, p. 178–179). "Sacrifice, loyalty and teamwork" were suddenly in vogue as opposed to the usual trappings of professional sport such as statistics and standings (Longman, 2001, p. 174).

Ideal heteronormative femininity and consumption community

Much has been made of the construction of an ideal heteronormative feminine identity by the hegemony. In large part, this construction has served the needs of corporations, allowing the shaping and manipulation of purchasing habits as women seek to conform to ideal heteronormative femininity. Sport has been an eager and active participant in the construction of this "consumption community," with entities eagerly accepting an exchange of cash or other considerations for access to lucrative consumer markets. Women's football has been no different, with its purveyors and participants pushed as or encouraged to function as the ideal heteronromative feminine role model to be aspired towards.

Ideal masculinity is constructed through ideals of physical strength, large, hulking stature, and aggression. By contrast, feminine ideals are seen as being "beautiful, small, thin, and, perhaps most importantly weak" (Roth & Basow, 2004, p. 249). To meet this ideal, women often diet, exercise, remove hair, and use make-up (Bartky, 1998). Masculine and feminine ideals are transmitted through family, religion, the workplace, and the media to the point that being "feminine" or "masculine" becomes a key for the identity of women and men (Bartky, 1998; Roth & Basow, 2004).

Wolf (1991) argues that women (and men) are encouraged to look certain ways, because meeting the masculine and feminine ideals of society takes money to purchase products and use services. McCaughey (1997) claims that sport may be a way of fueling capitalist needs by selling products to new markets and not as a tool of liberation. Goldman (1992) refers to this as "commodity feminism," with advertisers using visual touches to make distinct styles that allow women and men to "do" feminism and masculinity.

Despite the destruction of many myths, Carl Cannon claimed that people expect women to play sports like men but still "retain some of the traditional notions of femininity" (Grainey, 2012, p. 174). To conform to societal norms, women athletes must be "both strong and soft" to negotiate the dichotomy of strong athlete and patriarchal definitions of femininity (Markula, 1995). In effect, women athletes must play sport like men, with power and tenacity, but also retain their femininity to be acceptable to hegemonic forces (Christopherson et al., 2002).

While some companies' devotion towards promotion of women's sport and advertisement targeting women has been commendable, others have ascribed a more nefarious motive. Instead of breaking through patriarchal gender norms, critics like Goldman (1992) have argued that giant conglomerates such as Nike are interested in the bottom line, namely increasing their profits. The media has shown favor towards physically attractive athletes regardless of skill, emphasizing and exploiting heteronormative femininity (Grau, Roselli, & Taylor, 2007; Spencer & McClung, 2001).

Advertisements have played into heteronormative ideals of femininity, including "traditional" heterosexual roles for women while also targeting products for women with female athlete endorsers (Cuneen, 2001; Lynn, Walsdorf, Hardin, & Hardin, 2002; McGinnis, Chun, & McQuillan, 2003). Sports that emphasize traditional femininity, such as ice skating and gymnastics, have been most popular with marketers in the past (Duncan & Hasbrook, 1988; Kane, 1988, 1999; McGinnis et al., 2003).

Some advertisements for the 1999 WWC that flaunted USWNT members' traditional femininity and heterosexuality in an attempt to appeal to the heterosexual male demographic were met with mixed reactions. One of the most talked about advertisements fitting this description involved Brandi

Chastain, who posed "crouched behind a football ball wearing only her cleats and her rippling muscles," in a spread that appeared in *Gear* magazine (Markovits & Hellerman, 2004, p. 27). While the advertisement drew the attention of the masses, opinions varied as to the merit of such an ad towards promoting the game.

As was the case with the WUSA, WPS touted the traditional femininity of its players. League outfitter Puma introduced uniforms that, in their words, "Fuse Performance with Fashion, Bold Color and Feminine Flair" but which was panned by many (Sigi, 2009b). It was likewise with pink goalkeeper shirts not popular with some of the players, including outspoken goalkeeper Hope Solo. Some of the features produced by teams blatantly pandered towards promoting players' heterosexuality, such as Boston's "Battle of the Brides" featurette, which saw some players trying on wedding dresses.

Methodology

The purpose of this study was to examine the marketing of professional women's football through themes of feminism. In this research, a case study was developed (Yin, 2013). This study uses a single case study with multiple settings, which allowed the researchers opportunities for analysis and insight into specific issues (Denscombe, 1998; Yin, 2013). Case studies allow for the gathering and analysis of detailed information on subjects and for researchers to hone in on relationships pertinent to research goals, such as the relationship between marketing officials of a team and their core audience. Additionally, interviews through case studies make it easier to analyze and interpret unforeseen events (Denscombe, 1998; Yin, 2013).

Research context and data collection

Beginning play in 2013, the NWSL saw eight founder clubs with top players having salaries subsidized by international federations, while other players saw salaries cut greatly from previous leagues. Founder clubs varied greatly, with one affiliated with a MLS club, while others were holdovers from previous leagues. Variability between clubs in areas such as attendance, facilities, and infrastructure was massive, while the league as a whole suffered from a lack of media coverage that has plagued women's sports as a whole.

An effective way to examine feminist themes is through qualitative interviews with stakeholders (Alasuutari, Bickman, & Brannen, 2008). In a women's football marketing context, this was accomplished by speaking with marketing officials of clubs from the current professional league in the U.S., the NWSL, to analyze their perspective and experiences in dealing with feminist issues. Five interviews were conducted with NWSL marketing managers in the summer of 2014. Interviews took between 22 and 95 minutes.

Data for this research were gathered through these interviews and the collection of archival material, including league and team press releases and print and electronic media marketing artifacts. Some of the print documents examined included newspaper and magazine clippings detailing the league and its clubs, as well as any physical press releases sent out by the clubs and league, while some of the electronic artifacts examined included electronic news articles from third parties, team produced audio-visual content, and social media activities. The researchers collected approximately 194 pages of archival material.

For data gathering, interviewees were selected from a pool of willing participants associated with NWSL clubs in a management and marketing capacity. Potential participants were e-mailed through publicly accessible accounts found on official team websites with information on the research study. Participants were asked questions from an interview guide cultivated through literature review and background research that focused on the marketing of their team and the league as a whole with an emphasis on marketing through feminist themes. Examples of questions include: "What is your opinion on the traditional media's portrayal of your players?" and "What is your opinion of cause marketing as far as promoting women's football is concerned?"

Data analyses

The objective of the data analysis for this research was to identify common themes emerging from the data involving the marketing of women's football through feminist themes. The researcher conducted content analysis using the qualitative data analysis software ATLAS.ti 7.0 while completing a thorough review of interview transcripts and documents. The researchers focused on developing descriptions for each case setting in regards to their strategy and practices of marketing their product through the use of the specific feminist themes from the researcher's proposed theoretical framework.

The researchers utilized a cross-setting analysis to compare and contrast emergent themes between the different settings to see how different clubs utilize similar or different strategies and practices in their marketing through the feminist themes outlined previously (Yin, 2013). As data from interviews and from archival material was collected, they were both inductively and deductively analyzed through the guidelines established by Miles, Huberman, and Saldana (2013), as well as through the constant comparison protocol devised by Glaser and Strauss (1967).

The researchers began the content analysis through a process of open coding, using some of the terminology and themes (e.g., developing media relationships) gathered from the literature review to help begin the process of grouping and categorizing gathered data. Data was coded simply and succinctly, using short, descriptive phrases as codes. Following the process of open coding, the researchers engaged in axial coding to examine relationships and trends that may have risen to the surface after open coding (Corley & Gioia, 2004; Leopkey & Parent, 2009). This evolving process of coding provided more nuanced analysis of the data, enabling a more precise picture of the findings and how they related to the proposed theoretical framework. For the sake of consistency, the researchers used the constant comparison techniques set out by Glaser and Strauss (1967), comparing the already gathered literature, the archival material collected, and the interview data.

Results

Three prominent themes emerged from the data analysis: (a) inequity of rules, resources, and coverage, (b) embracing of motherhood, family values, and role models while shunning the "other," and (c) the existence of ideal heteronormative femininity and a consumption community. The following section examines each of these three themes in detail.

Inequity of rules, resources, and coverage

From the data, the researchers found numerous examples of an inequity of rules, resources, and coverage that can be categorized into disparities in budgets and resources, salaries, venues, and media coverage.

Budgets and resources

While nobody can doubt the financial challenges facing the NWSL, some interviewed club officials distanced themselves from using those challenges as a pre-determined excuse. Brian Budzinski of FC Kansas City was one such official, claiming he would not use the club's existence as a professional women's team as a reason for failure. The FC Kansas City general manager noted that "business is a business" and that the difference in using female athletes and male athletes did not necessarily place one above the other in his eyes (personal communication, July 24, 2014). Budzinski argued vehemently of having the best women players in the world as an advantage for the league, even with financial roadblocks.

For most of the league, resources pale in comparison to those available to professional men's teams. Marketing through old media has often proven to be difficult, with multiple interviewees indicating a lack of finances to produce advertising content for newspapers and television. Wood noted that former full-time staff positions in the early WPS days were now largely part-time. Alyse Lahue of Chicago noted that her organization at times felt they didn't have the staffing they needed or wanted.

The decline in budgets has largely handcuffed clubs as they try to produce marketing content. While men's professional clubs have only dumped more money into marketing, women's clubs have largely lived off of scraps. Ryan Wood of the Boston Breakers spoke of being able to call upon advertising agencies to develop content in WPS but seeing the money for those efforts vanish in NWSL.

Salaries

One of the most notable areas in which the financial pinch has been felt is with player salaries. Wood of the Boston Breakers noted that it was "almost embarrassing that you have to offer fifteen thousand dollars to someone who could get probably triple that in Europe" (personal communication, July 23, 2014). Salaries were uniformly lower than those of WPS, except for players whose salaries were being subsidized by their respective national teams. Some American players have eschewed playing in NWSL in favor of European leagues, where Wood quotes one player as making "probably five times more than she would have made," in Boston (personal communication, July 23, 2014). Lahue argued that this was unavoidable, as some Americans were always going to be lured by perks of European play.

As a result of the salaries, which go as low as $6,000, players have had to take part-time jobs during the season and full-time jobs after it or look for overseas playing opportunities after the end of the NWSL season. Wood noted that many players without a spouse or with low salaries have found themselves beholden to host families that allow the players to live with them and provide some food. Lahue spoke of the league instituting a housing cap, limiting the amount of money teams can spend on housing for players, another measure which can put pressure on players needing places to live during the season. At the same time, Lahue did note that housing payments on top of salaries for top players did seem reasonable to her, though the majority of the league's players remain underpaid.

Others have been forced out of the game due to financial hardships. Wood noted a personal friend who had to, "essentially retire from the job she's always wanted, because it just doesn't pay" (personal communication, July 23, 2014). Wood's Boston side also felt the sting recently of having a top draft pick from 2014 retire after one season to take a job with Amazon. Lahue echoed this noting that older players face decisions as to whether it's still worth it to keep on going for "the love of the game," as she noted that "you're not making a living off of doing this" (personal communication, July 31, 2014). The Chicago Red Stars general manager was more than sympathetic to the plight of the players on the lower end of the salary scale but noted that clubs had to keep salaries realistic given the revenue coming into the club, though Lahue did note a desire to get the minimum salary "much, much higher" (personal communication, July 31, 2014). However, Lahue was pessimistic about salary equity with men's professional players in the short-term:

> I should never say never, but we're not going to compete on a scale close to what men's professional players make. I just don't think that's a reality of the next five to ten years for us.
>
> (personal communication, July 31, 2014)

Like Wood, Lahue acknowledges that some of her club's players with lower salaries have part-time and full-time jobs on the side to make ends meet.

Venues

Other inequities have been felt by clubs through their venues. While men's MLS clubs began life at older multipurpose stadiums, including cavernous football stadiums, the growing trend has been for clubs to play at smaller, football specific stadiums. On the women's side of the game, stadiums and corresponding amenities have shrunk with time. Even as recent as the WPS days, clubs like Chicago were sharing space with their MLS cousins, often at great financial cost due to having to pay rent for the venue.

As a result of budget cutbacks, many NWSL clubs without affiliations with MLS teams have played in spartan accommodations compared to both men's professional football teams and previous women's professional teams in earlier leagues. These cutbacks have led to clubs having to balance between being fiscally responsible while also providing an atmosphere that will attract fans. In some cases, atmosphere has been muted due to the small venues. In other cases, like Boston's, a stadium that far outstrips demand can also diminish atmosphere, though Wood claimed the Breakers still had a charged atmosphere in cavernous Harvard Stadium.

Wood noted one of the major reasons Boston switched stadiums between 2013 and 2014 was a lack of parking and suitable public transportation that forced fans to arrive early. A clear emphasis was put on copious (and affordable) parking being available for Boston in their choice of going to Harvard as the club's home stadium in 2014, while proximity to public transport was also vital.

Budzinski noted that FC Kansas City also was forced to prioritize what was important in terms of venue choice between the 2013 and 2014 seasons. Atmosphere was also a consideration for the club in their switch from 2013 venue Shawnee Mission District Stadium in Overland Park, Kansas to Durwood Stadium in Kansas City, Missouri for 2014. Budzinski claimed that the new stadium provided a better atmosphere, no doubt due to the lack of a running track that had kept spectators far from the action.

Additionally, Budzinski stated that "the turf was not a high enough qual-ity for our players," with Durwood Stadium possessing a better brand of artificial turf, as well as a lack of distracting football lines that always irk football fans (personal communication, July 24, 2014). Problems with play-ing surface also came to the forefront in stadium discussions with Chicago's Alyse Lahue, who claimed that the city, despite being a football hotbed, did not have moderately sized venues with a good grass field around the city, or even suitable turf fields, complicating the club's search for a permanent home, and in effect turning the organization into nomads. Jim Gooley also indicated that the quality of turf was a major factor in Sky Blue FC choosing their venue at Rutgers University. Besides being a natural grass surface with no football lines, Gooley indicated that the drainage of the field was crucial, as cancellations are severely detrimental to a club's finances.

Lahue ruminated that there were trade-offs in the search for a permanent home for the Chicago club. The team's current home in Bridgeview, Illinois lacks the greater seating capacity of other clubs in the league and has lim-ited expansion possibilities. Some deficiencies affect the match-day sched-ule, as the distance between the field and locker rooms for have necessitated 20-minute halftimes instead of the customary 15. Earlier venues have been without concessions and/or lacked parking, leading to the team having to choose the lesser of many evils in their pursuit for a suitable home.

Other representatives spoke about their own clubs' trade-offs in seeking venue improvements. FC Kansas City may have moved to a venue with bet-ter field quality in their second season but also grappled with smaller capac-ity and limited audiovisual capabilities. Sky Blue FC's Jim Gooley noted that his club's venue at Rutgers University was easy to get to and had copious parking, though the club still struggled at the gate. Ironically, another club, Chicago, found old methods to be a partial solution, as they worked with the Chicago Fire MLS side to put on a doubleheader for one day at the club's old Toyota Park venue, eventually leading the Red Stars to once again play full-time at the stadium in 2016.

Media coverage

Another area where the difference between men's professional sports teams and NWSL teams is keenly felt is in the depth of media coverage. Whereas men's professional sports teams, especially in the bigger cities, are explored and analyzed in exhaustive detail, professional women's football teams in America have always been fighting battles to get covered by the traditional media. This has been especially apparent in the biggest markets containing NWSL teams, as representatives from Boston and Chicago echoed these sen-timents. The latter's Alyse Lahue expressed some disappointment at the lack of coverage and noted that the club "[doesn't] appear on the news, our scores don't appear on the ticker tape, we can't get in the Chicago Tribune to get our scores reported," reasoning that market saturation made getting media coverage particularly difficult (personal communication, July 31, 2014).

Lahue also spoke of the difficulty of commanding media attention, even when hiring a PR firm to partner with. She noted that the Red Stars were forced to resort to buying time on the news to get coverage from major media outlets. This is in stark contrast to men's professional teams, where media entities fall over themselves in trying to gain access for coverage. Boston's Ryan Wood lamented his club's inability to pry media attention away from his city's major men's clubs as well. Still, Wood claimed that "if for some reason the Red Sox aren't playing, Bruins and Celtics aren't playing, then you'll see like the Herald and Globe show up" (personal communication, July 23, 2014). Wood noted that for TV coverage "all the other major sports come first," unless the game was close to a WWC or Summer Olympics (personal communication, July 23, 2014). However, Wood was quick to mention that articles that were published were met with enthusiasm by the general public and friends, underlining the importance of such publications.

Whereas MLS has enjoyed an expanding television profile, the NWSL has had to make do with partial season deals that usually encompass just a handful of regular season matches along with the league's three playoff matches. FC Kansas City, Houston, and Portland have inked regional television deals, but production values are generally akin to that of the league's streaming efforts on YouTube, a far cry from the efforts of standard men's games' broadcasts. Gooley criticized the quality of these streams, noting the absence of flourishes (e.g., multiple camera angles, replays, overlays, etc.) that highlight production of men's games.

He went into more detail:

> I think that we should be micing the goals, I think that we should be micing players. I think we should be showing slow motion hits, show the drama of the game and present it more like a Hollywood production than a simple ninety minute game.
> (personal communication, August 13, 2014)

Gooley claimed that discussions to improve the standard of broadcasts have happened but that it was still an uphill climb to meet the standards of men's broadcasts.

Club officials were quick to point out their happiness with coverage they did receive, pointing out that overall player portrayals were largely positive. Budzinski claimed that FC Kansas City was happy with local coverage that had exceeded their expectations. Portland's Golub was happy as well, claiming the city's media had fully embraced the team, while noting that national coverage had been attentive, fair, and favorable.

Some club marketing officials expressed their disappointment that Nike had not been more proactive with their efforts in assisting the NWSL with marketing, despite the sporting giant's contributions with merchandise. Ryan Wood of the Boston Breakers mooted whether Nike could plunge some of their money into billboards promoting the league in major cities, which would appear to be little trouble considering the company's vast outlays at promoting men's professional sports in a similar manner.

Embracing motherhood, family values, and role models

From the collected data, the researchers found repeated instances of clubs embracing motherhood, family values, and role models while shunning the 'other' through creating a harmonious atmosphere, selling the player, portraying players as role models within the community, and using 24/7 messaging, while also negotiating portrayals of "the other."

A harmonious atmosphere

Much of the allure created by clubs revolves around what has been billed as a "family friendly atmosphere," touted by Wood as also being a big factor in pitching the club towards potential sponsors (personal communication, July 23, 2014). He noted that a main goal of the club was to promote such an atmosphere "that extends all the way down to not just the product on the field and the game-day experience but to the players themselves" (personal communication, July 23, 2014). Wood also noted that this line of thought did not just run through management but also through coaches, who desired, somewhat paternalistically, a club where "No one gets in arguments, everyone gets along," believing that such harmony would provide a good game day experience and product for fans (personal communication, July 23, 2014).

Alyse Lahue of the Chicago Red Stars noted that keeping a "good dynamic" was a crucial part of building the team, with players, coaches, and management all involved in choosing players to represent the club (personal communication, July 31, 2014). Jim Gooley of Sky Blue FC echoed this sentiment as well, extending it to the club's players' social media activities, claiming that players are told to always be positive and to support their teammates and the league.

Wood and Budzinski both acknowledged that portraying players as role models was a standard way of attracting the youth market, a key to the viability of teams. Part of that process occurs even before the club signs players, as Wood indicated that the Breakers look far beyond actual on-field talent when they try to recruit new faces for the playing roster, with the background of a player and their overall personality being put under a microscope. Jim Gooley of Sky Blue FC also was insistent on deep diving into players' background before signing them. Notable was Gooley's insistence that club looks at if players are good with kids, which could be construed as a positive attribute for a club that also holds clinics and camps for kids as part of its business model.

Selling the player

Gooley notes that his club does not just look at off-field behavior when looking to recruit new players. He noted that he tries to "find out everything I possibly can about that player on and off the field," including things like family background and anything the club could use to, in Gooley's words, "leverage her story to build the brand of Sky Blue" (personal communication, August 13, 2014). In a sense, the club is doing everything in its power to ensure players' narratives resonate with the public, which ultimately helps the club.

Gooley also talked of going against the grain of what doesn't "look like" a traditional role model (personal communication, August 13, 2014). He brought up former Sky Blue FC player Natasha Kai, a Hawaiian with copious body art and tattoos who he referred to as "a little bit nutty on the field" (personal communication, August 13, 2014). Gooley detailed the decision to heavily market Kai:

> Well, do you lead with that, do you advertise with that, well is that a good thing to do? Well, her tribal tradition say that the body should be decorated in this way, and OK, that's part of a culture, OK let's put it out there. [. . .] And what do you know, that sells tickets. It does.
> (personal communication, August 13, 2014)

By diversifying marketing beyond the normal role model archetype, Gooley and his club may be able to appeal to a more diverse market. Chicago has taken some of the unknown variables out of recruiting new players, as they have gone after many players with Midwestern ties. Lahue notes that:

> We have a lot of local players, [. . .] So they have a strong connection to the community, and I think with that comes sort of an added level of really caring about the team and caring about the team's success.
> (personal communication, July 31, 2014)

Additionally, Lahue touts organizational familiarity with players retained from past professional incarnations or developed through their amateur youth programs.

Role models and the community

The vetting process for Chicago goes beyond local ties and past experience with the club. Lahue asserts that players have to fit the personality of the team so that they "have the utmost faith in the people that we select in making sure that they're good people, again, good role models" (personal communication, July 31, 2014). While some might argue that this typecasts players, Lahue proudly owns the fact that her players are looked at as role models. She elaborates:

> If you have the option between that your daughter looking up to a Red Stars player or looking up to some of these the female singers nowadays, I won't name any, but I think we provide a pretty wholesome product for them to aspire to. And going along themes of staying fit and going to college and working towards your dreams.
>
> (personal communication, July 31, 2014)

Budzinski of FC Kansas City notes that acting as a role model is an expectation for his players, claiming "every player that comes into our club knows that we're gonna be out in the community a ton" (personal communication, July 24, 2014). In this sense, personal appearances with sponsors in the community and other role model duties are just as much a part of the job as playing in matches. Lahue noted that Red Stars players were expected to "be willing to get out in the community and be willing to market the team and that are going to really fit what it means to be a Red Stars player," with these obligations part of being a Chicago player (personal communication, July 31, 2014). Jim Gooley of Sky Blue FC went a bit further, claiming that for one of the club's major sponsors, ShopRite, the players and club were the faces of the brand, making personal appearances, going to food banks, etc.

Golub spoke glowingly of Portland's relationship with the community at-large, praising his organization in "giving back" to the community, claiming "it's the right thing to do" (personal communication, July 30, 2014). While such interaction has clear altruistic purposes, Golub did not gloss over the business implications of being constantly engaged with the community and talked up the club constantly being in the public's eye. Having "role models" on the team to help with this community engagement makes it credible and effective. Golub emphasized the desire for players being "good people" (personal communication, July 30, 2014). The Thorns president spoke of emphasizing the importance of making sure the "people who represent the organization on and off the field are doing the right things" (personal communication, July 30, 2014).

Gooley provided a stark example of who embodies the role model archetype on his Sky Blue FC club in the form of Nadia Nadim. Nadim overcame incredible hardship in fleeing Afghanistan and the Taliban, moving to Denmark and excelling in a game that players in her old country never played. Nadim is not just a great athlete but also a great student, ticking another appealing box for families. And after football, Nadim plans on becoming a plastic surgeon, a profession in which she can enrich the lives of others.

With these desirable traits, Nadim is exalted as a player that young girls can aspire to. Gooley spoke of some of his conversations with Nadim about her role:

> I say "this is an opportunity for girls to see you play, back, back home," she says, "yes, of course." And I said, "OK, well this is our, this is whether you like this or not Nadia, you're an ambassador, you're a role model, and once you step on the field at your level, there are girls and families inspired by you."
> (personal communication, August 13, 2014)

The "role model portrayal" relationship is a two-way street, as players are also dependent in some measure upon the veracity of their perception as role models. Wood notes that many players also make extra money through youth camps and clinics. Thus, players must conduct themselves in a manner befitting a customary "role model" to retain access to an additional market whose patronage may be necessary financially for the player to continue to play for a meager playing salary. Playing the part of a squeaky clean role model can also pay off for players in this reciprocal relationship between them and the club, as such players according to Wood was were "the people you always see on promotional material," thus offering up more exposure and potentially more opportunities for endorsements down the line (personal communication, July 23, 2014).

24/7 messaging

Another aspect of successfully portraying players as role models has been accomplished by tailoring the message used in marketing. A major theme used throughout the rise of women's sports in the United States has been sport as a vehicle of female empowerment that has allowed participants to break through various pernicious myths about women that had been used to keep them from participating in sport. Wood explained that the Breakers organization benefitted from previous associations with marketers who highlighted the athleticism of players in promotional material. Wood mentioned posters that "kind of showed like players like going into a tackle and just proving like these players are just as tough and can play, can play the sport just as aggressively as men can" (personal communication, July 23, 2014).

The natural assumption is that the women's players of NWSL clubs are designed to serve as role models for young girls, a reputation fostered by past marketing. However, Wood noted that the Breakers positioned themselves as role models for young girls *and* boys. He noted that the Boston youth academy fielded teams for both boys and girls, with Breakers players often coming to practices for teams of both sexes. Wood believed that sometimes young boys may think that women players are not skilled or tough until having their mind changed by actually seeing them play in person.

Fulfilling the "archetype" of the role model is not just a task for off-days, either. Budzinski of FC Kansas City claims that the club asks players to be as accessible as possible to fans, all the way through to the end of game nights where players on both home and visiting teams stay behind to sign autographs and take photos. Gooley claims that young girls "respond with shrieks" when they get autographs and pictures from their role models (personal communication, August 13, 2014). In reference to post-match autographs, Wood claims that:

> We told the players at the beginning of the season that "hey, there's an autograph section after the game. We're not requiring you to do it, but it's something that the team has . . . kind of promotes and does every year." Every single year, every single player goes there after the game, and the opposing players sometimes go there as well.
>
> (personal communication, July 23, 2014)

While Wood insists that the autograph session is optional, incidents where star players have failed to sign autographs have drawn scorn from fans and media alike on social media. While much of the willingness to sign autographs may come from appreciation for the fans' support, a cynical view may see some players fearful of deviating from the image of the gracious, humble athlete that has now become the norm. Wood also noted that when they do receive media coverage, it has usually been positive, a fact he attributes to "the players for keeping a level head on the field and being smart off the field," further underlining pressure on players to fulfill a duty as a "role model" (personal communication, July 23, 2014).

At the end of the day, Gooley regretted that an emphasis on presenting the players as role models played such a predominant role in marketing strategy. He claimed that:

> I personally would love to be able to just put the role model thing on the shelf, yes, we're that too, but stop leading with that. I want to lead with "amazing professional football performers," I want to lead with the matchups. We do not have that. We're not at the point.
>
> (personal communication, August 13, 2014)

While Gooley felt that the league was making progress towards being able to focus on game-related storylines, he was realistic in knowing that there was a long way to go. Ideally, Gooley felt the role model aspect should be backstory, with performance narratives taking center stage. However, clubs appear to still have a long way to go to realize that ambition.

The "other"

A great deal of conflict has stemmed over the lack of a voice for the Lesbian, Gay, Bisexual, and Transgender (LGBT) community within professional women's football, despite mounting evidence of an audience for the sport within the group. Lahue of Chicago spoke about the LGBT community having been a good target in terms of previous support of professional women's football in the U.S. Gooley claimed appealing to the LGBT community was a "part of the whole celebration of the game" (personal communication, August 13, 2014). While the first two professional women's football leagues largely ignored the LGBT community, a plurality of NWSL clubs has, at the very least, welcomed that community into the fold, with a few stridently marketing towards the community. All clubs interviewed seemed willing, at the least, to be accommodating to the community.

Perhaps most open have been the Portland Thorns. Organization president Mike Golub proudly touted being the first professional sports team in the United States to endorse equal marriage rights. Additionally, Golub mentioned the club's openly gay players as another point of pride for the organization. Based on informal evaluation and the testimony of others like Sky Blue FC's Gooley, Portland's crowds have often been replete with rainbow colored flags and other items commonly associated with the 'pride' movement as well.

Lahue indicated that Chicago had become very involved in catering to the LGBT community, holding a formal pride night in 2014 in June. The Red Stars organization reached out to all of the Chicago area's LGBT organizations, as well as the LGBT Chamber of Commerce in helping put together the event at a match in 2014 that went well according to Lahue. The pride night was also listed as the catalyst to forging relationships with LGBT groups, such as a suicide prevention organization that Chicago hopes will bear future fruit for the organization. Such participation allows organizations like Chicago to show their commitment in being a totally inclusive environment and speaking to a demographic that clubs in previous leagues have largely ignored. Lahue noted that the LGBT population has typically supported sports, making them an ideal marketing target for clubs and the league as a whole.

Gooley spoke of problems Sky Blue FC faces in marketing to the LGBT community based on location. While Gooley claimed there was a LGBT presence in the New Jersey area where the club is based, it also was not a highly marketable place for the community in his eyes. Gooley elaborated on how much easier it would be to attract the LGBT community if the club was closer to New York City:

> I could go into New York City and put together packages and bring out a larger contingent to come to these games, but I wouldn't do that

> normally for any club, only because of the geography and the reach, it's just beyond, it's a little beyond reasonable to come to New York City to come to our games. If we were playing in New York City, no problem, and no problem. I just walk up and down Christopher Street and with a megaphone, "come on out and celebrate yourself, come celebrate with us now."
>
> (personal communication, August 13, 2014)

Given the perceived importance of drawing the LGBT community, it will be interesting to see if NWSL clubs can find a happy medium in attracting that audience, even with geographical roadblocks.

While Wood of the Boston Breakers acknowledged the presence of lesbian players in the league was hardly a shock, he noted some reticence within his club in fully advocating towards the LGBT community. While Wood did not overtly refer to potential homophobia within the club's fan base, he claimed "a lot of the parents that come to the games have that old school mentality where we feel we have to be kind of cautious about the way we approach things and the way we promote things," a rather blatant coding of some fans being uncomfortable with what they see as a "different" lifestyle (personal communication, July 23, 2014).

An example of caution was evident in a marketing example provided by Wood relating to the promotion of couple Lianne Sanderson and Joanna Lohman, who both played for Boston. Specifically, the pair appeared in *People* magazine, with an article detailing their engagement and life as a couple. Wood describes speaking with league officials about promotion of the article:

> So I think we had a talk with the league and was like, "as much as it is to say 'hey,' go tweet something, go pick up the latest People magazine to see Jo and Lianne," it was like "People is big enough, it'll promote itself, and we don't have to."
>
> (personal communication, July 23, 2014)

Wood expressed frustration, noting that he doesn't think players want to be pigeonholed into certain typecast roles, but that being in *People* magazine is nonetheless a huge honor (personal communication, July 23, 2014). But Wood noted that among the market for the league's product are "adults who feel like their kids are going to be wrongly influenced by knowing all this," in reference to the LGBT community (personal communication, July 23, 2014). Despite what some would label a regressive viewpoint, Wood was optimistic in hoping that things would change and that overt promotion of LGBT content like the *People* magazine article would become more accepted with time.

Ideal heteronormative femininity and consumption community

From collected data, the researchers found repeated examples of the reproduction of an ideal heteronormative femininity and the creation of a consumption community, often through marketing aimed directly at women and the often controversial presence of provocative pictorials.

The consumption community

Many activities around a game day are built around fostering a consumption community amongst a prime target market: young girl and boy football players. Giveaways are frequent, with sponsors quick to give out items enjoyed by children like miniature football balls. When products are not being offered, clubs are eager to offer services targeted towards the youth market such as football "skills" games in pavilions and birthday parties with player visits. Such fan service both brings in extra revenue and builds brand loyalty for repeat business from families.

In large part, merchandise being sold is often targeted to what Alyse Lahue of Chicago had previously dubbed "low-hanging fruit," the youth players and clubs that the Red Stars have traditionally targeted (personal communication, July 31, 2014). Besides the youth merchandise that Lahue points to as big sellers, Chicago also does great business with merchandise targeted towards women according to the Red Stars general manager.

Aiming for the women's market

The symbiotic relationship between teams and apparel sponsors can best be seen within the partnership between the NWSL and leading corporate sponsor Nike. FC Kansas City general manager Brian Budzinski spoke of a relationship beyond just outfitting teams. He recounts that "Nike's came out and done some testing on the players themselves so they can, here in Kansas City, so they can improve their gear for the women's game" (personal communication, July 24, 2014). In effect, clubs are getting the highly coveted Nike gear for their players to use and to sell to fans but also the credibility that comes with being associated with a respected brand. For Nike, they get to associate with some of the best known players in the world in women's football and can develop and refine products and merchandise that will let them capture the growing women's market.

Gooley asserted the importance of merchandising based on thoughts about some of the club's female target market. He crowed:

> If you think about our fanbase, and how they behave at games, women have this joy for shopping, that even just browsing. I don't know what

it is, I don't have it, but I recognize it. When we open up our gates, our fans flock to the merchandise tent, and the merchandise tent is busy all game. And we make money there. It's great, I would love it if we could have that tent open all year long.

(personal communication, August 13, 2014)

Gooley also ruminated about some of the more "feminized" products the club was looking to offer besides football apparel, such as jewelry and shoes, trying to capitalize on objects made desirable by messengers of heteronormative femininity (personal communication, August 13, 2014).

Additionally, Gooley was quick to tout the growing market of "feminine" clothes that Sky Blue FC has been adding (personal communication, August 13, 2014). Gooley claimed that "girls like to wear feminine clothes" and that Nike's offerings had largely come up short in this regard (personal communication, August 13, 2014). He detailed his urging the club to capitalize on this gap in the merchandise market, bringing in products like "special running tops that are very feminine" that Gooley claimed sold well (personal communication, August 13, 2014). In large part, Gooley and his club are selling a product line that allows young girls and women to "do" femininity in heteronormative terms while still promoting athleticism, something long associated with Nike.

Who is put front and centre when pushing products has been a source of debate through incarnations of professional women's football in the United States, with a battle between promoting heteronormatively "feminine" players and the most athletic players, regardless of whether they meet the definition of heteronormative femininity. Lahue refused to separate the two categories into a stark dichotomy, noting that her Chicago club "[doesn't] think that we differentiate between the two very often" (personal communication, July 31, 2014). Lahue claims that it's a choice between three-dimensional female athletes that "all bring something very different to the table," that the club can use in a variety of marketing (Lahue, personal communication, July 31, 2014).

Provocative pictorials

Whereas professional women's football players posing nude or in revealing attire has been a divisive issue, most of the interviewees approached the issue magnanimously. Previously, mixed messages have been sent by leagues, such as when WUSA used promotional material featuring players in alluring poses while also not strenuously objecting to a Playboy offer to star player Heather Mitts to pose nude. However, critics were vehemently against such activities claiming that they cheapened the sport.

Ryan Wood of the Boston Breakers was conflicted on whether posing in revealing attire or tastefully nude in ventures was beneficial. Wood noted those opportunities were big boons for players in terms of exposure in a sport struggling for attention. Brian Budzinski of FC Kansas City also was neutral towards such magazine spreads. He explained that:

> each player they have the ability to market and promote themselves that'll better, better themselves financially, that's, that's for them to make their choices on what type of marketing they do about themselves. Whether that's a product they align themselves with or a modeling type of situation.
>
> (personal communication, July 24, 2014)

Budzinski as well as Chicago's Lahue and Portland's Golub were all adamant that such decisions and promotion of those spreads were ultimately up to the players. Gooley of Sky Blue FC echoed the thoughts of players who had previously posed for such pictorials, claiming that these athletes had worked hard to get in this physical shape and that their bodies were "showpieces" (personal communication, August 13, 2014).

Lahue presented a spirited defense of the adage of "any publicity is good publicity," claiming pictorials were "just going to open us up to a whole different realm of possibilities in terms of new fans or people that may get interested in the game" (personal communication, July 31, 2014). The Chicago general manager made it clear that she had no qualms about where new fans came from, even if they arrived after viewing players in a pictorial. Lahue believed that pictorials in magazines like *Sports Illustrated* and *ESPN The Magazine* could unlock new markets for the league and that they did not want to be pigeonholed into appealing solely to the youth market.

However, how much the league is willing to associate itself with such efforts was brought into question by a Wood anecdote about the league's attitude towards promotion of then Boston player Sydney Leroux's appearance in the *ESPN The Magazine Body Issue*. Wood recounts a conversation with NWSL league official Patrick Donnelly:

> I had a long talk with Patrick Donnelly from the league office about promoting it. It's the first year of NWSL, new league, you get your biggest star in the body issue which is one of the most, next to the swimsuit issue, in terms of sport magazines, like special editions, it's, I mean people look forward to it every year. So it was "hey, let's, should we promote this and say 'look, one of the Boston Breakers is in ESPN the body?'" And from our, our angle, we said want just to, just to let fans know that it's available, that's she's in it or what not. The league was like, "No, absolutely not. We don't want to promote anything like this."
>
> (personal communication, July 23, 2014)

Wood claims the reasoning was that the product would sell and promote itself and that the Breakers were told explicitly to not promote Leroux's appearance in the body issue, as the league catered to a "younger audience" (personal communication, July 23, 2014).

Wood spoke of the league only having an interest in actively promoting publicity that does not have the potential to offend, in their eyes, a lucrative youth and family market. On its face, the league and its clubs would appear to be glad for the attention from the "heterosexual male gaze" that such photo spreads can bring, as long as it can distance itself from critical or media backlash over such photos. Lahue of Chicago also was wary about focusing on sex appeal when promoting the club's players to the public. She notes that the club "[wants] to focus more on the women as athletes, not necessarily showcasing their sex appeal too highly," though she also notes that any notion of "girl power" as a theme has been overdone a bit in the past (personal communication, July 31, 2014). Still, Lahue admits sex appeal is still "a part of the game", and stressed that the Red Stars "focus on the fact that these are elite athletes and they're really strong women," and called such a truth "beautiful" (personal communication, July 31, 2014).

Discussion and conclusion

This research examined the marketing of NWSL clubs through feminist themes. Despite the popularity of the USWNT and of football as a participation sport in the U.S., research into the marketing of the sport has been sparse and anecdotal (e.g., Grainey, 2012; Longman, 2001). Feminist enquiry into women's football (e.g., Caudwell, 1999; Christopherson et al., 2002; Elling, 1999) has largely focused on the game outside of the U.S. despite repeated attempts at making a professional league work in the U.S. Data suggested the use of feminist themes in the marketing of professional women's football is prominent, while many challenges in equality brought to light by feminist sport marketing literature are still being contended with.

Given the failures of the first two professional women's football leagues in the U.S. due to haphazard and ineffectual marketing, a coherent marketing plan is crucial to the NWSL's viability. This study of marketing through feminist themes expands the sport management literature by explaining: the effects of an inequity of rules, resources, and coverage on marketing strategies for NWSL clubs; the embracing of motherhood, family values, and role models while shunning the 'other' and how that has changed recently with NWSL clubs; and the use of ideal heteronormative femininity to construct a consumption community and its effect on the marketing of NWSL clubs.

In the past, the patriarchy controlling football controlled the game as played by women, using outdated myths to implement humiliating rules differences as compared to the men's game involving the timing of the game and the equipment used (Lisi, 2013; Longman, 2001). While embarrassing alterations in rules due to perceived physical deficiencies in women have stopped, a lack of equality in funding and media coverage in comparison to men's sport that has plagued women's football was still found to be rampant (Blinde, Greendorfer, & Shanker, 1991; Duncan & Messner, 1996).

Within the NWSL, the internet has served as an equalizer in terms of coverage, with the profligation of niche sites devoted to women's football offering coverage that previous leagues could only dream about. The "highly stereotypical feminized" type of coverage seen in past tournaments has also dissipated, with more of the media regarding women's football as a 'serious' sport (Kane & Greendorfer, 1994, p. 36). However, in other areas, the NWSL has lagged behind rather than progressed. The television prospects of pro women's football in the U.S. have regressed with time, with the amount of televised games dropping while being relegated to lesser networks. The lack of a consistent television deal and struggle to gain local media attention has hampered opportunities for growth according to the interviewees in this study. Given the importance of the media in influencing public perception, winning that struggle has to be key for the NWSL (Fortunato, 2000).

League-wide, there is the brutal reality of salaries for non-subsidized players being low enough that some need part-time or full-time jobs to supplement their playing income. In this respect, depressed salaries may have been necessary for viability, but it has also placed an enormous burden on players. The salary battles of the past faced by the USWNT have been magnified for the rank and file of the NWSL, with a permanent solution not in sight (Longman, 2001).

It is clear from this research that the ability of clubs to portray players as role models to help attract families remains a key crux of marketing strategy. Despite criticism of a reliance on such a market in past leagues (Knoppers & Anthonissen, 2003; Longman, 2001; Martinez, 2008), nearly all interviewees noted needing to grab that market but also were aware of needing to capture a more adult market to thrive. Such a narrow focus worked for past short-term tournaments but are not viable in the long-term (Christopherson et al., 2002; Longman, 2001). In this respect, clubs with MLS ties such as Portland have benefitted from a carryover audience from their men's team who may also attend women's games.

Attitudes towards those not fitting in the typical heterosexual, heteronormative feminine template have softened. Homophobia has plagued women's sport for decades (Griffin, 2002; Longman, 2001). While homophobia was less overt surrounding the USWNT and early pro women's football leagues, much of the early marketing and media coverage of these ventures shied away from implications of homosexuality, touting aspects such as "motherhood" and being proper role models (Christopherson et al., 2002; Lipsyte, 1999). Though the degree to which clubs appeal to the LGBT community varied greatly amongst interviewees, all seemed at least tolerant of the community, while some had made marketing towards the LGBT community a key plank in their marketing. Additionally, as society has changed, so has the attitude towards the sexuality of players. Sexuality is no longer taboo in most circles, with many players openly gay.

Attitudes towards off-the-pitch displays of ideal heteronormative femininity have also shifted. Previous magazine pictorials of scantily clad players have been met with hyperbolically negative responses (Longman, 2001; Markovits & Hellerman, 2004). However, now, such pictorials are often met with a laissez-faire attitude from team officials, happy that players are able to draw attention in a saturated media environment. However, marketing officials also noted the league still wanted no part in actually actively promoting such magazine spreads, indicating attitudes have not fully changed.

In regards to merchandising, some clubs have actively sought to make more "feminine" products available, with initial efforts proving to be successful sellers. Akin to other efforts to target products towards women, such efforts allow purchasers to "do" heteronormative femininity at their leisure, all while building the brand of the clubs, creating a viable consumption community. For decades, corporations have sought to angle their way into a lucrative market by selling products appealing to women's desires to be able to "perform" femininity (Bartky, 1998; Wolf, 1991). With companies having previously used female athletes to help sell products towards women, the NWSL appears to be continuing a long tradition of a mutually beneficial relationship between corporate America and women's sport that allows companies to reach a lucrative market while boosting league coffers (Cuneen & Spencer, 2003; Lumpkin, 2007).

Managerial implications

Marketing is the lifeblood of sport clubs and leagues, and nowhere is it more important than in an embryonic league littered with past examples of failure. Past experiences and present initiatives in marketing through feminist themes can go a long way towards putting women's football clubs and leagues on a road towards success.

While a lack of funding equal to that of men's teams and leagues is unquestionably unfair, it is reality for the NWSL. Many of the interviewed marketing managers accepted it as such and noted that business was business. While gaining an association with a MLS team has helped Portland, other clubs have worked to find creative solutions to problems. One problem that has not been solved is that of player pay, which is frighteningly low for most and an issue that will have to be addressed if the NWSL is not to become a transient league with the majority of players drifting away after a few seasons.

The embrace of new and social media has proven to be a critical development in the marketing of women's football, giving a chance for smaller leagues like the NWSL to close the coverage gap. Teams have used social media to keep fans informed as well as push their product, practices that must continue considering the sparse coverage from traditional media. However, considering the positive opinions of those who did attract traditional media, a concerted effort at a well-rounded media strategy encompassing both new and traditional media should be in every NWSL club's plan.

The onus on a strategy to bring in more than one target market was also notable. While it was clear that a focus on continuing to bring in families is necessary as they are the most likely spectators to attend, all interviewees acknowledged that appealing to an older audience was a must if the league were to gain long-term traction. Again, this is an area in which MLS affiliated clubs have an advantage, in the form of an existing adult base already engaged with the organization.

A renewed commitment towards marketing to the LGBT community has also paid dividends for clubs who have fully embraced such initiatives. With the turn in public sentiment towards the LGBT community, the rewards of actively marketing to that community outweigh any negative consequences from a dwindling minority of offended parties. The positive results of early marketing initiatives indicate that more of such initiatives are on the way from prudent organizations.

The cognitive dissonance between clubs and the league on pictorials of players in swimsuits or revealing attire needs to be resolved sooner rather than later. As it stands, the league looks to be benefitting from the attention gained by such pictorial spreads while also telling teams to keep quiet about the spreads to prevent any potential blowback. Such a stance would make it seem that the league's official's desire being able to profit off the attention of the heterosexual male gaze while also protecting the sanctity of their status as a purveyor of "wholesome" family entertainment. It is a messy contradiction and one which the league must address.

The continued growth of a "consumption community" also bears watching as, for the first time, a professional women's football league has backing from one of the world's top apparel manufacturers in Nike. Nike has been overt in their appeals to capture the female market by marketing products enabling women to "do" heteronormative femininity, while this study also shows evidence NWSL clubs are getting into the game. How clubs try and capture the adult female market bears watching.

Future directions

Studying the marketing of professional women's football through feminist themes has provided valuable insight into the marketing of women's football in the United States, an under-investigated subject despite the existence of three professional leagues and a lucrative national team. This research serves as a starting point, with further research into the marketing of women's football through feminism necessary as the game continues to grow.

There are still gaps in the literature, as well as voices that need to be heard in piecing together a narrative.

One of the voices often unheard from in previous research into women's football marketing is the players themselves. A systematic campaign of research with players could help reveal insight into some issues raised by this research. Specifically, an inquest into the challenges facing less well-known players seems prudent given some of the financial realities about players that were revealed by marketing officials for this study.

Another voice that needs to be heard is that of the fans. While sport marketing research involving fans has been a constant in sport management literature, there are still notable gaps within said literature for the sport of women's football. Use of this study as a guide to examine issues brought up by this research could help fuel examinations into fan perceptions of the effectiveness of marketing efforts of the NWSL and its clubs.

References

Alasuutari, P., Bickman, L., & Brannen, J. (2008). *The SAGE handbook of social research methods*. Los Angeles, CA: Sage.

Bartky, S. L. (1998). Foucault, femininity, and the modernization of patriarchal power. In R. Weitz (Ed.), *The politics of women's bodies: Sexuality, appearance, and behavior* (pp. 25–45). New York: Oxford University Press.

Birrell, S. (2000). Feminist theories for sport. In J. Coakley & E. Dunning (Ed.), *Handbook of sport studies* (pp. 61–76). London: Sage.

Blinde, E. M., Greendorfer, S. L., & Shanker, R. J. (1991). Differential media coverage of men's and women's intercollegiate basketball: Reflection of gender ideology. *Journal of Sport and Social Issues, 15*, 98–114.

Bryson, L. (1987). Sports and the maintenance of masculine hegemony. *Women's Studies International Forum, 10*, 349–360.

Burstyn, V. (1999). *The rites of men: Manhood, politics, and the culture of sport.* Toronto, ON: University of Toronto.

Butler, J. (1990). Performative acts and gender constitution: An essay in phenomenology and feminist theory. In S. Case (Ed.), *Performing feminisms: feminist critical theory and theater* (pp. 270–282). Baltimore: Johns Hopkins University.

Butler, J. (1993). *Bodies that matter: On the discursive limits of "sex".* New York: Routledge.

Caudwell, J. (1999). Women's football in the United Kingdom: Theorizing gender and unpacking the butch lesbian image. *Journal of Sport and Social Issues, 23*, 390–402.

Caudwell, J. (2011). Gender, feminism, and football studies. *Soccer & Society, 12*, 330–344.

Christopherson, N., Janning, M., & McConnell, E. D. (2002). Two kicks forward, one kick back: A content analysis of media discourses on the women's world cup Soccer championship. *Sociology of Sport Journal, 19*, 170–188.

Connell, R. W., & Messerschmidt, J. W. (2005). Hegemonic masculinity: Rethinking the concept. *Gender & Society, 19*, 829–859.

Corley, K. G., & Gioia, D. A. (2004). Identity ambiguity and change in the wake of a corporate spin-off. *Administrative Science Quarterly, 49*, 173–208.

Cox, B., & Thompson, S. (2004). From heydays to struggles: Women's Soccer in New Zealand. In H. Fan & J. Mangan (Eds.), *Soccer, women, sexual liberation kicking off a new era* (pp. 205–224). London: Frank Cass.

Cuneen, J. (2001). Advertising sports-products to girls and women in a new era: A farewell to genderised visuals connoting stereotypical messages? *International Journal of Sport Management, 2*, 101–107.

Cuneen, J., & Spencer, N. E. (2003). Gender representations related to sport celebrity portrayals in the milk moustache advertising campaign. *Sport Marketing Quarterly, 12*, 140–150.

De Varona, D. (2004). Introduction – 'm's' in football: Myths, management, marketing, media, and money. A reprise. In H. Fan & J. Mangan (Eds.), *Soccer, women, sexual liberation kicking off a new era* (pp. 7–13). London: Frank Cass.

Denscombe, M. (1998). *The good research guide for small-scale social research projects*. Buckingham, U.K.: Open University.

Duncan, M. C., & Hasbrook, C. A. (1988). Denial of power in televised women's sports. *Sociology of Sport Journal, 5*, 1–21.

Duncan, M. C., & Messner, M. (1996). The media image of sport and gender. In L. A. Wenner (Ed.), *MediaSport* (pp. 170–185). New York: Routledge.

Dure, B. (2013). *Enduring spirit*. Seattle: Amazon Digital Services.

Elling, A. (1999). "A little rough, I like that": About the images of and experiences in women's soccer. *Tijdschrift voor Gender Studies, 2*, 25-35.

Evans, J. (1995). *Feminist theory today: An introduction to second wave feminism*. London: Sage.

Festle, M. J. (1996). *Playing nice: Politics and apologies in women's sports*. New York: Columbia University Press.

Fields, S. K. (2006). *Female gladiators: Gender, law and contact sport in America*. Chicago, IL: University of Illinois.

Fortunato, J. A. (2000). Public relations strategies for creating mass media content: A case study of the National Basketball Association. *Public Relations Review, 26*(4), 481–497.

Gill, R. (2007). Postfeminist media culture: Elements of a sensibility. *European Journal of Cultural Studies, 10*, 147–166.

Glaser, B., & Strauss, A. (1967). *The discovery of grounded theory: Strategies for qualitative research*. New York: Aldine.

Goldman, R. (1992). *Readings ads socially*. London: Routledge.

Grainey, T. (2012). *Beyond bend it like Beckham: The global phenomenon of women's Soccer*. Lincoln, NE: University of Nebraska.

Grau, S. L., Roselli, G., & Taylor, C. R. (2007). Where's Tamika catchings? A content analysis of female athlete endorsers in magazine advertisements. *Journal of Current Issues and Research in Advertising, 29*, 55–66.

Griffin, P. (1998). *Strong women, deep closets*. Champaign, IL: Human Kinetics.

Griffin, P. (2002). Changing the game: Homophobia, sexism, and lesbians in sport. In S. Scraton & A. Flintoff (Eds.), *Gender and sport: A reader* (pp. 193–208). London: Routledge.

Hargreaves, J. (2000). *Heroines of sport: The politics of difference and identity*. London: Routledge.

Heywood, L. (1997). *Third wave agenda: Being feminist, doing feminism.* Minneapolis: University of Minnesota.

Kane, M. J. (1988). Media coverage of the female athlete before, during, and after Title IX: Sports illustrated revisited. *Journal of Sport Management, 2,* 87–99.

Kane, M. J. (1989). The post Title IX female athlete in the media. *Journal of Physical Education, Recreation and Dance, 60,* 58–62.

Kane, M. J., & Greendorfer, S. (1994). The media's role in accommodating and resisting stereotyped images of women in sport. In P. Creedon (Ed.), *Women, media, and sport: Challenging gender values* (pp. 28–44). Thousand Oaks, CA: Sage.

Kane, M. J., & Lenskyj, H. J. (1996). Media treatment of female athletes: Issues of gender and sexualities. In L. A. Wenner (Ed.), *MediaSport* (pp. 186–201). New York: Routledge.

Knoppers, A., & Anthonissen, A. (2003). Women's Soccer in the United States and the Netherlands: Differences and similarities in regimes of inequalities. *Sociology of Sport Journal, 20,* 351–370.

Leopkey, B., & Parent, M. M. (2009). Risk management in large-scale sporting events: A stakeholder perspective. *European Sport Management Quarterly, 9*(2), 187–208.

Lipsyte, R. (1999, July 11). Sports and sex are always together. *New York Times,* p. 13.

Lisi, C. (2013). *The U.S. women's Soccer team: An American success story.* Lanham, MD: Taylor Trade.

Longman, J. (1999, July 12). Women's world cup: Day in the sun for the girls of summer after a riveting championship run. *New York Times,* p. D1.

Longman, J. (2001). *The girls of summer.* New York: HarperCollins.

Lumpkin, A. (2007). A descriptive analysis of race/ethnicity and sex of individuals appearing on the covers of sports illustrated in the 1990s. *Physical Educator, 64,* 29–37.

Lynn, S., Walsdorf, K., Hardin, M., & Hardin, B. (2002). Selling girls short: Advertising and gender images in Sports Illustrated for Kids. *Women in Sport & Physical Activity Journal, 11,* 77–101.

Madsen, D. L. (2000). *Feminist theory and literary practice.* London: Pluto.

Markovits, A., & Hellerman, S. (2004). Women's Soccer in the United States: Yet another American 'exceptionalism'. In H. Fan & J. Mangan (Eds.), *Soccer, women, sexual liberation kicking off a new era* (pp. 14–30). London: Frank Cass.

Markula, P. (1995). Firm but shapely, fit but sexy, strong but thin: The postmodern aerobicizing female bodies. *Sociology of Sport Journal, 12,* 424–453.

Martinez, D. P. (2008). Soccer in the USA: "Holding out for a hero"? *Soccer & Society, 9,* 231–243.

McCaughey, M. (1997). *Real knockouts: The physical feminism of women's self-defense.* New York: New York University.

McGinnis, L., Chun, S., & McQuillan, J. (2003). A review of gendered consumption in sport and leisure. *Academy of Marketing Science Review, 5,* Retrieved from www.amsreview.org/ articles/mcginnis05–2003.pdf

McRobbie, A. (2009). *The aftermath of feminism. Gender, culture and social change.* London: Sage.

Messner, M. (1992). *Power at play: Sports and the problem of masculinity.* Boston: Beacon.

Messner, M. (2002). *Taking the field: Women, men and sports*. Minneapolis, MN: University of Minnesota.

Miles, M. B., Huberman, A. M., & Saldana, J. (2013). *Qualitative data analysis: A methods sourcebook* (3rd ed.). Thousand Oaks, CA: Sage.

Roth, A. R., & Basow, S. A. (2004). Femininity, sports, and feminism: Developing a theory of physical liberation. *Journal of Sport and Social Issues, 28*, 245–265.

Scraton, S., Fasting, K., Pfister, G., & Bunuel, A. (1999). It's still a man's game? The experiences of top-level European women footballers. *International Review for the Sociology of Sport, 34*, 99–111.

Shaw, S. (2006). Scratching the back of "Mr. X": Analyzing gendered social progresses in sport organizations. *Journal of Sport Management, 20*, 510–534.

Sigi, F. (2009b, June 22). *Peter Wilt, WPS, and women's rights*. Retrieved from https:// soccer.fakesigi.com/peter-wilt-wps-and-womens-rights.html

Spencer, N. E., & McClung, L. R. (2001). Women and sport in the 1990's: Reflections on "embracing stars, ignoring players". *Journal of Sport Management, 15*, 318–349.

Wolf, N. (1991). *The beauty myth: How images of beauty are used against women*. New York: Doubleday.

Yin, R. (2013). *Case study research: Design and methods* (5th ed.). Thousand Oaks, CA: Sage.

Chapter 12

General game support programs associated with professional team sports

Kevin K. Byon, Mandy Y. Zhang, Noah Y. Hsu, Dan Drane, Brenda G. Pitts, and James J. Zhang

Introduction

Today's sports organizations face increasing competition for gaining market share. Thus, retaining existing consumers rather than attracting new consumers seems more imperative for the financial stability of sports organizations. Indeed, research has shown that retaining consumers is approximately five times less expensive for a service business than attracting prospective consumers (Kotler & Armstrong, 1996). Therefore, it is important for sports organizations to understand the underlying causes and antecedents of variables that may influence repatronage intentions (e.g., game attendance). The perception of service quality has been identified as one of the most salient variables that may affect not only customer retention but also customer attraction in the marketing literature (Brady & Cronin, 2001; Grönroos, 1984; Parasuraman, Zeithaml, & Berry, 1988). The concept of service quality has been examined extensively in various contexts, such as hospitality (Choi & Chu, 2001); fitness, leisure, and recreation services (Alexandris, Grouios, Tsorbatzoudis, & Bliatsou, 2001; Chelladurai & Chang, 2000; Lam, Zhang, & Jensen, 2005; Yu et al., 2014), and spectator services (Greenwell, Fink, & Pastore, 2002; Min, Zhang, Kim, & Kim, 2015; Tsuji, Bennett, & Zhang, 2007; Zhang, Lam, Connaughton, Bennett, & Smith, 2005; Zhang, Smith, Pease, & Jambor, 1998; Zhang et al., 2004). Some of the identified consequences derived from good service quality include customer loyalty (Petrick & Backman, 2001; Yu et al., 2014), repatronage intentions (Wakefield & Sloan, 1995), word-of-mouth (Wakefield & Blodgett, 1999), and satisfaction (Zhang et al., 2011), which in turn help sustain long-term profitability of an organization.

According to Kotler and Armstrong (1996), a service is defined as "any act or performance one party can offer to another that is essentially intangible and does not result in the ownership of anything" (p. 455). This definition implies an important distinction between a service and a product. A service deals with intangibility, which consumers cannot possess before the consumption stage. In addition, a service is regarded as inseparable from the core product, perishable when it is rendered, and variable among individuals. Therefore, service quality can only be measured by an individual's perceptions towards a service received (Parasuraman et al., 1988); whereas, tangible products can be more objectively assessed based on their qualities, such as toughness, durability, or defects (Crosby, 1979).

In service marketing, the term "service quality" has been more frequently used than a general term "service" when it comes to assessing the "service" from the consumer's perspective (Parasuraman et al., 1988). Based on the confirmation-disconfirmation paradigm (Oliver, 1980), Parasuraman et al. defined service quality as the comparison of a consumer's evaluation of the service performance to his/her pre-expectation of the service. This definition of the gap model between expectation and perception has been widely adopted in the marketing literature (Alexandris et al., 2001; Brown, Churchill, & Peter, 1993; Carman, 1990). However, due to lack of predictive validity and measurement reliability, this gap model has been widely criticized (Buttle, 1996; Cronin & Taylor, 1992), and researchers have recommended using a performance-only model by viewing service quality as an attitudinal construct (Cronin & Taylor, 1992; Zhang et al., 2005). Empirically, Cronin and Taylor compared the performance-only measure with the gap model and found that the performance-only measure was superior in all four industries to which a measurement was applied. Based on the performance-only measure, service quality is operationalized as a consumer's perception towards a service performance received by the consumer.

Theoretically, one of the most important reasons to examine service quality is its prominent explanatory power on outcome variables, such as purchase intentions (Petrick & Backman, 2001), cost (Crosby, 1979), profitability, customer satisfaction (Bolton & Drew, 1991; Cronin & Taylor, 1992), and word-of-mouth referrals (Petrick & Backman). The practical importance of investigating service quality lies in the fact that a superior quality of service will produce a competitive edge, which will be directly related to revenue generation (Zhang et al., 1998). Furthermore, accurate and periodic assessment of service quality would provide management with feedback by pointing out areas in which improvement can be made.

Studying service quality has significant implications for effective operations of sports programs. According to Wakefield and Sloan (1995), study on sports service quality has been a largely unexplored area when compared to other topic areas in spectator attendance research such as consumer psychology (e.g., team identification and motivation) and sociodemographic variables (e.g., gender, ethnicity, income, and education). Zhang et al. (2004) argued that services in relation to a sporting event are usually manifested through game support and operation programs, which are considered extensions of the core product (i.e., game itself). Examining service quality of those game support/operation programs would provide sports marketers and program administrators with needed consumer feedback and information for immediate attention. During a sports event, the game itself is usually the primary responsibility of the coach, athletes, and referees; whereas, sports marketers and program administrators essentially have little authority over how the game is played. Conversely, the attributes relevant to the quality of game support and operation programs can be controlled, manipulated, and improved by sports marketers and team administration. Therefore, examining service quality towards game support and event operation programs would have a great deal of practical relevance and value for the game management.

For the past two decades, service quality research has essentially been guided by two theoretical paradigms: (a) the American point of view that is represented by the SERVQUAL scale (Parasuraman et al., 1988) and its numerous modifications (Brown et al., 1993; Carman, 1990) and (b) the European point of view that is referred to as the Nordic model developed by Grönroos (1984). Nonetheless, both scales were developed based upon Oliver's (1980) disconfirmation paradigm; thus, they are not drastically different in their essential nature. In terms of the SERVQUAL, Parasuraman, Zeithaml, and Berry (1985) proposed a conceptual model that included ten factors that were purported to measure service quality. The ten factors were as follows: Reliability, Responsiveness, Competence, Access, Courtesy, Communication, Credibility, Security, Understanding/Knowing the Customer, and Tangibles. Later, Parasuraman et al. (1988) conducted two studies to empirically examine the viability of the ten-factor model. A preliminary scale with 34 items under the ten factors was developed, which was administered to 800 customers of four nationally known firms, including a bank, a credit card company, an appliance repair and maintenance firm, and a long-distance telephone company. Measurement properties in terms of factor validity, internal consistency, and predictive validity were examined through an exploratory factor analysis, alpha reliability, and regression analyses. The items were clustered into five factors: Reliability, Assurance, Tangibles, Empathy, and Responsiveness. Reliability referred to how dependably and accurately the service was performed. Assurance was defined as the courtesy, knowledge, and trust of employees. Tangibles were related to the appearance of physical facilities and communication items. Empathy was defined as the offering of caring and attention to customers. Responsiveness referred to the extent to which a service firm displayed a willingness to help and provide timely service to customers.

Numerous researchers in the disciplinary areas of leisure and sports management have adopted the SERVQUAL as the theoretical framework in their studies of service quality (e.g., Chelladurai & Chang, 2000; Howat, Murray, & Crilley, 1999; Papadimitriou & Karteroliotis, 2000). In the context of fitness centers operated in Korea, Kim and Kim (1995) followed the SERVQUAL concept and developed the Quality Excellence of Sports Centers (QUESC) that included 33 items under 12 dimensions. The twelve dimensions derived from an EFA were as follows: Ambiance, Employee Attitude, Employee Reliability, Social Opportunity, Information Available, Programs Offered, Personal Considerations, Price, Privilege, Ease of Mind, Stimulation, and Convenience. However, most of the factors showed low internal consistency reliability as the alpha coefficients were below .50. In an attempt to apply the QUESC scale to Greek private fitness centers, Papadimitriou and Karteroliotis (2000) conducted a study that involved 487 attendants of fitness centers. Findings of the study failed to confirm the factor structure of the QUESC; instead, the researchers identified a parsimonious model with 24 items under four factors: Program Availability, Other Services, Instructor Quality, and Facility/Attraction Operations. In the context of Australian recreation centers, Howat, Absher, Crilley, and Milne (1996) developed a scale that contained 15 items under five factors: Core Services, Staff Quality, General Facility, Secondary Services, and Knowledge. In an attempt to define more parsimonious dimensions, Howat et al. (1999) tested the five-factor service quality model and concluded with a three-factor model instead, including Core, Peripheral, and Personnel. Later studies that conducted confirmatory factor analyses revealed that the three-factor model was of stable psychometric properties (Howat & Crilley, 2007; Howat et al., 2002). Chelladurai and Chang (2000) developed a five-factor model pertaining to assessing service quality in recreation and fitness settings, which included Core Service, Interaction between Employee and Client, Interaction between Client and Client, Context, and Client Participation. While the proposed factors appear relevant to the recreation and fitness industry, the conceptual model has not yet been empirically validated. Adopting the SERVQUAL concept in a spectator sports setting, McDonald et al. (1995) developed the TEAMQUAL™ scale to assess service performance during a sports event, which included 39 items under the same five factors as the SERVQUAL scale. Although the authors took into consideration the nature of spectator sports and management of a sports event when developing the scale, measurement properties of the TEAMQUAL™ scale was never empirically validated. An assumption was made that measurement properties of the SERVQUAL would remain for the TEAMQUAL™.

The SERVQUAL scale was developed to measure functional quality of generic service aspects in general business and service settings (Parasuraman et al., 1988). Its application in specific contexts has been criticized by various researchers (e.g., Carman, 1990; Cronin & Taylor, 1992). Carman attempted to apply the SERVQUAL to measure service quality in a hospital setting. The researcher failed to confirm the five-factor structure; instead, nine factors emerged in a factor analysis, indicating the scale did not capture the various aspects of hospital services. When applying the SERVQUAL scale to a retail apparel store, Gagliano and Hathcote (1994) reexamined the factor structure of the scale and identified 19 items under four factors: Reliability, Tangibles, Personal Attention, and Convenience. Even so, as the original authors of the SERVQUAL scale, Parasuraman, Berry, and Zeithaml (1993) also acknowledged that the scale should be modified to be relevant to the context in which it is being adopted, indicating the limitation associated with a general scale for assessing service quality. Likewise, in sports management studies, numerous researchers supported the notion of developing industry-specific factors of service quality due to the different nature of services among sports organizations. For instance, services in spectator sports are more likely to deal with intangibles related to event operations than services in durable goods, such as sports apparel. The attributes measuring service quality should be those relevant to the context in which the service is to be employed (Greenwell, et al., 2002; Lam et al., 2005; Murray & Howat, 2002; Zhang et al., 1998, 2004). This notion is consistent with the indications of Nunnally and Bernstein (1994), who explained that measurement properties are both population and situation specific.

With modified adoption of Oliver's (1980) disconfirmation paradigm, Grönroos (1984) proposed a two-dimensional model that included technical quality and functional quality. Technical quality was defined as the outcomes of the service, which reflects tangible aspects. Grönroos (2005) elaborated that technical quality ". . . is what the customer is left with, when the service production process and its buyer-seller interactions are over" (p. 63). Functional quality was related to intangible aspects, such as the consumers' perception as to how the service was delivered. The uniqueness of Grönroos's theory was the recognition, inclusion, and emphasis of the technical quality aspect, where key service elements were specified. The functional quality was similar to the aspects in the SERVQUAL concept (Parasuraman et al., 1993, 1988). As an important aspect when defining a service, functional quality is the interaction between the service provider and the customer that takes place while the service is delivered (Brady & Cronin, 2001). McDougall and Levesque (2000) used the term "relational quality" as they defined the functional quality while taking into consideration the interaction aspect of the service. Surveying 447 church members, the researchers examined the relative importance of technical service quality, functional (relational) service quality, and perceived value on customer satisfaction, which was hypothesized to directly affect behavioral intentions. The results of the study indicated that core service quality, relational service quality, and perceived value were directly related to customer satisfaction, which in turn influenced behavioral intentions.

Following the technical vs. functional service quality concept (Grönroos, 1984), Lam et al. (2005) developed the Service Quality Assessment Scale (SQAS) to evaluate the service quality of health/fitness clubs. Through a review of literature, field observations, interviews, modified application of the Delphi technique, and a pilot study, a preliminary scale with 46 items was formulated. The preliminary scale was administered to members of one health/fitness club. By conducting an EFA of the pilot test data, six factors emerged, with 40 items retained. Next, the revised scale was administered to members of various health/fitness clubs. The data set was split into halves: one was for EFA and the other was for CFA. Six factors emerged in the EFA: Staff, Program, Locker Room, Physical Facility, Workout Facility, and Child Care. The fit indexes from the CFA indicated that the model was permissible. All the factors had acceptable alpha and construct reliability coefficients. The model was then tested for invariance across gender; nine items were eliminated due to a lack of invariance for factor loadings or tau coefficients. The 31-item scale with six factors displayed sound psychometric properties and invariance for factor loadings and tau coefficients and can be utilized to evaluate service-quality issues in various health/fitness club settings.

Taking into consideration the specific nature and activities during a spectator sports event, Zhang et al. (1998) adopted the Grönroos' (1984) technical vs. functional service quality concept and developed the Spectator Satisfaction Inventory (SSI) that contained 24-items under five factors: Satisfaction with Ticket Service, Satisfaction with Audio Visuals, Satisfaction with Accessibility and Parking, Satisfaction with Arena Staff, and Satisfaction with Event Amenities. As a result of an EFA and calculation of alpha coefficients, the scale displayed good factor validity and internal consistency reliability. The SSI scale was found to be the first instrument that was developed for measuring spectator service quality towards game support programs. The SSI scale has been adapted to the contexts of NBA professional basketball game (Zhang et al., 2004) and minor league hockey game (Zhang et al., 2005) settings. In an attempt to apply the SSI scale to the NBA context, Zhang et al. (2004) examined spectator satisfactions towards game support programs of a professional basketball team and their relationships with game consumption. The researchers modified the items in the SSI scale and developed the Spectator Satisfaction Scale (SSS) that included 18 items under four factors, including Satisfaction with Ticket Service, Satisfaction with Amenities of Game, Satisfaction with Audio Visuals, and Satisfaction with Accessibility Condition. Factor analyses, alpha reliability, stepwise multiple regression, and Kruskal-Wallis analyses overall indicated that the SSS scale were of good measurement properties, including predictive validity with 16% game attendance variance explained by the game support programs (i.e., event management activities). Utilizing a more advanced factor analysis method (i.e., CFA), Zhang et al. (2005) developed the Scale of Game Support Programs (SGSP) to measure spectator satisfaction associated with game operation of minor league hockey games. A preliminary scale consisting of 28 broad game support activities was developed through literature review, field observations, and interviews with administrators. Following an EFA, the data were reduced to 23 items under four factors: Satisfaction with Ticket Service, Satisfaction with Game Amenities, Satisfaction with Arena Service, and Satisfaction with Arena Accessibility. Following a CFA, the items were reduced to 22, retaining the same factors. The CFA also revealed that the SGSP was of good convergent and discriminant validity, as well as construct reliability. Overall, the factor structures and concepts among the scales developed by Zhang and associates (1998, 2004, 2005) were essentially similar and consistent although slight differences existed.

Statement of problem

While developing context-specific measures of spectator sports services help make improvements in event operations (Greenwell et al., 2002; Zhang et al., 1998, 2004, 2005), previous studies were usually conducted for a specific professional sports, such as minor league hockey games (Greenwell et al.; Zhang et al., 2005) and NBA games (Zhang et al., 2004), lacking generalizability and general application to a broader service environment of professional sports. Availability of a generalizable service quality measure at a particular competition level, for example professional sports, would help formulate theories, develop practical guidelines, train and communicate with employees, and most importantly pinpoint key service areas for improving the quality of event operations. In fact, both general and unique characteristics associated with professional team sports should be incorporated when developing a scale to assess the quality of support programs of general game operations. Therefore, the purpose of this study was to develop the scale of general game support programs (GGSP) related to professional team sports. With the intention to achieve good measurement properties and practical applicability for the developed scale, it was anticipated that the GGSP would be useful for researchers and marketers to examine the perceptions of consumers towards the quality of services offered by professional sports teams.

Conceptual framework

Following the Nordic model (Grönroos, 1984) as a primary theoretical framework and incorporating specific characteristics concerning game support programs of professional team sports (Zhang et al., 1998, 2004, 2005), a four-factor model was conceptualized to represent game support program quality of professional team sports in this study. The four factors were Ticket Service, Game Amenities, Venue Service, and Venue Accessibility. Each of these dimensions is discussed below.

Ticket service

Ticket Service refers to the various channels of ticket sale services, including such variables as phone order, mail order, box office, ticket personnel friendliness, personnel knowledge and training, web order procedures, convenience of ticket sale locations, and/or will call. It is imperative for sports organizations to provide effective ticket services in order to enhance the perceived service quality by sports consumers. Because ticketing is necessary for all spectators to get into a venue, the ticket office is usually the first contact location with a sports organization for most spectators, whether through phone, web, mail, or in-person contact (Mulrooney & Farmer, 1996). Previous studies concerning ticket service revealed its positive relationship with game consumption (Zhang et al., 1998; Zhang, Connaughton, & Vaughn, 2004). Zhang et al. (1998) found that ticket service was positively predictive of future game attendance of minor league hockey games. In an attempt to predict NBA season-ticket holders' sports consumption, Zhang, Connaughton et al. (2004) examined the roles of special programs and services for season ticket holders and found that ticket service personnel attributes were positively related to the consumption levels of both live and broadcasted game events. Contrary to these findings, Zhang et al. (2004) found that ticket services were not a statistically significant predictor of NBA spectators, which might have been attributed to outsourcing ticket sales to a nation-wide ticket distribution company, such as Ticketmaster. Thus, online ticketing should be taken into consideration in the measurement of game support programs.

Game amenities

Game amenities are defined as entertainment and promotional activities offered during the course of a game. Music, public announcements, scoreboard, promotions, and entertainment programs prior to, during, at halftime, and after the game, dance/cheerleading activities are examples that have been identified as contributing variables of game amenities. A number of studies have found that game amenities variables were related to game consumption (e.g., Greenwell et al., 2002; Wakefield, Blodgett, & Sloan, 1996; Zhang et al., 1998, 2004, 2005). Wakefield et al. (1996) found that scoreboard was related to affective reaction (pleasure), which in turn influenced game consumption in the context of college football and minor league baseball. Greenwell et al. supported this notion by finding that scoreboard quality was positively related to minor league hockey spectator satisfaction. Zhang et al. (1998) found that overall game amenities were an important predictor of game attendance of minor league hockey games. The positive relationship between high quality game amenity programs and spectator consumption levels were further confirmed by the findings of Zhang et al. (2004) and Zhang, Piatt, Ostroff, and Wright (2005) in their studies on NBA game consumers.

Venue service

Venue service is defined as the physical surroundings of service encounters that spectators experience as a part of game spectating. Service quality of the venue operations can be represented by such variables as concessions, venue cleanliness, restroom cleanliness and accessibility, and/or in-arena staff courtesy.

Previous studies concerning stadium or arena services revealed its positive relationship with game consumption (Wakefield & Sloan, 1995; Zhang et al., 2004). In the context of college football spectators, Wakefield and Sloan found that food, drink, venue cleanliness, and in-arena staff courtesy were statistically significant predictors of the desire to remain as consumers. Similarly, Zhang et al. (1998) found that the stadium service factor had a positive relationship with game attendance of minor league hockey game spectators, which was also the case for NBA game attendants (Zhang et al., 2004).

Venue accessibility

Venue Accessibility refers to the degree of convenience to access the stadium or arena. A wide range of variables have been identified as significant attributes. These may include, but are not limited to, parking, niceness of venue, security, ticket takers, ushers, and/or ease of entrance. The stadium accessibility factor was identified as a distinct factor in Zhang et al.'s (1998) minor league hockey consumption study. Wakefield et al. (1996) found that stadium accessibility had a positive impact on event enjoyment levels of college football spectators. This finding was supported by Zhang et al. (2004), who found that the stadium accessibility factor was positively related to game attendance of NBA spectators.

   In brief, games are the core product function of a professional sports team; the coaching staff, athletes, and referees are primarily responsible for producing the core product. When operating games, team management usually has little involvement in this process of the core product. Instead, the team management primarily works on other product functions related to game support programs, such as ticket service and stadium quality. The quality of support programs often affects the overall operational effectiveness of a team, and even promotes the consumption levels of consumers (Pitts & Stotlar, 2012). Game support programs are a form of customer service and are usually intangible issues that are based on individual perceptions, inseparable from the core product of the game, perishable as a game event ends, and variable among individuals with different backgrounds (Kotler & Armstrong, 1996). Overall, the four proposed factors represent the essence of game support programs that are provided by a professional team sports organization and empirical evidence derived from previous studies revealed that they were important aspects of sports event operations that affect consumption levels of professional sports spectators.

Method

Participants

A community intercept sampling method was employed to include professional team sports spectators from diverse backgrounds. Research participants (N = 453) were residents in four southeastern United States metropolitan cities, or within close proximity of these cities, where one or more professional team sports were franchised at the time this survey was conducted. Participation was completely voluntary and a participant had to be 18 years of age or older. To qualify for participation in the study, an individual must have also attended at least one professional team sports event within the previous 12 months. These sampling conditions enabled the research participants to be familiar with the game services of professional team sports events.

As shown in Table 12.1, the characteristics of respondents were consistent with those general backgrounds of professional sports consumers

Table 12.1 Frequency distributions for the sociodemographic variables (N = 453)

Variables	Category	Frequency (%) (N = 453)	Cumulative %
Gender	Male	274 (60.5)	60.5
	Female	179 (39.5)	100.0
Age	18–22	41 (9.0)	9.0
	23–30	175 (38.6)	47.7
	31–40	151 (33.3)	81.0
	41–50	58 (12.8)	93.8
	51–65	28 (6.2)	100.0
Household Size	1	90 (19.9)	19.9
	2	112 (24.7)	44.6
	3–4	179 (39.5)	84.1
	5–6	62 (13.7)	97.8
	7–8	7 (1.5)	99.3
	9 or more	3 (0.7)	100.0
Household Income	Below $20,000	23 (5.1)	5.1
	$20,000–39,999	79 (17.4)	22.5
	$40,000–59,999	128 (28.3)	50.8
	$60,000–79,999	81 (17.9)	68.7
	$80,000–99,999	56 (12.4)	81.0
	$100,000–149,999	42 (9.3)	90.3
	$150,000–199,999	27 (6.0)	96.2
	Above $200,000	17 (3.8)	100.0
Marital Status	Single	241 (53.2)	53.2
	Married	195 (43.0)	96.2
	Divorced	17 (3.8)	100.0
Education	In School Now	1 (0.2)	0.2
	High School Graduate	47 (10.4)	10.6
	In College Now	45 (9.9)	20.5
	College Graduate	265 (58.5)	79.0
	Advanced Degree	95 (21.0)	100.0
Ethnicity	Caucasian	259 (57.2)	57.2
	African American	61 (13.5)	70.6

Variables	Category	Frequency (%)	Cumulative %
		(N = 453)	
	Hispanic	87 (19.2)	89.8
	Asian/Pacific Islander	40 (8.8)	98.7
	American Indian	2 (0.4)	99.1
	Interracial	2 (0.4)	99.6
	Other	2 (0.4)	100.0
Occupation	Management	79 (17.4)	17.4
	Technical	28 (6.2)	23.6
	Professional	128 (28.3)	51.9
	Sales	60 (13.2)	65.1
	Clerical	12 (2.6)	67.8
	Education	111 (24.5)	92.3
	Skilled Worker	30 (6.6)	98.9
	Non-Skilled Worker	3 (0.7)	99.6
	Other	2 (0.4)	100.0
Attended Game	AFL	15 (3.3)	3.3
	MLB	99 (21.9)	25.2
	NBA	117 (25.8)	51.0
	NFL	203 (44.8)	95.8
	NHL	18 (4.0)	99.8
	MLS	1 (0.2)	100.0

as described by the Simmons Market Research Bureau (2007). In terms of the sample size required for CFA, Kline (2005) suggested that at least 10 respondents are desirable for each observed variable. Considering that the preliminary GGSP scale had a total of 38 observed variables, this study targeted a minimum number of 380 participants. A total of 470 question-naires were collected. Of those, 17 were eliminated due to having non-sporadic missing values; thus, a total of 453 questionnaires were included in subsequent data analyses. Missing values were rarely spotted within the remaining sample of 453 respondents. Among those occasional missing data points, there were no Not-Missing-At-Random (NMAR) data (Schafer & Graham, 2002). Only a few Missing-At-Random (MAR) were detected. For those MAR data, mean substitution was applied.

Instrument

Game support programs were operationalized as the controllable service activities related to game operations such as ticket services, venue accessibility, venue services, and game amenities to support the production of the core product. Factors and items for the GGSP were formulated based on a comprehensive review of literature, on-site observations of professional sports events, and interviews with administrators of professional sports teams. Of the literature reviewed, three scales were primarily taken into consideration due to their direct relevance and conceptual comprehensiveness, including the SSI (Zhang et al., 1998), the SSS (Zhang et al., 2004), and the SGSP (Zhang et al., 2005). These scales were generally developed through systematic measurement procedures that usually included review of literature, formulation of a theoretical framework, qualitative research, test of content validity, EFA, CFA, and tests of reliability. Adoptions and modifications of items from previous scales took into consideration the following: (a) uniqueness in the technical and function features of professional team sports, (b) general nature of this study with an attempt to represent all professional team sports, and (c) validity and reliability evidence of related factors and items. To ensure a wide range inclusion and representation of various professional sports and their event operations, the researchers attended a number of professional football, basketball, hockey, and baseball games. In terms of interviews, an open-ended survey was conducted for identifying additional items with five practitioners who were event operation coordinators in NFL, NHL, MLB, and a major intercollegiate athletic department. Consequently, a total of 38 items related to game support activities were included in the preliminary GGSP that had four factors: Ticket Services (ten items), Game Amenities (12 items), Venue Services (six items), and Venue Accessibility (ten items). The items were arranged in a random order and a Likert 5-point scale was adopted for each item, ranging from 1 = 'Very Unsatisfied' to 5 = 'Very Satisfied'. The preliminary GGSP items were preceded by a statement that guided a respondent to assess game support activities in the general context of all professional team sports. For the purpose of sample description, the following demographic background variables were included in the questionnaire: gender, age, number of people in the household, household income, marital status, education, ethnicity, and occupation.

Procedures

The process for conducting this study was approved by the institutional review board for research involving human subjects. To test content validity, the preliminary questionnaire was submitted to a panel of ten experts that contained five university professors who specialized in marketing and sports management and the same five practitioners who were event operation coordinators in NFL, NHL, MLB, and a major intercollegiate athletic department. Each panel member was requested to examine domain relevance, domain representativeness, and domain clarity of items under each of the stipulated factors. Following feedback from the panel members, minor changes were made for a small number of items in the areas of domain relevance and wording clarity. With the improved version of the instrument, a pilot study was conducted involving a sample of 32 sports consumers who attended one or more professional team sports events within the last 12 months. At this stage, suggested changes and improvements were all minor and primarily related to word clarifications.

To ensure a good representation of professional team sports consumers with different backgrounds in the main sample of study, data collections were conducted on both weekdays and weekend days. The questionnaire was passed out at seven sports bars, three shopping malls, one grocery store, one community park, and one college campus in the four southeastern United States metropolitan cities (Atlanta, Jacksonville, Tampa, and Miami) or within close proximity of those cities. A potential participant had to answer two screening questions: (a) is he/she 18 years of age or older? and (b) had he/she attended at least one professional team sports event within the previous 12 months? After an individual provided positive answers to both questions, he/she was asked to sign an informed consent form indicating his/her willingness to voluntarily participate in the study. Completing the questionnaire, on average, took approximately 15 minutes.

Data analyses

The total sample of 453 was randomly split into two halves. The first set ($n = 231$) was used for conducting an EFA of the game support variables. The second data set ($n = 222$) was utilized for conducting a CFA for the measurement model of the GGSP that would be resolved in the EFA. Procedures in the SPSS version 20.0 (SPSS, 2012) were carried out to calculate descriptive statistics of sociodemographic and game support variables, execute the EFA, and calculate Cronbach's alpha coefficients. Although the factors and many of the items in the GGSP were adopted and modified from previous scales, additional items from other related studies were also incorporated into the preliminary instrument. Due to this compilation process, an EFA was deemed necessary as the initial step for examining the factor structure of the GGSP. The main purpose of the EFA was to identify a simple factor structure that was of the potential to be generalized to a universe of variables from a sample of variables, so as to reduce redundant assessment and minimize inter-factor correlations. The Kaiser-Meyer-Olkin (KMO) and Bartlett's Test of Sphericity (BTS) were first examined to ensure that assumptions for a factor analysis were met (Kaiser, 1974). Alpha factoring extraction (Kaiser & Caffrey, 1965) and promax rotation (Hendrikson & White, 1964) were applied to maximize the generalizability of the factors. The promax rotation was developed by combining the advantages of varimax (orthogonal) and oblique rotation techniques (Fabrigar, Wegener, MacCallum, & Strahan, 1999). This rotation method is first started with an orthogonal solution; the factor matrix is then rotated to the best least-square fit to the ideal solution by the procrustes procedure (Hurley & Cattell, 1962). The following criteria were adopted to determine the factors and retain items: (a) a factor had an eigenvalue equal to or greater than 1.0 (Kaiser,), (b) an item had a factor loading equal to or greater than .40 (Nunnally & Bernstein, 1994), (c) a factor had at least three items (Hair, Black, Babin, Anderson, & Tatham, 2005), (d) an identified factor and retained items must be interpretable in the theoretical context, and (e) the scree plot test was also utilized to help make a determination on the number of extracted factors (Cattell, 1966). Alpha coefficients for the identified factors were calculated to examine internal consistency reliability (Cronbach, 1951).

Procedures in the AMOS version 7.0 (Arbuckle, 2006) were executed to conduct a CFA for the retained game support programs factors that were resolved from the EFA. Following the suggestions of Hair et al., (2005), multiple fit indexes were adopted, including chi-square statistic (χ^2), normed chi-square (χ^2/df), root mean square error of approximation (RMSEA), standardized root mean residual (SRMR), comparative fit index (CFI), and expected cross validation index (ECVI) (Bentler, 1990; Bollen, 1989; Hu & Bentler, 1999). Generally accepted values for each of these fit indexes are as follows: (a) for the chi-square statistic (χ^2), it is expected to have non-significant difference. However, it has been criticized that chi-square statistic is too sensitive to sample size (Kline, 2005). Bollen suggested that cutoff values of less than 3.0 for the normed chi-square are regarded reasonable fit. Browne and Cudeck (1992) indicated that any RMSEA values less than .05 shows a close fit; with a slightly liberal criterion, Hu and Bentler (1999) suggested that RMSEA value of .06 as a close fit. Any values of RMSEA between .06 and .08 indicate acceptable fit. Values of RMSEA between .08 and .10 show mediocre fit. Yet, values greater than .10 indicate unacceptable fit (Hu & Bentler, 1999). SRMR indicates how large residuals are. Therefore, smaller values of SRMR show good fit. Any values from 0.10 to 0.05 are considered as an indicative of an acceptable fit, while values below 0.05 indicate an excellent fit (Hu & Bentler, 1998). A rule of thumb for CFI is that any values larger than .90 indicate an acceptable fit, and values greater than .95 indicate a close fit. Lastly, the expected cross validation index (ECVI) has no set criteria. Generally, smaller values are considered better fit of the model.

Cronbach's coefficient alpha (α) values and construct reliability (CR) were examined to measure the reliability of the identified factors. Fornell and Larcker (1981) suggested .70 as the cut-off value for Cronbach's coefficient alpha and CR. Since the AMOS program did not provide CR values, CR coefficients were calculated using the formula outlined by Fornell and Larcker. To determine convergent validity, indicator loadings and significant z-values were evaluated (Anderson & Gerbing, 1988; Hair et al., 2005). Meyers, Gamst, and Guarino (2006) have suggested that if an indicator loading is equal to or greater than .50, it indicates that the pattern coefficient achieves meaningful significance. For the significant z-values, Anderson and Gerbing (1988) stated that "convergent validity can be assessed from the measurement model by determining whether each indicator's estimated pattern coefficient on its posited underlying construct factor is significant" (p. 416). Additionally, discriminant validity was examined using two methods: (a) an interfactor correlation is below .85 (Kline, 2005) and (b) a squared correlation between two constructs is lower than the average variance extracted (AVE) value for any one of the two constructs (Fornell & Larcker, 1981).

Results

Descriptive statistics

Descriptive statistics for the game support programs are reported in Table 12.2. Of the 38 items, 33 had a mean score greater than 3.0, the midpoint on the Likert 5-point scale, indicating that overall game support variables were evaluated with satisfaction by the professional team sports consumers when assessing their game attending experiences. Five items had a mean score that was slightly lower than the midpoint. Of all the variables, 'scoreboard information' item had the highest mean score ($M = 3.98$; $SD = 0.86$), and 'mail order' had the lowest mean score ($M = 2.53$; $SD = 1.12$). Additionally, skewness and kurtosis for the items were examined. For the skewness cut-off value, an absolute value of 3.0 would be considered extreme. For the kurtosis threshold value, an absolute score greater than 3.0 would be considered extreme (Chou & Bentler, 1995). In this study, all skewness and kurtosis values for the game support variables were well within the acceptable threshold (Table 12.2).

Exploratory factor analysis

An EFA was conducted for the purpose of identifying a simple structure among the game support variables (Stevens, 1996). The KMO measure of sampling adequacy value was .862, which exceeded the cut-off value of .50, indicating that the degree of common variance was meritorious (Kaiser, 1974). As a result, the sample was adequate for a factor analysis. The BTS was 1962.95 ($p < .001$), indicating that the hypothesis of the variance and covariance matrix of the variables as an identity matrix was rejected. Therefore, a factor analysis was deemed appropriate. In the EFA, five factors emerged with 21 items retained, explaining a total variance of 51%. The scree plot test also suggested that a five-factor model was most interpretable. The rotated pattern matrix from promax rotation is reported in Table 12.3. Based on the predetermined criteria, nine variables were eliminated due to not having primary loading on one of the five identified factors (i.e., replay screens, convenience of ticket sale locations, mail order, food and drink price, ticket personnel friendliness, music selection, ticket agencies, public transportation, and web/online order procedures). Five other items had factor load values lower than the predetermined criterion of .40

Table 12.2 Descriptive statistics for the game support programs variables (N = 453)

Variable	M	SD	Skewness	Kurtosis
1. Phone order service (TS1)	2.8381	1.05699	−.002	−.211
2. Will call service (TS2)	3.0703	1.01743	.019	−.188
3. Ticket exchange program (TS3)	3.0740	1.08765	−.245	−.217
4. Ticket agencies (TS4)	2.9046	1.05939	−.205	−.355
5. Game calendar and schedule (TS5)	3.9508	.81864	−.467	−.140
6. Ticket personnel friendliness(TS6)	3.7562	.92849	−.457	−.139
7. Convenience of ticket sale locations (TS7)	3.5258	.98321	−.486	.201
8. Web (online) order procedures (TS8)	2.9748	1.00301	−.094	−.191
9. Mail order (TS9)	2.5324	1.12279	.111	−.715
10. Efficiency of ticket office (TS10)	3.5442	.96554	−.185	−.544
11. Music selection (GA1)	3.6777	.91804	−.283	−.259
12. Public address system (GA2)	3.7020	.98289	−.505	−.266
13. Replay screens (GA3)	3.5366	1.12114	−.499	−.452
14. During game shows/entertainments (GA4)	3.5982	.93704	−.384	−.330
15. Post-game shows/entertainments (GA5)	3.2993	1.14694	−.314	−.591
16. Give away/prize(GA6)	3.2345	1.10624	−.179	−.660
17. Music volume (GA7)	3.8407	.91028	−.687	.429
18. Scoreboard information (GA8)	3.9779	.86446	−.639	.242
19. Pre-game shows/entertainments (GA9)	3.4568	.96155	−.484	−.096
20. Intermission/half-game entertainments (GA10)	3.4181	.96392	−.384	−.112
21. Dance/cheerleading activities (GA11)	3.5565	1.00805	−.507	−.245
22. Concourse entertainment activities (GA12)	3.3166	.88871	−.089	−.039
23. Food and drink quality (VS1)	3.5022	.91267	−.252	.137
24. Arena/stadium cleanliness (VS2)	3.7345	.91707	−.434	−.114
25. Restroom cleanliness (VS3)	3.2301	.98672	−.211	−.497
26. Food and drink price (VS4)	3.0310	1.20615	−.174	−.898
27. Restroom availability (VS5)	3.6049	.89772	−.372	−.124
28. Staff courtesy (VS6)	3.7439	.88285	−.251	−.474
29. Parking (VA1)	2.9467	1.18688	.056	−.891
30. Newness of arena/stadium (VA2)	3.5398	1.02435	−.486	−.075
31. Security (VA3)	3.7450	.88207	−.448	.019
32. Ticket takers (VA4)	3.6991	.90851	−.489	−.028
33. Traffic/crowd control (VA5)	3.4204	1.08299	−.382	−.431
34. Public transportation (VA6)	3.1327	1.10767	−.271	−.388
35. Niceness of arena stadium (VA7)	3.8514	.89621	−.444	−.437
36. Ushers (VA8)	3.4614	.83689	−.014	−.246
37. Ease of entrance (VA9)	3.5762	1.01605	−.373	−.454
38. Seating directions (VA10)	3.7441	.88886	−.575	.331

Note: TS = ticket service; GA = game amenities; VS = venue services; VA = venue accessibility.

Table 12.3 Factor pattern matrix for the game support programs variables: alpha factoring with promax rotation

	FI	F2	F3	F4	F5
Game Amenities (6 items)					
Pre-game shows/entertainments	**.856**	.036	−.059	.031	−.083
Post-game shows/entertainments	**.795**	.080	−.149	−.136	−.017
Dance/cheerleading activities	**.720**	−.184	−.005	.072	.096
During game shows/entertainments	**.668**	−.036	.027	.248	−.015
Intermission/half-game entertainments	**.627**	.042	.105	.070	.159
Concourse entertainment activities	**.600**	.129	.205	−.066	−.088
Venue Services (5 items)					
Arena/stadium cleanliness	.034	**.673**	−.211	.084	.056
Restroom availability	−.140	**.656**	−.117	.205	.085
Restroom cleanliness	.005	**.653**	.018	−.086	.188
Parking	.163	**.628**	.031	−.222	.063
Ease of entrance	−.118	**.444**	.360	.246	−.252
Ticket Service (3 items)					
Ticket exchange program	.083	−.049	**.769**	−.098	−.058
Will call service	−.221	−.099	**.756**	.138	.116
Phone order service	.127	−.055	**.635**	−.136	.048
Venue Convenience (4 items)					
Scoreboard information	−.001	−.058	−.108	**.704**	.125
Game calendar and schedule	−.039	.006	−.054	**.598**	.077
Security	.185	−.070	.111	**.565**	−.053
Staff courtesy	.096	.161	.075	**.550**	−.090
Venue Accessibility (3 items)					
Public address system	.020	.025	.401	.078	**.539**
Traffic/crowd control	−.054	.183	.169	−.125	**.535**
Seating directions	.049	.074	−.197	.236	**.525**

Note: FI = game amenities; F2 = venue services; F3 = ticket service; F4 = venue convenience; F5 = venue accessibility.

and hence they were eliminated (i.e., give away/prize, ushers, food and drink quality, music volume, and ease of entrance). Additionally, due to double loading and lack of interpretability and relevance, three items were removed (i.e., newness of arena/stadium, efficiency of ticket office, and niceness of arena/stadium). Consequently, a total of 21 items were retained under the five factors that were labeled as Game Amenities (six items), Venue Services (five items), Ticket Service (three items), Venue Convenience (four items), and Venue Accessibility (three items). Alpha coefficients for the factors were .88, .77, .73, .74, and .66, respectively, indicating that they were of acceptable internal consistency. Although the resolved factor structure was slightly different from the proposed four-factor model, it was essentially consistent. The slight difference might be an indication that unlike previous studies that focused on a specific sports event, the current study examined game operational activities from a general perspective that covered all professional team sports events.

Confirmatory factor analysis

Data for the retained five factors with 21 items were submitted to a CFA, using the ML estimation method (Hair et al., 2005). Goodness of fit indexes revealed that the five-factor measurement model did not fit the data well. Values of model fit indices were as follows: $\chi^2 = 482.84$ ($p <$ .001); $\chi^2/df = 2.70$; RMSEA = .088 (90% CI = .078 – .97); SRMR = .077; CFI = .78; and ECVI = 2.66. The model fit tests suggested a need for respecification. Based on Meyers et al. (2006) criterion that item loading should be equal or to .50, a number of low indicator loadings also supported a model respecification. In this process, six items were eliminated (public address system, scoreboard information, traffic/crowd control, seating directions, game calendar and schedule, and restroom cleanliness). Consequently, a four-factor model with 15 items was respecified: Game Amenities (six items), Ticket Service (three items), Venue Service (three items), and Venue Accessibility (three items). Consistent with the recommendations of Bollen (1989), each factor consisted of at least three items. This four-factor model with 15 items was further submitted to a CFA. Overall goodness of fit indexes revealed that the four-factor model fit the data reasonably well (Table 12.4). Chi-square statistic was significant ($\chi^2 = 212.44$, $p < .001$). The normed chi-square ($\chi^2/df = 2.53$) was lower than the suggested cut-off value (i.e., < 3.0; Bollen,). The RMSEA value indicated that the four-factor model had an acceptable fit (RMSEA = .083, 90% CI = .069 – .097; Hu & Bentler, 1999). SRMR (.068) was of a good value ($\leq$ .10; Kline, 2005). CFI was .89, which was marginally acceptable (Meyers et al., 2006). ECVI was 1.29, which indicated a much better fit than that of the five-factor model.

Unlike EFA, CFA allows comparing various competing models. Noar (2003) noted that "by testing various models against one another, one can

Table 12.4 Model fit comparison among the correlated five factors, uncorrelated four factors, second-order correlated four factors, and correlated three factors of game support programs

Model	χ^2	df	χ^2/df	RMSEA	RMSEA CI	SRMR	CFI	ECVI
Correlated Five Factors	482.84	179	2.70	.088	.078–.097	.077	.82	2.66
Uncorrelated Four Factors	453.44	98	4.63	.128	.116–.140	.220	.70	2.25
Second-Order Factor	275.83	86	3.21	.100	.087–.113	.085	.84	1.56
Correlated Four Factors	212.44	84	2.53	.083	.069–.097	.068	.89	1.29
Correlated Three Factors	219.04	87	2.52	.083	.069–.097	.070	.89	1.29

CI = confidence interval.

glean further details about how the items and constructs of a scale are related to one another" (p. 633). Following Noar's suggestion, we tested three competing models (i.e., uncorrelated four-factor model, correlated three-factor model, and a second-order model), along with the correlated four-factor model with 15 items. Theoretical justification for the uncorrelated four-factor model would imply that each of the four dimensions would be unrelated to one another. Zhang et al. (1998, 2004), in their scale development studies, adopted varimax rotation, which was an orthogonal solution implying that the dimensions were mathematically independent of one another. Theoretical support for the correlated three-factor model is that Zhang et al. (2005) found that interfactor correlation between Arena Service and Arena Access is rather high ($r =. 78$), suggesting that the two factors be combined together. Lastly, support for the second-order model would be that all the four factors were purported to measure game support programs that were all tied to event operations of various professional team sports. Therefore, a second-order model, called Peripheral Service Quality that represents all factors, was hypothesized. The competing models were analyzed using the previously outlined data analysis procedures. Comparatively, the uncorrelated model showed worst model fit, followed by the second-order model. The overall model fit of the correlated three-factor model remained almost the same as the correlated four-factor model (χ^2 = 219.04, $p < .001$; χ^2/df = 2.52; RMSEA = .083, 90% CI = .069 – .97; SRMR = .07, CFI = .89, and ECVI = 1.29). However, after examining model estimation, it was found in the correlated four-factor model that the interfactor correlation between Venue Service and Venue Accessibility was excessively high (1.06), suggesting that the two factors be combined into one factor, which was labeled as Venue Quality. Since the three-factor model was statistically more feasible in the current study, the three-factor model was adopted for subsequent analyses (i.e., reliability, convergent, and discriminant validity).

A convergent validity test was conducted by evaluating indicator loadings and significant z-value. All of the factor loadings were statistically significant with z scores ranging from 5.70 to 10.75 ($p < .001$). All indicator loadings were above the modest criterion of .50 (Meyers et al., 2006) except for one item on Venue Quality (i.e., 'ease of entrance' with a value of .44). A decision was made to retain the item due to its high theoretical relevance to the Venue Quality factor. Overall, the three-factor model of the game support programs showed acceptable convergent validity (Table 12.5).

Interfactor correlations were .36 (between Ticket Service and Venue Quality), .49 (between Game Amenities and Venue Quality), and .63 (between Game Amenities and Ticket Service), respectively, indicating excellent discriminant validity. The Fornell and Larcker's test found that all squared correlations in the scale were less than AVE value for respective construct, indicating robust discriminant validity (Table 12.5 for AVE). As a result of the two factor analyses (i.e., EFA and CFA), a construct validity test,

Table 12.5 Indicator loadings, critical ratios, Cronbach's alpha, construct reliability, average variance extracted for the game support programs

Variables	Indicator Loadings	Critical Ratios	Cronbach's Alpha	Construct Reliability	Average Variance Extracted
Game Amenities (6 items)			.85	.86	.52
During game shows/ entertainments	.71				
Post-game shows/ entertainments	.60	8.20			
Pre-game shows/ entertainments	.78	10.54			
Intermission/half-game entertainments	.79	10.75			
Dance/cheerleading activities	.68	9.24			
Concourse entertainment activities	.70	9.60			
Ticket Service (3 items)			.74	.72	.47
Phone order service	.69				
Will call service	.65	7.54			
Ticket exchange program	.76	8.18			
Venue Quality (6 items)			.77	.80	.41
Staff courtesy	.70				
Restroom availability	.70	8.70			
Arena/stadium cleanliness	.72	8.90			
Ease of entrance	.44	5.70			
Security	.61	7.76			
Parking	.52	6.69			

and reliability tests, it was found that the three-factor model with 15 items was the most appropriate model measuring general game support programs associated with the events of professional team sports.

The reliability of the factors and respective items was evaluated by Cronbach's alpha and CR. Cronbach's alpha values for the three-factor model indicated that all factors were well above the acceptable threshold (i.e., greater than .70) suggested by Hair et al. (2005), ranging from .74 (Ticket Service) to .85 (Game Amenities). The CR values for the three constructs of game support programs were all above the recommended cut-off criterion (Fornell & Larcker, 1981), ranging from .72 (Ticket Service) to .86 (Game Amenities). Based on the overall information of reliability, the determined factors were deemed reliable (Table 12.5). A graphical representation of the three-factor model of the GGSP is presented in Figure 12.1.

Discussion

As market competition becomes more intensified in professional team sports, it is imperative for both researchers and practitioners to identify

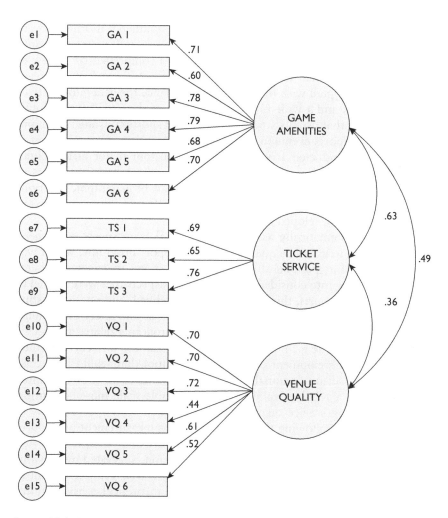

Figure 12.1 First-order CFA for the GGSP

those variables that directly and indirectly influence game consumption (Hansen & Gauthier, 1989). Findings of previous studies revealed that game support programs were important predictors of sports spectator consumption behavior (Murray & Howat, 2002; Wakefield & Blodgett, 1996; Zhang et al., 1998, 2004). However, these studies have usually been studied in the context of a specific profession sports (e.g., Wakefield & Sloan, 1995; Zhang et al., 2004). Thus, it was necessary to conduct this study that incorporated the attributes of service attributes and product extensions of professional team sports. By following the Nordic model (Grönroos, 1984) as a primary theoretical framework and the performance-only paradigm

(Cronin & Taylor, 1992; Zhang et al., 2005) as the assessment format, rigorous psychometric testing procedures were conducted in this study to develop the GGSP scale. Systematic procedures were undertaken to formulate the preliminary instrument, which included a comprehensive review of literature, test of content validity, and a pilot study. A community intercept approach was adopted with the intention to enhance the generalizability of research findings and a wide-range applicability of the GGSP scale. Unlike previous studies that usually studied professional sports consumers at a limited number of sports events in one geographic location, data collection in this study was conducted at various locations in four major metropolitan areas to support the intention of enhanced generalizability. Consumers of comparatively more diverse backgrounds in terms of geographic locations and sports types participated in the study in an effort to improve the external validity of the developed scale.

This study systematically assessed professional team sports consumers' perceptions towards service quality of game support programs, which was at times referred as peripheral activities in the sports management literature. While taking into consideration the unique aspects that were related to professional team sports, this study adopted, modified, and revised existing scales and also generated items through observations and interviews. Unlike previous studies that measured game support programs related to specific professional games (e.g., minor league hockey games), the current study emphasized the development of an assessment tool that would be precise and useable for all professional team sports. Zhang et al. (2004) pointed out that having a reliable, valid, and generalizable scale must be a priority when studying service quality issues associated with specific areas of event operations. Following this notion, rigorous measurement procedures were conducted in this study. A five-factor model first emerged that was essentially consistent with the theoretical dimensions suggested by previous studies (Zhang et al., 1998, 2005). The dimensions were reduced to four in the initial CFA. Following careful statistical and theoretical considerations, three competing models were also generated and tested. Eventually, the correlated three-factor model with 15 items (Game Amenities, Ticket Service, and Venue Quality) was found to be superior to other hypothesized models. One noticeable solution that emerged at this stage of the study was that two separate factors, Venue Services and Venue Accessibility, were combined into a single construct, Venue Quality.

Although somewhat different from the findings of previous studies, the resolved factor structure in this study still reflected those factors derived in previous studies (Zhang et al., 2004, 2005). For instance, in a minor league hockey study, Zhang et al. (2005) found high interfactor correlation between Arena Services and Arena Accessibility; thus, the researchers commented that "the two factors can be merged to form one single construct or they may be influenced by another latent variable" (p. 64). Another possible explanation may be related to respondents' memory decay. Unlike previous studies, the current study recruited respondents who reported that they attended one or more professional team sporting event within the past 12 months at the time when the survey was conducted. With the passing of time, consumers might have had a difficult time to clearly distinguish between the Venue Service and Venue Accessibility factors, particularly when both of these factors assessed attributes related to services and accessibility. Nevertheless, further studies are suggested to confirm the factor structure of the two latent constructs. Although the current study showed a slight difference compared to previous studies with regard to factor structure of the game support programs, findings of this study has its uniqueness in that the GGSP scale resolved in the current study is viable and feasible in the general settings of professional team sports. To a great extent, this study has helped fill a void that there have been no scales developed of this nature. The sample characteristics in the current study represented sports consumers who had attended game events in six professional sports leagues (i.e., NFL, NBA, MLB, NHL, AFL, and MLS). Thus, the factors and respective items derived from the current study can be used in more general professional sports settings.

The three resolved factors (Game Amenities, Ticket Service, and Venue Quality) in the GGSP are common game support factors that have been repeatedly found to be related to game consumption level in previous studies (e.g., Greenwell et al., 2002; Wakefield & Sloan, 1995; Zhang et al., 1998, 2004). Findings of this study have reinforced the importance of these three factors in the planning, preparation, and operation of a professional sports event. While making efforts to maintain and improve delivery quality of these three functional areas, professional team sports organizations may highlight their quality and efficiency in marketing campaigns through such procedures as printed materials, broadcasted messages, and online information. In addition to applying the GGPS scale to measure common factors of game support programs during professional sports events, the three resolved factors have implications for job classification, work duties, and human resource recruitment, placement, and training. Work forces and job duties may be organized, departmentalized, and coordinated according to the three-factor structure. Within each dimension of game support programs, there were inherent relationships; thus, activities within a dimension also define the job span for employees, volunteers, and student interns working in that unit. Some cross-training of duties within a dimension appear necessary. These three dimensions also represent fundamental activities of event operations that are common to all professional team sports organizations, indicating their importance to the success of hosting an event. Professional team sports organizations need to prepare well for the programs and activities under the three dimensions in an effort to achieve sustained success in event operations.

The fact that this study was unable to distinguish between Venue Service and Venue Accessibility factors indicated that future studies are necessary to further examine the dimensionality of these two factors. In previous studies, researchers found that service quality of game support programs affected consumer behaviors (e.g., Wakefield & Sloan, 1995; Zhang et al., 2004); however, the current study did not examine the predictive validity of GGSP on sports consumer behaviors, such as game attendance level. Future studies should look into this measurement aspect by examining the impact of GGSP on various affective and behavioral consumption variables that logically represent the consequences of service quality, such as game attendance (Greenwell et al., 2002; Zhang et al., 2004), customer loyalty, purchase intentions, referrals (Petrick & Backman, 2001), repatronage (Wakefield & Sloan, 1995), and overall customer satisfaction (Bolton & Drew, 1991; Cronin & Taylor, 1992).

Additionally, since only one half of the entire data was used for CFA, the authors could not perform a cross-validation to further ensure the model's generalizability of the factor structure. According to MacCallum, Ronznowski, and Necowitz (1992), any model that went through model respecification should be further confirmed by an independent sample. Although, the measurement model in the current study displayed good psychometric properties, more validation studies are always constructive. Along with the GGSP factors, future studies may also examine the influences of market demand factors associated with the core product elements of a sports event (i.e., the game itself) and how they function together and lead to elevated consumption levels at professional team sports events.

References

Alexandris, K., Grouios, G., Tsorbatzoudis, H., & Bliatsou, H. (2001). Relationship between perceived constraints and commitment to recreational sports participation of university students in Greece. *International Journal of Sports Management*, 2, 282–297.

Anderson, D. R., & Gerbing, D. W. (1988). Structural equation modeling in practice: A review and recommended two-step approach. *Psychological Bulletin, 103*, 411–423.

Arbuckle, J. L. (2006). *AMOS 7.0 user's guide*. Chicago, IL: SmallWalters Corporation.

Bentler, P. M. (1990). Comparative fit indices in structural models. *Psychological Bulletin, 107*, 238–246.

Bollen, K. A. (1989). *Structural equations with latent variables*. New York: John Wiley & Sons.

Bolton, R. N., & Drew, J. H. (1991). A multistage model of customers' assessments of service quality and value. *Journal of Consumer Research, 17*, 375–84.

Brady, M. K., & Cronin, J. (2001). Some new thoughts on conceptualizing perceived service quality: A hierarchical approach. Journal of Marketing, *34*(3), 34–49.

Brown, M. W., & Cudeck, R. (1992). Alternative ways of assessing model fit. *Sociological Methods and Research, 21*, 230–258.

Brown, T. J., Churchill, G. A., & Peter, J. P. (1993). Improving the measurement of service quality. *Journal of Retailing, 69*, 127–139.

Buttle, F. (1996). SERVQUAL: Review, critique, research agenda. *European Journal of Marketing, 30*, 8–32.

Carman, J. M. (1990). Consumer perceptions of service quality: An assessment of the SERVQUAL dimensions. *Journal of Retailing 66*, 33–55.

Cattell, R. B. (1966). The scree test for the number of factors. *Multivariate Behavioral Research, 1*, 245–276.

Chelladurai, P., & Chang, K. (2000). Targets and standards of quality in sports services. *Sports Management Review, 3*, 1–22.

Choi, T. Y., & Chu, R. (2001). Determinants of hotel guests' satisfaction and repeat patronage in the Hong Kong hotel industry. *Hospitality Management, 20*, 277–297.

Chou, C. P., & Bentler, P. M. (1995). Estimates and tests in structural equation modeling. In R. H. Hoyle (Ed.), Structural *equation modeling: Concepts, issues and applications* (pp. 37–55). Thousand Oaks, CA: Sage.

Cronbach, L. J. (1951). Coefficient alpha and the internal structure of test. *Psychometrika, 16*, 297–334.

Cronin, J. J., & Taylor, S. A. (1992). Measuring service quality: A reexamination and extension. *Journal of Marketing, 56*(3), 55–68.

Crosby, P. B. (1979). *Quality is free: The art of making quality certain.* New York: New American Library.

Fabrigar, L. R., Wegener, D. T., MacCallum, R. C., & Strahan, E. J. (1999). Evaluating the use of exploratory factor analysis in psychological research. *Psychological Methods, 4*, 272–299.

Fornell, C., & Larcker, D. (1981). Evaluating structural equation models with unobservable variables and measurement error. *Journal of Marketing Research, 18*, 39–50.

Gagliano, K. B., & Hathcote, J. (1994). Customer expectations and perceptions of service quality in retail apparel specialty. *Journal of Services Marketing, 8*, 60–69.

Greenwell, T. C., Fink, J. S., & Pastore, D. L. (2002). Assessing the influence of the physical sports facility on customer satisfaction within the context of the service experience. *Sports Management Review, 5*, 129–148.

Grönroos, C. (1984). A service quality model and its marketing implications. *European Journal of Marketing, 18*(4), 36–45.

Grönroos, C. (2005). *Service management and marketing: A customer relationship management approach.* Chichester, UK: John Wiley & Sons.

Hair, J. F., Black, W. C., Babin, B. J., Anderson, R. E., & Tatham, R. L. (2005). *Multivariate data analysis* (6th ed.). Upper Saddle River, NJ: Prentice Hall.

Hendrikson, A. E., & White, P. O. (1964). Promax: A quick method of rotation to oblique simple structure. *British Journal of Statistical Psychology, 17*, 65–70.

Howat, G., Absher, J., Crilley, G., & Milne, I. (1996). Measuring customer service quality in sports and leisure centers. *Managing Leisure, 1*, 77–89.

Howat, G., & Crilley, G. (2007). Customer service quality, satisfaction, and operational performance: A proposed model for Australian public aquatic centers. *Annals of Leisure Research, 10*, 168–195.

Howat, G., Crilley, G., Mikilewicz, S., Edgecombe, S., March, H., Murray, D., & Bell, B. (2002). Trends in service quality, customer satisfaction and behavioral intentions of Australian aquatic centre customers, 1999–2001. *Annals of Leisure Research, 5*, 51–64.

Howat, G., Murray, D., & Crilley, G. (1999). The relationships between service problems and perceptions of service quality, satisfaction, and behavioral intentions of Australian public sports and leisure centre customers. *Journal of Park and Recreation Administration*, 17(2), 42–64.

Hu, L. T., & Bentler, P. M. (1998). Fit indices in covariance structure modeling: Sensitivity to underparameterized model misspecification. *Psychological Methods*, 3(4), 424–453.

Hu, L. T., & Bentler, P. M. (1999). Cutoff criteria for fit indexes in covariance structure analysis: Conventional criteria versus new alternatives. *Structural Equation Modeling*, 6, 1–55.

Hurley, J., & Cattell, R. B. (1962). The procrustes program: Producing direct rotation to test a hypothesized factor structure. *Behavioral Science*, 7, 258–262.

Kaiser, H. F. (1974). An index of factorial simplicity. *Psychometrika*, 39, 31–36.

Kaiser, H. F., & Caffrey, J. (1965). Alpha factor analysis. *Psychometrika*, 30, 1–14.

Kim, D., & Kim, S. Y. (1995). QUESC: An instrument for assessing the service quality of sports centers in Korea. *Journal of Sports Management*, 9, 208–220.

Kline, R. B. (2005). *Principles and practice of structural equation modeling* (2nd ed.). New York: Guilford.

Kotler, P., & Armstrong, G. (1996). *Principles of marketing*. Englewood Cliffs, NJ: Prentice-Hall.

Lam, E. T. C., Zhang, J. J., & Jensen, B. E. (2005). Service Quality Assessment Scale (SQAS): An instrument for evaluating service quality of health – fitness clubs. *Measurement in Physical Education and Exercise Science*, 9, 79–111.

MacCallum, R. C., Ronznowski, M., & Necowitz, L. B. (1992). Model modifications in covariance structure analysis: The problem of capitalization on chance. *Psychological Bulletin*, 111, 490–504.

McDonald, M. A., Sutton, W. A., & Milne, G. R. (1995). TEAMQUAL™: Measuring service quality in professional team sports. *Sports Marketing Quarterly*, 4(2), 9–15.

McDougall, G. H. G., & Levesque, T. (2000). Customer satisfaction with services: Putting perceived value into the equation: An empirical examination. *Journal of Services Marketing*, 14, 392–410.

Meyers, L. S., Gamst, G., & Guarino, A. J. (2006). *Applied multivariate research: Design and interpretation*. Thousand Oaks, CA: Sage.

Min, S. D., Zhang, J. J., Kim, M. K., & Kim, C. (2015). Understanding consumers of Asian female sports: A case study of the Women's Korean Basketball League (WKBL). *International Journal of Sport Management and Marketing*, 15, 19–35.

Mulrooney, A., & Farmer, P. (1996). Managing the facility. In B. L. Parkhouse (Ed.), *The management of sports: Its foundation and application* (2nd ed., pp. 223–248). St. Louis, MO: Mosby.

Murray, D., & Howat, G. (2002). The relationships among service quality, value, satisfaction, and future intentions of customers at an Australian sports and leisure centre. *Sports Management Review*, 5, 25–43.

Noar, S. M. (2003). The role of structural equation modeling in scale development. *Structural Equation Modeling*, 10, 622–647.

Nunnally, J. C., & Bernstein, I. H. (1994). *Psychometric Theory* (3rd ed.). New York: McGraw-Hill.

Oliver, R. L. (1980). A cognitive model of the antecedents and consequences of satisfaction decisions. *Journal of Marketing Research*, 17, 460–469.

Papadimitriou, D. A., & Karteroliotis, K. (2000). The service quality expectations in private sports and fitness centers: A reexamination of the factor structure. *Sports Marketing Quarterly*, *9*, 157–164.

Parasuraman, A., Berry, L. L., & Zeithaml, V. A. (1993). More on improving service quality measurement. *Journal of Retailing*, *69*, 140–147.

Parasuraman, A., Zeithaml, V. A., & Berry, L. L. (1985). A conceptual model of service quality and its implications for future research. *Journal of Marketing*, *49*(3), 41–50.

Parasuraman, A., Zeithaml, V. A., & Berry, L. L. (1988). SERVQUAL: Multiple-item scale for measuring consumer perceptions of service quality. *Journal of Retailing*, *64*, 12–40.

Petrick, J. F., & Backman, S. J. (2001). An examination of golf travelers' satisfaction, perceived value, loyalty, and intentions to revisit. *Tourism Analysis*, *6*, 223–237.

Pitts, B. G., & Stotlar, D. K. (2012). *Fundamentals of sport marketing* (4th ed.). Morgantown, WV: Fitness Information Technology.

Schafer, J. L., & Graham, J. W. (2002). Missing data: Our view of the state of the art. *Psychological Methods*, *7*, 147–177.

Simmons Market Research Bureau. (2007). *Study of media and markets*. New York: Market Research Bureau.

SPSS. (2012). *SPSS 20.0: Guide to data analysis*. Upper Saddle River, NJ: Prentice Hall.

Stevens, J. (1996). *Applied multivariate statistics for the social sciences* (3rd ed.). Mahwah, NJ: Lawrence Erlbaum.

Tsuji, Y., Bennett, G., & Zhang, J. J. (2007). Consumer satisfaction with action sports event. *Sports Marketing Quarterly*, *16*, 199–208.

Wakefield, K. L., & Blodgett, J. G. (1996). The effect of the servicescape on customers' behavioral intentions in leisure service settings. *Journal of Services Marketing*, *10*(6), 45–61.

Wakefield, K. L., & Blodgett, J. G. (1999). Customer response to intangible and tangible service factors. *Psychology and Marketing*, *16*, 51–68.

Wakefield, K. L., Blodgett, J. G., & Sloan, H. J. (1996). Measurement and management of the sportscape. *Journal of Sports Management*, *10*, 15–31.

Wakefield, K. L., & Sloan, H. J. (1995). The effects of team loyalty and selected stadium factors on spectator attendance. *Journal of Sports Management*, *9*, 153–172.

Yu, H. S., Zhang, J. J., Kim, D. H., Chen, K. K., Henderson, C., Min, S. D., & Huang, R. H. (2014). Service quality, perceived value, customer satisfaction, and behavioral intentions among elderly consumers at a sport and fitness center. *Social Behavior and Personality*, *42*, 757–768.

Zhang, J. J., Connaughton, D. P., & Vaughn, C. E. (2004). The role of special programs and services for season ticket holders in predicting game consumption. *International Journal of Sports Marketing and Sponsorship*, *6*, 99–116.

Zhang, J. J., Lam, E. T. C., Cianfrone, B. A., Zapalac, R. K., Holland, S., & Williamson, D. P. (2011). An importance-performance analysis of media activities associated with WNBA game consumption. *Sport Management Review*, *14*, 64–78.

Zhang, J. J., Lam, E. T. C., Connaughton, D. P., Bennett, G., & Smith, D. W. (2005). Development of a scale to measure spectator satisfaction towards support programs of minor league hockey games. *International Journal of Sports Management*, *6*, 47–70.

Zhang, J. J., Pease, D. G., Smith, D. W., Wall, K. A., Saffici, C. L., Pennington-Gray, L., & Connaughton, D. P. (2004). Spectator satisfaction with the support programs of professional basketball games. In Pitts, B. G. (Ed.), *Sharing best practices in sports marketing: The Sports Marketing Association's inaugural book of papers* (pp. 207–229). Morgantown, WV: Fitness Information Technology.

Zhang, J. J., Piatt, D. M., Ostroff, D. H., & Wright, J. W. (2005). Importance of in-game entertainment amenities at professional sporting events: A case for NBA season ticket holders. *Journal of Contemporary Athletics, 2,* 1–24.

Zhang, J. J., Smith, D. W., Pease, D. G., & Lam, E.T.C. (1998). Dimensions of spectator satisfaction towards support programs of professional hockey games. *International Sports Journal, 2*(2), 1–17.

Index

Note: Page numbers in **bold** indicate tables and page numbers in *italics* indicate figures on the corresponding page.

For Product Safety Concerns and Information please contact our EU
representative GPSR@taylorandfrancis.com Taylor & Francis Verlag GmbH,
Kaufingerstraße 24, 80331 München, Germany

Printed and bound by CPI Group (UK) Ltd, Croydon, CR0 4YY
01/05/2025
01858412-0001